THE DARKNESS CRUMBLES

By the same author

From the House of War
Behind Iranian Lines
The Disappeared: Voices
From Argentina's Dirty War

THE DARKNESS CRUMBLES

Despatches from the Barricades
Revised and Updated

The darkness crumbles away –
It is the same old druid Time as ever.

From *Break of Day in the Trenches*
by Isaac Rosenberg

JOHN
SIMPSON

HUTCHINSON

LONDON

This edition first published in 1992 by
Hutchinson

Random Century Group Ltd
20 Vauxhall Bridge Road, London SW1V 2SA

Random Century Australia (Pty) Ltd
20 Alfred Street, Milsons Point, Sydney, NSW 2061, Australia

Random Century New Zealand Ltd
PO Box 40–086, Glenfield, Auckland 10, New Zealand

Random Century South Africa (Pty) Ltd
PO Box 337, Bergvlei, 2012 South Africa

A CIP catalogue record for this book is available from the British Library

Phototypeset in Plantin and Bembo
by Raven Typesetters, Ellesmere Port
Printed and bound in Great Britain by
Clays Ltd, St. Ives PLC

ISBN 0 09 177252 4

For great empires, while they stand, do enervate and destroy the forces of the natives which they have subdued, resting upon their own prospective forces; and then when they fail also, all goes to ruin, and they become a prey. So was it in the decay of the Roman Empire: and likewise in the empire of Almaigne, after Charles the Great, every bird taking a feather.'

Sir Francis Bacon, 'Of Vicissitudes of Things'.

CONTENTS

PREFACE

When the first edition of this book was published in July 1990, I wrote in the Preface that I thought there were only two people on earth who had been at all the events with which the book was concerned: the massacre in Tiananmen Square, the quiet revolutions in Poland and Hungary, the breaching of the Berlin Wall, the collapse of Communist rule in Czechoslovakia, the violent overthrow of Nicolae Ceausescu in Romania, and the evolution of power in the Soviet Union. I was one of them, I wrote, and an American photographer, Peter Townley, was the other. In fact there was a third: Peter's identical twin brother David. I found this out as I stood alongside them in the cafeteria of the Supreme Soviet building in the Kremlin, drinking tea and eating some unspeakable cake in the interval of a long debate on the future of the Soviet Union in the wake of the attempted coup in August 1991: yet another event which the three of us saw for ourselves.

I would like to be able to claim that being at these transcendently exciting moments conferred some amazing insight on me. On the contrary, there were times when it would have been far less confusing to have been sitting in a newsroom somewhere, reading the agency despatches and watching the BBC World Service. Nowadays, indeed, I sometimes feel like the character in 'Le Rouge et le Noir' who has reminisced so often about being at the battle of Waterloo and heard the experiences of so many others, that he begins to wonder if he really was there after all.

Yet I have my notebooks to prove to myself that I was: scruffy, sometimes mudstained affairs in which I jotted down not only what people told me but also what I was feeling and seeing at moments of importance. It is the small details – the smells, the sounds, the look on someone's face or the precise words used – which vanish from the memory first. I was often bemused, tired or scared when I went through the experiences recorded in this book, and my impressions at the time sometimes turned out later to have been wrong. Yet what I jotted down at the time has something of the effect of a snapshot: blurred and ill-composed perhaps, but capable of conveying things which a more considered portrait might leave out.

A successful revolution is the moment when the trappings of state fall
to the ground, and the men and women who have sheltered behind
them are revealed to be exactly such poor, bare, forked animals as the
rest of us. In the pages that follow there will be great tyrants who
mishear messages, mix up their papers at news conferences, forget what
they mean to say, lose their temper or their nerve or their sense of
proportion, and escape in ordinary little cars with their wife nagging at
them like any other back seat driver.

With the exception of China, whose moment cannot surely be
delayed much longer, each of the revolutions I describe were joyful
events which delighted most of the people who saw them or merely
heard them described. Mankind cannot unfortunately exist at this
emotional pitch, however, and without exception each of the successful
revolutions I describe was soon to be followed by gloom and disillusion.
Many people thought the act of revolution would of itself be enough to
ensure a prosperous and contented future. The realization that it was
not – that it could sometimes be followed by worse poverty – has been a
bitter one. But in the months between May 1989 and February 1990
(with a brief reprise in Russia in August 1991) I witnessed more
concentrated happiness, enthusiasm and hope than I expect to see again
in my lifetime. This book is an attempt to recall those moments, as well
as to explain them and look briefly at what followed.

More than a hundred friends of mine in various countries have
helped me in this. I have quoted many of them, but a sizeable number
found it hard to shake off the nervousness of a lifetime, and I have not
named anyone who was unwilling to be named. I have disguised them as
I thought necessary; but if the labelling has been tampered with, the
contents have not.

I shall not go into great detail with my thanks and acknowledge-
ments. Some of the episodes I first described in articles for *The
Spectator, Granta, The Independent, The Times, The Weekend Guardian*
and *The Listener* in Britain, and *Harper's* and *World Monitor* in the
United States. Elizabeth Nash and Wenlan Peng read the original
manuscript and give me extremely valuable advice. Those individual
friends who checked the chapters on Poland, Czechoslovakia, East
Germany, Romania, Russia and China I have thanked privately. My
greatest thanks should properly go to the BBC, which acted as my
sponsor, travel agent and publisher in each of the adventures I describe.
If it had not been for Tony Hall, Chris Cramer, Mike Robinson, John
Mahoney, Tim Gardam, Mark Thompson, Nick Guthrie and other
good friends and colleagues in 'The Corporation', I should merely have
watched the whole business enviously from a distance. Jacintha

Alexander has been the best agent a writer could have, and I remain most grateful to Shusha Guppy for putting us together. Richard Cohen was a wonderfully thoughtful and patient editor for the original version, and to Neil Belton's kindness and generosity that version owes its new and updated pair of legs. Without Tira Shubart's companionship and support the entire endeavour would have been unthinkable.

J S
London
February 1992

INTRODUCTORY: FROM
LENINGRAD TO ST PETERSBURG

After 74 years of silence the past is readmitted into our lives and so is our awareness of Russian tradition. I hope we may open up a new era in which our cultural, religious and spiritual traditions will come back to life.

ANATOLY SOBCHAK, Mayor of St Petersburg, at the banquet for Grand Duke Vladimir, November 1991.

'No one wants this kind of stuff now,' said the dealer in paintings, wheezing a little as he pulled a gigantic canvas through the doorway of his bedroom, in a dreary, badly lighted flat on the outskirts of Moscow. It was a week after the failure of the coup against Mikhail Gorbachev in August 1991. The painting seemed almost as big as the flat itself: a nearly life-sized depiction of a group of revolutionaries about to charge across the Square to the Winter Palace in Petrograd in 1917. My friend had haggled over it for a quarter of an hour, made as if to leave, then finally settled on a price of $300: an amount which would take several months for most Russians to earn, if they were honest. Once the transaction had been done, the dealer wasn't worried about talking down his wares any longer. 'Even since the coup, this kind of stuff is finished. Who wants anything to do with the Revolution now? It's all in the past, thank God.' He started taking the canvas off the stretchers.

I looked at the painting. The flashes from the exploding shells fired by the battle cruiser *Aurora* glittered in the eyes of the almost life-sized revolutionary in the foreground. His mouth was half-open with excitement, his head was thrown back heroically, his rifle was held out menacingly in front of him. A band of vivid scarlet was tied around his upper arm. Ahead of him lay Palace Square, with the Winter Palace beyond. Fires were burning, of the same brilliant colour as his armband. His objective was to destroy, once and for all, the old outmoded structures of the world. He was the vanguard of Marxism-Leninism, and the moment of revolution had come. He prepared to charge. The world was about to be shaken.

It was nothing like that in reality, of course. The *Aurora* certainly opened fire, but the troops who took over the Winter Palace marched quietly across the square and queued up to enter through the kitchen door which someone had forgotten to lock. Once they were inside and made their way through the building, the defenders surrendered immediately and the old regime was finished. Not a drop of blood was shed. The photographs and newsreel pictures which later illustrated the official versions of the revolution were all taken from Eisenstein's excellent but misleading film about it; Stalin, who approved the project, would not have been content with anything less than maximum heroism. Yet on the night of 25 October 1917 (corresponding to 7 November in the modern calendar) all that happened was that the stop-gap system which had tried to govern Russia since the February revolution and the abdication of the Tsar simply collapsed through its own feebleness.

That night a small, unrepresentative group of conspirators whose leader, nine months before, had said 'We of the older generation may not live to see the decisive battles of this coming revolution,' took power in the name of the working-class, consolidated it with the utmost ferocity, invented a whole range of romantic myths about the origins of their revolution, grew in strength and influence until many people thought they would dominate the world, and then, in their turn, collapsed through something of the same feebleness. For a doctrine which claimed to be the final answer to the economic and intellectual problems of the world, the Marxist-Leninist revolution had not lasted long: 74 years from start to finish, the span of an average man's life in the Western world. Thanks to the brutal carelessness of the Soviet system, the average life of a man under Soviet rule was likely to be significantly shorter.

If there was a single day on which it could be said that the Marxist-Leninist system came to end in Europe, it was 7 November 1991, the anniversary of the charge across the square. On that day the city which had been Petrograd at the time of the revolution and Leningrad after 1924, formally resumed its original name of St Petersburg. The ceremony was performed in the presence of the Grand Duke Vladimir Kyrillovich Romanov, first cousin once removed to the last Tsar, Nicholas II, and claimant (though his right was much challenged) to the crown. By a fitting congruence, the Grand Duke was 74: he, like the revolution, had been born in 1917, and now he had outlived it.

Together with the Grand Duchess, a member of the princely Bagration family and (to the dismay of many Romanovs) a divorcee, the Grand Duke had flown by chartered plane to the capital city of his family two days earlier. 'This,' he was quoted as saying during the flight, 'is the moment I have been waiting for all my life.' As he drove through the streets of the city he had never seen, his pale, sad, haunted face glimmered at the window of the vast black official Chaika, looking out at the grand but decaying buildings and smiling at the occasional groups of by-standers who waved the old Russian flag of white, blue and red. Most people took little notice of the cars as they passed: life was hard in the new St Petersburg, and the queues were longer than at any time since the end of the Second World War. Eggs, meat, tea, sugar and butter were all rationed; there were rumours that bread would be next.

On the anniversary itself the crowds started assembling in Palace Square before 8 a.m. There seemed to be almost as many children as adults: this was a day which everyone wanted to be remembered for generations to come. November is a dreary month in St Petersburg, and it was cold and gloomy, though sometimes it seemed as if the sun might break through the thin white cloud-cover. Each of the statues of the Tsars, almost all of which had been left in place throughout the years of Bolshevism, was garlanded with wreaths and flags. There was an atmosphere of great suppressed excitement: from time to time someone would throw a handful of papers into the air, and they would drift down on the heads of the people below. There was laughter and a kind of determined gaiety.

A far smaller demonstration was going on not far away: the few vociferous, faithful Communists who were not prepared to give up the faith in which they had been raised gathered to celebrate the anniversary of the revolution, singing the Internationale, waving red flags and hoisting pictures of Lenin above their heads. It was a show of defiance as much as anything: the feeling that there was something unworthy in giving up a principle for which so much had been sacrificed for so long. There were, at most, several hundred of them; but many thousands of others, who did not themselves want to turn out, shared their view that the terrible privations of the 900-day siege of the city during the Second World War should not be forgotten in the rush to return to the city's historical roots, and that these were best honoured by leaving the name of Leningrad as it was.

In Palace Square there were all kinds of excitements: parachutists landing among the crowds carrying vast pre-revolutionary flags; speeches by politicians, appearances by celebrities, free food and drink, a chance to see the Grand Duke himself. It wasn't that people thought things would get better as a result of having the Romanovs back or changing the name of the city to what it had been; it was simply a feeling that the wrongs of the past were being undone, and the flow of Russian history was at last being restored. That night there were magnificent fireworks: towering rockets that exploded into gigantic red and white chrysanthemums in the sky. The rockets had been ordered for the usual celebration of the revolution, but the abortive coup and the subsequent collapse of the Communist Party had changed all that. In the interval between the planning of the occasion and its taking place, the revolutionary fireworks had turned into loyalist ones.

To call the collapse of Marxism-Leninism in the Soviet Union a revolution is to dignify it beyond its deservings. The coup of 19 August 1991 was a despairing attempt by those who were still loyal to an older, more dictatorial system of government to rescue the Communist Party from the slow death which they rightly anticipated. All they achieved was to kill it off quickly instead: their coup fell apart within three days. Yet it was not defeated by a popular uprising, despite the myths which quickly took root about the vast crowds at the barricades. The great mass of the Soviet people remained as passive as they had throughout the period of Bolshevik rule.

Marxism-Leninism died in different ways in different countries. In Poland and Hungary, where past history might have indicated that it would be swept away on a tide of blood, it was eased out constitutionally. In the German Democratic Republic it was killed by its own economic failure and (in the final instance) because of a miscalculation by the Party leadership; in Czechoslovakia it fell to the reawakened sense of identity among the people at large; in Romania it was pulled down by the despair of hungry crowds; in Bulgaria it faded tactfully away; in Albania the idiosyncratic national variant died from the general democratic infection; in Yugoslavia it, and the state, collapsed in violence together. Further afield, it simply disappeared in Ethiopia, Angola and Afghanistan when the supply of weapons and money from Moscow dried up. Countries with Marxist-Leninist tendencies suddenly ceased to exhibit them. In Britain and half-a-dozen other Western countries the Communist Party simply voted to close down and re-open for business under a new, non-Bolshevik title.

Suddenly, there was no enemy for NATO and no ideological competition for the capitalist liberal democracies. The planners were taken by surprise: Britain had signed a contract to upgrade its Polaris-armed nuclear submarines with Trident; France had invested heavily in a new system of short-range nuclear weapons which could reach no farther than the eastern part of a now reunited Germany – its closest ally. The significance of the sudden end to the old super-power rivalry was overlooked by President Saddam Hussein of Iraq, who expected Soviet acquiescence in his invasion of Kuwait in August 1990, and found instead that Moscow backed every one of the resolutions against him which were proposed by the Americans at the United Nations.

After the failure of the coup in Moscow, there were sets of *matryushka* dolls for sale in the likeness of various hate-figures; Saddam Hussein and Yasser Arafat nestling inside Hitler and Napoleon. Only a short time before, Saddam and Arafat had been valued clients of the Soviet Union.

The 1980s effectively killed off Marxist-Leninism, even though it was far from obvious until the end of the decade that this was happening. After 1985, when Mikhail Gorbachev came to power, it seemed as though Soviet power was developing and changing, not that it was dying. Most people still remembered that the Soviet system had apparently been at its height only ten years before. In the 1980s it seemed that the West was trying to push back some of Moscow's advances of the Soviet Union, nothing more. Those who visited the Soviet Union were aware of the growing culture of democracy and of the advancing arteriosclerosis which was crippling the economy; but very few of them anticipated that the collapse would be so quick, or so devastating. The events of 1989–91 showed that Marxism-Leninism had reached no deeper into the national life of the countries involved than the surface: a crust, which broke almost immediately. It never commanded the loyalty of the people who figured so much in its rhetoric and so little in its daily practice. For those of them who lived in the satellite countries of central and eastern Europe the system meant nothing more than an updated form of colonization; for the people of the Soviet Union itself – soon to collapse into its component parts – it was a new tyranny by yet another unelected group of autocrats.

As the archives opened, the precise effects of this colonial rule began to emerge: mass murders, imprisonment on a large scale, phoney election results, corruption on a large scale, the lives of hundreds of millions distorted by a few careerists. One example can stand for all of them. In 1968 Gerd Poppe, a young medical student doing his national service in the East German army, was part of a contingent which was ordered into Czechoslovakia to crush the liberalization movement. He hated the job he was told to do, and talked about it openly with his fellow-soldiers. Someone reported him to the authorities. The Stasi, East Germany's secret police, opened a file on Gerd Poppe, and a Lieutenant Zoennchen of Section XX was put in charge of the case. It was the start of a long and careful war which lasted for years. As part of it, Lieutenant Zoennchen tried to break up Poppe's marriage and turn his children against him. He approached Poppe's wife, Ulrike, and told her that if she would leave Gerd she could go back to university as a post-graduate student, earn a good salary, and be provided with a well-to-do and utterly loyal lover: a judge called Harald. Ulrike Poppe turned the offer down, and the marriage was saved. Lieutenant Zoennchen, only one of 85,000 Stasi agents, had to turn his attentions to someone else. No doubt he succeeded in plenty of other cases.

It was the Lieutenant Zoennchens of Marxism-Leninism that caused the collapse of the system, because they gave so many people a reason to hate it. Its architects never envisaged that the time would come when they would need genuine popular support. When the time did come, the Party offices were empty and the people – the real people – were in the streets.

INTRODUCTION: THE
SPRINGTIME OF NATIONS

'When a government, like an old-fashioned building, has become crazy and rotten, stops the way of improvement, and only serves to collect diseases and corruption, and the proprietors refuse to come to any compromise, the community proceed in this as in some other cases; they set summarily to work – they pull down the house, they abate the nuisance.'

WILLIAM HAZLITT on the French Revolution, 1828

On the morning of 14 July 1989 I walked to work.

Along the Champs-Elysées Algerian huxters were selling rosettes, Phrygian caps of liberty, and copies of the Declaration of the Rights of Man. There was almost nothing that couldn't be overprinted with some memento of the French Revolution, from handkerchiefs to condoms. The crowds smiled and stretched in the early sunshine. Most seemed to sport a ribbon or a cockade in revolutionary red, white and blue. Many people had bought cardboard periscopes to make sure of seeing something of the parade, hours before there was anything to see. Others sat at the tables outside Fouquet's or the Café Georges V drinking coffee and eating a tricoloured mixture of ice creams called a *Drapeau Patriotique*.

In the Avenue itself soldiers brushed the faint dust of the morning from the armour that had been assembled there: tanks, armoured cars, armoured personnel carriers, motorized artillery. *Agents de police* watched indulgently as people climbed on the barriers to get a better view. They moved forward only when someone stepped on the sacred roadway itself, and even then they smiled and apologized. There were thousands of soldiers on the streets, in plumes and breastplates or camouflage and berets, but not one in a hundred was armed. Soon the President of the French Republic would be driving down the Champs-Elysées in an armoured car with a hundred men and horses of the *Gardes Républicaines* behind and in front of him, to celebrate the two hundredth anniversary of the most significant revolution in the world's history.

Afterwards President Mitterrand was to chair a summit conference of the seven leading economic powers in the newly completed Arche de la Défense. I left the Champs-Elysées before the great march took place and with the Arc de Triomphe behind me began the long walk down the Avenue de la Grande Armée towards the Arche. Everything here was closed, even the bars. People were hurrying past me up the gradient towards the Étoile, anxious not to miss anything. They were unaware that the crowds were already six or more deep down the full length of the parade, and the supply of periscopes was running out.

There was thunder in the clear sky: formations of interceptors, strike aircraft, bombers, transport planes and helicopters made their way in line astern from west to east along the precise direction of the avenue down which I was walking. As they flew over the Arche de la Défense and roared towards us, the lead aircraft broke out red, white and blue smoke behind them. Little children sitting on their fathers' shoulders clapped to see them, ducking their heads because the planes seemed so low.

That the leaders of the West's seven leading economic powers were meeting in Paris that day was a piece of political grandstanding by François Mitterrand. Yet with hindsight the two hundredth anniversary of the French Revolution was perhaps the single moment which best reflected the triumph of Western liberal democracy over all rival systems of government. The wealth, the grandeur, the personal liberty, the prestige and power which were on display were greater than the world had ever seen before. Soon, indeed, the rose was to become a little blown. The decline in the influence of the United States became more obvious. Margaret Thatcher seemed unassailable as Britain's prime minister, but would be politically vulnerable within sixteen months. The Franco-German relationship would soon diminish. The West wouldn't necessarily be weaker, but the power relationship between the different countries was changing, and so was the position of the individual politicians.

By contrast the Soviet Union, the West's great competitor for forty-five years, was almost on its knees. Gorbachev had declared the Cold War over when he met George Bush in the saloon of a Soviet cruise ship berthed at the island of Malta the previous December. What he meant was that the Soviet Union had been obliged to give up its attempt to compete with the United States both militarily and economically. For some time, Gorbachev and his foreign minister, Eduard Shevardnadze, had been doing their best to calm tensions in places where the superpowers had once competed. In each case – the Middle East, Africa, Central America and in Europe itself – the Soviet Union gave up its old positions, told its friends it could no longer back them so strongly, and began to open relations with countries it had once abhorred: South Africa and Israel in particular. It was done partly from a genuine desire for peace. It was also done because the cost of keeping its side of the conflict going was too great.

The Soviet Union had reached its own high-water mark fourteen years earlier. In November 1976 there had been a gloomier and more threatening parade than the one the world was witnessing in Paris. As the tanks and mobile missiles rumbled over the cobblestones in Red Square, Leonid Brezhnev, appearing with the rest of his Politburo on the balcony of Lenin's tomb was old, sick and had an attention span estimated at fifteen minutes in every two hours. Yet the military and political authority of the Soviet Union, as represented by the parade in honour of the anniversary of the 1917 Revolution, was at its greatest since the 1940s. The United States had been soundly beaten in Vietnam, and country after country in South-East Asia had fallen to the Communists. The MPLA, backed by Moscow, was winning the war in Angola. Soon there would be a concerted attempt to break NATO and neutralize the entire central part of Europe.

When the crucial moment came, however, the Western alliance stuck together. The men who ensured that the competition between capitalism and Communism would eventually be won by the West were President Jimmy Carter and Chancellor Helmut Schmidt – Carter for identifying the deployment of Cruise missiles in Europe as the key to the continuing strength of the Alliance, and Schmidt for forcing it through against considerable opposition in West Germany, the one country where it mattered. Having remained together politically, the West had out-produced, out-earned, out-thought, out-grown and out-performed the Soviet bloc ever since. By the time a new Soviet leader came to power in 1985 the battle had been thoroughly lost. He might want to retain some aspects of Marxism-Leninism, but they wouldn't include the old economic system or the old idea of thought-control.

So here were the seven leaders of capitalism, having preserved themselves from the power of revolutionary Marxism, gathering in celebration of the two hundredth anniversary of another revolution. In its way the French Revolution had often been cruel, ugly and mindless, a release of the worst forces in society and an affront to the principles which many of the leading revolutionaries professed. The joyful sense of release which marked 14 July 1789 was followed inevitably by the Terror, the Directory and the Bonapartist seizure of power. The aftershocks of 1789 continued throughout the nineteenth century and well into the twentieth. The near-revolution of 1968 was one of them.

Margaret Thatcher disapproved of the whole business. Her gift to François Mitterrand on this transcendent occasion was a first edition of Dickens' *Tale of Two Cities*: inexpensive, and not very good as history. There was a considerably more suitable present from George Bush: the key to the Bastille, taken originally to the young United States by Lafayette. Mrs Thatcher's view was that evolution was greatly preferable to revolution; which may well be true, but is of little help to those who live in an autocracy which refuses to evolve.

When the seven leaders met, 1989 was more than half over. No one around the conference table at the Arche suggested that it might turn out to be a year of revolution on the scale of 1789. No one, indeed, suggested that there would be any revolutions in Europe in 1989. There was evolution, in Hungary and Poland. There was something that was starting to pass for evolution in Bulgaria. There was evolution in the Soviet Union itself. There, it was felt, the process ended. The rest of Central and Eastern Europe seemed fixed in political permafrost. The conventional wisdom was that the current generation of leaders – Honecker, Ceausescu and the rest – would have to die off before there could be any change. At the Sommet de l'Arche, the world was still divided into three parts: the West, the Communist bloc and the uncommitted Third World. That division did not last out the year.

Later the falling of the dominoes came to seem inevitable. At the time it did not appear like that. Days before the revolutionary process began in Czechoslovakia, those who knew the country best believed the old system had at least eighteen more months to run. Even after the process had begun in Romania, the best-informed estimate was that if his health lasted Ceausescu would still be in power by the mid-1990s. There was no single cause for these changes. Small things played a disproportionately important part in them: a misplaced document in East Berlin, an erroneous broadcast in Prague, a whispered aside in Bucharest. But these were merely the sharp rocks which finally wrecked the boat. It was already being propelled down the stream by a combination of political currents faster than anyone realized.

One of these currents was unquestionably the political and economic strength of the West as represented at the Arche. Later, some politicians tried to claim the credit for this; but by standing near the old Reichstag in Berlin and saying 'Mr Gorbachev, take down this Wall!' Ronald Reagan – or rather, his speechwriter of the moment – simply showed he had no understanding of how the Wall might eventually come down. It wasn't Mrs Thatcher's economic principles which caused the changes in the Soviet bloc, nor the diplomacy of Hans-Dietrich Genscher and Helmut Kohl. It was the simple, verifiable fact that Western capitalist society was effective, rich and reasonably free, while the countries of the socialist bloc were manifestly not.

For it wasn't just capitalism that had won, it was the Western concept of representative democracy. Ordinary Russians, Chinese, Czechs and Romanians all knew that people in the West were freer than they were. The demand for greater democracy in Tiananmen Square in 1989 had a considerable effect elsewhere in the socialist world. After all the years in which the Chinese had appeared to be the most mechanical and unthinking supporters of the system, a million people demonstrated to demand something better than Marxism-Leninism. That, and the savage end of the demonstrations, had a profound effect everywhere. It placed a particular emphasis on the value of demanding greater democracy. During 1989 the feeling grew in many countries that democracy was an idea which, if the circumstances were right, was worth coming out on to the streets for. In 1989 there was something of the same revolutionary contagion which there had been in Europe in 1848–49, 1917–19 and 1968.

All empires come to an end. Nowadays it is fashionable to say that this happens when they overstretch themselves militarily and financially. Maybe, though, the process can happen the other way round: it becomes obvious that they have overstretched themselves because they have run their course. The old will to power, the old self-belief, the ability to force people to make the sacrifices which are necessary to keep an empire going, all start to fade. The burden of empire becomes harder to bear; the overstretching begins to hurt, and therefore is seen to exist. This is what happened in the Soviet empire in Europe. Moscow tried to ease the burden, and it slipped.

The burden of empire in Central and Eastern Europe has been borne on other shoulders in this century: by the Emperor of Austria-Hungary and by the German Führer. When the Austro-Hungarian Empire collapsed in 1918, it gave place to a series of small, independent states which had mostly tried for self-determination in 1848 and failed. There was a new springtime of nations, more successful than in 1848 – for a time. If it had not been for Stalin's strategic interests at the end of the Second World War there would have been another springtime when Hitler's European empire collapsed. The year 1989 represented a return to the pre-1938 order in Europe; a return, indeed, to an older, pre-1914 order.

The Soviet empire in Europe was never a natural entity. If it had been predominantly Slavic or had consisted of territories which imperial Russia once controlled it might have been more coherent. Instead there were only two elements that held it together: the fact of Soviet military power and the fiction that each country had voluntarily chosen the Communist way. The old Marxist maxim was that capitalism would die of its own contradictions. As it turned out, it was Marxism-Leninism's contradictions which killed the Soviet empire.

As with most empires, it required someone with the courage to begin the process of decolonization. There is evidence that Mikhail Gorbachev came to power realizing that Soviet control in Europe (though not in Central Asia) would have to disappear. It was the only empire in modern history where the possessions were richer and more developed than the imperial power itself; now it was turning out to be more interested in personal freedom than were the governments of the subject peoples.

People throughout the Soviet bloc took Gorbachev at his word. They watched him withdraw his forces from Afghanistan in February 1989. They believed that he sympathized more with the Prague Spring of 1968 than with the men who sent in the tanks, for instance; and they believed him when he said there would be no tanks again. If Honecker, Jakes and Ceausescu had no Soviet tanks to back them, then the only bar to greater freedom was their security police and their army. Gorbachev may have actively undermined all three; and it was clear he would have preferred to be free of them. The Marxist-Leninist system itself made revolution rather than evolution necessary. It failed to evolve a convenient means by which the men who had fought their way to power and stayed there for years could be constitutionally removed. Since the system was incapable of change, it was necessary to get rid of it and start again.

*

The only country where the system evolved away from Marxism-Leninism was Hungary. In a sense it happened because of the horrors of the past. Conditions after the Communist take-over of 1947 by Matthias Rakosi were in some respects worse than those elsewhere in Eastern Europe. At the concentration camp in Recsk, in the Matra mountains north of Budapest, political prisoners worked for fifteen hours a day, winter and summer, cutting andesite from the quarry and carrying it with their bare hands. The uprising of 1956 was a reaction to such excesses. People believed the West would help them. They also believed that the Soviet leader Nikita Khrushchev, who had spoken so movingly a few months earlier about the horrors of Stalinism, would accept the democratic changes which Imre Nagy, the Hungarian prime minister, was seeking to introduce. Perhaps, also, they thought Khrushchev was simply weak.

But Nagy was thirty years too early. Khrushchev was no Gorbachev, and the 1950s were not the time for a satellite country like Hungary to slip into neutrality. Moscow's suppression of the independence movement was savage. Two thousand tanks were used, three thousand people died. The Soviet ambassador, Yuri Andropov (who later became Chairman of the KGB and General Secretary of the Communist Party), tricked some of the Hungarian leaders into coming to discuss a truce over dinner at the embassy. Men of the Soviet secret police burst in and arrested them. Nagy and his defence minister, Pal Maleter, were later hanged.

The man whom Moscow selected to govern Hungary and return it to orthodoxy was a strange, secretive figure. Janos Kadar might have been undistinguished as a political thinker, but he was a survivor whose ideas evolved remarkably over the years. He had suffered personally under Stalinism. He usually kept his hands hidden when he met foreign visitors, but if you looked closely you could still see the marks where his finger-nails had been torn out by the secret police in Rakosi's time. When he was imposed on Hungary in the immediate aftermath of the 1956 uprising he was loathed by the great majority of his people. Yet Khrushchev had chosen well. Kadar was never loved, but by the mid-1960s he had shown sufficient independence to earn the grudging support of many Hungarians.

Eventually, moving with immense care and slowness, he edged away from the rest of the Soviet bloc in economic terms. Managers ran their own factories with minimal interference from the Ministry of Heavy Industry in Budapest. Workers were given access after hours to the machinery at their plant so that they could produce goods which they could sell privately. The authorities had realized the workers were doing it anyway, so they tried to make sure it happened only during their time off. Farmers sold to a free market. None of it worked particularly well, but it was a great deal more efficient than any other socialist economy. Leonid Brezhnev recommended the Hungarian way as the model for the Soviet Union and the rest of his allies, without seeming to realize that it undermined the old system of centralized planning. When Margaret Thatcher visited Hungary in 1984, she received a rapturous reception from ordinary people when she walked down the main shopping street of Budapest. Kadar, hearing of this, tried the same thing a few days later. No one took any notice of him.

Within the Hungarian Socialist Workers' Party there were new men and women who wanted to move much farther than Kadar. I first met Imre Poszgay, who was to become the effective leader of the HSWP, in 1983. He talked like an Austrian socialist. On one occasion, Kadar had referred to him as 'impertinent'. No one was ever quite sure whether this was supposed to be affectionate or savage. Poszgay had avoided getting involved on either side in the 1956 uprising because he was based in a provincial town at the time. A fat, jolly man with a deceptively open manner, an intellectual by instinct and training, he worked his way up through the system, until in May 1988 he and those who thought like him in the Party were strong enough to call a special congress and vote Kadar out of power.

Kadar's place was taken by Karoly Grosz, and Poszgay became a member of the Politburo. Soon he and not Grosz became the dominant figure in the leadership. Changes began to happen fast. Poszgay, acting on his own initiative, announced in February 1989 that the events of 1956 had been a popular uprising rather than an attempt at counter-revolution. Although Kadar had gone it was still by far the most delicate subject in Hungarian politics. Even then the Party Central Committee could not be induced to go as far as Poszgay; but in June 1989 permission was given for the bodies of Imre Nagy and the other leaders of the 1956 uprising to be exhumed. Nagy's body was found buried in waste ground at the Ujkoztemeto cemetery, wrapped in tar paper. On 16 June his coffin lay in state in Heroes' Square before being formally reburied.

At last Hungary had come to terms with its past. Its future was secured by a decision, taken by the Central Committee, to introduce a multi-party system. Poszgay's own position often seemed closer to that of the opposition Hungarian Democratic Forum than to his own party, the HSWP. Later that summer, again at his instigation, Hungary opened its borders with Austria. People from the German Democratic Republic were able to flood through to the West in such numbers that the entire future of the state was called into question. By November the position had become so bad that the government in East Berlin could think of nothing better than to allow its citizens to move freely to the West. Liberalization in Hungary led directly to the breaching of the Berlin Wall.

By the time President Bush visited Budapest in July 1989 Hungary had effectively ceased to be either a Communist country or a Soviet satellite. Senior politicians talked seriously of joining the European Community, and even their jokes about joining NATO weren't entirely fanciful.

I stood on the balcony of a flat overlooking the square in the centre of the city where President Bush was due to make a speech. The anachronistic red star on the roof of the Parliament building would shortly be removed. It was the last outward sign of the years of

Marxism-Leninism, apart from the drabness of the city and the bullet marks from 1956. Beside me was the man who lived in the flat, an Anglophile in his mid-forties from a wealthy background. The rooms were dark and in need of decoration, but the furniture was extremely grand and the paintings on the walls were good ones. There were English touches: mementoes of visits by at least two generations of the family. I thought I spotted an oar on the wall of a distant room, from some college regatta perhaps. He wore a cravat, like a star from a Pinewood film of the 1950s. From his balcony he looked down at the enthusiastic crowds which were starting to gather.

'These little Communists of ours are acting like real politicians,' he said; 'they're giving people what they want, instead of what they ought to want. The trouble is, they can never give us so much that we can forget that they are Communists.'

He pulled out an antique bottle of Bell's Scotch Whisky. It was strangely shaped, and looked as old as the doctor.

'My father put this away in a cupboard in 1947,' the doctor said. 'He said he wouldn't drink it until the day the Russian soldiers left our country. Before he died he made me promise to do the same. Maybe quite soon now. . . .'

He made a little glass-lifting motion with his hand and laughed. Early in 1990 the Soviet Union reached agreement with Hungary to withdraw its troops.

He was right about the fundamental unpopularity of the Party. I went to see Imre Poszgay a few days later and asked him whether he and his colleagues would really be the beneficiaries of the changes they were introducing. He smiled a cheery, deceptively innocent smile.

'Who can say? Naturally I hope so. That's why we're doing these things. But to be honest with you, there's nothing else we can do. Even if others win the elections, there's no serious alternative to doing what we have done.'

When the final round of elections came, in April 1990, the reformed Communists won only 8 per cent of the seats, and Poszgay and his colleagues were out of office. A centre-right government came to power. As in 1918, Hungary had emerged from an empire and found itself on its own; though this time, unlike the violence and destruction which followed the abortive Communist republic of Bela Kun in 1919, the transition was peaceable and relaxed. Hungary's economy and environment had been horribly damaged by thirty-three years of Marxism-Leninism; but now, at least, it had shown the way to the rest of Central and Eastern Europe. There are dozens of men and women, maybe more, who had a part in encouraging the revolutions that will be described in this book. But the stout figure of Imre Poszgay who lost his job and was obliged to stay at home and cook for his family, is one of the more important of them.

When the Soviet troops began leaving Hungary I telephoned my Anglophile friend to see if he had broached his father's bottle of Scotch.

'Pure nectar, my dear fellow,' he said.

PART I
THE ANCIEN REGIME

1
THROUGH THE LOOKING-GLASS

'All our principles were right, but our results were wrong. . . . Our will was hard and pure, we should have been loved by the people. But they hate us. Why are we so odious and detested?'

ARTHUR KOESTLER, *Darkness At Noon*

YOU ARE NOW LEAVING THE AMERICAN SECTOR
ВЫ ВЫЕЗЖАЕТЕ ИЗ АМЕРИКАНСКОГО СЕКТОРА
VOUS SORTEZ DU SECTEUR AMERICAIN
SIE VERLASSEN DEN AMERIKANISCHEN SEKTOR

The Friedrichstrasse crossing-point at Checkpoint Charlie was always an eerie, unpropitious place. A war might have broken out here. It was the boundary of the known world: everyone who crossed into East Berlin knew that. This end of the street was secure and safe. At the other end, everything was uncertain. In the warmth of their huts in the middle of the road American, British and French military policemen chatted, their feet on the table. They were not border guards, because the Allies maintained that Berlin was legally undivided. They took no notice when the occasional car or pedestrian penetrated the West from the Communist side.

I made the crossing for the first time in the late 1970s. As I passed the huts, heading eastwards along the Friedrichstrasse, the lack of alertness on the western side seemed like a paradigm of the West in general: too relaxed, too unconcerned about its long-term safety. I wanted NATO soldiers to watch over my progress down this narrow, undistinguished little street. It was night, but the East German searchlights made the crossing-place bright as day. Their beams reached into the West and illuminated the house which had been turned into a museum dedicated to the people who had lost their lives at the Berlin Wall. To walk past it, eastwards, felt like defecting.

I had a suitcase in each hand, and a knapsack slung over my shoulder. It was cold, but I was sweating. The Wall was smooth and grey, and its run through the city was broken here for only the width of the street. To left and right lay no-man's-land, swept clean by bulldozers, lit by arc lamps, guarded by machine guns. From here on, everything would seem as grey and forbidding as the Wall itself.

I looked up. High above my head on the side of the first building in the Eastern bloc was an old, peeling sign advertising an East Berlin newspaper: NEUE ZEIT. New time. I was passing through the looking-glass. Here, new time meant old time, democratic meant autocratic, the People meant the Party, freedom meant dictatorship, independence meant Soviet control, a sovereign republic meant an artificial statelet. If you wrote 'East Berlin' on an official form here, they would tear it up. This, supposedly, was Berlin *tout court*, the capital of the German Democratic Republic. It was also Looking-glass Land. Any resemblance to a real state was purely imaginary. Any reference to a state of reality would get you into trouble.

Checkpoint Charlie was open and exposed. I knew I was being watched. Ahead of me, a yard or two on the Eastern side, a sentry-post jutted out onto the pavement. It was necessary to walk round it. Behind the thick greenish glass a uniformed soldier and a man in civilian clothes, silhouetted by the light behind me, stood up as I approached. The civilian began taking photographs of me. The camera was intimidatingly big, its lens a huge, shiny eye registering everything about me, searching out my intentions. The motor drive whirred in the silence of the street.

A man in uniform stood in my path. He hand rested on his pistol holster. He didn't move, and he didn't speak. I tried to shuffle past with my luggage.

'*Moment, bitte.*'

I stopped.

'*Reisepass.*'

I put down my cases and searched for my passport. It took a little time. He was impatient: his breath fled from him in the cold air, he tapped his holster. He glanced through the passport as though it were worthless, then handed it back dismissively. There seemed no purpose in the exchange. It was control for controlling's sake.

Ahead lay a door with blistered paint. The policeman nodded towards it. Inside, several people in bulky clothes were sitting on a bench: Westerners, waiting to pass through. They looked as if they had been there a long time. Occasionally someone would be allowed in, and the next person would stand up and walk over to the counter. It was half an hour before I reached that stage.

'Why are you here?'

I explained as best I could. The man behind the counter was boorish, middle-aged, his fingers nicotine brown. He scarcely listened. At the end he tossed my passport and my letter of invitation from GDR Television back across the counter.

'What happens now?'

He looked away, and I had to work out the next stage of the process myself. The path led to a pimply border guard of eighteen or nineteen in a wooden booth. He examined my passport and visa form. My every feature was scrutinized: colour of hair, colour of eyes, age, any distinguishing marks. Behind and above me was a mirror, so he could check that I wasn't carrying anything. He asked all the question the other man had already put to me. It was minutes before he stamped my passport.

The next stage was the customs inspection. Two unsympathetic characters looked through my cases and my kitbag. My books received detailed inspection: for political content, decency, hidden messages. They passed, and the inspectors seemed disappointed. Everything went back into my cases, a great deal less neatly than before, and there were two more gates and another police checkpoint before I was considered worthy of entering the German Democratic Republic. Overhead hung the East German flag, a black, red and gold tricolour with a hammer and a set of compasses imposed on it: the nation of workers with hand and brain.

I was back in the Friedrichstrasse. But it too had passed through the looking-glass. Now it was dingy and dark and there were very few cars. They wheezed asthmatically past: feeble two-stroke Trabants, for the most part, which took ten years to buy and lasted a good deal less than that. There were no taxis around. The Trabants, though slow, were not prepared to stop. My shadow was thrown by the arc lights of Checkpoint Charlie onto the dilapidated walls, long and irregular, like an early Fritz Lang film. The electricity used up along the Wall seemed to have drained the current from the rest of East Berlin. In the gloom, I started to walk to my hotel.

In the early 1980s the East Germans realized the need to present themselves better. Checkpoint Charlie was smartened up and the police were told to be more polite. It had little effect, but the crossing itself took on a more normal appearance. The city of East Berlin itself began to improve. Money was spent on new buildings, to compensate the citizens who were never allowed to go to the West. But it remained a strange, truncated place where through-roads became sudden dead ends, and people could die trying to leave in the wrong way. For the rest of its time as the pretend capital of a pretend state it kept its air of nasty absurdity, as unnatural as a garden of plastic flowers.

Then, in a matter of months in 1989 and 1990, it ceased to be a

separate entity at all: it became merely a shabby section of town, which
had once protected its shabbiness by bright lights and machine-gun
bullets. Nowadays the very idea that you might cross a frontier when
you walk down the Friedrichstrasse seems as unlikely as being greeted
by a British immigration official in Rangoon, or an Austrian one in
Venice. The German Democratic Republic, a state that was neither
democratic nor properly German, is back in the historical lumber-
room; and the Soviet empire in Central and Eastern Europe has gone
the way of the Sublime Porte and the Kingdom of the Two Sicilies.

*

Like East Germany, the entire Soviet system was based on a political
metastasis. Things were the opposite of themselves. 'WAR IS PEACE'
was the slogan in Orwell's *1984*. Within the Soviet empire the unspoken
slogans were 'Autocracy is Freedom'; 'Poverty is Wealth'; 'Selfishness
is Brotherhood'. In a political system supposedly governed in the
interests of the workers and the peasants, the workers and the peasants
did worse than under most contemporary forms of capitalism. In the
political system created to destroy privilege, a political caste was
provided with shops, hotels, farms and entire factories to meet its every
need, while ordinary people suffered hardship and shortage. A society
supposedly based on equality and fraternity operated on the basis of
grab what you can and the weakest to the wall. The people of Moscow
and Warsaw and Prague were even ruder and more aggressive than
those of New York or Paris. You had to fight to get what you needed,
because everything was in short supply.

And all the time the system declared that it was better and more
moral than any other. Vaclav Havel, the opposition playwright, who as
a result of the upheavals of 1989 became Czechoslovakia's president,
wrote: 'A power grounded in an omnipresent ideological fiction . . . can
rationalize anything without ever having to brush against the truth.'

The active principle at the heart of the system, which operated from
the Friedrichstrasse to the farthest reaches of Soviet Asia, was mistrust.
Nothing was to be taken on credit. A sense of watchfulness, of dubiety,
operated at every level of life. Foreign visitors to the Soviet bloc
assumed it was directed particularly at them. They created legends
about microphones in their hotel rooms and spies in the street. But the
legends were only occasionally true. In a society where consumer goods
were of poor quality and in short supply, Westerners could not escape
notice, so they rarely needed to be followed. It was the ordinary
population which was under observation. Every block of flats, every
street, every district had its active Party members, its local Committee,

its People's Militia, its organization for the defence of the revolution. Each reported back on people who were unenthusiastic, who lacked the proper class credentials for advancement, who were too interested in the things of the West. The revolution had to be defended against them.

And it was in need of defence. It would never have taken place naturally in any of the countries which came into the Soviet Union's orbit between 1945 and 1948. The largest percentage of the vote which the Communist party obtained in elections which were genuinely or relatively free in those first post-war years was the 38 per cent in Czechoslovakia in May 1946. In each of the other countries the figure was much smaller, until the Communists took control and awarded themselves ludicrously high levels of support.

So the people were not entirely reliable. After the riots in East Germany of 1953, when the writers' union accused the people of forfeiting the trust of the government, Bertolt Brecht wrote his scathing poem, quoted so often it has become hackneyed, suggesting that the government should dissolve the people and elect a new one. Marxism-Leninism is a system which aims at the social, moral and political fulfilment of mankind, and yet it has consistently failed to reach its aim. Since the governed are too frail to do what Marxism-Leninism tells them is in their own best interests, they have to be forced into it. A fundamental mistrust arises, which under Stalin reached the level of paranoia. His successors, from Khrushchev to Chernenko, were more balanced men, but the feeling that socialism had to be maintained in spite of the people continued. Even Party members had to be watched with the greatest care.

May Day in Moscow was a pleasant holiday – an opportunity for workers to turn out and celebrate the day which is dedicated to them. In Red Square the arrangements followed an exact pattern, year after year. On the cobblestones were the indelible painted marks which showed the groups involved where to take up their positions. It was a highly orchestrated business. As the floats went past and the crowds cheered you could hear another, slightly different form of crowd reaction. It took a little while to realize that this different applause and cheering came from the loudspeakers, just in case the real thing was insufficiently enthusiastic.

The only people who could take part in the May Day celebrations were Party members, chosen by local Party committees all over the Soviet Union for their dedication to the cause. Even so, each year there were no fewer than seven security checks on the way in to Red Square, to ensure that the faithful comrades were not carrying weapons which they might turn on their leaders. And once, when I had to leave the

Square early, a friend of mine took me over to one of the gates of the Kremlin as we were walking out. Inside were several hundred para-military policemen in full riot gear. They had been stationed there, as they were every year, just in case the hand-picked, thoroughly reliable Party members taking part in the celebrations should use the occasion to stage a *coup d'état*.

In 1959 Nikita Khrushchev went to New York and prophesied that by 1980 the Soviet Union would overtake the United States in economic terms. Long before the date arrived it was clear that no such thing would happen. Marxism-Leninism had succeeded in turning a vast, backward country into a super-power; but it could not ensure that it remained one. Too much was lost in the process of trying to catch up. Sometimes it became necessary to select specific, clearly-defined areas where the socialist countries could succeed better than any other country on earth. Sport was a particular favourite. The GDR selected athletics, Czechoslovakia tennis. The less attractive the regime, the more it needed the ring of ersatz success.

And just as Marxism-Leninism claimed that failure was success, so it claimed that success was failure. Official propaganda harped on the failings of capitalism. One particular Soviet television correspondent who specialized in reports on urban decay and race violence in the United States became well known in the black districts of New York City. He would speak privately of his affection for the United States and insist, when times grew easier in Moscow, that his editors had demanded that kind of reporting from him.

But the propaganda was overdone. In Central Europe especially, where many people had relatives in the West and had sometimes been able to visit them, the exaggerated accounts of decline and social decay did not ring entirely true.

> Did you know that in the city of Baltimore, in Maryland, America, two thousand people have no beds to sleep in at night, and there is no running water for eight thousand households?
>
> (From a Slovak magazine)

The figures may well have been accurate, but the constant repetition was in itself enough to make readers doubt them; especially when it was known that a third of all households in the Soviet Union were without running water.

'At one time here you couldn't open a newspaper without finding news items which were really bad about the West.'

The speaker was a taxi-driver I had found in Wenceslas Square in

Prague. He was a slow, gentle man: the very reverse of a taxi-driver in a big Western city.

'We never believed them. In fact, maybe it made us think the West was better than it really was, because whatever we read, we thought the opposite about it. So when it said in our newspapers that thousands of kids went to school with no shoes, or without having anything to eat, we would just think, "They're telling us this because they know it happens here, and they're trying to make us feel better about it." It meant that we thought even worse about our system, and even better about the way things were done in the West.'

In every country of this curious empire, where the imperial masters were poorer, less educated and less advanced than any of the countries they controlled, you would find a powerful sense of inferiority to the West. In the Soviet Union, where it dated back at least to the time of Peter the Great, people often took this inferiority to absurd lengths.

'How are you flying back to London?' a woman in her sixties asked me at a party given by a group of Moscow dissidents in 1978. She wasn't a dissident herself. She was related to the host, and just happened to be visiting. I told her I was taking an Aeroflot flight the following morning. She grabbed my hand earnestly.

'I beg you, don't do it. Put off your journey. Aeroflot has so many crashes, and we only hear half of them on our news. They hide the others, because it would look bad for us. Take a Western plane. That's the only way you'll be safe.'

Exaggerated propaganda had resulted in exaggerated disbelief.

Throughout the Soviet bloc, beginning in the early 1950s, schools had a weekly air raid practice. Children were herded out of their classrooms and into shelters, where they were given lessons on the effects of nuclear radiation. Much the same thing happened in American schools, though not Western European ones. But whereas the United States mostly abandoned the practice in the late 1960s, air raid practices for schools in the Soviet bloc continued into the 1980s. They were accompanied by lectures about the danger of invasion from the West, and particularly from the Federal Republic of Germany. It made a deep impression on one Hungarian office-worker, now in her mid-forties:

> In my school they took it really seriously. Maybe it was because of the Revolution [in 1956]. Perhaps they wanted to make sure we didn't have good ideas about the West. I don't know. But they would tell us endlessly about what the Germans did during the War, and how they were planning to do the same things now. It used to scare me a lot. My grandparents lost their house in the War, and they used to tell me about it, though they never said

exactly how it happened. I used to think the Germans were coming back at any time, and we'd lose everything. And I used to hate the West because they were on the side of the Germans.

And then, when I was around eleven or twelve, my father told me what had happened. It wasn't the Germans who had destroyed our house, it was the Russians! And once I knew that, everything I'd been taught at school started to look phoney. I couldn't believe it any more. And I soon found out that a lot of my friends felt the same way. I tell you, by the time we were in our teens we didn't believe anything we heard from any of those people any more – our teachers, our government, none of them. If you're looking for reasons why we Hungarians split off from the Russians, that's why. They told us lies. And when we found out they were lies, that was it. Finished.

Marxism-Leninism is the most pervasive political system yet devised. By comparison the right-wing dictatorships of Latin America, or South Africa under apartheid, have had nothing like the extraordinary levels of control which the Soviet Union invented and imposed on its satellites. Not even Hitler's Germany aspired to the same level of control. Over the years this led to a quiet, unspoken intensity of hatred among the people whose lives were dominated and distorted by them. But until the great uprisings of 1989 the hatred had seemed dormant. In their everyday lives most people were resigned to the restrictions and the self-censorship which they experienced every hour of the day. The dissidents in each country were few in number and had no real influence over the population as a whole. The only exception was Poland, where dissent grew steadily until it reached the point where Solidarity represented a large part of the entire nation.

For decades, the vast majority accepted the system because there was no practical alternative to it. People joined the Communist Party, and sometimes rose high in its ranks, out of pure opportunism. It was simply a way of getting on in life, but it did not necessarily involve any intellectual or political commitment. So the Communist Party, which had always been able to call on the greatest idealism, had turned into a useful career system for cynics.

The notion of brotherhood and comradeship was equally put through the looking-glass. Since goods of most kinds were in short supply, people had to fight to get them. Lining up to buy goods in an ordinary shop was a Hobbesian experience, a war of every man against every man. It is true that people would pick up things for their friends and relatives, and carry string bags wherever they went in order to take advantage of the sudden appearance of special goods in the shops. But you had to build up your network of friends and relations precisely because that helped you to compete better in the Hobbesian war. And at the same time everyone knew that the senior levels of the Communist system, the Nomenklatura, were able to use special shops where they could exercise the privilege of being more equal than others. In these stores there were attractive goods in abundance, queuing was rare and there was no unseemly pushing. Here at least the ideal was realized, for the few if not for the many. The basic principle on which Marx had built his philosophy had passed through the looking-glass.

There was always an unspoken sub-text of life in Central and Eastern Europe: within the new socialist man and woman as created by the social engineering of Marxism-Leninism an awareness of the old national life remained. The great majority of people remembered in silence what had been done to their country by the Russians after 1945. As in France after the loss of Alsace-Lorraine in 1870 (though for very different reasons) the principle was: think of it always, speak of it never.

During the nineteenth century the countries of Central and Eastern Europe which were later to come under Soviet control were mostly divided up among three great empires: the Austrian, the Russian and the Ottoman. East Germany alone had not been subject to one or other of these groupings; indeed, as Prussia, it had maintained something of an empire itself. But when, in 1918, the great wave of nationalist renewal swept across Europe as a result of the Allied victory over the Central Powers, the newly independent countries which emerged did not for the most part turn naturally to parliamentary democracy. Poland, Hungary, Romania, Yugoslavia and Bulgaria all became autocracies of one kind or another: some with kings at their head, some with generals or marshals. Only Czechoslovakia became a natural parliamentary democracy in 1918, and it remained democratic until Britain, and France under British pressure, abandoned it to dismemberment by Hitler twenty years later.

During the Second World War, each one of the countries which later formed part of the Soviet empire was occupied by Nazi Germany, or governed by Nazi sympathizers. None of them therefore emerged from the process of liberation with its old pre-war political system intact. Everywhere except Romania the Communist Party had played a significant part in the resistance to Hitler, and demanded its political reward. As the former wartime allies increasingly fell out with each other and the Cold War began, the political doodlings of Churchill, Roosevelt and Stalin at Tehran, Yalta and elsewhere about the future percentages of Soviet and Western influence in Eastern and Southern Europe ceased to have any serious meaning.

Between 1945 and 1948, country after country fell into the Soviet sphere. East Germany was Stalin's by right of conquest; until 1972 the

West German name for it was the Soviet Occupation Zone (SBZ). The old pre-war *Kommunist Partei Deutschlands*, boosted by sizeable numbers of Soviet German agents who had spent the War in Moscow and were sent into Berlin as early as May 1945, merged forcibly with the German Democratic Party, the SDP, to form a new grouping in 1946: the *Sozialistische Einheitspartei Deutschlands*, or Socialist Unity Party of Germany. Its leaders took over the main offices of state, and reduced the civil service and the other political parties which remained to the status of mere figureheads. Its constitution made it clear that all fundamental human rights were subject to 'the concrete conditions under which the proletarian revolution must triumph' (Article 19).

The borders of Poland, so often shifted in the past at the whim of its neighbours, were altered radically yet again at the end of the War. The effect was to shift Poland bodily westwards on the map. On the eastern side it lost 46.5 per cent of its territory, which was incorporated by Stalin into the Soviet Union. To the west, Stalin compensated Poland with most of East Prussia, the entire part of eastern Germany to the Oder-Neisse Line, and the city and surroundings of Szczecin (formerly Stettin). The result was to reduce Poland in size by a fifth. But in spite of Soviet domination and the merciless elimination of all rivals to the (Communist) Polish Workers' Party and its leader, Wladyslaw Gomulka, Poland assumed the characteristics of a Communist state only slowly. The Polish Peasants' Party, led by Stanislaw Mikolajczyk, put up a stubborn resistance. Gomulka set up a rival Peasants' Party under Communist domination to confuse the voters; then, before the election of January 1947, he unleased a wave of terror against the Polish Peasants' Party. Even so, it was necessary to rig the result. Gomulka's Democratic Bloc was declared to have won 80.1 per cent of the vote. The Peasants' Party was awarded only 10.3 per cent. Soon afterwards Mikolajczyk fled to the West, and what remained of his party was forcibly embodied into a National Unity Front. Article 1 of the Constitution of 22 July 1952 said that all power was vested in 'the working-people of town and country'.

In 1945 Hungary was treated by the victorious Red Army as a defeated ally of Nazi Germany. The country suffered greatly from its new masters, and was obliged to pay the costs of the Soviet occupation as well as heavy war reparations. At first, the hostility to the Russians and the memories of the destruction caused at the time of the short-lived Communist republic of Bela Kun after the First World War meant that the small and ineffective Hungarian Communist Party could do little to establish itself in power. It remained moderate in its policies and aims, and compromised with the non-Communist parties of the wartime resistance. Meanwhile it infiltrated its supporters into key positions in the government and the trade unions. In the election of November 1945 the conservative Smallholders Party won 57 per cent of the vote, while the Communists could only achieve 17 per cent.

But the presence of the Red Army made the eventual outcome certain. Soon the Communist Party switched to tougher tactics. With considerable brutality, the Hungarian army's Communist-controlled political squads and the security police began arresting people accused of conspiring against the state. The Smallholders Party was effectively destroyed. In new elections in August 1947 the Communist-dominated People's Front won 60 per cent of the votes. Soon the other groupings within the Front effectively ceased to exist. A further election in May 1949, completely manipulated, gave the People's Front 95.6 per cent.

Romania had only a small Communist Party, and there have been suggestions that during the war Moscow connived with the fascist regime in Bucharest to liquidate Communists who were operating inside Romania. When the fascists surrendered in 1944 those Romanian Communists who had spent the war in Moscow moved in. Under pressure from the Soviet military authorities the Communists were given the key ministries in the government. In the November 1946 elections the parties which supported the National Democratic Front polled nearly 80 per cent of the votes, but a year later most of the groups which had formed the Front were dissolved. On 30 December 1947 King Michael I was forced to abdicate. Romania became a 'people's republic' and soon adopted a constitution along the lines of the Soviet Union.

The Soviet army effectively dictated the Communist take-over in Bulgaria as well. Here the Communist Party quickly dominated the other parties in the Fatherland Front, and by taking over the key ministries of justice and the interior it was able to hunt down groups and individuals who were said to have been pro-German or anti-Communist. Bourgeois elements in the army and the civil service were purged. The election of October 1946 was manipulated, and the Fatherland Front won 80 per cent of the votes cast. The previous month the monarchy had been abolished. Another 'people's republic' came into being.

The last piece of the jigsaw to fall into place was Czechoslovakia. It was considerably more advanced than countries like Romania and Bulgaria, and its democratic tradition resisted the implacable demand of the Soviet Union for Communist control longer than the others. But the actual seizure of power by Klement Gottwald took only six days in February 1948. The pre-war President, Eduard Benes, who had been based in London during the war, believed he could manipulate the Communists and opened negotiations with Gottwald on the creation of a National Front government. Benes became President again in May 1945, and the Communists were given eight out of twenty-five ministries including that of the Interior. In the elections of May 1946 the Communists received 38 per cent of the vote; they formed a coalition with the Social Democrats, and Gottwald became prime minister.

In the months that followed, the Communists began the infiltration of the trade unions and the police in earnest. By February 1948 the position was so serious that twelve non-Communist ministers resigned, thinking they would bring down the government and force new elections. But the threat of a general strike and of violence by the police and the armed workers' militia seemed to indicate that widespread fighting might break out, leading perhaps to civil war. Benes accepted Gottwald's plans for a new cabinet. Soon all the institutions of the state were thoroughly purged. The pro-Western foreign minister, Jan Masaryk, died in circumstances which indicated murder. Within six months Benes had resigned and was dead too. A ferocious series of show trials ensured that Czechoslovakia became Stalin's most obedient vassal. His enormous statue overlooking the Vltava River was not destroyed until 1962, six years after his condemnation by Khrushchev. The buttons on its jacket were as big as loaves of bread.

Stalin may not have planned the take-over of Central and Eastern Europe in detail beforehand. Parts of it happened without the need for prior planning. But it was an ugly story of deceit, intimidation and brutal violence. The new leaders were not subject to any check except the fear of Stalin. Each of them knew that the next purge, whether of Titoists or Jews or bourgeois nationalists, might sweep him away too. The Gottwalds and the Gomulkas and the Rakosis committed great excesses to prove their loyalty. In Czechoslovakia in 1949 the religious orders were closed down; troops and secret police units raided every monastery and nunnery in the country. Monks, nuns and priests were driven off in closed trucks, some to prison and some to work in the uranium mines. They were given no protective clothing there, and a large number died of cancer. That, it seems, was the intention.

After the initial clear-out of the army, the civil service and the police, the purges which followed were mostly of senior people within the Party. As the socialist system settled down, ordinary people had relatively little to fear in the way of thought-crime unless they chose to take a deliberate stand against the government. But there was always the danger of being reported for lesser offences, always the need to guard what you said and what you did. Utter conformity in thought and deed might not always be necessary, but it was always safer. Most people preferred to be safe. In every country, as the years passed, conditions became gradually easier. It was no longer dangerous to wear Western clothes or listen to Western music, though such things were often deeply disapproved of. It became easier to listen to Western radio stations.

There were some benefits to living in a socialist society. Medical care, though not always good, was entirely free. Those who needed care at health spas could receive it free of charge. Holidays were often provided for workers and retired people. Old people's homes were usually well run, and available to all. Pensions were adequate. Maternity leave was generous, and jobs were held open for women after they had brought up their children. Education was usually good. The streets were relatively clean, and the cities much freer of crime than those in the West. But it was all done in an environment which demanded complete conformity.

If you insisted on going to church or having your children baptized or confirmed, if you kept in contact with relatives abroad, if you had affairs outside marriage, if you were homosexual, if you were a close relative of someone who defected to the West, if you openly preferred the West to socialism, you were liable to suffer up and down the full length of the Party's reach. You would not receive suitable housing. You would not be promoted. You might lose your job and not be able to find another, and thereby lay yourself open (in a system where unemployment did not exist) to the charge of social parasitism, which was punishable by imprisonment. Your children, and the children of your relatives, would not receive a university education and would not themselves be eligible for decent jobs.

In schools and universities, there were benefits for those who studied Russian and built-in obstacles for those who studied English, French or German. Societies were established to promote friendship and under-standing with the Soviet Union. In the 1950s, when fear and conformity were at their height, the membership in each country was in the millions. After the invasions of Hungary and Czechoslovakia and the crises of the 1970s they dwindled to a few hundred thousand in most countries. Part of their function was to counter negative stereotypes about the Soviet Union, and even to prevent the use of words which carried unfortunate connotations. In Poland, for instance, the natural translation for the adjective 'Soviet' (sowiecki) was dropped because between the wars it had taken on a pejorative meaning. Instead, the adjective 'radziecki' (from the noun meaning 'council') was adopted. 'The Soviet Union' became 'The Councillar Union'.

Regardless of history or national style, the towns and cities of each people's democracy imitated the look of the Soviet cityscape. The only acceptable architectural style was the grey functionalism of new Soviet building. The only permissible decoration in terms of painting or sculpture was socialist realism. Until well into the 1970s Eastern European city authorities were constructing vast stone or metal statues to impersonal concepts: the Victory of Socialism, the Friendship of the Socialist Peoples, and so on. In Bratislava, the capital of Slovakia, the arrival of the Red Army in 1945 brought violence, pillage and rape and led to political servitude for two generations. An enormous, inartistic sculpture was erected on the hillside overlooking the city to show the gratitude of the local population to the liberators. Right up to the day when Communist rule collapsed in Czechoslovakia newly married couples, following Soviet custom, laid the flowers from their wedding ceremony at the eternal flame burning there.

The Soviet Union enmeshed its allies in a complex skein of treaties and agreements, covering mutual assistance in defence, mutual trade, cultural co-operation. There was nothing on paper to indicate that the Soviet Union held a controlling interest: all was done in terms of respect for each other's rights. But Moscow laid a more fundamental reliance on the system of control that lay below the surface. The NKVD, and later its successors the MVD and the KGB, heavily penetrated each of the equivalent organizations in satellite countries.

In the West, during the 1970s, the nervousness and moral indignation which the Soviet take-over in Central and Eastern Europe had aroused began to fade. So did memories of the Soviet invasions of Hungary and Czechoslovakia. To challenge the Soviet system, or to harp on its failings, was reminiscent of the old Cold War attitudes which most people wanted to leave behind. There was never any shortage of sympathy for organizations like Charter 77 and Solidarity which strove for greater freedom. But the left in Western Europe believed that disarmament was the main priority, and that if there were too much criticism of the Soviet bloc's internal policies the whole process of détente might be jeopardized.

No one imagined until the last moment that the socialist system would be swept aside by overwhelming popular hatred. It was more reasonable to assume that it would slowly become more liberal and make the lives of its citizens easier and freer. And because the Soviet bloc looked as though it were permanent, it was natural to deal with it as it was, rather than as Western governments and individuals would have preferred it to be.

In most of the countries of Western Europe, however, there were men and women on the left who went further. Trade union delegations went on fact-finding trips where the facts were usually favourable to the host regime. Union officials were given free holidays. Groups of left-wing doctors, journalists or social scientists were guests at symposia which were often directed against NATO and the United States. There were peace conferences which concentrated solely on the nuclear threat posed by the West. Not that the guests were by any means always fellow-travelling dupes. At an international conference in Prague, for example, a British nurse insisted on being taken to the nearest hospital, rather than the one the organizers had chosen. It proved impossible to stop her, and she and the group she was with were appalled by the poor standard of cleanliness and the out-of-date equipment they found. But in general there was a tendency on the left in Europe to equate the admitted shortcomings in the Soviet bloc with human rights violations in countries supported by the United States, as though the existence of the one cancelled out the need for concern about the other.

For up to forty-five years – more, if Lithuania, Latvia and Estonia are included – the Soviet Union forced Marxism-Leninism onto countries which had previously been successful market economies. It could only be done with immense violence to the individual rights of millions of people. During Stalin's lifetime the suffering was as bad as anything experienced under Hitler. Lives were wrecked casually. As with Nero, *proximis saevi ingruunt*: those who were closest to the centre of savagery, which in this case meant the Communist Party, suffered particularly badly. Stalin purged and repurged the Party several times over, and even men like Nikita Khrushchev who toadied to him most were sickened by what they did on his orders. After the fall of Communism in Central and Eastern Europe the mass burial grounds in country after country were pinpointed and the details of the concentration camps came to light.

Life under Stalin was dangerous for everyone. The father of the Czech film-maker Jana Bukova supported a friend who had recognized his boss as a former *capo* (a trusty with special privileges) in a Nazi concentration camp. The ex-*capo* had influence in the Party and had them both gaoled. A Pole spent years in gaol for insulting Stalin, when something he said was misconstrued. A Prague woman found out thirty years later that her habit of wearing a hat in the street in the early 1950s had caused the local Party informer to denounce her as a bourgeois element. As a result, her husband had been refused promotion, her children's education had suffered, and they had never been allocated suitable housing. As in Mao's China, children were rewarded for informing on their parents. Anything but utter obedience was dangerous. George Orwell's gloomy view of the triumph of socialism, *1984*, which he laboured over in the BBC canteen, was an accurate one.

> In our world there will be no emotions except fear, rage, triumph and self-abasement. We have cut the links between child and parent, and between man and man, and between man and woman. If you want a picture of the future, imagine a boot stamping on a human face – forever.

Yet it proved to be less a picture of the future so much as of Orwell's present. Elements of *1984* remained true for the entire period of Soviet rule, but after the death of Stalin the tide of savagery began very slowly to ebb. Marxism-Leninism changed over the decades. To the moment when it ceased to be the ruling ideology of the eastern part of Europe it was still capable of damaging people's lives in ways which freer societies would regard as intolerable. But with certain exceptions it had ceased to be actively cruel and was mostly just repressive.

The big demonstrations which brought the system down in country after country, and the derisory results obtained by the Communist Party wherever free elections were held, were a judgement on the past as well as the present. Most people believed that the Communist system had been actively harmful. The gangsterism of the past, as well as the serious environmental consequences of too much inefficient heavy industry and the degree to which the Eastern bloc had fallen behind the West in the creation of wealth, were causes of anger and shame. Most people, in the aftermath of the revolutions of 1989–91, seemed to feel that they had suffered personally from Marxism-Leninism.

In the wake of the revolutions, as I went from country to country in what had been the Soviet empire, almost everyone I spoke to could show lives that had been warped in some way by the old system. Those who had suffered greatly were few in number, and their sufferings tended to be similar to each other: periods of imprisonment, beatings up, the loss of jobs and privileges. In a way, the lesser effects reveal more about the nature of a society. The three cases which follow – those of a Czech, a Pole and a Romanian – are relatively mild, though that of the Romanian is worst because under Ceausescu Romania itself was worst. But they each reflect the small cruelties or distortions of life as it affected them.

*

We were in the dingy staff room of a junior school in a featureless suburb of Prague. The only bright object in the room was a brand new poster of Vaclav Havel, which someone had bought that morning and stuck on the wall. From what I had seen on the way in, though, the children were better behaved than they would have been at similar schools in most Western countries, and the standard of teaching was high. But Anna, the teacher who had brought me here, felt that her life was hard, and that as a woman she suffered considerable discrimination. Most of the other women teachers agreed. Officially, the Communist authorities accepted that on average women were paid a third less than men for doing the same jobs. At their school, the teachers felt the gap was worse than that.

Anna is married now, but for some years she brought up her eldest daughter, the child of an old boyfriend, on her own. She has the drawn look of someone who never gets as much sleep as she needs, and sleep is what she talks about almost obsessively. She gets up before six each morning, and is never in bed before eleven at night. The problem is not her working hours, but the time she has to spend shopping in a system which produces endless queuing for small quantities of poorly produced goods. She feels bad because her children are not looked after properly.

'I cannot be a proper mother to them.' It is a continual source of guilt, and there are more personal difficulties too. Contraceptives are expensive and difficult to buy, but she has already had three abortions and agreed with her husband after the last one that they would never let it happen again. She is in constant fear of getting pregnant once again.

Hers has not been an easy life. Her parents, devout Catholics, threw her out when she became pregnant for the first time. She moved into a two-roomed flat with an elderly friend of the family, but the woman died soon afterwards. When the authorities found out, they took her to court because she had no permission to live there. The lawyer in the case promised vaguely to help her, but used that as a pretext to blackmail her.

'That's a nice table,' he would say when he came to discuss the case. 'It'd look very nice in my front room.'

She gave him most of the things he asked for, except sex. In spite of his supposed help the case against her proceeded. Finally she found out precisely whom she needed to bribe. Five thousand crowns, the equivalent of three months' wages, paid to a secretary ensured that the relevant documents were 'lost'.

To Anna, there was nothing surprising in any of this. The malignity of officialdom is something she grew up with. Her parents were lower middle class people who were troubled for years by accusations that they were hostile to the regime. Their church-going did not help. The hostility of the woman who acted as the Party informant in the block of flats was enough to prevent Anna from being given an exit visa in 1965 to go on holiday to Italy, where a relative of hers lived. The disappointment seems to have soured her. She could, she says, have escaped from Czechoslovakia for good. Over the years Anna was placed under heavy pressure to join the Communist Party, but she never gave in to it. Yet she is not a brave woman; it took her a long time to join the demonstrations against a system she loathed, and she was always worried about being under surveillance. Even now that the Communist system has gone for good she lowers her voice when she talks about her dislike of it.

She is, naturally, delighted at what has happened. She and her friends exchange anecdotes about the relaxed and unstuffy ways of Havel and his government, compared with the dourness and pride of the Communists. She is something of a snob too. Havel and the others speak better Czech, and they are educated men. A teacher does an impression of one of the old Communist ministers, and she laughs with the others but not as loudly.

'Of course it's wonderful, what's happened here,' she says to me afterwards, as we drive along the gloomy suburban streets. 'But, you see, I can't help remembering that I've lived my whole life under these bastards. My life has been wasted. And now it's all over, I'm too old to change. I think I shall always be afraid they'll come back. I can't get over that feeling, you know. They've damaged me for ever.'

It's meant as a joke, but her voice trembles a little. You can tell that it is entirely true.

*

The sulphurous air caught at our throats and dirtied our clothes. It was so thick we could see it. As Karol and I walked in the cold across one of the vast, empty areas that Communist architecture seems to aim for, he was in full flight, outlining a new area of his general theory about his native Poland with the zest that an enthusiastic gardener might bring to planting a newly dug bed with flowers. It is a good theory.

Poland, Karol says, has a mother complex. The result is a nation of Polish males who see themselves as warriors, with the task of fighting and dying, if necessary, for their motherland. They are subordinated to the mother-image, just as, in Polish Catholicism, Christ is subordinated to His Mother. By contrast God the Father, the eternal law-giver, is a distant figure of little immediate relevance, largely undefined and rarely seen. It is to this absence of the father-figure that Karol ascribes the Polish lack of respect for the strict forms of law. 'We live by double standards,' he says, thinking always of the next analogy, the next irony.

'We tried to cheat the Communists, and we've ended up like them as a result.'

Karol has not ended up like them at all. A writer and an intellectual from a well-to-do family, his rejection of Communism and all its works has left few outward scars on him: except, perhaps, for an inability to settle. He remains an outsider, formulating his theories to explain the inexplicable: how decent men believed the god of Marxism and failed to abandon it when it failed them. The subject has brought a deep hostility between him and his father. During the war his father played a noble part in sheltering Jews and helping them escape from Poland. He was not a Communist, but a Social Democrat. Nevertheless when the Communists took over in 1945 he and some of his colleagues sided with them, thinking they could tone down their new rulers' excesses.

Instead, he was trapped by Stalinism and was lucky to escape its habit of devouring its own. In 1948, the year Karol was born, his father was arrested and interrogated during the first of the big purges in Poland. He survived to become part of the elite. As a child, his son was taught to believe implicitly in the goodness of the system, and the love which Stalin had for all of them. At that age Karol was ignorant of political realities; but by the age of nine or ten he learned that there was something below the surface – something they didn't tell you, like finding out about sex at school. The Communists maintained a double standard which no one was allowed to speak about. You could laugh at them, but only in secret.

His father rose higher and higher, his politics by now indistinguishable from those of the Communists. He and his son parted company on the question of religion, for Karol was developing deep religious feelings. But the real divide between them came in March 1968, as it did for Poland generally. The trouble started when students like Karol protested against the banning of the play *Forefathers*, written by the great nineteenth-century Polish poet Adam Mickiewicz about the arrests of students in Tsarist Russia. The authorities used savage measures to repress the students. There was a distinctly anti-Semitic tone to the repression, and many of Karol's Jewish friends were forcibly deported from the country of their birth.

This was the moment when Karol finally turned his back on socialism and on politics in general. But his father, the man who had risked his life to save Jews during the Second World War, now sought to justify everything. He reasoned that if he were to resign, as many other men and women did, worse people would come in his place. He wouldn't be a Don Quixote, he said, so he kept on supporting what the Communists did, and he kept on doing his important job. In 1981 he accepted

martial law too. He believed there was no alternative to co-operating
with Moscow. Karol says that to co-operate with Moscow was to co-
operate with cancer. He has nothing to do with his father now.

He turns back to the grand theory of the mother-worshipping Poland
– extended now to take in Russia, with its Orthodox worship of God the
Father, stern and unforgiving and set on domination. In 1980, Karol
says, the rise of Solidarity restored to Poland a measure of masculinity.
Fathers and sons: the nature of every relationship has been funda-
mentally affected by the experiences of forty-five years of state
socialism.

*

You can usually find Jimmy in the InterContinental Hotel in Bucharest.
He is either in the coffee shop, making an expensive, bad-tasting
cappuccino last an hour, or he is in the lobby. He moves from group to
group among the foreign journalists, offering services, making deals.
Discreet wads of money are stuffed into his pockets, or pulled out of
them. This is his natural habitat, the life he was created for. Nowadays
it is easier and safer, because the Securitate, who once preyed on people
like him, has become extinct. He prefers the nickname Jimmy to his
Romanian name, because it emphasizes his difference from other
people. He likes to think of it as his Englishness. He sports a dark blue,
broad-brimmed hat. A trophy of some deal with a French magazine
correspondent in the first days of the Revolution, it has a raffish air and
makes him look a little less seedy. But the drooping moustache gives his
face a gloomy cast, and the deep parallel lines which a hard life has
gouged down his cheeks make him look a good ten years older. He is
only thirty-one.

When he told me that his life had been a hard one I believed it. He
had spent seven years in prison for various offences, each sentence
detailed in his identity card for any policeman or prospective employer
to read. They were petty crimes. He didn't like Communism, and he
didn't like Ceausescu. He was an outsider, an instinctive, habitual
criminal. He had been gaoled for theft, and for trying to escape from
Romania. Once he succeeded in getting to Yugoslavia, but the police
there beat him up badly and handed him back to the Securitate, who
gave him a worse beating. His limp was genuine: it continued even
when he forgot that he'd told me about it. Because he would not
conform, the system forced him further and further towards its outer
edge, until there was no acceptable way for him to avoid starvation
except through methods the system identified as criminal. He became a
black marketeer. Maybe he stole things, though he denied it. Every

time he saw something new – a Walkman, a radio, a pack of batteries – he would ask if he could have it. He promised to get us a four-wheel drive vehicle to take us across the snow-bound mountains. In the meantime, he had a story to tell me.

He claimed that two days earlier, at the height of the Revolution, he had broken into a flat which five Securitate snipers were using to fire down at the street below. Armed only with a knife, he had lunged across and caught the nearest Securitate man around the neck. He had stuck his knife into the soft underpart of the man's chin and screamed at him to drop his gun if he didn't want his throat cut. The man had dropped his gun, the others had run for it. He saw that I didn't believe him, and became aggressive.

'Come and see. You must bring your television camera. I will show you everything.'

It was part of Jimmy's method to hector you into doing what he wanted; the wheedling came later.

A cameraman and I went with him. It was snowing hard, and he had problems in finding the place. I started to get angry. Then we came across a group of soldiers round an armoured personnel carrier which hadn't yet been withdrawn because its tyres had been shot out in the battle. The officer in charge threw his arms round Jimmy and kissed him.

'He is hero of Romania,' the officer shouted, and Jimmy's dark blue hat fell in the snow while the other soldiers gathered round admiringly.

The officer told us where the flats were. An old man answered Jimmy's knock, and welcomed him with something of the same enthusiasm. The flat was almost burned out; the Army had poured fire into it when they spotted the Securitate snipers. We stood on the sodden carpet, near the gaping hole in the wall where the window had once been, and I asked him questions while the cameraman filmed.

'You had nothing but a knife, and you knew they had Kalashnikovs. Why did you come into this room and attack them?'

You couldn't miss the anger and violence in his face then. What he was saying was the truest thing in his life.

'I did it because I hated them. Because it was my chance to hit back at them. I wanted to kill them all. They took away seven years from me. They took away my whole life. I wanted them to pay.'

We left the flat where Jimmy had been the hero of Romania and went back to the InterContinental, where he was just another hustler. We arranged the details about the four-wheel drive vehicle and said goodbye to him. At eight o'clock the next morning he failed to turn up. There was no four-wheel drive. Probably there never had been. He didn't come to see me to apologize. If he caught sight of me across the lobby of the hotel during the next few days he would turn his back and start talking to someone. The system had made him an outcast, a small-time enemy of the state, untrustworthy, wheedling, weak. And yet for an instant, goaded by the violence which the system had engendered in him, he had done something as brave as I had ever come across.

2
FINAL APPEARANCE

Much, if not most, of the Communist Party's loss of internal energy stemmed from its monopolistic position in our political system. The lack of a need to fight for voters undermined the spirit of innovation, intellectual intensity and proletarian liveliness that distinguished the Party until the first few years after the 1917 October Revolution.

ALEKSEI IZYUMOV, *Komsomolskaya Pravda*, February 1990

It was the day after Solidarity's victory in the Polish elections of August 1989. In spite of the legal gerrymander by which the Communists had reserved 173 out of the 460 seats in the Sejm, the lower house of the Polish parliament, their defeat had been total. In the Senate, Solidarity, under the title of Citizens' Parliamentary Club, had won 99 seats. An independent who was pro-Communist had won one seat. There were only a hundred in all. General Woyciech Jaruzelski, having presided over this defeat, was in a state of great gloom. He had already told his two closest colleagues, Jerzy Urban and Mieczyslaw Rakowski, that he was thinking of resigning. At the time, he meant it.

A small group of editors from the official Communist newspapers and from television had gathered at the Central Committee headquarters to discuss the position with Jaruzelski. Since their task was to put the best possible face on things, they asked Jaruzelski if he wanted to give a press conference, or maybe take part in a television interview, so that he could set out his defence. But he was sunk in the deepest depression and seemed incapable of making a decision about anything. Finally someone asked him what Moscow was saying about it all. Jaruzelski answered gloomily that he had been given a completely free hand. President Gorbachev had made it clear that it was up to him to do what he thought best in the circumstances. The pace of political change, even the very nature of political change, was a matter for his own judgement. There was silence. Each of the editors listening to him was no doubt reflecting on the awkwardness of the position. He was a man set under authority, as they were. None of them would have found it very easy under the old system to be told to say exactly what they thought was right. Then Jaruzelski started speaking again.

'Sometimes,' he said, 'the silence of the telephone is terrifying.'

The silence of the telephone brought about the end of Soviet rule in Central and Eastern Europe. Once the Soviet Union stopped giving orders, direct or indirect, to its satellites, then the Communist leadership in each of those countries was effectively left isolated. And since none of them existed there by popular will, it was only a matter of time and chance how they collapsed. If Soviet troops were not there to shore up the threatened regimes, there was no serious consideration which could prevent ordinary people from demanding change. What had happened in East Germany in 1953, Hungary and Poland in 1956, Poland and Czechoslovakia in 1968 and Poland in 1981 would not happen again. Each individual leader in the satellite states was on his own now.

When empires fall, the subject peoples take advantage of the increasing lack of will at the imperial centre: in Sir Francis Bacon's phrase, every bird takes a feather. But in the case of the Soviet empire Gorbachev clearly signalled that he wanted a new relationship with Central and Eastern Europe. He initiated the decolonizing process himself, by a change of attitude. At the annual summits of the Warsaw Pact he was content to be *primus inter pares*, rather than the imperial overlord. He showed favour to those leaders who were doing most to achieve reform: chief among them Hungary and Poland. He made it clear that he had little in common with conservative leaders like Honecker; he played an active part in forcing Gustav Husak out of power in Czechoslovakia; his distaste for Nicolae Ceausescu and the regime he ran in Romania was evident.

` Honecker, Husak and Ceausescu all issued coded warnings about the effects of what he was doing. Any change in the Soviet imperial approach was a threat to them. The Brezhnev Doctrine had been their guarantee of security, and once it was gone their days in office were bound to be numbered. From now on the rulers of Eastern Europe existed purely on sufferance: they would continue for as long as the people they governed chose to put up with them, and not a moment more.

The Warsaw Treaty of Friendship, Co-operation and Mutual Assistance, known to the West as the Warsaw Pact, held what proved to be its last annual political consultative committee meeting in Bucharest in July 1989. The chairmanship rotated according to the alphabetical order of the member country's name, and in 1989 it was held by the Socialist Republic of Romania. The chairman was Nicolae Ceausescu. The Committee meeting to which he welcomed his fellow presidents and Party general secretaries took place on 7 and 8 July. None of the seven leaders who attended it can have had the slightest suspicion that within six months all of them except Gorbachev himself would have been swept away; nor that the Warsaw Treaty itself, although still formally in existence, would have ceased to be an effective military alliance.

Even in the summer the streets of Bucharest looked grey and poverty-stricken; but the big hotels were filled to capacity with the delegations. Food was flown in from West Germany, and the shop windows along the main thoroughfares were stocked from the special stores available to the Securitate, Ceausescu's street police. The lobbies of the better hotels were stocked with prostitutes, also by courtesy of the Securitate. Most of the prostitutes and all the goods which filled the windows disappeared on 9 July, when the delegates left.

There were enthusiastically worded signs of welcome everywhere. The entire Romanian people, it seemed, extended the hand of friendship to the leaders of the Warsaw Pact. Romanian television, which broadcast for only three hours a night because of the shortage of electrical power, showed a great many pictures of Ceausescu and his wife welcoming the guests and opening the first formal session. The others were shown in proportion to their popularity with the Ceausescus. The viewers saw quite a lot of Erich Honecker, the East German leader, and Milos Jakes and Gustav Husak, respectively the Party leader and President of Czechoslovakia. Both countries formed a conservative alliance with Romania against the reforms emanating from Moscow.

There were almost as many pictures of Todor Zhivkov, the Bulgarian leader, because he was felt to be a conservative at heart, even though he was wavering. Of Mikhail Gorbachev and his prime minister, Nikolai Ryzhkov, there had to be a certain amount of television coverage, since the Soviet Union could scarcely be ignored at a Warsaw Pact summit. But the editors at Romanian Television had instructions not to linger on them. Little was seen of General Jaruzelski, the Polish Party leader, since he sided with Gorbachev but was less important. One leader appeared only in group scenes: Rezsoe Nyers, the leader of the Hungarian Party. Everyone knew there would be serious rows at the summit, and that on each of the questions at issue Ceausescu and Nyers would be on opposite sides.

Ceausescu stood in the conference hall of the presidential palace in the centre of Bucharest, greeting the leaders one by one. He looked uneasy, especially when Gorbachev and Nyers arrived. Everyone else received a kiss from him. So did Gorbachev, after an instant in which the television viewers thought that Ceausescu was going to pull back. Nyers received only a curt handshake.

Although Ceausescu must have believed that the situation in his country was totally stable and his own position as strong as ever, it was plain that Gorbachev's new thinking had already caused him problems. From 1968 onwards, when he had supported the reformers in Czechoslovakia, though not the reforms, and had defiantly stood up to the Soviet Union and the Brezhnev Doctrine, Ceausescu had been regarded with favour in the West. Successive American presidents had given him the kind of attention and support which a much larger country might have expected. Over the years, governments in Britain, France and West Germany courted him. He was regarded as an independent voice within the Warsaw Pact, a kind of Tito in the making, who might at some stage be induced to take his country out of the Soviet bloc altogether.

There were those who said that his independent policies – maintaining diplomatic and trade links with Israel, China and pre-revolutionary Iran, for instance, at a time when the Soviet Union had its difficulties with all three – were not independent at all but provided Moscow with a useful route for back-door diplomacy. Still, he was his own man, which was welcome to the West at a time of confrontation between the West and the Soviet Union. But once Gorbachev had come to power, Ceausescu's independence from the new Soviet Union which was being created was of little value.

Only then did many politicians in the West choose to notice that from the late 1960s Ceausescu had run a regime which had become increasingly repressive. He had always demanded grovelling adulation from his Party officials. When he entered a conference hall they were expected to follow him with their eyes, smiling and clapping in time to their chanting of the syllables of his name: CEA-U-SES-CU, CEA-U-SES-CU, CEA-U-SES-CU. They were also expected to give him at least fifty standing ovations during a major speech.

Moreover, Ceausescu's ministers were obliged to stand on a specified circle of carpet twenty feet from his desk at the office he used at the Central Committee headquarters. When he consented to give a television interview, the questions had to be submitted in advance; any refusal meant the cancellation of the interview. Half an hour before it was due to begin, his officials came and set up the chairs: one for the President, one for the interviewer. The first official agreed to place the two chairs four feet apart. A second official, ten minutes later, winced and placed them seven feet apart. Finally, just before the great man arrived, another official widened the gap to ten feet. Ceausescu himself was cold and unyielding when he arrived, but protocol demanded that the entire interview team should be photographed with him.

The next day's edition of *Scinteia*, the feeble, poorly-produced four-page newspaper of the Romanian Communist Party, filled its front page with an exact transcript of the President's remarks. The questions, which had often been critical, were edited down or sometimes simply replaced by harmless ones of *Scinteia*'s own devising. Only the camera-man appeared in the accompanying photograph in the newspaper: he was 5′ 6″, a couple of inches taller than the President. Everyone else in the team had been much bigger. They were accordingly airbrushed out. Nicolae Ceausescu, the shoe-maker's apprentice who had made it to the presidency, disliked having to compete with anyone else.

At the Warsaw Pact summit there was to be a good deal of competition. There was a serious row between Ceausescu and the Hungarians about the oppression suffered by the 700,000 Hungarian-speaking people of Transylvania. At a private meeting with Nyers, Ceausescu refused even to discuss Hungary's demand that the curbs on travel for the Hungarian-speakers should be lifted. And when Nyers suggested that a group of international experts should study the question, Ceausescu shouted out that he would never allow them into the country. The Hungarian foreign minister said relations with Romania had reached their nadir.

But the major source of disagreement was over the pace and nature of reform within the Warsaw Pact countries. Gorbachev was worried about the prospect of increasing integration in Western Europe after 1992; it seemed likely to him that the Soviet Union would be left even further behind, unless the partitions between the eastern and western wings of what he had so often called 'our common European home' could be broken down. For that to happen, the nature of the Warsaw Pact itself would need to change. He had strong support in this from the Poles and the Hungarians. The Hungarian foreign minister told a television interviewer later:

> While the Soviet, Polish and Hungarian delegations emphasized the extraordinary importance of the whole transformation process, the renewal of socialism and the maintenance of values, some countries took the unambiguous position that their previous way of doing things need not and must not be changed, and that socialism has proved its vitality, its viability and so on. Well, we believe that history and the current situation prove something else.

Ceausescu was the most outspoken of the other leaders about this revisionist approach. At the end of June he had said he was 'puzzled and even concerned by the tendencies recorded in some countries to weaken the Communist Party's leading role'. At the summit Ceausescu could count on the support of the East German and Czechoslovak delegations. Zhivkov, the Bulgarian leader, did his best to stay neutral. His instincts were with Ceausescu, but he knew that he had to keep in with Moscow.

Gorbachev himself had come to Bucharest from Paris, where he had received a rapturous reception but had not made as much political progress as he would have liked. It was important to him for domestic reasons that the Warsaw Pact summit should go well, and seem like a victory for his ideas. Although there was no one as conservative as Ceausescu and the East German and Czechoslovak leaders at the top of the Soviet Communist Party, there were plenty of doubts in Moscow about the direction Gorbachev was taking. A successful defence of those policies in Bucharest was important.

The Warsaw Treaty countries had never been so divided. Not even the crises over the Hungarian invasion of 1956 and the Czechoslovak invasion twelve years later produced as many mutually incompatible policies among the member countries. Gorbachev had abandoned the idea that there was a single acceptable pathway to socialism. As he spoke from his place halfway down the long table in the conference room which had once been the banqueting hall of King Michael I of Romania, before he abdicated in 1947, Gorbachev talked of the changes which were taking place within the alliance:

> There is a new spirit within our Treaty with moves towards independent solutions to national problems. Life changes, and this organization will change as well, but it still has a role to play.

Plainly, he wanted the Pact to move away from being a predominantly military alliance – each delegation round the table had its defence minister there, most of them in general's uniforms – and turn itself into a predominantly political and economic one.

*

But the three hostile delegations at the table saw no reason for the slightest change in the Warsaw treaty. They anticipated only trouble for themselves and their position if this happened. During Gorbachev's speech Ceausescu, sitting at the head of the table in the chairman's seat, fidgeted and looked annoyed. To his left, separated from him by Todor Zhivkov and the Bulgarian delegation, sat the Czechoslovaks. Their leader was the little-known and uninspiring Milos Jakes, who had been given the general secretaryship of the Party partly because of his seniority and partly because the other candidates were unacceptable to a majority within the Czechoslovak Politburo. It was Jakes who, after the Soviet invasion of 1968, had taken responsibility for the wide-ranging purge throughout the whole of Czechoslovak society. Hundreds of thousands of careers and lives were wrecked by Jakes in the service of the Party he had now, for a short space of time, risen to lead.

Beside him sat the enigmatic figure of Gustav Husak who, thanks to pressure from Moscow, had had to stand down as General Secretary two years before. He was here less in his capacity as Czechoslovakia's president than out of deference to his continuing political influence. He was said to have taken the loss of his previous power very hard. It was Husak who had made Czechoslovakia what it had been ever since 1968: politically paralysed, lacking any serious opposition, a completely safe ally of the Soviet Union. A sombre man, without a spark of obvious character, his life had been marked by personal unhappiness and public humiliation. His mother died in 1914, a year after he was born. His father, who worked in a stone-quarry in Slovakia, joined the army and was sent off to the front a few months later. Husak was brought up in an atmosphere of considerable poverty, and won his way to university through his own ability. As a committed Communist, he played a part in organizing the Slovak National Uprising against the Nazis in 1944. After the political coup which brought the Communists to power in Czechoslovakia in 1948, he rose quickly in the Party ranks and was then caught up in the Stalinist purge of 1950. In the following year he was found guilty of Slovak 'bourgeois nationalism', and was sent to prison. He stayed there until 1960, and it was three more years before he was rehabilitated.

Husak's part during the Prague Spring was an ambiguous one. At the time he gave the impression that he sided with Alexander Dubcek and supported his reforms; though he slipped in sufficient warnings about the speed and direction of reform for his official biography to be able to say later that he 'spoke out publicly against the destructive activities of the right wing in the Party and against the anti-socialist forces which threatened the foundations of the socialist system in Czechoslovakia and its external political ties.' The biography manages to deal with the events of the period without even mentioning the Soviet invasion. Husak soon began to side with the invaders, and took over Dubcek's job in April 1969.

In the treacherous political times in Czechoslovakia in the late 1960s, Husak was skilfully Laodicean. He had not been an enthusiastic reformer, but he did not sign the invitation to the Russians to invade. He enjoyed little loyalty or affection from those who worked with him, and aroused more indifference than anything else among ordinary people. When he was eased out of the leadership at Gorbachev's urging, the Soviet Politburo sent a sharply worded message of congratulation to Jakes, as his successor, saying it hoped he would ensure the revival of socialism in Czechoslovakia. At this Warsaw Pact summit he said almost nothing. He was an embarrassment: a gloomy, depressing reminder of the past, a symbol of everything Mikhail Gorbachev was attempting to do away with.

Down at the far end of the table, opposite Ceausescu, sat the East German delegation headed by Erich Honecker. He combined the roles of General Secretary of the Party and Chairman of the Council of State: in effect, though not in title, he was the president of the country. He had the perennial look of a faithful deputy who had taken over the top job: which is precisely what had happened. He was not a natural leader, and the role seemed never to come easily to him. Non-Communists in East Germany used to find his long speeches intolerable, partly because his accent made him slur the words *Deutsche Demokratische Republik*, which naturally occurred with great frequency whenever he spoke.

Like Husak, Honecker had risen by sheer ability, but he had never suffered the same setbacks; the purges of Stalin's period did not reach down to his level. Walter Ulbricht, the General Secretary of the Party in the GDR, used him for the two most unpleasant tasks of the 1960s, both of which he performed with skill and distinction. In 1961, when people started flooding across to West Berlin in search of jobs and a better life, it was Honecker who laid the plans for the Berlin Wall. It was organized and built so quickly and with such secrecy that it took the West almost completely by surprise. It was Honecker, too, who gave the order that anyone trying to cross the Wall should be shot.

Seven years later, when the reforms of the Prague Spring began, Honecker was the man who was entrusted with the job of attacking the actions of the Dubcek government in public. And in August 1968, when Soviet troops were preparing to invade Czechoslovakia, he was placed in charge of preparing the military force which the GDR sent to accompany them. Soon his position was strong enough for him to be able to challenge Ulbricht for the leadership. With the help of Moscow, to whom he had shown himself so useful, he succeeded.

Now, as he sat at the Warsaw Pact summit in Bucharest, Honecker was strongly allied with the Czechoslovak leadership, which he had done his bit to set up, and with the Romanians. He may well have been mildly uneasy about the link with Ceausescu; whatever the faults of men like Honecker, Husak and Jakes, they were not personal dictators along Ceausescu's increasingly absurd lines. But the speech Gorbachev had just delivered confirmed that he would require all the help he could get now. Like Ulbricht before him, Honecker knew that the GDR required considerable propping up if it were to survive. Having no objective reasons for its existence apart from the fact of having been conquered by the Soviet Union forty-five years before, it could not survive on its own. As early as 1958 Honecker had said, 'The tensions in Germany can never be relaxed until the German Democratic Republic is secured and strengthened on all sides.'

Now, thirty-one years later, he was obliged to sit and listen while Mikhail Gorbachev undermined its entire foundation. The stress and perhaps the anger he felt must have been considerable. He was not a man who easily disagreed in public with anything a leader of the Soviet Union said. Now he was obliged to make a short speech which, while not openly hostile, dissociated him from almost every idea Gorbachev had put forward. But the speech seemed to cost him a good deal of effort, and later, as the first day's session approached its end, he started to show signs of real distress. He was experiencing acute pains in his side and back. His face went white. He remained conscious, but could no longer sit upright in his chair. His breath came in long wheezing gasps. As the men sitting round the long table looked on, two attendants came hurrying in and carried Honecker into another room. A special ambulance which had been on standby for the summit was called, and he was driven to hospital along the centre lanes Ceausescu normally reserved for his own use. At first it was thought that Honecker was suffering from kidney stones, but when he was flown back to East Berlin it became clear he had a cancerous tumour which required surgery.

It was symbolic of what was happening to the Warsaw Pact. The Pact existed in the form it did because of the Soviet Union's old desire to protect itself with a *cordon sanitaire* against the West in general, and the Federal Republic of Germany in particular. Its first line of defence, therefore, was the Berlin Wall. The strong implication of much of what Mikhail Gorbachev was saying was that the Wall was no longer necessary: that a new form of alliance should be created, which would not necessarily confront Western Europe in military terms. Erich Honecker was obliged to sit there and listen to the funeral sermon for the system he had helped to create and maintain, for the Wall he had constructed and for his own career. Once he had been carried out of the conference hall in the presidential palace in Bucharest, he was never again to regain full control of his country.

The events which led to the breaching of the Wall four months later had been set in train. There was no one sitting round the table who would not be affected, and by the end of a year the only country still nominally Communist would be the Soviet Union itself. Jaruzelski would still be in place, but would have ceded control to ministers from

Solidarity. Honecker would be saved from gaol only because of his illness. Zhivkov would be in disgrace and under investigation for corruption. Jakes and Husak would be swept out of office by a tidal wave of public anger. And Ceausescu, who had felt so strongly about the changes which Gorbachev was introducing, would be chased out of his palace, deserted by his closest associates, and shot dead by a firing squad of his own soldiers. The phoney Communist revolutions of the immediate post-war period in Eastern Europe were about to be reversed even more quickly than they had originally taken place.

3
SLIPPING THE LEASH

There is only one road: from totalitarianism to democracy, and we have covered a great length of it. If you compare the way in which we live today – this very conversation, here – with the times when for a word, for a joke, one went to prison, you will see that we live in a different country, in a different social order.

JACEK KURON, interviewed for British television in 1988

It is All Souls' Day, the first of November 1989: cold, grey, gloomy. A mist hangs over Warsaw. The snow, speckled with pollution, lies on the ledges of buildings and in strips along the roads. A tide of people flows towards the city's graveyards, holding bunches of flowers, potted plants or wreaths to remember their dead. For all its life and wit, Poland is a nation of mourners. The culture is one of sacrifice and unforgotten loss. There is much to remember. In 1939 the population of Warsaw was 1.5 million. By the end of 1944 half of them were dead and the other half were forced by the Nazis to leave the city. Many were sent to labour camps. Warsaw, already in ruins after an uprising which had lasted for 62 days, was destroyed building by building with flame-throwers and explosives. One tragedy had followed another. First the ghetto was liquidated, in the spring of 1943. A year and a half later the Warsaw uprising was quelled. The Poles had fought the Germans while the Russians watched from the other bank of the Vistula.

Altogether Poland lost six million citizens during the Second World War, half of them Jews. Its soldiers fought from the first day of the War to the last, on all fronts, in all the Allied armies, and in the Polish underground itself. Ordinary, moderate language is insufficient to cope with the scale of what the Poles suffered. 'Abandoned by the West in 1939, butchered by the Nazis, sold at Yalta in 1945, raped by the Soviet "liberators" who incorporated one third of its territory.' None of these expressions, used by the Polish writer Jacek Dobrowolski, is too strong.

In the cemetery two Dominican monks sweep the accumulated leaves from the grave of a prior. There is a noise of boots on gravel: a platoon of soldiers marches, guns at the port, to the grave of a Second World War general. They lay down their wreaths by number, bending awkwardly at the waist. The officer calls out a command, muted in the graveyard atmosphere. The soldiers salute a man who has been dead for twenty years, then turn and march away.

Everywhere the old, the middle-aged and the young are kneeling and gardening and sweeping. Weeding tools clink against marble and granite. Wanda A., born 1918, died 1940, her short life coinciding almost exactly with the brief time of Poland's independence. Mieczeslaw W., born 1818, died 1907: eighty-nine years during which Poland did not exist as a state. Advocate this, Aircraftman that, Bishop the other, all living out their lives in the wider context of Poland's national tragedy. A late-Victorian cherub kneels, headless through some accident or weakness in the stone. Patience on a monument stoops, her left hand missing but four fingers still sculpted to her temple. An entire family smiles out at us from a chocolate-coloured oval photograph set into the headstone, father, mother, two sons, all young and happy and full of life. Died 5 March 1944, 8 March 1944, 20 April 1944, 17 August 1944.

Crows drop heavily from the bare trees and fly low, like laden bombers, to land on a cross or the head of an angel. When they caw, you can see their breath. On the wall of the church is a cross, and a series of numbers: 140,000 at Majdanek, 100,000 at Treblinka, and so on. These are not Jews but Catholics. On this dark morning the wall is the only place of warmth and light. Dozens of little candles are burning in glass jars, their flames obeying the direction of the wind. Above them, cemented into the foot of the wall, are small tablets each bearing the name of an individual, and each with a single word and date in common: Katyn, 1940, where Stalin destroyed an entire military caste, more than 15,000 men. An army officer looks on thoughtfully. An old woman wipes away tears of sadness and cold with a sleeve. Broken glass from the little jars in which commemorative candles float crackles underfoot like ice on the hard ground. A crow dips its beak appreciatively in the candle fat, and no one chases it away.

★

The Catholic faith in Poland was as tenacious against Soviet Communism as it was against Tsarist imperialism, and ultimately as successful. The collapse of the last remnants of Marxism-Leninism in Poland was the victory of the Church. It would not have happened as it did without the election of a Polish pope, or the imprisonment of a Polish cardinal. Cardinal Stefan Wyszynski, who was held in the same prison as Wladyslaw Gomulka, became the rallying-point for people's private sense of nationality in the 1950s, when it was too dangerous to be an open nationalist. The election of Karel Wojtyla to the Papal throne rekindled the sense of pride and resistance. After the Solidarity movement, the direct result of that rekindling, was stamped out by martial law in 1981 it was the Catholic Church which provided consolation and a sense of identity. And when Solidarity's candidates won the 1989 election, it was the final ideological victory of Polish Catholicism over Polish Communism.

The fabric of Marxism-Leninism in Poland had begun to unravel as early as 1956, when Gomulka was rehabilitated and given back his old job as General Secretary of the Communist Party after being arrested and imprisoned under Stalinism. For a brief moment, it seemed reasonable to hope that reform meant something, that a man who had once suffered for his relatively liberal beliefs would put them into practice. But the system was not to be shifted in that direction. Gomulka gradually became as hidebound, as unreasoningly conservative, as the others; so that there had to be a new palace revolution in 1970, triggered by strikes in Gdansk and Szczecin which swept him away and put Gierek in power in his place. The same thing happened again.

After that, nothing could be expected from any further changes within the system, and everyone knew it. By the mid-1970s the division between Poles and their government was becoming absolute. Neither seemed to be of any importance to the other. They had become mutually irrelevant. People wrote, and taught, and bought and sold, and worked and refused to work, without reference to the complex rules which were supposed to cover every aspect of life in a Marxist state. They were clocking on at factories and working long hours using the machines for completely different, private enterprise jobs, while elaborate efforts were made to give the impression that the factory's production quotas were being met. 'We pretend to work and they pretend to pay us' was a familiar joke in Poland. By the late 1970s it had become 'We pretend to be governed and they pretend to govern us.' There was no breakdown of law and order. People did roughly what they were supposed to do, outwardly at least. But it was absurd and pointless, and everyone knew it: not only the supposedly governed but the supposed governors as well. There was no need for a revolution in Poland in 1989; the system crumbled away.

It is difficult now to find a Marxist who will defend the way things were run in Poland towards the end. In 1981 many of them believed that martial law was necessary to hold the country together and prevent the Russians from invading. General Jaruzelski, however, having made himself a military dictator, failed to use his new powers to bring about the necessary changes in the economy. He simply tied Poland closer than ever to the Soviet Union with agreement after agreement. The chance was lost. In the end, even true believers were alienated by the system, just as everyone else had been years before.

When a revolution takes place the overthrow of the old regime seems an end in itself. But what looks like a solution merely turns out to pose a new series of questions to a new set of politicians. In Poland, the most immediate of these questions is, how do you create a new system which people can accept and become part of? It involves everything from establishing an economy which doesn't have to be undercut and industry where people do the work they're paid for to reinventing the kind of government which seems to reflect what the electorate wants. After the years of 'We pretend to vote and they pretend to represent us' such things are not easy.

In Warsaw the winter sky hangs heavily over the city. Days which begin with sunshine are grey and dank by ten in the morning. A mist of watery cloud and pollution cuts off the tops of the buildings and levels out at the first crown of the Stalinist Gothic cathedral which is the city's 'palace of culture', built in the last year of Stalin's reign. Along the main Jerozolimskie Avenue, in front of this palace of Communist culture, is a hoarding which carries a big poster. It says 'PORNO' in fat pink letters: 'FILM EROTYCZNY'. Small political posters on the walls have been systematically attacked. A long downward strip has been torn on each of them, an identectomy which removes all knowledge of the man – that it was a man you can tell from his suited shoulders which remain – and whatever political programme he might have offered.

Two large crowds have gathered, not at the food shops which are full of produce and largely empty of customers, but at the currency exchange offices and the bookstalls. *Animal Farm*, Josif Brodski and Solzhenitsyn are piled up as casually as if they've always been permitted; yet there is still a residual wariness about the men who pull the cardboard boxes full of books out of the back of their vans. They can't help looking round to check for policemen. Poland is a country where literature means something; you don't find people queuing for books in Britain or the United States, or black marketeers supplying them.

The buildings along Jerozolimskie Avenue are formless, ugly and grey: all that Communism had the imagination and the money to build, on the rubble-strewn sites left them at the end of the war. They re-erected the old city, like the Campanile in Venice, *com' era, dov' era*: as it was, where it was. Then they ran out of energy, time, inspiration, cash. All along here there are men in their twenties and thirties standing around watching the passers-by. As a foreigner approaches them a quiet litany begins:

> '*Entschuldigung, bitte.*'
> '*Wechsel?*'
> 'You change money?'
> 'Mark, dollar?'
> '*Entschuldigung, bitte.*'
> '*Entschuldigung.*'

For them, all foreigners are likely to be Germans. They hope so, because Germans change the most money. Four policemen walk by in a line, their hands on the white truncheons stuck in their belts. Out of habit the money-changers drop their voices even lower, but do not actually stop offering. The policemen are laughing, and take no notice anyway. No one seems certain whether changing money is entirely legal or entirely illegal. No one cares.

Ahead is a pedestrian underpass, which takes the crowds of shoppers beneath Jerozolimskie Aveune. The entrance to this one is covered with posters and graffiti:

RAP CLUB – VIDEO CONCERTY
White Power
Russian tanks to the Volga!
Anarchy
LECH.

There are underpasses in all modern cities, but socialist town-planners made a particular feature of them. It is, perhaps, part of a genuine effort to look after the interests of people without cars, of whom there are a great deal more than in Western countries. The result, in Peking, in Moscow, in Warsaw and Prague and a dozen smaller and less attractive cities, is that an elaborate subterranean life sprang up in these tunnels. Out of reach of the weather, people could take shelter, meet, sell each other things, hold impromptu political meetings and paste up endless posters. They were underground figuratively as well as literally: in Prague and Warsaw, in particular, small opposition groups would meet in the passageways beneath the main streets. The most radical posters were usually to be found there, and they tended to survive longer. The police patrolled the underpasses less frequently.

The time is November 1989, and this particular one has a life of its own. Under the low ceilings, in the dankness, small traders arrive early in the morning and stay all day, selling whatever they can gather together. The choice is often pathetically small. One man offers a single packet of 20 'Carmen' cigarettes, three tins of boot polish, all black, and an old-fashioned pair of men's hair clippers from a barber's shop. An elderly man with a bent back and a long nose with a permanent drip has a stock of large pink and black plastic lady-birds, which he winds up and sets buzzing around his feet. From time to time one that is less well aimed escapes and heads off into the crowd. There is a dispute when a woman treads on one, but she pays a third of the price and he continues to offer it for sale when she has gone.

There are elderly women selling a single item of poor quality lace, and younger ones selling Palestinian k'firs. One man has a single item of stock: a set of chrome taps for a wash-basin. When he sells it he moves away fast, bequeathing his place to someone with a couple of Solidarity T-shirts. Next to them is a man with a hi-fi set, smart enough to look at but of a little-known brand: Anitech, it says. Everyone examines it but no one asks the price. A woman sets out her stock of underwear on a blanket laid out on the floor. The generous cups of brassieres stick up into the air like puddings on a plate. Above the constant shuffling of feet in trainers – the almost universal footwear – is the music of a band. It is only the length and elaborate nature of the tunnels that damp down the sound. There are eight of them: three on concertinas, one on a double bass, a couple on banjos, a violinist and a drummer. None is younger than sixty. A singer belts out pre-war songs about pretty girls, the longing for home, mother and the need to dance. The singing is uniformly jolly, whatever the subject matter, and an old woman selling strings of garlic cloves nearby joins in the choruses in a cracked voice that sounds as though it was last used when the song was written. Three men with physical disabilities limp around with tambourines, collecting low-denomination zloty notes from the crowds shuffling past.

Farther along are four public telephones in a line. Four women of varying ages are standing there, patiently putting in their five-zloty coins (worth so little that twenty of them would not buy you a cup of coffee). The estimate is that only one out of every twenty-six attempts to dial is successful. In the ten minutes while I stand and watch them, only one of the people using the telephones gets through. They reach the third or fourth digit, then ring off and start again. People say the phones are always worse when it rains. At the exchanges, most of the equipment was designed in the 1940s or early 1950s, and everything that the Polish genius for improvisation can do with wire and string has to be done to keep the system going. It is a wearing business for those who use it and those in charge of it alike: just one of the small pinpricks of everyday life which makes things cumulatively intolerable.

Above everything there is the insistent, sweet odour which pervades the public places of Poland and the Soviet Union, and of nowhere else I know. It is composed of sweat, cigarettes and perhaps a kind of cheap scented soap. It is the very smell of Communism, and is fading as Communism fades: though not until the old women who sweep out places like the underpass have gone. Amid the smell and the shuffling one man does modest but consistently good business. He holds out a veined old hand, the fingers as nicotine-brown as thin cigars, with medallions in white metal dangling from it. I assume at first that they are either religious or Solidarity medals. But Solidarity is not doing so well now that it is in government, and the customers who stop are mostly younger men. Closer to, I can see the characteristic soup-strainer moustache and heavy disapproving eyebrows of Marshal Pilsudski, socialist turned military dictator of Poland between the wars; the man who told the Social Democrats:

> Gentlemen, I am no longer your comrade. In the beginning we went in the same direction, and took the same red-painted tram. But as for me, I got off at the 'Independence' stop.

The words fit post-Communist Poland with some accuracy; and it is not surprising that Pilsudski, the autocratic father of a newly independent country, appears everywhere: in brass on the counters of souvenir shops, on stamps, on lapel-pins, on the medallions dangling from the hand of an old man in a pedestrian underpass. Why, I asked a young bright-looking man who had just bought one of the medallions, was he so interested in Pilsudski?

> Because he is the greatest man Poland has produced this century. And because we need someone strong to lead us now. Poland is in a real mess. We've got to get out of it somehow.

The underpass hints at the mess, and at the degree to which the old system has broken down, with nothing to take its place. Groups of youths stand around the battered electronic games which have been set up in one of the outlying tunnels. They shout and bang the controls, elbowing each other aside to take their place. One of them moves away from the Satan of Saturn machine and looks across at me. He speaks good English for a seventeen-year-old.

> What else do we have to do? I hate it here, but I can't get the money to go abroad. Poland is dead. Dead and buried. I got an uncle in Chicago, he's

gonna get me a green card. I'll work as an electrician, I guess. America is the place.

For the citizens of the former Soviet empire, America is what it always was: the hope of the world's huddled masses. It is as though the events of three decades have entirely passed them by: the decline of the United States in economic and political terms, the increased barriers to immigration. An American visa and a green card are the first prize in the post-revolution lottery. Second prize, some way down, is the chance to work in West Germany. After that, it seems, nothing much counts. Getting out is not an obsession with Poles as it became with East Germans, but it is always there as an option, and returning Poles find it hard to admit that life in the United States didn't match up to their hopes. If you do not succeed there, you keep quiet about it and live on the dollars you bring back with you.

Behind the seventeen-year-old is a notice board where typed postcards offer work, flats for exchange in Warsaw – and a questionable ticket out.

Canadians, Americans and Poles living in North America offer marriage to Polish men and women. Write, enclosing a photograph and a description of your figure, to the Lolita Agency, Vancouver, British Columbia.

Yet the Western world lies only a few hundred yards from the steps of the underpass. The large hotel there is built as an oasis from the reality of life outside its walls. There are green plants everywhere, and pastel colours, and people who smile and bow and call you 'sir'. English is the first language here: English English, American English, German and Swedish and Dutch English. Around the atrium, sub-classical music flows from a pianist, a violinist and a cellist, chosen for their looks as much for as their playing. A cup of Earl Grey tea and a pastry at one of the tables on the open mezzanine floor cost the equivalent of a weeks' wages in the grey, damp world outside. The hotel's windows are of suitably darkened glass.

Only three types of Pole come through the doors: those who have hard currency or vast amounts of zlotys to spend, those who work here, and some extremely attractive women. These are not members of Djilas' New Class, the old, successful Party members, who simply enjoyed the kind of standards which a more genuinely socialist society would have made available to everybody. In the atmosphere of anger and resentment which followed the collapse of Communism in Poland and everywhere else, the privileges which the Party awarded itself are seen as nothing less than corruption. The people who are allowed into the hotel are different. They have to provide Westerners with what they want. It can be trade, or information, or services of some kind. Or it can be sex.

Before the big changes in Warsaw, the big hotels employed porters who could spot at a glance whether or not someone belonged there; but most Poles would keep away from hotels where Westerners stayed anyway. They didn't want to attract the attention of the security policemen who always hung around such places, and they didn't want the humiliation of being turned away by the porters on the door. Nowadays the porters at the big hotels are still alert, but the criteria have changed a little:

Nobody ever told me who not to let in. I just know. It isn't just the clothes they wear. I never worked at another hotel before this one. They like to have people who are new to the business. The don't want them working here with all the old ways – you know, telling people everything they can't do, and that kind of stuff, like they used to. Even so, I know which kind of guys wouldn't have been allowed in here in the past: guys with jeans and beards. Poles, I mean. Now, I don't just automatically stop them. They could be computer scientists, they could be artists. I watch them. Only if I think they've come to change money or sell something, I throw them out. But there's selling and selling. I guess it depends on how much you're selling for. Five dollars, not enough. A hundred dollars, okay. I'm not talking about the girls. I don't want to talk about them. No one tells me what I should do about them, either. Maybe I think it's not my business.

All this was accompanied by a look that said it was not my business either.

*

When I first went to Gdansk I had not expected it to be beautiful. The films of Wajda, the television news pictures and the very name of the Lenin Shipyard summoned up grainy, black-and-white images: dirty snow, ugly buildings, crude exploitation, water cannon and police baton charges. The shipyard was certainly a place where labour was exploited, and there was occasional ugliness. But the suburbs were graced by the grand suburban houses of nineteenth-century ship-owners, the exploiters of their day, and the city itself, which was Danzig in its former incarnation and so powerful it did not need to be a member of the Hanseatic League, now has better mediaeval buildings than are left in Bremen or Hamburg. The houses are florid in a Germanic way, and the elaborate towers of the churches have a Protestant look;

though almost all the churches in the city are Catholic and the Protestant German settlers are long gone. This is the city in which Günter Grass was born, and which he describes in his novels:

> Like Westerzeile which ran parallel to it, Osterzeile was perpendicular to Baerenweg, which ran parallel to Wolfsweg. When you went down Westerzeile from the Wolfsweg and looked leftward and westward over the red tiled roofs, you saw the west side and front of a tower with a tarnished bulbiform steeple. . . .

The streets and the roofs and the bulbiform steeple are there still, but the names have disappeared. There are no wolf's or bear's ways in Gdansk now.

Our minds associate size with importance, but the Lenin Shipyard itself is smaller and less significant than you would expect. I came there in the autumn of 1988, not long before the great political upheavals began in earnest. I was following a foreign dignitary who had come to pay homage at the birthplace of Solidarity. The workforce crowded the place to cheer and throw flowers. No matter that Margaret Thatcher was an advocate of closing down old industries like shipbuilding if they were uneconomic, nor that the Polish government, still in Communist hands, had just announced that the shipyard was to be closed. For the workers of Gdansk, she represented radical, crusading anti-Communism. They cheered and threw their flowers as hard as they could, and those who were closest to her leaned out to shake her hand or kiss it.

While they waited in the low October sunshine they chanted the slogans elaborated during years of political activism:

'Lenin is yours, the Shipyard is ours.'
'Gdansk Shipyard.'
'No freedom without Solidarity.'
'Urban [the government spokesman] lies.'
'Down with Communism.'
'One day Communists will hang from the trees like leaves.'

At that time, 1988, there was nowhere else in the Soviet empire where such things were chanted so openly. The police, long since accustomed to the virulence of Solidarity supporters, lounged around and grinned at the insults. The crowd, completely unreconciled to the decaying system operated from Warsaw, did not grin back. These things were meant. At the same time there was a yearning in their faces and on the banners they held up: 'Mrs Thatcher, don't let them close down the shipyard', 'Mrs Thatcher, don't forget us Poles'. But other banners showed that some people in the crowd had already moved out of the socialist system altogether. There were nationalist groups, and groups of young conservatives – tough-looking right wingers wearing boots and carrying staves for use, if necessary, against the police. And again and again came a football chant, which I had last heard on the Champs Elysées when Mitterrand was re-elected in 1987, and was to hear again fourteen months later in the towns and cities of Romania when Ceausescu was overthrown. Picked up by football crowd after football crowd across the face of Europe, it was a full-blooded chorus, capable of being belted out indefinitely, an enduring song of protest and support, and eventually of revolution:

'*Olé, olé, olé, olé*,
We won't give in.'

At last the man who had embodied the anger and desire for independence of these people emerged. 'Lech, Lech, Lech Walesa,' they chanted when they saw him. Now he was pale and heavy, and the famous moustache was streaked with white. Lech Walesa had diabetes, stomach ulcers, a bad back, and a heart condition. He found it hard to stand for more than half an hour at a time. Some of this was the result of his time in prison under martial law. But neither prison nor illness undermined his certainty, during the difficult years between December 1981 and the gradual easing of conditions in 1983, that Solidarity had a future as well as a past. Scarcely anyone else in Poland believed it, and Walesa's most important achievement was not so much in climbing over the Lenin Shipyard wall in 1980 and being elected the leader of what became Solidarity, but his refusal to give up the movement when it was generally thought to be dead.

Even so, it would not have risen again without the action of thousands of miners in Silesia, steel workers in Stalowa Wola, and dockers and shipyard workers in Szczecin and Gdansk in August 1988, whose strikes threw the government into a panic. The strikers were mostly younger men with little organization behind them. The strikes sprang from the problems of their everyday working lives: low pay, poor conditions, long hours, unsafe machinery. As for Solidarity and its leadership, they regarded them as played out and largely irrelevant. But the government, which at that time was led by General Kiszczak, called in desperation on the only man they could think of: Lech Walesa.

Once they had dismissed him as a sparrow trying to be an eagle, but on 31 August 1988 Kiszczak invited him to a government villa on the outskirts of Warsaw and made him an offer. The government would agree to legalize Solidarity and open round-table talks with Solidarity itself, with Catholic politicians and with non-Communist groups, if he would persuade the miners and the dockers and the shipbuilders to return to work. It took Walesa precisely three days to achieve his side of the bargain. Solidarity, thanks to the prestige of Lech Walesa's name and his unbroken faith that the movement could once again be the force it had been in 1980 and 1981, was effectively reborn. In less than a year it would be running the country.

The concept of negotiations at a round table, rather than the standard confrontation between two sides, was an intelligent one. It seems to have been suggested in the first place by Jaruzelski. The effect was to emphasize and encourage co-operation between the various parties rather than competition. Early on, the various groups came to refer to each other as 'partners' – the word Mikhail Gorbachev was already using about the United States and its allies at the various negotiations on arms control.

At the round table talks, Solidarity had two big advantages. It wasn't obliged to look over its shoulder all the time to make sure that its followers liked what it was doing, since its political base was largely undefined. Second, it was plain to everyone that the (Communist) Polish United Workers' Party was running out of ideas, influence and people. A new government was formed on 14 October with Mieczyslaw Rakowski, the Party's propaganda chief who was bitterly opposed to Solidarity and much hated by it, as prime minister. By sitting down to negotiate with Solidarity, however, the Communists had shown they were unable to govern the country without Solidarity's agreement. At that stage the leading figures in Solidarity didn't expect that they would soon be part of the government. The collapse of will within the PUWP took them by surprise. They had expected a return to the days immediately before martial law, with legalized trade unions, greater freedom for the media, the promise of radical reforms in the economy, but all done with the Communists in the positions of power.

*

It was a national holiday when I went to see Mieczyslaw Rakowski in the prime minister's office, where he had been installed two weeks earlier. Inside the entrance to the building three soldiers lounged about, listening to a football match on the radio. It wasn't easy to get their attention. They were not interested in the fact that my colleagues and I had come to film an interview with the prime minister. The only other people in the building, apart from the soldiers and ourselves, were three low-ranking officials and the prime minister himself.

Rakowski was a flawed and interesting man. He seemed a natural liberal, in Communist Party terms, but in 1981 he was a fierce advocate of martial law, and at the time the Solidarity leadership believed he had deliberately misled them in negotiations in order to trap them more effectively. Now, the empty building emphasized his isolation. The office he used was immense, void of any personal touch. On the walls were various bland canvases displaying landscapes under snow. Ornate, official furniture broke up the empty spaces. It had the air of a crematorium: functional, tidy, dead. In one corner Rakowski shifted around in his Third Empire chair, a nervous, energetic man who relied on jokes when the questions became difficult. His hands shook visibly, and he chain-smoked until our camera was switched on. Directly it was switched off he began smoking again. The year before he had called Solidarity 'a closed chapter in our history'. Now he called it 'a group of intellectuals who are experienced but lack a broader following'. He was sharp and bitter. Months before the collapse of the government he led, and of the party he belonged to, he could sense that there was no future.

No one, certainly not Solidarity, expected the results of the 1989 elections to be so sweeping. They knew they would do well; they had no idea it would be on this scale. Most members of the Solidarity leadership thought they would win 65–75 of the hundred seats in the Senate. They won 99. If it had not been for the reserved seats which the PUWP had arranged for itself beforehand it would have disappeared as a political force then and there. Lech Walesa declined the difficult job of prime minister. One of his main advisers, Tadeusz Mazowiecki, a Catholic intellectual and magazine editor, took it on instead. For the first time since 1939 Poland had a (fairly) properly elected government which – except for the unrepresentative quota of Communist MPs in the Sejm – reflected the wishes of its people.

The ministries of the interior and defence, the key departments which the Communists had always insisted on acquiring when the countries of Central and Eastern Europe were absorbed into the Soviet empire, remained in Communist hands; but everyone knew it was simply to calm any anxieties in Moscow. It was a sop, not a threat. Soon the statue of Feliks Dzierzynski, the Polish nobleman who founded the Soviet secret police, was destroyed, and people took home pieces of it as mementoes. It was the NKVD, the successors of Dzierzynski's Cheka, which massacred the Polish officer corps at Katyn. Soon, too, big state enterprises which bore the name of Lenin, including the shipyard in Gdansk, struck out the name. The big letters were taken down. Brass bands played, a thousand cameras snapped to catch the moment.

In other empires there would have been a ceremony. A new flag

would have been run up to replace the old one. Perhaps there would
have been a new national name. Settlers would have left, people of
another race would have taken over the government offices. Poland's
independence, the first to be achieved fully in this particular empire,
was not to be celebrated like that. There were some changes, even to the
national symbols: the crown reappeared on the Polish eagle. The state's
name was altered from The Polish People's Republic to The Republic
of Poland. The word 'socialist' began to go from brass plates and
letterheads. But there was no colonial governor to give a last salute.
What had gone in Poland was the habit of dependency – the concept
that the national political life was grounded on what Moscow believed,
and on what Moscow wanted.

*

The Palace of Culture and Science, at pl. Defilad, was built between 1952
and 1955 as a gift from the Soviet Union (817,000 cubic metres; height 234
metres; 3,288 rooms). It houses branches of the Polish Academy of Science,
exhibition halls, four theatres, four cinemas, Museum of technology, Youth
Palace with swimming pool and Congress Hall with seating accommodation
for 3,000. The 30th floor offers a magnificent panorama of the city and
vicinity.

Thus the official guidebook, on the absurd Stalinist Gothic cathedral
which dominates the centre of Warsaw, to the city's disadvantage. This
vast confection is familiarly known as The Pastrycook's Nightmare.
Inside the monstrous doors, though, the proportions are suddenly
inverted. The grandeur is all on the outside. The hallway is small and
dark, with inferior marble. Statuary glimmers at the stairheads, also on
a small scale. The 3,288 rooms seem mostly to be low and curiously
shaped.

I had come to see a professor of social psychology, whose office was
on the tenth floor of the extraordinary construction. But Janusz
Reykowski was more than that. He had been an adviser to the Interior
Ministry for twenty-five years, and a member of the last Politburo
before Poland ceased to be Communist. He was small and smiling and
dressed largely in brown, and had the face of a better-looking Erich
Honecker. He was prepared to be remarkably frank about the death of
the Party and his feelings about it.

During the 1980s, after martial law was imposed, those men in the
leadership who were opposed to all change – we called them the beton-
concrete group – gradually lost ground. The main credit for that belongs to
Jaruzelski. He eliminated them, bit by bit. But by 1988, when major steps

towards economic reform were taken, it was clear the Party had failed. The problems, in the economy and in society, couldn't be solved by this government. It simply didn't have the support in the country to deal with them.

So the Party either had to find some way of getting support to make radical reforms or Poland would drown economically. The political elite took the decision that it would have to change its approach to Solidarity, and accept that it wasn't just a marginal force. There was a lot of internal opposition in the Party to this. Don't forget, many people in the Party thought that Solidarity was just a group of foreign agents and adventurers. But by the end of 1988 the final decision was taken that agreement was the only peaceful solution, in fact the only solution of any kind to Poland's problems. The day that the prime minister, General Kiszczak, first met Lech Walesa was the day the old Party died in Poland.

For a man who has supported the Communist Party for nearly half a century, he seems to accept the position remarkably well. But then, of course, he is not simply a former member of the Politburo, he is a psychologist and a scientist. Marxism-Leninism may have ceased to exist as a serious force, but people's reactions to that are behavioral phenomena, which it is his duty to observe with dispassion.

At first, when the election results came in and it was plain how badly the Party had done, it was a very dramatic moment. There was a temptation in some minds to try to abolish the results. There was a wave of attacks on the Party leadership, with people demanding that the leadership should do something about the situation. But there was no one who could do anything about it, and we couldn't get any support from Moscow. Many party members found that unintelligible. To them it seemed like a stab in the back.

Why, I asked him, had Marxism-Leninism failed? In his view, the failure was not by any means complete.

If you compare Poland with, say, Latin America, and look at the social structures there, you can see that different social groups have benefited from the process here. In Poland and the Soviet Union the poorest groups in society have benefited and the middle class and the intelligentsia have lost. There were six million peasants in Poland before the war, and they lived at a very low level, without even having enough to eat. People like that have advanced tremendously. You only have to look at Mexico or Argentina to see what has happened to the same sort of people without the benefit of socialism.

But it became unable to change itself, to move to another stage of social and economic development. After the initial progress, socialism lost the ability to develop fast. Still, the historical process isn't finished yet. People thought in the 1930s that capitalism would never recover after the misery of the depression. The old form of socialism is dead now. Whether other forms will arise, I can't say. What I do know is that these problems of economic and social development aren't easy to solve.

He looked out from his window on the tenth floor of Stalin's gift to the people of Poland at the darkness of Warsaw. The outer office was empty: the secretary had left, and so had all the other secretaries in the building. Not even the wheezing old lift operator was still at his post. The corridors with their highly polished floors ran off into the shadows. The building was dark and echoing, and the small statues were hard to make out. The Poland which Stalin had forced his men to create in the likeness of the Soviet Union was finished.

A few days earlier, in this same building, the PUWP had reorganized itself, adopted another name, agreed on new and more democratic goals. The leadership passed to a younger generation. Mieczyslaw Rakowski, the former prime minister, seemed lonelier when he announced the name of the new leaders of the Party than he had when we interviewed him in his empty office building a year before. The tears welled up in his eyes. Everything he'd worked for had gone.

In an office in another part of Poland Lech Walesa sat preparing a speech for television. Not having wanted the job of prime minister after the 1989 election, he was now aiming at the Presidency. His appearance seemed subtly different. His moustache was bushier, and came lower down on each side of his mouth. Behind him, on the wall, was a photograph of a man who looked faintly similar. It was the face I had seen on the medallions in the Warsaw underpass: Marshal Pilsudski, saviour of the nation and ex-socialist who ran Poland with an attempt at military precision in the 1920s and 1930s. When Walesa made his television appearance, he was accompanied by martial music associated with Pilsudski's army.

'But of course,' said one of my politically-minded friends, 'all Polish history is cyclical. Didn't you realize? They've called us the doormat for invading armies, the sick man of Europe, and the Christ of the nations. But now we've slipped the leash.'

PART II
PEKING –
SETTING AN EXAMPLE

4
THE RIVER OF PROTEST

The water can carry a boat; it can also capsize it.

Proverb quoted on a banner carried in Tiananmen Square, May 1989

With hindsight, the morning of Saturday 13 May saw the last hours of the old China: the China created and irrevocably damaged by chairman Mao Zedong (Mao Tse-tung), the China which Deng Xiaoping had liberalized and tried to salve. For weeks now, there had been demonstrations. They had started after the death of Hu Yaobang, the former general secretary of the Party, on 15 April. Hu Yaobang was certainly liberal-minded (he was the first member of the leadership to wear Western suits) but he was never regarded as a supporter of democracy until his fall from office in 1987. Slowly he came to be seen as a martyr, sacked unfairly by the bureaucrats. He was adopted as a symbol of liberalization and as a supporter of greater democracy, and it had been for that reason that he had been disgraced two years earlier. He was also regarded as honest, and everyone knew that the current leadership was not. Several times since Hu's death, university students had taken to the streets, occupied Tiananmen Square, and brought the traffic to a halt throughout the centre of the city. But on the surface, things were calm and orderly in Peking that morning.

The surface was all I could judge. I had never been to China before, and had no informed knowledge of its culture or politics. I was there to report on the forthcoming visit by Mikhail Gorbachev, which was intended to bring to an end nearly twenty years of hostility between the People's Republic of China and the Soviet Union. As far as I was concerned, the visit was an important moment for Soviet foreign policy; and that I did know something about. If Chinese students chose to demonstrate during the Gorbachev visit – and not everybody thought they would – that was someone else's concern. It was impossible to believe that the demonstrations might be more significant than the diplomatic *rapprochement* between Moscow and Peking.

It was a difficult city for a newcomer to understand. Wide boulevards with vast modern buildings overshadowed side streets which were dark and narrow. It teemed with life, but in ways I could scarcely comprehend. As my taxi drove me to what I understood to be the geographical centre of Peking, I found it hard even to work out where we were on the map. I had only two words in common with the driver, 'Beijing' and 'hotel'. I asked him to take me there. The Beijing Hotel was, I understood, a short walk from Tiananmen Square.

I walked along Chang'an Avenue, trying to come to terms with it all. It was placid, yet teeming with people: people for whom I was apparently as interesting as they were to me. We walked in columns, east to west along one side of the pavement, west to east along the other, two streams of a divided river. People craned their heads to examine me as I passed. Even in this main avenue of the city foreigners were a rarity. There was no hostility, no intentional rudeness; if I smiled, people smiled back in friendly, embarrassed fashion. There was a harsh smell in the warm air.

In the road beside me there was a continual fluttering of bicycle bells which arose from two other, much greater rivers, running east and west along the roadway. Each bicycle carried a number-plate and a fantastical maker's name painted in roman letters: 'Forever', 'Flying Pigeon', 'Phoenix'. The bicycles rode at a common speed, just as we were walking at a common speed, slow and undemanding. No one overtook or barged into the cyclists or the pedestrians on either side. Social orderliness lay across the place like a meteorological depression.

The people in the various rivers alongside me were better off and more at ease than at any time in China's history. There was no longer a social and political impulsion to merge into the crowd. Only older men wore Mao jackets; only the poorest of the young men wore green army trousers. The rest were cheaply but brightly dressed as they strolled along in the May sunshine. Some were eating the ice cream sold in the stalls along the way. It had, I later found, an acrid aftertaste. Others chewed away at thin pancakes coated with paste which had no discernible taste at all. There was a great deal of hawking and spitting.

It was a day for families. People walked in threes: man and woman and only child. The children who were in the stream coming towards me carried toys bought at stalls inside the Forbidden City, little mechanical helicopters that whizzed around a stick, or toy guns of the most rudimentary kind. The children were usually so well wrapped up against the gentle spring day that their arms stuck out at the sides. On top of everything some of them wore little imitation People's Liberation Army caps. The PLA seemed remarkably popular.

The people around me seemed to be savouring the feeling that life could be counted on to get better, a little at a time. The freedom to hold hands with your girlfriend or boyfriend in public, wearing whatever clothes you chose, was just a dozen years old in China. Before that, young couples could walk together only if they were engaged, Little Red Sentinels were trained to inform on their parents and friends, and children sang 'Father is dear, Mother is dear, But Chairman Mao is dearest of all.' It was different now.

A man in a T-shirt that read 'SPORT' in badly printed English passed me. He carried a child on his shoulders who looked like the Last Emperor in a little woollen hat, and his wife wore a neat blue dress. They had the air of people who had carefully amassed the social gains they had been allowed and were making the most of them: small investors in personal freedom. The man half-inclined his head to me, and the limp form of the Little Emperor above him made me an exaggerated bow. I bowed back. People around me tittered.

Along Chang'an Avenue, moving among the bicycles like fat carp among the minnows, were cars. Not small family ones, but large saloons, advertising the wealth of the people inside them. There were Toyota Crowns, Volvos, Mercedes, each costing a great deal in foreign exchange. The Red Flags, immense gimcrack automobiles of antique design which China manufactured itself, seemed to have vanished from the streets. It was a sign of the times. Peking had the air of a place that had suddenly come into money, but not honestly. As I walked along, the skyline in every direction was fringed with giant cranes; hotels and office blocks were going up with no thought of the number of businessmen and tourists who might occupy them.

During the period of Deng Xiaoping's power the great organs of state which controlled access to real estate had been allowed to act as developers themselves; thus, the hotel I was staying in had been constructed as a joint venture between the People's Liberation Army and a Japanese construction company. The management organization was based in Manila, and there was a persistent rumour that Imelda Marcos, the widow of the deposed President of the Philippines, had a stake in it. It looked out at another, equally under-occupied, in which the Security Police had a stake. '*Qanmin jingshang*' was the official slogan which had been used when such examples of private enterprise had started: 'everybody doing business'. The benefits filtered downwards, if thinly.

I wandered into the Forbidden City, the huge complex of palaces belonging to the emperors of the Ming and Qing dynasties. Over the Gate of Heavenly Peace there hung the portrait of Chairman Mao, the founder of a new dynasty. I was unable to take my eyes off it. It was a masterwork of utter blandness. This was the man whose whims had cost more lives than Stalin's, and yet there was no expression whatever:

no cunning, no anxiety, no past. It was a portrait of facelessness, and yet it was exactly true to life. I passed through the archway, where people stopped to pat the brasswork on the giant gates, shining it with their collective touch. In the courtyard the little shops and stalls were doing good business, selling the toys and hats I had seen on Chang'an Avenue. Children were being dressed up as princes and princesses, to be photographed by a professional photographer with an ancient camera on a tripod. The children never cried, and never spoke. They sat astride wooden horses or lay back in carriages and endured the business of being robed and presented as though they were taking part in some palace ritual.

Away from the crowds in the central avenues of the Forbidden City the long, near-identical buildings of the old palace with their yellow roofs and complicated carvings were bewildering. I could make nothing of their original purpose, nor their modern function. Staircases of white marble with carved animals at their extremities led nowhere. It was easy to accept the old idea that China was impenetrable; that the experience of its people was somehow different from the experience of people living under other forms of totalitarianism.

I left the palace and went out again under Mao's portrait, over the little marble bridges where people were taking each others' photographs. No one walked on the grass, or stepped over a boundary chain, or dropped litter. There was a rational, law-abiding feel to everything. The policemen who were strolling around were never troubled by anyone's behaviour. Heading on my own across Chang'an Avenue, which everyone else crossed by an underpass, I raised a storm of warning from the fluttering bicycle bells.

Tiananmen Square opened out ahead of me. Loudspeakers on the lamp posts played empty official music. It was a vast parade-ground, bordered by ugliness: the Great Hall of the People on the western side (eleven acres in size and built in eight frenetic months during the Great Leap Forward of the 1950s) and the mausoleum on the southern side where Mao's waxen body was on permanent display. In the centre was the Monument to the People's Heroes. The People appeared a great deal in all this, but only in name.

The Square was the heart of Communist China, and its emptiness seemed to match the spiritual emptiness of Deng Xiaoping's system. It was an open air stage on which, from time to time, actors portraying the People would represent their gratitude to the Party and its reductionist system. The play had gone on for forty years, but now it was emptier than ever. What was unclear to me was the degree to which people, The People, realized that it was empty. I assumed that few did.

Yet Tiananmen Square could also witness genuine shows of sorrow and of courage. In 1976 people had risked their freedom and their lives here to show their respects to the dead Zhou Enlai, and to call for the arrest of the Gang of Four. This was where the students had mourned the death of the former leader Hu Yaobang in April, and had begun calling openly for more democracy. It was difficult to sort out, this contrast between the utter obedience on the one hand, and the open defiance on the other.

I strolled across the Square towards the Monument. At that stage I knew nothing of its significance: not even that the calligraphy on it was Zhou Enlai's. It was guarded by a few men in uniform. One seemed nervous. He was listening to a walkie-talkie, and craning his head in the direction of the Gate of Heavenly Peace. I walked round. Several people came close to the Monument so their friends could photograph them against it. A young soldier, his head so recently cropped that you could still see the abrasions, stood to attention, his cap under his arm, while his mother focused the camera. They were both very proud.

A summer wind was blowing. It was warm, and it brought a curious musty odour: the odour of Peking. It also brought an unfamiliar sound. The policeman with the walkie-talkie spoke a couple of staccato words into it, his voice ending high. The sound was a distant crowd of people, singing.

. . . *L'Internation-a-a-le* . . .

Scarlet banners were crowding round the corner of the Square from the Avenue. They showed up against the maroon walls of the Forbidden City like blood on an old coat. A big crowd of demonstrators was heading towards the Monument. They were singing the one song which, after forty years of the People's Republic, everybody could be counted on to know. Around the edges of the Square a few old men and their grandchildren had been flying little kites in the afternoon breeze: cormorants and owls, butterflies and dragons, fluttering and swooping above their heads. Now the red banners caught the same breeze, and the old men hauled in their kites to watch. It was the approach of an army without weapons, which had no intention of fighting. Its strength came from a vague undefined wish for something better.

The students marched towards us in orderly fashion. The serious faces in the front ranks broke into smiles as they approached. They were starting to raise their hands in the Victory sign. Close to, many of the banners were tattered. They looked like regimental battle- standards from a cathedral, and the paper carrying the big Chinese characters was peeling off them. These were the banners from the time of Hu Yaobang's funeral in April. They bore nothing but the name of Peking Normal University and the faculty of the students who were carrying them.

Ever since the beginning of the year there had been rumours that the students of Peking would stage something on 4 May, the seventieth anniversary of the student demonstrations against the government of the old republic. The death of Hu Yaobang had triggered the protests early, and provided an initial rallying-point. Soon the protest took on a life of its own, with new reasons for people to join the demonstration. Some of the banners the students carried into the Square reflected the latest cause for anger.

'The Students Are Patriotic!'

'We Demand The Withdrawal Of The People's Daily Editorial!'

'Dialogue Now!'

Those dated from the demonstration of 27 April, the day after the *People's Daily* had carried a powerful attack on the student movement. The editorial was said to have been dictated by Deng Xiaoping himself. It referred to 'a planned conspiracy and a disturbance' created by 'a handful of people'. In the semiotics of Chinese Communism these were serious accusations. Many students felt then that they had to force a retraction.

This demonstration contained a new element. At the head of the marchers came a group of two or three hundred young men and women with white bands round their heads. On each headband were two Chinese characters: 'hunger' and 'strike'. They were the shock-troops of the latest protest. They looked like kamikaze pilots or Islamic martyrs, but they were quiet and unemotional. As the front of the demonstration reached the foot of the Monument they sat down in a group. One unfurled a white flag he'd been carrying over his shoulder: it said in English 'Fast to the Death'. Others in the crowd pushed the police aside and jumped over the low chain around the steps at the foot of the Monument. They swarmed up the broad steps, laughing and shouting.

Their enthusiastic faces stood out against the grim marble reliefs around the base of the Monument behind them. The People's heroes were frozen in mid-bayonet charge during some revolutionary battle, teeth gritted and eyes rolling fiercely. The excited, flushed young faces contained no such ferocity, but the low chain which the students had leaped over was the line between quiet obedience and all-out political challenge. The Monument was holy ground, on which few feet were supposed to tread. In less than three days' time Mikhail Gorbachev was due to lay a wreath there. The stakes were very high this time.

Soon the great empty public space, barren and tidy, had taken on the noisy, unkempt, cheerful atmosphere of a travelling fair. A man pedalled laboriously through the crowd on a kind of flat-bed rickshaw.

It was carrying large cardboard boxes full of blankets and sleeping bags, surmounted by two flag-waving students. 'We Want A Dialogue!' said the identical slogans on the identical white T-shirts they were wearing over their ordinary clothes like mediaeval surcoats. Everybody clapped and cheered.

'We don't want to challenge our government,' an English-speaker explained to me. 'We just want them to talk to us. We want to explain that we aren't unpatriotic.'

They believed that if they simply demonstrated their goodwill the representatives of an old, entrenched system would acknowledge it.

The warm afternoon drew on. People were still moving around, greeting their friends and enjoying themselves. The outright challenge to authority had brought a sense of liberty. Little groups had gathered all round the Square, listening to discussions. I stayed as long as I could, and could not resist coming back later. At two in the morning, the meetings were still going. The students were arranging places to sleep, chattering and laughing, laying out their things.

It all had the air of a temporary protest which might end at any moment. There was a heavy smell of food frying in cheap butter. It came from the stalls which had already gathered to cater for the multitude. I noticed that the street vendors, who were making good money, stayed away from the Monument. They were the small businessmen whom Deng Xiaoping had allowed to operate under the new economic liberalism. They knew better than most that the margin of liberty might be reduced at any moment. They wanted to be able to get away fast if it happened.

The first night was cold and windy, and few of them had thought to bring sleeping bags or warm clothing. But having established their position, no one wanted to leave. It was an adventure. Before I left the Square that night I made a point of visiting the hunger strikers. They lay in rows, their white headbands showing up in the pale light. Most seemed to be lying on their backs, still awake. They were looking up at the sky. There was little talking here.

Over the following days and weeks the aims and demands of the students had a notably elevated tone. They were challenging an entire system on behalf of democracy and freedom. But at the same time the conditions under which they lived their daily lives played a part in their discontent. Their dormitories were small and uncomfortable: a room twenty feet by ten would house half a dozen students, whose bunks constituted the only living-space they owned. There was nowhere to hang clothes or store private possessions. A guitar, a few books, a teapot and a couple of cups, a towel: that was all. Washrooms were usually spartan and very cold in winter, with bare stone floors and a line of dirty, cracked hand basins. There were often just two lavatories for a hundred or more people. The dormitories were bad-smelling, gloomy places, which only the habitual friendliness and jollity there made bearable.

The students were not protesting about these conditions. Most of them seemed scarcely to notice that they were bad. But the conditions intensified their receptiveness to revolutionary ideas, in much the same way that the skilled workers of Petrograd were receptive to revolutionary ideas in 1917. Chinese students regarded themselves as being in the vanguard of political progress. Mao Zedong had used them in that way during the Cultural Revolution in 1966, and the predisposition to political action was still there. Ideas and information funnelled into the crowded dormitories of the universities in Peking. Opinions were standardized and differences over tactics diminished. It was difficult for anyone to opt out of the general movement. When the students marched to the Square the dormitories were almost entirely empty.

Only the graduate students among them had even been born at the time the Cultural Revolution was at its height; but the Tiananmen Square demonstrations were the last faint aftershocks of the earthquake. Mao Zedong's name was often mentioned with respect in the speeches of the students and on their banners. The Cultural Revolution by contrast was regarded with embarrassment by the government and loathing by the generation which had suffered from it. The students were the next generation down. Because the government had placed such heavy emphasis on the economy, education in general had been neglected, and political instruction often hardly existed. In the universities there was something of a spiritual vacuum, surrounded by fantasies of instant wealth and success.

People who knew precisely what they thought a decent society should be were hard to find. The word 'democracy' was used continually, but it rarely meant pluralism along Western lines. Instead it meant the right to express criticisms of the Communist Party, which would eradicate the ills from which it was suffering. For most students this would strengthen the Communist Party. They wanted it to be more accountable to the people. When the student leader Chai Ling was asked if democracy and Communism were mutually compatible, she replied:

I don't think there is any fundamental rift between democracy and Communism, but I haven't researched that problem. I can say that we seek something that is fundamental and natural. We aren't looking for new 'isms'. Our struggle is for individual human rights. We want to participate in the running of the country. We want to decide who our leaders will be. Democracy is our natural right. We must become our own masters.

The students no longer wanted to be dictated to. They wanted an end to the pressure for conformity, to a government which no one believed in, to a system which could manipulate the idealism of millions of ordinary people for its own cynical reasons. They were not protesting against Communism as such. Indeed, the songs they sang were the songs Communism had taught them. Nevertheless they knew what had happened at the time of the Cultural Revolution, and they blamed the system for that, even though Deng Xiaoping had himself been a victim of it. The protests in Tiananmen Square were in some ways a late aftershock from the Cultural Revolution. Later, a woman in her thirties who was in the Square with the students explained to me how her own youthful excitement and energy had been wasted:

> I was only twelve. They had brainwashed me completely. I really believed I was serving Chairman Mao faithfully by informing on my parents. It was a kind of competition between us. I even exaggerated the things they did that were counter-revolutionary, so that I would be better than the other children. My parents were dragged out of the house, attacked, and I was there shouting with the others. I thought I was being really good. Nothing very bad happened to them, apart from being beaten up and paraded around. I heard of cases where people were killed, but it didn't happen in our school. My parents have forgiven me now. They understand it was just an illness, and I was one of the patients. But once you've done something like that you know how bad the system can be. I never want that sort of thing to happen again. I tell all my students about it. That's why we must have democracy in China.

The Cultural Revolution had used the Red Guards as its puppets. Their idealism had simply been turned into a political tool to further the careers of some leaders at the expense of others. The demonstrations after Hu Yaobang's death were partly a declaration of independence against all that. They represented the rebirth of idealism. The system under Deng Xiaoping operated as it had always done on the principle known as '*guanxi*': 'connections'. You had to know people to get on. It was inherent in China's essentially feudal culture, where favours are granted in return for absolute obedience and unswerving loyalty. The natural instincts of the students to look to something outside themselves and their studies, something grander and more inspiring, was unsatisfied. There was no political cause in modern China which was worthy of their self-sacrifice. It was necessary for them to create one themselves.

Peking Normal University was much less radical than Peking and Qinghua Universities, and did not attract the cream of the intelligentsia. Its students were trained to be teachers in colleges and secondary schools: not very glamorous careers. Mao Zedong's daughter had graduated from there. The average age of the students was usually higher than elsewhere. Conditions were better, and there was less of a hothouse effect. Apart from brief flare-ups in 1986 and 1987 it had remained quiet. Now things had changed. The students at Peking Normal were determined not to be left behind this time. Two years before it had produced an outspoken and extremely liberal-minded male lecturer, Liu Xiaobo, who advocated complete Westernization. There were handwritten notices everywhere, of the kind known as big-character posters. They were continually being replaced by new ones. Students stood in front of them, copying the characters down so they could pass the messages on to their friends in other colleges and universities in the city. Once posters like these would have been written out to the dictation of the Party and the government. Now they were put there by the students, and they were fiercely worded.

There was a new spirit of courage and daring. The rally of 27 April, which brought 100,000 people into Tiananmen Square, had been organized from Peking Normal University. So had the march of the 10,000 bicycles on 10 May, when the students took a 40-kilometre ride around Peking and stopped in front of the *People's Daily* to insist that the offending editorial should be withdrawn. The usual fear of Chinese university students, that they would be assigned to bad jobs in unpopular places unless they behaved themselves, had gone. The quiet basketball court of a quiet university had become the place where the fundamental decisions on the initial course of the revolution were made. It was filled with fluttering red flags and echoed with songs.

The best known of the leaders of what became the Autonomous Student Federation, Chai Ling, was at Peking Normal University. She was a tiny, gentle woman in her early twenties. When I first met her, I thought she was a little girl. She was no more than four feet ten inches high, and she smiled a great deal. But there was an intensity about her which had infected the whole university, and was soon to influence the students' revolution as a whole. It showed itself in the arguments of 12 and 13 May which led to the take-over of Tiananmen Square.

The demonstrations of mourning for Hu Yaobang and the anti-government sit-ins and bicycle protests which followed had thrown up a collective leadership. The Peking University Students' Solidarity

Preparations Committee contained many of the leaders who were to run the great demonstration in Tiananmen Square: Wang Dan, Wuer Kaixi, Yang Tao, Li Lu, as well as Chai Ling and her husband Feng Congde. The fiercest argument came on the question of the hunger strike. It was a way of demonstrating total commitment, and it would draw on the reserves of self-sacrifice within the student movement. The threat to starve oneself to death has a particularly strong resonance in Chinese culture. It was the ultimate weapon the students had at their disposal.

Some of the leaders, including Wuer Kaixi and Wang Dan, felt that they should keep it in reserve. It was enough, they felt, to take over the Square. Chai Ling and Feng Congde were both strongly in favour of the hunger strike, and their determination swayed the meeting. But it required all Chai Ling's passionate rhetoric to persuade people to take part. At first there were fewer than a hundred volunteers, but by the next day, when the marchers moved off to take over the Square, four times that number put on the white head bands.

Wuer Kaixi and Wang Dan were very different in nature. Wuer came from Xinjiang. His real name was Uerkesh Daolet, but he used a form which Han Chinese could pronounce more easily. His features showed his Uighur origin. His father was probably a regional deputy. If Wuer was often unpopular with the other leaders, the students as a whole admired his dash and his witty, outspoken contempt for the Party leadership. He dressed and behaved in flamboyant fashion, and enjoyed the limelight more than any of the other leaders. He like to be around when the television cameras were there. Yet despite his outspokenness, his instinct in any debate on tactics was usually to be cautious.

Wang Dan was thin and languid, and extremely courteous. He seemed at first to be shy and tongue-tied, and he was a poor speaker, but he had strongly held convictions. He had been influenced by the dissident astrophysicist Fang Lizhi, who believed that students were the one group in Chinese society with the organization and drive to force the government to introduce greater democracy. Wang Dan had arranged seminars on democracy for the history students of Peking University, and his interventions in the debates on tactics were usually more thoughtful than Wuer Kaixi's and less radical than Chai Ling's.

Implicit in the decision to stage a hunger strike was another question: how long the students should remain in the Square. A hunger strike implied a long test of strength, lasting if necessary the full period of Mikhail Gorbachev's four-day visit to China. The leaders who were against the hunger strike were for the most part in favour of withdrawing at least partially from the Square to allow Gorbachev's visit to go ahead as planned. Wuer Kaixi was one of them. Chai Ling was strongly in favour of a total occupation.

No one saw any of this as an insult to Gorbachev. To the students, he was a hero. He had introduced in the Soviet Union precisely the kind of right of open discussion which they believed should exist in China. Yet although they admired him there was no suggestion that he should be invited into the Square to meet them. No one suggested placing him at the head of their protest. He was a valuable exemplar, and his visit offered them the perfect chance to draw everyone's attention to their protest. It went no further than that.

Some students argued that by occupying the Square during the visit of a Soviet president they would damage two particularly unpopular figures in the regime, Prime Minister Li Peng and President Yang Shangkun. Both had been educated and trained in the Soviet Union. But Deng Xiaoping would be the real victim of their action. The ending of the Sino-Soviet split was to have been his diplomatic master-stroke. That achieved, he would retire after a few months in his eighty-fifth year. This was his solution to the problem that faced every leader under the Marxist-Leninist system: how to arrange a peaceful and satisfactory transfer of power. By interfering with his plans the students were risking Deng Xiaoping's fiercest anger. Even at this stage there were people who warned that Deng might send in the army, and that there could be bloodshed on a big scale. But there was no real alternative for the students. Either they intensified their campaign to have the *People's Daily* editorial withdrawn or they gave up. There could be no half measure.

*

I went to see Gorbachev's official spokesman, Gennadi Gerasimov, in his hotel suite on the morning the main Soviet party arrived. Gerasimov had been in Peking for several days with the advance party. He looks like a leading man from the era of the black and white film, and the silk dressing gown he was wearing as he opened the door added to the impression. He was as skilful and smooth as ever. The problem with the students was, it seemed, merely something got up by Western journalists.

'I don't see why there should be a curious atmosphere. We've waited for this visit for thirty years. The students are just the backdrop for the media. The main concern is the summit; and it's long overdue.'

'Might it not,' I asked, 'distract the attention of the Chinese leadership?'

'It's no great surprise for them, you know, not something new. But the media can distract their attention. No, we have an agenda to discuss. If other things are happening in the country, so what? These are the problems that happen when you make reforms.'

He was right from his country's point of view. For Gorbachev the important thing was that the agreement with China should be signed. It would mean he could remove three-quarters of the Soviet troops stationed in Mongolia, on the Chinese border. If the Chinese leadership was in difficulties at home, that only made the process easier. For once, Mikhail Gorbachev would not be the sole focus of media attention; that was all.

That morning, the second of the occupation of Tiananmen Square, the students had woken to a fine clear sky. It had been chilly in the night and few of them had tents or sleeping bags. Almost as soon as they awoke, the dispute had begun again between Chai Ling and Wuer Kaixi about whether they should move back from the Monument to the People's Heroes and the Great Hall of the People and allow the authorities to welcome the Soviet leader as they welcomed far less important people.

Wuer Kaixi was in favour of moving back beyond the Monument and leaving enough room around the steps for the usual ceremonial guard when Gorbachev laid a wreath there. They could move back directly afterwards. Chai Ling had shaken her head and banged her fist against her side. If they moved back they would be lessening the pressure. They mustn't let up. They might as well leave the Square altogether as move away from the most important part of it. According to Li Lu, another of the student leaders, someone pulled out a knife and threatened to stab Chai Ling if she did not agree to withdraw; at the same time one of her supporters threatened to stab her if she did.

There was more shouting. In the end Wuer Kaixi stormed out and appealed to the bleary-eyed students to follow his lead. About a quarter of them did. The rest stayed with Chai Ling. After that the two leaders scarcely spoke to each other for several days. Some of Chai Ling's supporters suggested that Wuer had been in touch with his father, the local Party official in Chinese Turkestan. There was a half-suggestion left hanging in the air that no real Chinese would have done such a thing. It was several days before Chai Ling's supporters accepted Wuer's good faith again.

Those who refused to leave the Monument had to spread out to fill the gaps left by the others. As they were settling down again there was new excitement. Figures appeared on the roof of the Great Hall of the People, among them the distinctive balding head of Zhao Ziyang, the General Secretary of the Communist Party. He had come to see for himself whether it would be possible to welcome Gorbachev with the customary guard of honour in the Square in a few hours' time. He was holding a pair of binoculars, and for a few minutes he scanned the crowd carefully. There could be no welcoming ceremony there.

According to the Russians, it was Zhao who gave the order that Gorbachev's guard of honour should meet him at the airport. In a culture which sets as much store by ceremony as the Chinese, it was a stunning humiliation. The Square which lay at the heart of the Communist state was no longer in the hands of the government. It would have been embarrassing enough in a Western country. In China, it was a serious affront for which someone would have to pay.

But not yet. The reasons why the government did nothing to clear the students from the Square were complicated and concerned more than dissent in the streets. Immediately before Gorbachev's historic visit to Peking the delegates of the Asian Development Bank had arrived for the first of their annual meetings to be held in Peking. The Chinese government wanted to make a substantial bid for ADB funds, and needed therefore to convince the Bank's governors that its open policy would continue. There could be no bloodshed either during the ADB meeting or during Gorbachev's visit. The Chinese government could not admit to having serious internal problems. Second, intellectuals and university professors had given warning that if there were any brutality their support for the government's action would be withheld. Third, there was the historical parallel. The show of grief for the death of Zhou Enlai in 1976, which was against the orders of Madame Mao and the others of the Gang of Four, the left-wing clique which surrounded Mao in the months before his death, had been a spontaneous movement which had indirectly saved the political life of Deng Xiaoping, the natural heir to Zhou Enlai. To clear out the people now occupying the Square would have been to align himself with the Maoist old guard.

Finally, a complicated political battle going on behind the scenes made intervention of any kind impossible. Power in China lay not with the Communist Party Central Committee or even with the full Politburo; it lay with a five-man inner cabinet, the Politburo's Standing Committee, and with Deng Xiaoping, who held no constitutional or Party position. His only formal post was the chairmanship of the Central Military Commission, which effectively controlled the armed forces. Deng, shrewd, witty and vindictive, was the most influential figure in the leadership. Even so, the politics of China's leadership dictated that decisions had to be made unanimously. There could be no divisions, no suggestion of dissent. Divisions in the leadership, it was believed, led to chaos in the country. It was a principle which long predated Communism. Far from being an absolute monarch, Deng could work only with the agreement of a majority of the others.

His political career had been an extraordinary record of great heights and great depths. He was with Mao Zedong on the Long March, he fought the Japanese and then the Nationalists, making friendships within the army which were still effective forty years later. When the People's Republic came into being in 1949 he was one of its leaders. As General Secretary of the Communist Party he was one of the four most important men in China, together with Mao, Zhou Enlai and Liu Shaoqi. However, like Liu he was a victim of the Cultural Revolution. He was disgraced, purged, and banished. He lived humbly, first as a waiter then as a lathe-turner. He grew vegetables to feed his family and nursed his son who had been thrown from a window by the Red Guards and crippled. In the 1970s Deng was briefly rehabilitated, only to be purged again by the Gang of Four.

His luck turned. The Gang of Four was overthrown, and Deng rose to power again. He threw China open to new ideas. He visited the United States. For a time, a limited amount of free speech was allowed, until in 1979 he ordered the clearing of the Democracy Wall where students, and more particularly workers and unemployed people, had been putting up big character posters critical of the Communist Party. His enduring reforms were economic; he was simply interested in results, not in ideology. 'It doesn't matter if a cat is black or white, as long as it catches mice' was his famous way of encapsulating a new start for modern China. People frightened and exhausted by the faction fighting which had devastated the country's economy and led to the deaths and imprisonment of millions were deeply grateful. It was under his influence that China opened up to Western capital. Peasants were given the right to grow and sell food for their own profit. The countryside was transformed. For the first time in decades, the peasants began to make a decent living. Some became very prosperous indeed.

Still, Deng always saw economic liberalization as being different from political liberalization. His experiences in the Cultural Revolution had left him with a hatred of unbridled freedom, and he equated the right of people to criticize their rulers with open rebellion and violence. He introduced Gorbachev's notions of perestroika into China seven years before Gorbachev came to power, but he had no interest in glasnost. The tragedy which unfolded in China in May and June of 1989 was Deng Xiaoping's tragedy as well. He must have identified the student protesters with the Red Guards who had humiliated him and injured his son. He had suffered greatly and was determined to ensure that he never suffered again.

The political crisis in China was a drama with a very few characters on stage and enormous crowd scenes. Apart from Deng himself there was the elegant, corrupt Zhao Ziyang who dyed his hair and looked a great deal younger than his seventy-one years. Zhao had succeeded Hu Yaobang as the General Secretary of the Party and Deng's heir presumptive. In 1987 Deng had wanted to hand over all his posts to Zhao. But Zhao had no military experience, and was worried that he might not be able to control the People's Liberation Army. As a result he wanted Deng to continue as Chairman of the Central Military Commission. The conservatives in the leadership preferred this, since they felt their power had already been seriously diminished. In the months that followed, however, Zhao's position weakened. He had engineered an economic boom of sorts, but then it went wrong. He seems to have seen the reform movement as his chance to restore his position. As a result, he successfully vetoed any use of force against the students in Tiananmen Square.

The third of the central characters was Li Peng. Like Zhao, he had played little part in the great events in China before the 1980s. He was a bureaucrat with thirty years' experience in the electricity supply industry. His rise was due to an accident not of birth but of adoption. His father was a Communist who was killed by the Kuomintang, and Li Peng was adopted, together with a number of other orphans, by Zhou Enlai. He had never held a senior position in the political world, and Deng selected him partly because he was a technocrat who seemed to get things done. Unlike his adoptive father, though, his temper was short, and his judgement poor, and he had few liberal tendencies.

The fundamental battle on the Standing Committee was between Li Peng and Zhao Ziyang. The previous summer, at the leadership's seaside resort of Beidaihe, Li Peng had criticized Zhao fiercely over economic policy. He blamed him for the overheating of the economy and demanded retrenchment, while Zhao advocated an even freer market. His think tank, the Institute of Economic Structural Reform, is believed to have advocated total privatization as the only long-term solution to China's problems. Li Peng was widely regarded as incompetent, but the conservatives within the Communist leadership, among them the President, Yang Shangkun, used him as their mouthpiece. Now there was a new issue: how to deal with the challenge from the students. In all of this Deng Xiaoping seems to have been something of a bystander. He sided with Zhao on the economic issue, but cannot have done so on the issue of the demonstrations in Tiananmen Square.

Of the other members of the Standing Committee, Hu Qili and

Qiao Shi were popularly said to have belonged to 'the wind faction': they went with the prevailing current. Hu Qili in particular was an opportunist, though he did show some liberal tendencies. He played a part in the drafting of the *People's Daily* editorial which offended the students, but later he sided with Zhao Ziyang. Qiao Shi was more conservative by instinct, while the fifth member, Yao Yilin, was older and more conservative still. For the time being the leadership was deadlocked.

Gorbachev duly arrived, and was welcomed at the airport by President Yang Shangkun and a guard of honour. The scene was televised live so that everyone in the country knew the usual pattern of events had been disrupted. Since the Soviet group could not be taken to the Great Hall of the People immediately they were driven to the Diaoyutai state guest house. Later that afternoon there was a formal reception at the Great Hall, but the motorcade could not drive through Tiananmen Square to get there. Instead it had to go through the back streets to reach a rear entrance. They passed the little cook-shops and the cobblers in streets that were only a little wider than the official limousines and were littered with cabbage-leaves and heaps of rubbish. Our camera caught a marvellous shot of Gorbachev looking out in bewilderment at the extraordinary scene through the rear window.

In the Square, the students knew that their action was affecting the political balance between Deng and Zhao, though their main concern was still with their own dispute. They were as critical of Zhao's corruption as they were of Deng's old age. It was only later in the week that the attacks on Zhao faded; but Deng was always their main target.

I walked towards the Monument, edging my way through groups of students who were still arguing about the question of moving back from the Great Hall of the People. There was security of a kind now. They had blocked off the central area, standing along a perimeter tape which divided the outer areas from the inner one where the hunger-strikers lay. The students had been brought up in a system where rigid controls were the norm. Like the concentric rings of influence in the Square, with the masses of demonstrators, many of them factory-workers, on the outside, the hunger-strikers in the middle and the leaders beside the Monument at the heart of the protest, Tiananman Square was taking on the characteristics of the society against which it was reacting: outer circles and inner circles, security, restricted admission, identity controls. They were right to do it, in a way: the security police were moving around, taking photographs and jotting down names.

I showed my pass a few times, picking my way over the rubbish heaps and the abandoned banners. There was a gate formed by bamboo poles at the point where the tapes ceased. Over it hung a sign:

'We Are Fasting For The Liberty Of This Nation.'

Everywhere people wanted to explain themselves. Their very clothes carried messages. In the warmth of the summer morning many people were wearing T-shirts, on which they had written slogans, mostly variants on the same theme:

'I like rice but I like freedom better.'

'I love life, I need food, but I'd rather die without democracy.'

There was a sense of liberation, that just to be in the Square was a statement in itself. People smiled and shook my hand, and asked me to sign their books and T-shirts. Everyone, it seemed, listened to the BBC's Chinese language service. The gentleness, the smiles and the headbands were irresistibly reminiscent of the big rock concerts and the anti-Vietnam demonstrations in the 1960s. There was the same certainty that because the protestors were young and peaceful the government must capitulate.

'We Shall Overcome' read a patched-together sheet worn over a tracksuit.

'Love is great' read an armband.

'Peace in every country' read a flag hanging limply from a pole.

'Death if not freedom' read a handwritten T-shirt worn by a piratical character with a red headband.

'Democracy, Our Common Goal' read a banner.

Often the students spoke good English, but even those who didn't would insist on explaining at length their aims, their wishes, their lack of hostile intention. They would crowd around, grinning or earnest, to make their points.

'We just want to ask the government to talk to us. We aren't challenging the government, we just want a dialogue.'

'We Chinese are no worse than the other people of the world. Why should we have less freedom than everyone else?'

'The government is always putting us off. We're going to stay here until we get satisfaction, or until we starve to death.'

'This is not a demonstration against Gorbachev. Gorbachev is a very great man. But this is our opportunity to ask the government for talks.'

The opinions were often trite, and the range of views narrow. But it was an extraordinary thing for these people to find themselves talking to foreign journalists, expressing loud opinions about their own leaders, and finding themselves applauded for doing so. The experience was a liberating one. That was what made coming to the Square every day a singular pleasure. The disciplined rivers of well-drilled citizens I had seen on my first day in Peking had changed into an extraordinary flood of self-expression. The people in the Square were no longer merging themselves in the common stream; they were learning the dangerous attractions of standing out as individuals.

'Listen to me.'

People turned their heads. A fat man in his early forties had taken the microphone at one of the long meetings on the steps of the Monument. His tone was strong and aggressive. He made fierce chopping movements of his free hand at every sentence. His stomach showed itself between T-shirt and waistband. But he wasn't a figure of fun.

I'm not afraid of dying. I saw the demonstration of the students here on 21 April, and I was deeply moved. The next day I joined the students and I've been supporting them ever since. You plainclothes cops, can you hear me? My name is Wu Xitong. I'm a worker, and my unit number is 120989789. I'm not afraid of telling you who I am. The students are struggling for democracy. That's why they're here.

He turned in the direction of the upper windows of the Great Hall of the People, the sweat pouring off his ample forehead. Heads were visible, leaning out of the windows.

Come on, listen to the students. Join them. Our beloved Zhou Enlai always used to receive students if they asked to see him. Why don't you come down and meet them? And what about you, Li Peng? Why don't you come down too? It'd do you good.

Everyone laughed. The laughter and the applause encouraged him to one last rhetorical flourish.

I think every worker should come here and support the students. My heart beats with the students. Do you support me?

They roared their approval and shouted that they did. The fat worker was taking a serious risk by announcing his name and number. The security police were everywhere. It seemed as though every time I gathered a crowd of students round me and started talking to them, someone would appear and take snapshots of us. Often, no doubt, it was innocent enough, but some of the photographs were later used to identify students who had gone too far in breaking the rules.

No one attacked Marxism-Leninism as such until near the end of the protest. Specific reforms of the political system were only rarely demanded – by the students from the Central Party School, for instance, who sported a banner which read 'Abolish the Central Advisory Commission of the Chinese Communist Party'. The CAC was formed mostly of geriatric ex-members of the Politburo who had been shuffled sideways by Deng Xiaoping eighteen months early in order to bring in slightly younger men. But they continued to influence political life, and when the crisis reached its peak Deng Xiaoping was forced to turn to them to save himself. The students of the Central Party School were right to single out the CAC as something which needed urgent change. Yet this was not a movement with specific goals; it was an angry rejection of the tone and method of government in China.

Most of all, it was a protest against corruption. A system which operated on the principles of 'everyone doing business' and 'connections' was bound to depend heavily on graft and nepotism. Everyone had their examples, even if it were only the fact that Deng Xiaoping's son, Deng Pufang, who was permanently injured by his fall from a window during the Cultural Revolution, was head of the institute which looked after the disabled. He was chairman of Kanghua, a highly dubious company which traded in all manner of things. There were suspicions about the origin of Kanghua's capital, and suggestions that it might come from the Institute for the Disabled. But because it came under the chairmanship of Deng's son there was no question of checking its accounts. At the end of 1989, however, the government was obliged to look into this and other companies. Kanghua was suddenly and mysteriously dissolved before the government inspectors could see the books. But such cases aside, everyone knew that the members of the leadership lived in great style in Zhongnanhai and elsewhere, and they resented it. Mao Zedong had left behind him a legend of simple living. So had Zhou Enlai. Their successors were different.

Not far from the steps to the Great Hall of the People, an ugly man with protruding brown teeth was standing on the seat of a bicycle rickshaw and lecturing the crowd. His voice was harsh. Patches of sweat glinted on his shirt in the afternoon sun. He had brought a group of students to the Square from Peking Normal University, he explained, and he would not accept any fare. There was laughter at that. Rickshaw drivers enjoy little esteem in Peking. Many of them are former prisoners, and the job is regarded as degrading. ('You should be ashamed of yourself, pedalling white men around,' someone shouted out to a driver who took me along Chang'an Avenue the next morning.) They also tend to ignore Chinese passengers if there are foreigners around. This particular rickshaw man was nettled by the laughter, and his irritation inspired him.

All right, so I'm a humble man. But I have the dreams of an Emperor.

He stretched out his arms to encompass the group that had gathered to hear him, and beyond them the Square and the future of China itself.

I support the students, and, like them, I'm not afraid of death. And the reason is that I love my country and I can see that my country is in danger. That's why I've been driving these students to the Square for nothing. I hereby call on the Chinese people to rise up against the corrupt officials in our country. That way we can have a bright future and a proper democracy. There's a whole groups of people inside the Party who lead the same kind of luxurious life that bourgeois capitalists do.

'What sort of democracy do you mean?' someone asked. He paused impressively.

My understanding of democracy is that power belongs to the people, not to some tiny group which dominates the people. And the leaders of that democracy have to lead decent lives.

He had won the crowd over. They cheered and applauded him, and hands were raised out of the crowd to shake his. People told him he was a great man, and, better still, that he spoke the truth. He wiped his sweating forehead and climbed down, busying himself with the cushion he'd been standing on, too modest to accept the further congratulations of his audience.

A few days later we drove out of Peking to the incomparable Valley of the Ming Tombs to examine a prime example of the corruption that now existed. A Japanese company had received permission to create a golf course there. In the dryness of the Valley the golf course looked like an emerald dropped in the sand. The site was insensitively chosen. It was the place where in 1966 Mao Zedong and Zhou Enlai came to begin the digging of a reservoir with their own hands. They were inaugurating a self-help programme to teach the Chinese people to do without foreign machinery. In the place where Mao and Zhou acted out their simple way of living their successors were enjoying themselves in style.

The water from the reservoir was used to keep the golf course green. The peasants whose land had been compulsorily purchased worked to cut the grass, or sat in servile fashion around the edges of the greens while the Japanese played their shots. The peasants' wives and daughters wore yellow uniforms and acted as caddies. They had large veils like the protective headgear of beekeepers to protect their faces from the sun and from the stares of the Japanese golfers.

The Japanese Golf Company, Ltd, had created a useful meeting place for government ministers and Japanese businessmen to do business in the way both sides preferred: out of sight. They could discuss matters of mutual profit over a game of golf, or in one of the rooms set aside in the expensive clubhouse for bridge and poker. The manager, who was also Japanese, proudly showed us the membership board. Zhao Ziyang's name was at the head. Li Peng, the premier, and President Yang Shangkun were also there. So were many of the top civil servants. It was difficult for Westerners, and impossible for ordinary Chinese, to join.

*

Within a day or so of our visit to the countryside the Square had become the camp-site of an army. There were clearly defined areas for the students of different universities. Food was delivered on a regular basis. Ordinary people responded with generosity to requests for bottled water. Doctors set up a virtual field hospital. Inside the tents, hunger-strikers and people who were suffering from heat exhaustion lay on camp beds in the cool green light. Doctors and nurses moved quietly and efficiently up and down the lines of beds, pausing to glance at the flow of glucose or plasma to a patient.

The numbers on hunger strike were growing all the time: during the first three days of the protest they rose from four hundred to 3,140. For many of them the act of declaring a hunger strike was symbolic rather than literal. People wearing the white headbands would often pull out a bar of chocolate and eat it. Wuer Kaixi admitted that he ate a meal most evenings, in order to keep up his strength and efficiency. But most of the original core of four hundred ate nothing that entire week.

The atmosphere in the hot sun became oppressive. The smell of rubbish and of urine began to hang heavily over the Square, so that it soon became a test of determination to wander round it. Doctors warned the protestors that the bad air from so many people was dangerous, and urged anyone who felt ill to take oxygen or go to hospital. Soon there was an almost continual wailing from ambulance sirens, day and night. The students became skilful at keeping clear wide pathways through the crowds for their passage, and the constant flow of bicycles and people followed the lines laid out for them. The police abdicated all control, and stood marooned in their boxes like castaways. If you looked down on Chang'an Avenue from the height of the Beijing Hotel the empty ambulance lanes looked like sandbanks in the current of people, bicycles and vehicles. Marshals shouted angrily at anyone who ducked under the cordons of string to cross the empty spaces.

The visit which had occasioned the demonstrations continued. The television pictures of Gorbachev's meeting with Deng Xiaoping were a shock to many people. At a formal lunch, Deng looked old and fragile.

A dumpling fell heavily from his chopsticks as he was opening his mouth to take it. His speech was slurred and it looked as though he was no longer able to marshal his thoughts. Later, a senior official said privately he was under heavy medication. To the people all over China who were watching, Deng's days as leader seemed to be coming to an end. The students were scandalized and delighted in roughly equal measure. From that point onwards there was even more emphasis in their slogans and speeches on the need to get rid of the tired, incapable old men who were running China.

Zhao Ziyang, the reformist whose reforms had gone wrong, seems to have seen his opportunity in all this as well. When he and Gorbachev posed for the cameras at the start of their meeting he made skilful use of the fact that China Central Television had placed a live microphone close to them. He gave the impression he was chatting privately to Gorbachev. Instead he was broadcasting to the Chinese nation.

> In the name of all the members of the Central Committee, I extend our welcome to you. The meeting you had with Comrade Deng Xiaoping is the highlight of your trip to Peking. I am sure you understood that this meeting with Comrade Deng Xiaoping represented the normalization of the relations between our two Parties. As you know, Comrade Deng Xiaoping has been universally recognized as the leader of the Chinese Communist Party ever since the fifth session of the Communist Party Congress – although he retired from the position he held in the Chinese Communist Party and the government during the third session of the 11th Party Congress. But the Party as a whole cannot manage for an instant without his talents and leadership. There was an official decision on this matter, and though it wasn't openly published it was a most important decision. We need his helmsmanship on all the most important issues. This information has never been made public before. You are the first person I have told this to.

Gorbachev, who must also have known the microphone was live, thanked Zhao uncomfortably for passing on this confidence to him. There was nothing very startling in it, but Zhao seemed to be making the point that Deng Xiaoping, as the man in charge, was responsible for dealing with the problems which existed in Tiananmen Square.

In a closed society people have to look for the subtlest political signals. Zhao Ziyang's words seemed to hint at a weakness at the top of the leadership. Slowly the students changed their campaign away from attacks on the corruption represented by Zhao and his family and towards Deng's own position. The signals were confusing, but they all indicated that a struggle for power was beginning. Over the days that followed Deng's continued control of things became the central question; and as Zhao became politically weaker the students supported him more strongly. He might be corrupt, but he represented the way in which most students wanted China to go – the way of increased liberalization and openness. It may well have been a serious lack of understanding on their part to support Zhao by attacking the one man, Deng Xiaoping, who had the power to save him. But change was in the air. By Tuesday night throughout Peking people were making their minds up whether they should join the protest and so swing the balance in favour of radical reform.

Wednesday 17 May saw the outbreak of an entirely peaceful insurrection. Hundreds of thousands of people had decided to join in on the side which seemed certain to win. 'Hello Mr D and Mr S!' said some of the banners. 'D' stood for democracy and 'S' for science: the terms had originally been used by students and intellectuals in the 1930s. The major avenues of Peking were blocked by bicycles, cars, lorries, buses and flatbed trucks all heading for the Square, filled with people cheering, singing, playing musical instruments, waving flags, enjoying themselves. The racket of it all could be heard streets away. I watched as the entire workforce at a building site caught the fever from a passing truckload of people. They swarmed down the scaffolding, laughing and shouting, and lined up like schoolchildren on the pavement outside. Someone harangued them for a short while, and then they headed off in the direction the truck had taken. Cement-mixers, spades, hods of bricks, electrical gear were left where they lay. No one wanted to be left out.

Chang'an Avenue was almost impassable. The obedient streams had turned into a tidal wave which disregarded every one of the old rules. People were sitting and picnicking on the open tribunes on either side of the Gate of Heavenly Peace, where only senior Party officials, 'model workers' and foreign dignitaries could sit at the great parades of the Communist year. The policemen who protected them had vanished. The great curling red banners of rebellion were everywhere, waving, catching the wind. I had never seen so large a crowd so relaxed. Victory seemed a foregone conclusion; how could any government resist a popular uprising of this magnitude?

Earlier, people had been careful not to attack Deng Xiaoping too openly. Now he was the major target. People carried ludicrous caricatures of him, a squat dwarf with a black heart. 'What does it matter what colour the cat is, as long as he resigns?' said several placards, mocking Deng's best known saying. A manifesto was issued that day by a group of leading academics which said: 'The Qing Dynasty ended 76 years ago, but China still has an emperor even though he lacks the title of emperor, a senile and absurd autocrat.' Some people carried small cardboard effigies of Deng hanging from a gallows. And because Xiaoping means 'little peace' and the characters have the same sound as those for 'little bottle', it was a joke repeated innumerable times across the whole crowded plain of Tiananmen Square to drop little bottles and let them smash. Everywhere you went that day your feet crackled on the fragments of Deng's political career.

All levels of the great Chinese bureaucracy were represented. There were tax inspectors and customs officials and people from China's central bank. There were big contingents from state television and radio, and from the various newspapers. There was a sizeable group from the *People's Daily*, whose editorial had caused the demonstrations. A policeman was carried majestically along on the front of a lorry, holding a placard which read 'The Students Will Surely Win'. All the big hotels had sent delegations of workers to the Square. I caught sight of the bus carrying people from my hotel, but none of the managers was on board. They had carefully stayed away.

There were more workers than anything else, packed on to trucks over which flew proudly the name of their factory. By now ordinary people outnumbered the students. A thousand soldiers marched through the streets in uniform. They were political soldiers, from the logistics department of the General Staff. Most significant of all, heading for the whirlpool of the Square there was a contingent from the Central Committee of the Communist Party. When the banner they carried came into the Square a great roar went up from the students. If the Party itself was starting to come over to their side the battle was surely won.

All that was necessary was to keep up the pressure, and the students had the means to do that. The hunger strike was attracting greater numbers than ever, and in the heat and the foetid atmosphere of the Square 600 people had so far been taken to hospital. There was an hysterical edge to the way the nurses would run into the crowd to pick up someone who seemed to have fainted, then dash back to the waiting ambulances with them. It was an acting out of emergency, just as the hunger strike itself was an acting out of the business of starving oneself to death. It wasn't phoney – the medical conditions were real enough – but it was being done to demonstrate to the government and to the other protestors the extreme urgency of it all.

'If someone dies now, there will be a revolution,' said a respected academic who had come to the Square to show solidarity with his students. 'But of course if nobody dies Deng Xiaoping won't be under quite so much pressure.'

He looked away, unwilling to conclude the syllogism. Nobody died. Perhaps, after only a few days of hunger and thirst, it was unlikely that they would.

Mikhail Gorbachev, whose visit had precipitated the entire crisis, was meanwhile all but unnoticed. He met some students and was openly sympathetic to them. But at the press conference he gave he was careful to stay away from controversy.

> I wouldn't take it on myself to make judgements about what is happening here. A difficult process is under way in China. But dialogue is starting, and we have to welcome that. We hope that solutions will be found which will be acceptable to the Chinese people and to the Chinese government.

It sounded as though he too expected Deng to go soon. The demonstrations were spreading to other major cities in China. Change seemed inevitable.

*

Outwardly, the crisis reached a head on Thursday 18 May. The rumour spread through the Square that Deng would resign at 7 o'clock that evening. As each new group heard the rumour, it broke out into clapping and singing as if the resignation had already taken place. Even normally well-informed officials had no idea what was going on behind the scenes. That morning officials from the State Council, the Ministry of Foreign Affairs and the judges' vocational school – all people who kept in touch with what was happening – joined in the demonstrations on the assumption that Deng was about to resign. People with promising careers would not have risked them unless they thought they were safe.

The reality was different. Deng was not preparing to resign. He regarded the challenge to his power as being a repetition of his experiences during the Cultural Revolution, and saw the Red Guards rising up against him once more. But he kept his nerve. On Wednesday night he called together the five members of the Standing Committee of the Politburo and told them that he intended to call in the army. He had already made the arrangements through the Central Military Commission, of which he was head. Gorbachev was leaving Peking for Shanghai and the Soviet Union in a few hours' time. There was no reason why force should not now be used. The meeting seems to have been a painful and angry affair. Zhao Ziyang, who had once been his protégé, told Deng he could not agree and threatened to resign.

The code which enjoined the maintenance of complete unity on the leadership meant that until the dispute was fully resolved the various members had to keep up appearances. In spite of Deng Xiaoping's threat of force, the members of the Standing Committee continued with what seemed to be Zhao Ziyang's conciliatory approach towards the students. The difficult meeting with Deng went on all night. At 5 a.m. four of the five Standing Committee members, Zhao Ziyang, Li Peng, Qiao Shi and Hu Qili, went to a Peking hospital together with Rui Xinwen, the head of the Politburo's propaganda department. The television cameras of CCTV went with them.

The plan was for a well-publicized show of sympathy towards the hunger strikers. Li Peng and Qiao Shi had been strongly in favour of Deng's plan to call in the army against the students. Hu Qili, though an ally of Zhao's, lacked the courage to support him. And yet the whole group allowed themselves to be lectured by the students, and showed an exaggerated interest in their health and welfare. It showed the extent to which the students had won this part of the battle. Even the government had to acknowledge the rightness of their approach. Li Peng sat down beside one patient and patted his arm.

> Your mother must be very anxious about you. We will look very seriously into all the matters which you have raised and think out a way to solve the problems we are facing together.

He turned to the doctors and nurses who were standing alongside.

> As medical personnel, you know how dangerous this hunger strike is. You don't like to see these patients in this vulnerable condition. (To the patients) Have a good rest, keep fit, take care.

One of the students in particular wasn't prepared to be patronized.

> The Communist Party has got to rejuvenate its image in the minds of the people, to convince people that it still has something to offer. That way China will have something to offer. We've got to do like they do in the United States, and make the government popular. Do you agree?'

If the elder statesmen disagreed with this, and Li Peng and the other conservatives cannot have accepted that they should follow the United States in anything like it, they did not show it. 'We're all on your side,' someone said, off camera. 'We need to have a better understanding of each other,' said Qiao Shi, one of the advocates of using military force against them.

The television report allowed one of the students the last word:

I believe that high-ranking Communist Party members should make their own children set a good example. You must punish nepotism. This will help you to convince the people that you are clean.

The leaders of the country were accepting a public scolding from teenagers.

At midday Li Peng met a delegation of students in the Great Hall of the People. It was a curious affair, with most of the students, including Wuer Kaixi, dressed in pyjamas and attached to oxygen tanks. They had been brought direct from the hospital. Wang Dan had come from the Square. He was wearing a black leather jacket and had a red band tied round his head. At first the students thought it was the televised debate they had been demanding, but Li Peng began by lecturing them.

I want you to take some food so as to have something to sustain your lives. Then we can have a good talk and gradually solve our problems. I advise you to leave the Square as soon as possible, and then the government will be ready to talk to you. There are a few people who have been inciting you to go on hunger strike. I don't know what their motives are, but I'm strongly against this.

Wuer Kaixi began to say something at this point, and Li Peng showed his first sign of anger.

As a Communist Party member and head of the government I have to express my views. We had an agreement that you wouldn't interrupt me.

He banged his hand on the arm of his chair with annoyance.

Wuer Kaixi then became angry too. He snatched the tube from the oxygen tank away from his nose and started wagging his finger at Li Peng.

This meeting isn't just a little late, it's come too late. . . It seems to me that many of the leaders here haven't understood what I meant. The problem isn't to persuade the student representatives sitting here to give up the hunger strike and leave the Square, but how to persuade the students outside. Unless our requirements are met, they won't leave. . . What the government should do is to give a quick answer to our requests. If not, there's no point in sitting here and talking.

In the ordered, hierarchical society of China there was no precedent for speaking to an elderly government figure like this. The atmosphere was so tense that one of the student leaders, a man still in his early twenties, suffered a minor heart attack. At the end Li Peng stood up abruptly and walked out. He seemed extremely nervous about his failure to convince the students. But Wuer Kaixi had been quite right. He and Wang Dan went out into the Square when the meeting was over and argued for an end to the hunger strike, but the majority, headed by Chai Ling who had not been at the meeting with Li Peng, refused. It proved to be the last chance for a negotiated settlement.

That night there was another meeting of the Standing Committee of the Politburo. It failed to reach agreement, and Zhao Ziyang was once again in a minority of one. He knew that his only chance of rescuing his career had gone. He was close to exhaustion, but he agreed to make one last effort to persuade the hunger-strikers to give up. Li Peng, unwillingly, agreed to go with him. They drove down to the Square, and accompanied by their officials they each climbed on to one of the buses which had been brought up for the hunger strikers to shelter in at night.

Zhao was wearing a smartly pressed Mao jacket, but he looked terrible. Several times his voice broke and he seemed close to tears. He spoke through a loud hailer, because after three days and nights with scarcely any sleep he had very little voice left.

> Please be reasonable. Think about it hard and use your common sense. I'm not here today to have direct dialogue with you. I'm here to beg you to think hard about what you're doing. As you know, the whole nation, the government and the Party are in a state of great anxiety and the country is on fire. . . This situation can't continue. All comrades who are of good faith want to improve the situation in China, but things are getting worse every day. I say this from my heart: you must stop the hunger strike. . . You can't solve this problem unless you are reasonable. I was young like you once. I've been through all this. I myself lay down on the railway tracks and waited for a train to come along. I understand it very well. But do you really want to carry on with the hunger strike? If you want to see it all settled, you've got to live. Thank you very much.

It was a strange, rambling appeal and had no chance of succeeding. As Wuer Kaixi had explained, the students were too divided to call off the hunger strike at this point. Li Peng had also been speaking, though far more abruptly, on another bus in the Square. Now Zhao Ziyang signed a few autographs, climbed down from the bus and drove back to Zhongnanhai with Li Peng. It was the last anyone saw of Zhao. The next day, martial law was declared and he was under arrest.

5
DEATH IN THE SQUARE

There is chaos on the streets of Peking. The Chinese government will take steps to stop it.

LI PENG, Prime Minister, 19 May 1989

It was early that evening, Friday 19 May, that we began to get reports of troop movements, We had set up our office in a couple of rooms in the Great Wall Sheraton, and it had become a centre for information with people continually coming in or telephoning. The 27th Army, to the north of Peking, was on alert status. Fifty trucks with soldiers in them had been seen on the western outskirts of the city.

The student leaders had decided to give up the hunger strike but not to leave Tiananmen Square. It was a belated response to Zhao's final appeal, and an attempt to ward off military action. It was now being reported that Zhao had offered his resignation. Deng Xiaoping wasn't after all a weak figure who could easily be toppled. He was still in charge. There was a sense of panic among the academics and intellectuals who had joined in the demonstrations on Wednesday and Thursday. I rang someone we had interviewed two days before and asked him for another interview.

'It wouldn't be timely,' he said. He sounded deeply shaken.

Fang Lizhi, the respected scientist, was prepared to be interviewed. He had a record of taking risks. When the American embassy invited him to the Great Wall Sheraton for a banquet given by President Bush, he had turned up, only to be stopped by the police. Now he came to the Sheraton again. But he was so nervous, and his English became so confused, that he said nothing we could broadcast.

The leading figures in the Party held a joint meeting that evening with the military at the General Logistics department of the army in West Peking. Only four members of the Politburo Standing Committee were there. Zhao Ziyang had sent a message to say he was ill. It was both an affront to the others and an admission of defeat. The meeting took place in a large theatre with the members of the leadership sitting on the stage. The audience was composed of military officers and Party members. They sat separately, divided into units and areas. Television cameramen from CCTV moved up and down the aisles filming the speeches on the stage and the reaction from the audience.

At midnight, an hour or so after the meeting had ended, an edited version of the proceedings was broadcast on television. Li Peng, wearing a black Mao jacket as though to symbolize the return to tougher and more disciplined ways, read out a statement.

> Until now we've been lenient. We've restrained ourselves for over a month. But a government which serves the people must take strong measures to deal with social unrest. . . The fate, the very future of the People's Republic of China, built by many revolutionary martyrs with their own blood, faces a serious threat.

Then it was the turn of the President, Yang Shangkun. Instead of standing and reading his speech, he sat at the table and spoke without notes. There was a teapot beside him, and he toyed with a cup.

> To establish stability around Peking and to restore normal order, we have been obliged to move troops of the People's Liberation Army to the vicinity of the city. If things are allowed to continue as they are, then our capital city will not remain a capital city.

There was loud applause at that, and the cameras panned across the width of the auditorium to show the full extent of it. Yang Shangkun tried to draw a distinction between the ordinary students, who had received such support from the people of Peking in the previous few days, and the trouble-makers who had led them on: 'I would like to make it clear that by sending in the troops we are not intending to deal with the students.'

To those who listened over their radio sets in the Square, or heard it reverberating round from the loudspeakers near the Gate of Heavenly Peace, this was a clear declaration of war. Trucks full of supporters from schools, universities and factories headed for Tiananmen Square and drove wildly up and down the length of Chang'an Avenue, their great red and white banners floating in the wind. Groups of cyclists, hundreds at a time, bunched together and rode along at a stately pace, waving, chanting, singing, shouting. All over the city ordinary working class people, who had mostly taken little part in the demonstrations, decided it was time to stand up and be counted.

As the troop lorries moved in towards the centre of the city people came out onto the streets and blocked them. They argued and shouted at the drivers and at the soldiers sitting stolidly in the back. Officers shouted into their radios and tried to persuade the crowds to let them

pass. It was useless. Sometimes the soldiers themselves said they
sympathized with the crowds and had no intention of taking action
against them. Mostly they tried to ignore the shouts and insults. They
were helpless, marooned in a sea of excited people.

These were not students, aroused by the oratory of their leaders,
carried away by a quixotic demand for things they had only heard of in
foreign radio broadcasts. These were the working people of Peking.
Many of them were middle aged. For the most part they maintained an
eerie silence. As I walked through the crowd they fell back, politely, to
let me pass. They all stared at me, looking at my clothes, my features,
the notebook I was carrying. They were neither friendly nor hostile,
merely uncomprehending; but when someone gave me a Victory sign
and I returned it they exploded in cheering and applause.

I moved closer to the line of army lorries, which I could only dimly
see ahead of me. In the distance there was chanting and shouting: 'Go
home! Go home! Go home!' The soldiers from one lorry had jumped out
of their cramped seats and gathered round a short, heavily built woman
who had brought them a bucket with soup in it. They ate noisily and
greedily, while she watched and smiled. She wore short-sleeved blue
overalls and her thick arms, folded over her chest, were bare. Her
pleasant, jolly face was heavily lined. She smiled when we approached
her, and when she showed her brown teeth and spoke to me I was
enveloped by the smell of raw garlic:

> We are all Chinese. The soldiers are just human beings like us, and so I
> brought them some food. But I don't want them to go to the centre of the
> city. They are our children. They must love the students, not attack them.

It was hard to find anyone else who would talk to a Western camera
crew. These were not articulate students who felt it was safe to express
their views. Most of them remembered the days when speaking to
foreigners was a punishable offence. They would smile when I asked
them a question, moving away and shaking their heads. As for the
soldiers, they appeared to have withdrawn into a glum silence of their
own. It seemed cruel to try to make them speak. Their eyes followed
me, but they said nothing and scarcely moved. They were not in any
danger. They were humiliated but not threatened. There was no anger,
no passion in this entire crowd. They had simply decided that the army
would not get through.

Their motives seemed to be a modified version of those of the
students. They disliked the security police, they disapproved of the
stories of corruption in high places, they felt it was time for younger
people to take over the government. Nevertheless they didn't echo the

students' demands for democracy, and in the end they were prepared to use the fiercest violence against the army, when the students remained resolutely non-violent. These were the People, in whose name the Communist Party had done everything for forty years. It seemed to me that this was their revenge on the politicians who had used their name. They had had enough of a system which supervised their lives and disrupted them at its own whim. Without having any clear idea what they did want, they knew they no longer wanted this. Probably they never had wanted it.

For the government, a new and more dangerous element had entered the situation. A senior official privately quoted Deng Xiaoping as saying earlier in the week, 'As long as the workers and the peasants and the army are on our side, it doesn't matter about the students.' Now, it seemed, the workers and students were uniting to neutralize the army. It was a magnificent victory for unarmed people. Even tanks had been stopped by the crowds. It showed equally a lack of determination on the part of the soldiers. One of the rumours which was going around was that the general commanding the 38th Army, based on the outskirts of Peking, had refused to issue his men with live ammunition because his daughter was one of the students in Tiananmen Square. There were many such rumours. Most of them seemed to offer comfort and hope.

★

It was 5 o'clock on the morning of Saturday 20 May. At the eastern end of Chang'an Avenue the sky was taking on a lighter tone. The orange light from the high street lamps cast long, disturbing shadows. There were dozens of people on every street corner. They had been up all night, in case the miracle of the night before proved temporary and the tanks and trucks got through after all. A man laboured past me, pedalling a trishaw with six people on the flat wooden boards behind him. They grinned at me and raised their fingers in the Victory salute. It wasn't clear to me that the victory would last.

Once again I picked my way through the Square. The smell of disinfectant was strong, overlaying the other smells. In the dark I shuffled through the detritus on the ground: empty plastic bottles, cardboard from hand-drawn signs, leaves from the flowering cherry trees, bits of broken bamboo which had once carried banners, sticks from ice creams, cellophane bags from the frozen drinks the students endlessly sucked in the daytime heat.

There were sleeping bodies everywhere, wrapped in white banners with huge Chinese characters, or flags, or plastic coats the colour of condoms, or tarpaulins. A girl lay with her arm across her boyfriend's chest and her head on his shoulder. Some people were sitting up now, their arms round their knees, looking dubiously at the lightening sky as if they were worried what the day would bring. I edged my way towards the village of tents and teepees in the centre of the Square. A couple of marshals, their figures outlined against the sky, watched me coming and asked for my pass.

'BBC,' I said to them. I'd left my pass in the hotel.

'Ah, BBC.'

The word went round. People propped themselves up on elbows, sleepily, to look at this representative of an organization they all listened to.

Glass crunched under foot: Xiaoping, little bottle. The sky was beginning to take on a glorious lighter blue, the clouds pink from the coming sun. I edged my way through the centre of the Square, passing the Monument. Zhou Enlai's elegant calligraphy down its face glinted in the light from the sky. Ahead of me were the steps of the Great Hall of the People. There had been rumours that soldiers would come bursting out of the doors at sunrise. A hundred or so diehards sat on the lower steps to stop them. No soldiers appeared, and the sky was getting lighter by the minute.

People were thoroughly awake now, and a great cry went up as a truck with a hundred or so workers on the back careered down the street, sounding its horn. There were confused slogans, chants, bursts of laughter as it passed. Their faces were lit up by the dawn and by the exhilaration of it all.

The loudspeakers in the centre of the Square, which were controlled by the students, crackled and made an announcement. It must have been good news. Everyone cheered, and the noise awoke the late sleepers. Near me as I sat on a low wall a couple stirred at the noise. The girl half-cried with fatigue, and laid her head on her boyfriend's knees. He stroked her hair, looking across at the eastern sky. The red crest of the People's Republic over the Gate of Heavenly Peace, several hundred yards away, was still illuminated. The light from it shone faintly through the miasma that hung over the Square. The rising sun was taking over now. The blue flashing light of an ambulance passed me, and was obscured by a white banner. The disembodied light flashed eerily through the whiteness.

The street lights were switched off. I looked at my watch: 5.21. Even with the Square under occupation and the authority of the state challenged, the everyday routines were maintained. There was more crackling from the loudspeaker system: someone was putting on a tape. It hissed, and broke into the fourth movement of Beethoven's 9th Symphony.

'*Freude!*' the bass shouted.

The word echoed round the Square, reverberating from the ugly Stalinist buildings which were never designed to hear any such thing as Beethoven's notion of freedom. It was impossible for the heart not to lift at such a sound, at such a time. I watched the peaceful expression on the face of a man in his thirties who had spent the night on the pavement near me. He can have known nothing of Beethoven, but he pushed his conical straw hat back on his head and listened, the inevitable cigarette in his mouth.

The sound of morning coughing and hawking competed with the Ode to Joy. A man walked past me wearing a yellow head-band with a skull and crossbones on it. A couple sauntered along close behind him, chewing something. Apologetically they reached up and wiped their hands on a banner over my head that proclaimed 'Democracy or Death': something in the spirit of the man with the skull and crossbones.

Joggers were starting to appear on the edges of the Square now, men who had always come this way in the early morning and saw no reason why they should stop. A truck with reinforcements arrived, and young men and women dropped off the sides like people escaping from a burning ship. A cyclist circled round me and handed me a copy of *Beijing Science and Technology News*, which seemed to be all about the stopping of the army. The sun started to illumine the millions of shards of broken glass everywhere. It was morning. The army hadn't come.

*

There was martial law, but there was no force to back it. The suspension of everyday reality continued. The crowds stayed on the streets, the police wandered among them aimlessly, civil servants went into their offices and did no work, the shops stayed open. The patterns of everyday life continued, even though the government was unable to govern. At nine o'clock, a few hours after I watched the dawn in Tiananmen Square, the State Council issued four decrees:

Martial Law Order Number One. According to Article 89, Section 16 of the Constitution of the People's Republic of China, martial law is declared in the following eight districts of Peking municipality, with effect from 10 a.m. today, 20 May 1989.

The Peking Municipal Authority further issues the following three decrees.

1. Chinese citizens.
No Chinese citizen shall participate in any demonstration, protest or

march in the martial law area, nor take part in any strike in the said area. It is an offence under martial law regulations to spread false rumours. Anyone who violates these provisions shall be liable to arrest by the duly constituted authorities, that is the People's Liberation Army or the police.

2. Foreign citizens.
(i) All foreign citizens must observe the martial law provisions, and all other relevant decrees.
(ii) No foreign citizen shall involve himself or herself with any activities by Chinese citizens which might violate the martial law provisions.
(iii) The People's Liberation Army and the police are authorized to arrest any foreign citizen who violates this decree.

3. Foreign journalists.
(i) All foreign journalists are strictly forbidden to incite unrest or issue reports which exaggerate the situation.
(ii) No foreign correspondent (including those from Hong Kong or Macao) may enter the premises of any government organization, factory, mine or university to undertake reporting or filming, without official written permission.
(iii) Any foreign journalist violating these provisions renders himself or herself liable to arrest by the People's Liberation Army or the police.

I went out very cautiously that morning with a cameraman colleague. We took a small video camera in a shoulder bag and looked for places where we could film without being seen. It was soon clear that there was no need for such precautions. No one cared about the martial law provisions, even though the government loudspeakers at the northern end of Tiananmen Square repeated them again and again. The students' loudspeakers in the centre of the Square blared back Beethoven and messages of support from students in other cities across China. The war of the loudspeakers, which continued until the troops opened fire on the students on the night of 3–4 June, began in earnest that morning.

The danger hadn't receded. Overhead, helicopters buzzed the Square and dropped leaflets on the city which contained messages of support for Li Peng. People jumped into the air to grab them as they fell, then tore them into little pieces. Absurd fears were voiced over the students' loudspeakers:

Dear friends and fellow-students, this is to warn you of two dangers which we have been informed about. We are told there are army snipers in high buildings around the centre of the city. We have also been told that metal gratings in the streets may be electrified. Please be very careful.

That evening the students started building barricades. They dragged over the great concrete blocks with metal rails set into them which ran along the sides of Chang'an Avenue. Then they supplemented them with flimsier things: bicycles, blocks of wood, boxes, bricks and lumps of masonry from a building site beside the Beijing Hotel. There was a great deal of tension during the night, and few people slept well in the Square.

The next day, Sunday, a train full of soldiers pulled in to the main railway station. The students had ten or fifteen minutes' warning and headed to the station, which was less than a mile away, in sizeable numbers. The soldiers stayed gloomily, silently, in their carriages as the students besieged them. Later, the train pulled ignominiously away. A proclamation from something called, vaguely, 'Martial Law Enforcement Headquarters' put out a curious statement that afternoon which said that army manoeuvres had now been stopped.

> The People's Liberation Army should continue to follow disciplined procedures. The army should love the people and take care of the students, and educate them to observe the law. We oppose any activities which are contrary to this endeavour.

No one thought the battle had been won, but everyone knew that the great mass of the urban population was supporting the students. Soon signs of a very Chinese form of resistance began to appear. The announcement of martial law was made on television by two news-readers, Li Juanying and her male colleague Xue Fei. Xue read out the statement itself, never once looking at the camera and (most unusually for Chinese television) stumbling over the words. The following day a student banner appeared in the Square reading 'Long Live Xue Fei!' Xue did not appear on television again. China Central Television had taken a liberal turn in the year or so before the demonstrations, and had been airing a considerable range of different views. It had also broached some difficult topics: inflation, the grain crisis, the failings of joint ventures. During the hunger strikes in the Square the news programmes had shown pictures which had undoubtedly raised public sympathy for the students. They had also given a clear idea to the country at large of the size of the great anti-government demonstrations of 17 and 18 May.

There were other ways of fighting the government. There was sabotage in the preparation of the new banners which hung from buildings along Chang'an Avenue and elsewhere, enjoining citizens to avoid anarchy and obey the martial law decrees. Within a day or two, the squares of paper, each with a single character painted on it, began to curl and fall off. Guerrilla war was fought out in the pages of the newspapers. There was a constant flow of articles which presented the government's side, but even in the *People's Daily* there were other, contrary items. The sub-editors took to putting big, misleading headlines on foreign stories, as though they were commentaries on Chinese affairs. Thus:

MILITARY FORCE SHOULD NEVER BE USED AGAINST CIVILIANS

The Hungarian leader, Imre Poszgay, today commented on an official investigation carried out into the circumstances of the Soviet intervention in Hungary in 1956. It had been wrong, he said, for Moscow to send its troops in to suppress the Hungarian uprising.

Or:

OLD MEN SHOULD RETIRE FROM POLITICS

The Burmese parliament was told today that government ministers who reached the age of 75 should be encouraged to resign.

A newspaper in Shanghai carried a photograph of Winston Churchill giving a Victory sign. These gestures were like partisan raids into enemy territory. They kept up morale and made the government look stupid. Each new example was greeted with delight by the students.

*

The Great Wall looped over the ridges and hilltops like the cordons the students used to rope off Tiananmen Square. For the five thousand years of China's recorded history the farmers here had had to fight hard to make anything out of the harsh land. The countryside was as dramatic as the water colours Wen Chia painted to illustrate the work of the T'ang Dynasty poet Tu Fu: peaks, standing rocks, winding rivers, fir trees, hermits, distant travellers. As we headed out beyond the Wall I remembered some of Tu Fu's lines:

The Kingdom is ruined but the mountains and rivers survive.
In the city, spring grass and leaves grow thick.
Blossoms shed tears for the troubled times.

The valleys were filled with the sudden brilliance of paddy fields. The peasants were bent over, up to their calves in the green rice, splashing through the water. Political disturbances were things that passed them by. A Western author asked the people of a country village if they had ever seen a foreigner before. They said they had: Mongol troops had passed close to the village in the thirteenth century.

Eight-hundred million people out of a population of a thousand million live in the countryside. If the cities were full of discontent and foreboding, the peasants had a great deal to be grateful to the government for. Before the revolution in 1949 the life of the peasants was wretched. Then the Communists leased out the land to them and things became better. But Mao Zedong, whose family were farmers, introduced one of his immense schemes of social engineering which did such damage to China. Anxious to prevent any gap between rich farmers and poor ones, he introduced a commune system. It was deeply unpopular. Poverty and lassitude overtook the countryside.

In 1979 Zhao Ziyang and Deng Xiaoping dissolved the communes and leased the land to the villagers on the basis of the numbers in each household. Farmers were allowed to sell most of their produce on the open market. As food prices rose in the towns and cities, the peasants began to prosper. For the ten years between then and the troubles in Tiananmen Square, the peasants had approved strongly of Deng Xiaoping's government. The news from Peking bewildered them and made them angry.

We stopped in the village of Bohaishuo. It was a rambling place on a hillside, with dirt roads curving between the long, not unprosperous houses. It was like a village in Eastern Europe in the nineteenth century. Pigs rooted by the roadside. There was no electricity or mains water. In the middle of the village stood a mast with loudspeakers on it, which relayed the radio news every few hours. The whole village knew what was happening in Peking and the other cities of China.

Chickens and guinea-fowl scattered in front of us. Up the hillside, under the chestnut trees, goats were browsing. We were lucky in the house we chose first. The man who lived there was a sailor, and had travelled round the world to Europe. He had been to Antwerp. Southampton and Felixstowe. His face was pleasant and open over his dirty plaid shirt. Having seen so much of the world, he was less worried about talking to a foreign television crew at a time when Peking was under martial law.

Inside his house the straw burning under the cooking pot smelled almost like incense. He sat down on the family bed, which was a mattress laid over a clay-built stove to keep them warm in winter. Yes, he said, he did very well out of farming. His family earned 1,500 yuan a year, ten times what they had earned before Deng and Zhao reformed the agricultural system. He thought the students were stupid: they were putting everything in danger. Maybe China would sink back to the old ways if the present government was overthrown.

We filmed him pumping water from the well in the little courtyard. Then one of the neighbours arrived. The village Party secretary was worried that the sailor-farmer might be talking to the foreign television people. Not at all, said the sailor-farmer, they had just wanted to film him using the well. He looked at us expressionlessly.

I went with our translator to see the Party secretary. He was an engaging old man in his late sixties with a witty, evil face. His mouth was filled with ill-shapen, misplaced teeth, mostly capped with gold; he carried his savings round with him. He was badly wall-eyed, but he turned his strabismus to his own advantage. The translator and I sat on chairs side by side, and as he, too, perched on his bed above a clay stove he kept his left eye on me and his right on the translator. Over his head was a Chinese calendar with a picture of Marie Antoinette on it: a curious thing to find in the house of a Communist Party official. One of his many sons sat silently beside him. Every now and then he refilled our cups from a giant enamel teapot.

In village terms, Lie Qingshang was seriously rich. Taking one of his eyes off us and shifting it to his son, he told me he earned 10,000 yuan a year: a thousand from pears, a thousand from chestnuts, six thousand from chickens, two thousand from other things. The translator, who had been working out the amount of land Liu farmed with his sons, suggested that he probably earned 100,000 yuan a year. Liu laughed, pleased at the compliment.

'If I earned that much I'd go and live in Hong Kong.'

He had helped the resistance against the Japanese in the War, running messages and hiding weapons. I told him that my uncle had also fought the Japanese in the War.

'Salute!' he shouted, and slapped the palm of my hand with his.

I hoped this might encourage him to record an interview with me, but he was too canny for that.

'I follow Party discipline,' he said.

Since 1949 he had been purged no fewer than four times, and each time he had made a comeback. He was a village Deng Xiaoping.

'I'd be in Peking running the country if it weren't for one thing. Guess what it is?'

I looked at his dishonest, amusing face and tried to work it out.

'I can't read or write!'

He roared with laughter, perhaps at my discomfiture. His physical appearance apart – it was hard to think of him at the clubhouse of the Japanese Golf Company, Ltd – he would have made a good living out of the rich pickings which 'everyone doing business' offered.

Everyone here supports Comrade Deng Xiaoping. He's done everything for us. As for those students, they just piss in the bed and spoil it for everyone.

He pointed graphically at the communal bed he was sitting on. The words seemed familiar. Afterwards I remembered: Charles de Gaulle had used the expression *chie-en-lit* about the students in Paris in 1968. But Liu Qinshang wouldn't repeat even these loyal sentiments for our television camera. He was too canny for that. Four purgings were enough. Who knew what might happen next?

There was a great deal of handshaking as we left. With a kind of good-natured cunning he asked the translator for his name and work unit number. A report would have to be prepared about all this. The translator refused. He was a strange man, a poet and writer who had attached himself to us in a way which no one could now remember. His English was very good, but our other Chinese helpers were certain he was a spy and would sometimes refuse to talk if he were in the room. I found his company very pleasant, but even I became nervous when he wrote down everything we said in a large school exercise-book. When I asked him why he did, he said he was planning to turn his experiences with us into a short story. Here in the village, however, he became anxious when the Party secretary wanted to know his identity. I intervened.

'Who knows,' I asked the Party secretary, 'what might happen next?'

He laughed a great deal at that. He was still laughing as we drove off. I could see his straw hat waving for a long way down the road.

*

Tiananmen Square had changed. There were fewer people there now, and many of them came from provincial universities. The Peking students had mostly gone back to their studies, though they were ready to turn out again at the hint of trouble. The Square was less pleasant. The makeshift latrines stank with the sweetness of faeces and the acid of urine. The marshals were more officious in demanding passes. The leaders argued among themselves and were rarely seen.

It was a relief to walk down the western arm of Chang'an Avenue, past the Gate of Heavenly Peace, to the main entrance of Zhongnan-hai, the leadership compound. A thousand or so students were blockading the gateway, standing or sitting opposite it while twenty or more soldiers sat facing them under the portals of the gate. It was a gesture, nothing more; the Party and government leaders, who lived inside the compound, rarely used the formal front gate, and the side gates which they did use were free of demonstrators. Still, it was a serious indignity. Someone had hung placards round the necks of the two ceremonial lions on either side of the gateway. The slogans demanded the resignation of the government and the introduction of democracy.

There were speeches, and the occasional entertainment: dancing, drumming, flute-playing. The soldiers sat with their legs crossed, looking straight ahead of them. No one taunted them, but once when a soup kitchen handed out food to the students I saw a young man go up to the line of soldiers and offer them a bowl of rice and chopsticks. They continued to stare straight in front, and one of the student marshals pulled the young man away. Everything the students did in April and May was reminiscent of 1968 and the Woodstock period, but nothing was more evocative than this.

As we were filming the crowd from the vantage-point of the soldiers I saw an old man craning through the heads to watch these goings-on. You could tell from his wrinkled brown face he had never dreamed that ordinary people could be allowed to heap such indignities on the Party and the government. He was amazed and shocked and yet, I thought, felt a sneaking excitement at it all. Perhaps even the most timid and obedient servant of the state derived a private, guilty pleasure from the iconoclasm of others.

*

All this time the government had slowly been growing in strength. Military units were ordered to hold study sessions on the speech Li Peng had made the night before martial law was imposed. Messages of support came slowly and sometimes reluctantly for Li Peng. After four days only twelve out of thirty-nine provinces and major cities had given him their backing. Most of the local Party bosses were waiting to see which way the wind would blow. There was an attempt by Zhao Ziyang's allies to summon an emergency meeting of the National People's Congress, which would have brought things to a head and might have voted against Li Peng. The chairman of the Congress, Wan Li, had been on a visit to Canada and the United States and was now, according to Zhao's supporters, flying back to Peking to call a meeting. Instead, his plane flew to Shanghai, and he was said to be ill. A week after the introduction of martial law he issued a statement which said that while the students were patriotic the demonstrations were being manipulated by a handful of people.

Later, a high-ranking source which had usually been reliable in the past told us that Deng Xiaoping, who had not been seen in public since

Gorbachev's visit, had been travelling round the provinces demanding assurances of support from the senior commanders of the People's Liberation Army. On 18 May, we were told, he flew to the city of Wuhan where he summoned the generals commanding all seven of China's military regions to a conference. Six of them agreed to give him total support. The seventh was more equivocal. He was the general commanding the Peking region.

Slowly, the government machinery was starting to regain its self-confidence. There were more anonymous people with cameras in the Square, filming the leaders, especially when there were foreign journalists about. Strange incidents which placed the students in a bad light began to occur. On Tuesday 23 May a teacher, a journalist and a worker from Hunan, Mao Zedong's province, walked up to the gateway and threw ink at the huge portrait hanging over it. Mao's bland, moonlike face was not badly defaced – a blot hit his left eyebrow, and others spattered across his neck and jacket – but this was iconoclasm of a serious kind. A group of students standing nearby seized the three men and handed them over to the police. They were taken to a bus where a CCTV reporter interviewed them. None of them would say why they had done it. The students were certain they were agents provocateurs, whose task was to show that crimes against decency were being committed because of the occupation of the Square.

Later even more disturbing things happened. A lone soldier drove a truck into the Square, parked it, and ran off. The students examined it and found it was full of rifles, ammunition and hand grenades. Again, they handed it over to the police at once, and helped to unload it. A security policeman with a video camera filmed the incident. Later, when the government had regained control, CCTV broadcast a carefully edited video which purported to show that the students were armed and violent. This incident featured strongly in it. So did the defacing of Mao's portrait. There were also numerous shots which, the commentary said, showed foreign agitators suborning the students. I thought I recognized myself among them.

An hour after Mao's portrait was attacked the sky, which had earlier been clear, began to darken. Soon black storm clouds were heading from the West. We had come out to see the ink-spattered painting, but we found ourselves instead filming a wild storm. The rain fell harder and faster than I had ever seen. In a few minutes my thin tropical suit was soaked through, and a pen in my inside pocket started to leak ink all over my jacket like black blood. Truck-loads of demonstrators careered across the road, skidding on the wet surface. The wind whipped the red and white banners and sent them streaming across the Square. It lifted tents bodily and blew them away, leaving the people who had been sheltering in them exposed and frightened. It whipped up the rubbish and swept it out of the Square altogether. It lashed the Monument and blew down the teepees around it. The air was full of sticks and tarpaulins and sheets of plastic. They wrapped themselves round trees and street lamps, or flew off into the distance, like the spirits of the dead. The loudspeakers shook on their posts, pouring music and instructions into the rain and the empty Square. At last the stench of disinfectant and urine was washed away.

Most people fled when the wind came up and the sky darkened. They took shelter in the underpass which went from the Square to the Gate of Heavenly Peace: thousands of wet, dispirited people crammed together, their light clothes steaming. Some diehards rode out the storm. We filmed a man whose picture went round the world: naked to the waist, held in position by a friend, he perched on the marble rails of the Monument and defied the elements, his arms raised in twin victory signs. He was doing it for our benefit, but it seemed to symbolize the spirit of the entire protest.

Soon there were only a few dozen students left in the Square. A platoon of soldiers in sou'westers could have solved the government's problem. We were on the northern side of that vast expanse, obliged to stay there because the cameraman, Eric Thirer, was a perfectionist and the pictures were stunning. The wind lashed the rain at us, and whipped it towards us across the empty flat expanse of paving-stones. In the distance three figures came battling towards us, sometimes leaning into the wind, sometimes blown along by it as it veered. They tacked in our direction like small boats in a stormy bay. As they reached us one of the students started taking off his flimsy raincoat. It was a difficult operation, but when he had it free he thrust it towards me. It was a gesture of thanks to us for being there. I couldn't accept it: I was wet through anyway, and he had nothing on but a T-shirt and shorts. In the end he accepted it back, but knelt down in the rain and kissed my hand. In that storm I felt like Lear with Tom o'Bedlam.

*

I first heard about the statue in the house of one of the artists who had been working on it. It had to be created in great secrecy. The authorities would regard it as the ultimate provocation and would do everything they could to prevent its being erected. The idea had come, not from the student leaders themselves but from a small group of students at the Central Institute of Fine Arts. They constructed it from a small maquette model in a courtyard of the Institute, building it up with a mixture of fibre-glass and plaster of Paris. It was clearly inspired by the Statue of Liberty with its lamp, but in other ways the flowing hair and the girlish, European features owed something to the French figure of Marianne. Chai Ling, the student leader who had been most enthusiastic about the plan, called it a symbol for the movement. We smuggled her into our hotel shortly after the statue was erected and interviewed her. She sat smiling her gentle smile, her feet scarcely touching the ground. In the white top and green shorts she wore she looked like a schoolgirl. She was passionate about the statue. Was it a Statue of Liberty? Or the Goddess of Democracy?

> She is the Goddess of Democracy, of course. She is the symbol of our hopes and aspirations, she represents the fruit of our struggle. The government is making all kinds of slander and accusation about her, but we resist its propaganda.

On the night of 29 May the statue was brought into Tiananmen Square in three parts, on the backs of flatbed bicycle rickshaws. Flimsy-looking scaffolding was in place by the next morning. That evening there was a festival of drumming and dancing around the shrouded statue, and then she was uncovered. It was a master-stroke. People came flooding back to the Square in such numbers that Chai Ling and the other leaders called off their fruitless argument about whether and how they should abandon Tiananmen Square. Standing opposite Chairman Mao's portrait (a spare copy of which was raised into place within hours of the desecration) the statue held up her torch of freedom almost in his face. It was extremely effective, and deeply offensive to the government.

On the night of Friday 2 June the army moved in. This time they didn't come by truck and tank, they ran in groups of a hundred at a time. Choosing their routes carefully, they had worked through the side streets. By the time the students and those who supported them realized what was happening, they were almost in the Square. I ran too when I heard the news, following the sound of drumming. The streets were empty and dark, but I knew them well by now. I was alone, and hoped I would be able to find a camera crew.

I turned the corner into Chang'an Avenue. Heaps of equipment lay in the middle of the streets. Lines of young men were being forced down the farther side of the road. They'd moved the students out of the Square, I thought.

'What's happening? Does anyone speak English?'

No one spoke English. I pushed my uncomprehending way through the crowds. There were so many things I couldn't work out. Why were the crowds so big? Where were the guns?

Then I realized. The soldiers were the prisoners. The equipment was their equipment. They had been stopped again. You could see they were exhausted from running. They had no spirit in them. Down beside the Beijing Hotel several hundred of them were sitting down, some in the road and some in a building site. They were hemmed in by a thick crowd of exultant people. From time to time someone would grab a portable loudspeaker and boom some message at the luckless soldiers. As before, they sat there and took it. Their officers looked at the ground. They had no orders, no idea what to do next.

I met up with a BBC camera crew. We filmed the lines of soldiers on the other side of the road, though they were often hostile to us. Then we went back to the large group beside the Beijing Hotel, their white shirts and green jackets startlingly bright in the camera lights. The officers were negotiating with the student leaders. As we filmed, one of the officers shouted an order and about two thirds of the group stood up, stretching their aching legs, and formed up in the road. The others stayed where they were. They and their officers, it seemed, had sided with the crowd. The others were going back to their barracks.

They marched down the dark side-street. We followed, filming them as they went. They took no notice of us, and we moved in and out of the ranks. They were walking slowly, with little discipline. Bob Poole, the cameraman, found himself behind an NCO carrying a white plastic can. Perhaps it had contained drinking water. The camera light suddenly angered him. He lashed out at it with his plastic can. His act of resistance rallied the other soldiers. They gathered round us, shouting and pulling at us. The light came off the camera and was smashed. They began pulling at the cameraman, getting him away from me and the sound recordist. I was shouting now, at the soldiers and at the cameraman.

'Hold the camera down, Bob.'

He managed to lower it from his shoulder, and that calmed them for a little. But the man with the can came back and shouted at us, and the violence started again in the dark, narrow street. Bob was pulled away from us again, into the pool of green uniforms.

The next moment someone was shouting back at them in Chinese, and three students moved in between the soldiers and us. The soldiers released Bob. We got away quickly, back down the street towards the bright streetlights of Chang'an Avenue. I tried to thank one of the students. He shrugged.

'It's our duty,' he said.

The soldiers headed off into the darkness, disappointed at the failure of their momentary attempt at revenge.

★

The next night, Sunday 3 June, everyone was expecting them to come back. It was humid and airless, and the streets round our hotel were empty. We set out for the Square, a big conspicuous European television team: reporter, producer, cameraman, sound recordist, translator, lighting man, all complete with gear. A cyclist rode past, shouting and pointing. What it meant we couldn't tell. Then we came upon a line of soldiers. Some had bleeding faces, one cradled a broken arm. They were walking slowly, limping. There had been a battle somewhere, but we couldn't tell where.

When we reached Chang'an Avenue it was as full of people as it had been at the height of the big demonstrations. It was a human river again. We followed the flow of it to the Gate of Heavenly Peace, under the restored portrait of Mao. There were hundreds of small groups, each concentrated around someone who was haranguing or lecturing them, using the heavy public gestures of the Chinese. Other groups had formed around radios tuned to foreign stations. People were moving from group to group, pushing in, crushing round a speaker, arguing, moving on, passing new information.

For the most part these weren't students. They were from the factories, and the red cloths tied round their foreheads gave them a look of ferocity. Trucks were arriving from the outskirts of the city, full of young workers. They waved the banners of their workplace, singing, chanting, looking forward to trouble.

People were shouting: there was a battle going on between tanks and the crowd somewhere to the west of the city centre. Details differed. I had trouble finding out what was being said. I watched the animated faces, everyone pushing closer to each new source of information, pulling at each other's sleeves or shoulders. Tanks and armoured personnel carriers, they were saying, were heading for the Square. They were coming from two directions, east and west. The crowds couldn't stop them.

'It's a different Army. It's not the 38th.'

The man was screaming it, clutching at our translator, pulling his arm, wanting to make him understand the significance. It had been the 38th Army that had tried to recapture the city the previous night, and on the night before martial law was declared. The soldiers had been unwilling to do their duty. These were armies from the outside, the rumours said, savage armies that didn't care who they killed. It wasn't true. The soldiers that moved in to Tiananmen Square were indeed from the 38th Army. They were just as savage as any outsiders.

We pushed on towards the Square. Several thousand people were standing there motionless, listening to the loudspeakers high above our heads: the government loudspeakers.

> Go home and save your lives. You will fail. You are not behaving in the correct Chinese manner. This is not the West. It is China. You should behave like good Chinese. Go home and save your lives. Go home and save your lives.

The voice was expressionless, epicene, metallic, like that of a hypnotist. I looked at these silent, serious faces illuminated by the orange light of the street lamps, studying the loudspeakers. Even the small children, brought here with the rest of the family as part of an outing, stared intently. The words were repeated again and again. It was a voice the people of China had been listening to for forty years, and continued listening to even now; but no one did what the hypnotist said. No one moved.

And then suddenly the spell broke. People were shouting that the army was coming. There was the sound of violent scraping, and across the Avenue people were pulling at the railings set in concrete and dragging them across to form a barricade. Everyone moved quickly. The crowd was acting as one, suddenly animated. Its actions were fast and decisive, and sometimes brutal. They blocked off Chang'an Avenue. We began filming, flooding the sweating enthusiasts with our camera light. Young men danced round us, flaunting their weaponry: coshes, knives, spears, bricks. A boy rushed up to our camera and opened his shabby green windcheater like a black marketeer to reveal a row of Coca-Cola bottles strapped to his waist, each filled with petrol and plugged with rags. He laughed, and mimed the action of pulling out a bottle and throwing it. I asked him his age. Sixteen. Why was he against the government? No answer.

Our translator heard that the Army would move in at one o'clock. It was half past midnight now. In the distance, above the noise of the crowd, I thought I could hear gunfire. I wanted to find a vantage-point from which we could film without being spotted by the army. But the tension which bonded the members of the crowd together had a different effect on us as a team. It was hot and noisy. We argued about whether we should have interviewed an English-speaking doctor we had met a short time before. We started shouting. It was all very trivial. The producer wanted to gather more background material for the documentary we had been working on. I argued that we needed to prepare ourselves for the coming confrontation, worried that it would take us by surprise unless we had a plan of action. The cameraman, impatient with us both, wanted to get on with filming the scene in front of him. Both of them were right. Made angry and petulant by the airlessness, the heat and the sense of coming violence, I headed off on my own to find the doctor whom we should indeed have interviewed earlier.

I pushed through the crowds, immediately feeling better for being on my own. There were very few foreign journalists left in the Square by now, and I felt conspicuous on my own. Yet I also felt good. People grabbed my hand, thanking me for being with them. I gave them a Victory sign and everyone round me applauded. It was hard to define the mood. There was still a spirit of celebration because so many people were out on the streets in defiance of the government; but it was giving way to a terrible foreboding. There was also something else, something I hadn't seen before in China: a reckless ferocity of purpose.

I crossed into the main part of Tiananmen Square and headed for the village of tents. I had spent so much time in the Square that I felt I knew each tent, each smell. A young couple clung to each other, her head on his shoulder. I passed close to them, but they didn't look at me. I thought of passengers on a sinking ship, waiting for the killing shock of the cold sea. A student asked me to sign his T-shirt. It was a gesture from an earlier, happy time, and I suspected I would be doing it for the last time. I signed the loose material at the back, below the collar, and he turned to face me. He had thick glasses and a bad complexion.

'It will be dangerous tonight,' he said. 'We are all very afraid here.'

He grabbed my hand and shook it with a great intensity. His grip was bony and clammy. I asked what he thought would happen.

'We will all die.'

He straightened up and shook my hand again. Then he slipped away through the tents.

The camp was dark. A few students were left there, but most of them had gathered around the Monument in the centre. I could hear the speeches and the occasional burst of singing: the Internationale, as always. They were about to pay the price for rebelling against the Communist system, and they were singing the Communist anthem while they waited. Here, though, it was quiet. I looked up at the face of the Goddess of Democracy, thirty feet above me. The symbol of all our aspirations, the fruit of our struggle. I loved that statue. It seemed disturbingly fragile, very easy to tear down and smash.

The speeches and the songs continued in the distance. Then they stopped. There was a violent grinding and squealing: the familiar sound of an armoured personnel carrier. I heard screaming. Behind me in the Avenue everyone was running. The APC was driving fast down the side of the Square. It seemed uncertain of its direction, one minute driving straight for Chang'an Avenue, the next stopping, turning, stopping again, as if it were a big animal looking for a way of escape. There was a scream and a sudden angry roar. The vehicle had crushed someone under its tracks. It turned in my direction, and started moving. I felt another kind of panic now, but it wasn't fear for myself. The action was starting and I was separated from my colleagues. In times of danger, the professional code runs, you stay with your colleagues and help them. I didn't want to earn a reputation as someone who disappeared when the trouble started.

The vehicle went on careering back and forth. It must have knocked down six or seven people. Later I saw one of the bodies, the legs wrenched off at the knee by the metal tracks. By now the APC was being hit repeatedly by Molotov cocktails and was on fire. Somehow it managed to escape, barging its way through the crowds with a crowd of angry attackers behind it. It fled along Chang'an Avenue to the west.

Then a second armoured personnel carrier came along the Avenue, alone and unsupported like the first. The crowds knew that with their numbers and their petrol bombs they had the power to knock it out. They screamed with anger and hatred as it veered in different directions, trying to find its way through the crowd, not caring who it knocked down. The Molotov cocktails arched over my head, spinning over and over, exploding on the thin shell of armour that protected the soldiers inside. Still the vehicle carried on, zigzagging, crossing the Avenue, trying to find a way through the barricades. A pause, and then it charged head on, straight at a block of concrete – and stuck there, its engine roaring wildly.

A terrible shout of triumph went up from the crowd then, primitive and dark. The prey had been caught. The smell of petrol and burning metal and sweat was in the air, intoxicating and violent. Everyone round me was pushing and fighting to get to the vehicle. I resisted, and then saw the light of a television camera close beside the trapped APC. I guessed that my colleague, Ingo Prosser, was the only cameraman brave enough to be that close. Now I was the one who was fighting, struggling to get through the crowd, pulling people out of my path, swearing, a big brutal Englishman larger and stronger than any of them. I tore one man's shirt and punched another in the back, desperate to get to my colleagues.

All round me people seemed to be yelling at the sky, their faces lit up. The vehicle had caught fire. A man, his torso bare, scrambled up the side of the APC and stood on top of it, his arms raised in victory, the noise of the mob welling up around him. They knew they had the vehicle's crew trapped inside. Someone started beating at the armoured glass with an iron bar.

I reached the cameraman and pulled at his arm to get his attention. He scarcely noticed me amid the buffeting and the noise and the violence and just carried on filming. He and his sound recordist and the Chinese lighting man and I were a few feet from the burning vehicle: close enough to be killed if it exploded or the soldiers came out shooting, but I couldn't persuade them to step back. So we stayed there, with the heat beating against our faces as people continued to pour petrol on the bonnet and roof and smashed at the doors and the armoured glass. They wanted to get at the soft, vulnerable flesh inside. What must it be like in there? I could imagine the soldiers half-crazed with the noise and the heat and the fear of being burned alive.

The door at the rear of the vehicle opened a little. The screaming round me rose even higher then. A soldier pushed the muzzle of a rifle out, but it was snatched from his hands and suddenly everyone was grabbing his arms, pulling and wrenching until he finally came free. Then he was gone. I saw the arms of the mob flailing above their heads as they fought each other to get their blows in. He was unconscious or dead within seconds, and his body dragged away in triumph.

A second soldier showed his head through the door and was immediately pulled out by his hair and ears and the skin on his face. I could see him clearly for a few instants: his eyes were rolling and his mouth was open, and he was covered with blood where the skin had been ripped off. Only his eyes remained, white and clear, but then someone was trying to get them as well, and someone else began beating his skull till the skull came apart and there was blood all over the ground, and his brains, and still they kept on, beating and beating and beating at what remained.

Then the horrible sight passed away, and the ground was wet where he had been.

There was a third soldier inside. I could just see his face in the light of the flames, and some of the crowd could too. They pulled him out, screaming, wild at having missed out in the killing of the other soldiers. It was blood they wanted, I knew, it was to feel the blood running over their hands. Their mouths were open and panting like dogs, and their eyes were expressionless. The Chinese lighting man told me afterwards they were shouting that the soldier they were about to kill wasn't human, that he was just a thing, an object, an animal which had to be destroyed. And all the time the noise and the heat and the stench of oil burning on hot metal beat at us, overwhelming our senses, deadening our feelings.

Just as the third soldier was pulled out of the vehicle, almost fainting, an articulated bus forced its way fast through the crowd and stopped with great skill so its rear door opened just beside the group around the soldier. It was the students. They had heard what was happening, and a group had rushed over in the bus to save whomever they could. It was as noble an act, I think, as any I had come across. The students – there were four or five of them – tried to drag the soldier on board by force, but the crowd held on to him, pulling him back. By some mischance the bus door started to close. It seemed the soldier's life must be lost.

I had seen people die in front of me before, but I had never seen three people die one after the other in this way. Once again the members of the crowd closed around the soldier, their arms raised over their heads to beat him to death. The bus and the safety it promised were so close. I couldn't look on any longer, a passive observer, watching another man's skin torn away or his skull broken open, and do nothing. I saw the soldier's face briefly. It expressed only horror and pain as he sank down under the blows of the people around him. I started to move forward. The ferocity of the crowd had entered me, but I felt it was the crowd that was the animal, that wasn't human.

The soldier was hanging limply in the arms of the crowd and a man was trying to break his skull with a half-brick, bringing it down with great force. I screamed obscenities at him, stupid obscenities since no one could understand them, and threw myself at him, catching him with his arm up as he prepared himself for a final blow. He looked at me blankly, and I felt his thin arm go limp in my grasp. I stopped shouting. He let me take the brick away and I threw it under the bus. It felt wet. A little room had been created around the soldier, and the students who had tried to rescue him before were able to get to him and pull and push him on to the bus by a different door. The rest of the mob hadn't given up, and some of them swarmed on to the bus to try to kill him there, but the students formed a protective block around him and they gave up. He was safe.

The vehicle burned for a long time, its driver and the man in the front seat beside him burning with it. The flames lit up the Square and reflected on the face of the Monument where the students had taken their stand. The crowd in Chang'an Avenue had been sated. The loudspeakers had stopped telling people to save their lives. There was silence.

The students sang the Internationale. It sounded weak and faint in the vastness of the Square. Many were crying. Maybe some students had taken part in the violence, but those in the Square itself had been faithful to the principle of non-violence. I began to realize why the two armoured personnel carriers had been sent in on their own. They were intended to be sacrificial victims. The army commanders had known that one or both of them would be caught. It was a way of stirring up the emotions of the ordinary soldiers, so that when the moment came they would have no pity for the demonstrators.

My colleagues and I wanted to make sure our pictures survived if we were arrested or shot, and I told the others we should go back to the Beijing Hotel and come out again later. I feel guilty about that now. We should have stayed in the Square, even though all the other camera crews had left and staying might have cost us our lives. Someone should have been there with the demonstrators when the army moved in, filming what happened, showing the courage of the students as they were surrounded by tanks and the army fired into them as they advanced. One or two Western newspaper journalists stayed with them, anonymous in the crowd. With our conspicuous equipment, we could not have been hidden, but we should have stayed too.

We didn't. We took up our position on the fourteenth floor of the Beijing Hotel. From there we got the famous pictures that were seen all round the world. Everything in them seemed grey and distant, though. We saw most of what happened, but we were separated from the noise and the fear and the stench of it. We saw the troops pouring out of the Gate of Heavenly Peace, bayonets fixed, shooting first into the air and then straight ahead of them. They looked like automata, with their rounded dark helmets. We filmed them charging across and clearing the northern end of the Square, where I had seen the young couple sitting and waiting for the shipwreck. We filmed the tanks as they drove over the tents where some of the students had taken refuge. Maybe the young couple, or the boy who asked me too sign his T-shirt, were among them. Those who were closer than we were said they heard the screams of the people inside the tents. We filmed as the lights in the Square were switched off at 4 a.m. They were switched on again forty minutes later, when the troops and the tanks moved towards the Monument itself, shooting first in the air and then directly at the students, so that the steps of the Monument and the heroic reliefs which decorated it were smashed by bullets.

Once or twice we were shot at ourselves, and a Taiwanese photographer in a room two doors from ours died from a bullet wound as he stood on the balcony. During the night the security police came to arrest us in our room. The young Chinese student who had been our lighting man, Wang, had opened the door to them and then tried to shut it when he saw who was there. A uniformed hotel porter grabbed him by the sleeve, and two men in suits stood behind him. Wang shouted out and I ran over. I pulled him away from the porter, and confident in my ability to keep the door shut against the three of them if necessary I peered through the gap between the door and its frame. Wang kept trying to translate, but I pushed him away.

Foolish things come to one's lips at such times; I shouted out that the British ambassador would be very angry if they persisted in trying to enter the room, and that unless they left at once I would ring him myself. The threat was more than usually empty: I had not visited the British ambassador in Peking and knew nothing of him, but my experience of a number of his colleagues was that they wanted nothing to do with such difficulties.

Curiously, it worked; perhaps it was my tone of voice. The pressure on the other side of the door relaxed, and there was grumbling as the three of them moved away. They did not come back. After that, Wang stuck close to me, convinced that I exerted some occult power over secret policemen which would protect him. I liked him: he was bold and amusing, and stayed with us long after all our other Chinese helpers had evaporated.

Meanwhile the crowds below us had regrouped in the Avenue, shouting their defiance at the troops who were massing at the farther end. Every now and then the crack of a rifle would bring down another demonstrator, and the ambulances or the flatbed bicycle rickshaws would hurry them away to hospital. I had given up trying to clear the balcony of everyone except the cameraman and me. The Chinese who had taken refuge with us couldn't be prevented from seeing what was happening.

One of them was a student leader who had come to our room because we were foreigners. I shouted at her to get away, that it was too dangerous, that only those with a job to do should stay out there. She refused, turning her head away from me so I wouldn't see that she was crying, her hands clenched tight enough to hurt. She was determined to watch the rape of her country and the utter destruction of the movement she and her friends had built up in the course of twenty-two days in the Square.

I recalled the lines of another T'ang Dynasty poet, Tu Fu's friend and master Li Po: if you try to cut water with a sword it will just run faster. But the river of change had been dammed, and below me in the Avenue where it had run people were dying all the time. Beside me, the cameraman stirred and started filming. Down in the Square, in the early light, the soldiers were busy unrolling something and lifting it up. Soon a great curtain of black cloth covered the end of Tiananmen Square. What was happening there was hidden from us.

*

Chai Ling stayed in the Square until the end. Later she recorded her impressions of what happened, and the tape was smuggled out to Hong Kong. These are extracts from it.

> I was the general commander in the Square. There were also some other student leaders like Li Lu and Feng Congde [her husband]. At 9 p.m. all the students in the Square raised their right hands and made a vow: 'I swear to promote the democracy and prosperity of my country and to prevent it from being overthrown by a handful of people. I am willing to give my young life to protect Tiananmen Square. I am willing to give up my life and my blood to protect the people's Square until the last one of us dies.'
>
> We knew this was a war between love and hate. This was not a war of weapons against weapons. We knew that if we used truncheons, bottles and sticks to fight the speeding tanks and the sub-machine guns, our demonstration was bound to fail. We decided to sit there quietly and be prepared to be sacrificed for the peaceful pro-democracy demonstration. We embraced each other. Our eyes were full of tears. We were waiting for the moment to come.
>
> All the people on the outside edges of our gathering died. At least two hundred students in tents were rolled over by tanks and crushed to death. In the Square, nearly four thousand people died. After the massacre the executioners even burned all the corpses to eliminate the traces of their violence. The symbol of our movement, the Goddess of Democracy, was smashed to pieces by the tanks.
>
> For each and every Chinese who has a conscience, please put your hand on your heart, please think of these young children, hand in hand and shoulder to shoulder, sitting quietly beneath the Monument, watching the blows of the murderers with their own eyes.

A student from Qinghua University takes up the story:

> By 4 a.m. all the lights in the Square were turned off. The pop singer, Hou Dejian, decided to negotiate with the army for a peaceful withdrawal of the students. By 4.40 we were starting to withdraw. All the Square's lights were switched on again, and we saw endless lines of troops marching towards us fiercely. They held sub-machine guns and weapons I had never seen before. The police began hitting students fiercely with electric cattle prods and sticks with iron nails. Before long, scores of students were bleeding heavily. We were forced to retreat up the steps to the level of the Monument. We still held hands tightly and sang the Internationale.
>
> I then realized we were completely surrounded by soldiers. Only one small opening remained, in the direction of the Military Museum. The armed police kept hitting us with full strength, and we finally fell down into the Square. Then the sub-machine guns started.

We were forced to retreat back up the Monument steps. The troops started to shoot at us again. Groups of workers and citizens, not students, became really anxious and they took up wooden sticks and rushed towards the soldiers. The Autonomous Federation of Beijing University Students announced the students would leave. It was not yet 5 a.m.

By then the only opening in the lines of troops was filled by tanks. A group ran forward and tried to open an exit among the tanks for the retreating students. Most were shot and killed. We finally opened a small exit amidst the tanks. I and three thousand students escaped through that opening. We ran and ran without stopping amidst the shooting.

Chai Ling's estimate of the number killed in the Square was too high. When universities resumed in the autumn of 1989 the student roll-calls showed that relatively few were missing: perhaps several hundred in all. Most of them would have died in the Square. The most reliable estimate of deaths in Peking put the figure at between 1,500 and 3,000. Most of those were ordinary citizens, people who had come to hate the Communist system and the government, and who were not bound by the non-violent ideals of the students.

As the sun came up that Sunday I looked down at the Aveune which had become so familiar to me as it took on its latest, unfamiliar transformation: a field of fire for the army. Bicycles rode up and down, bells jangling angrily, swerving in and out among the lumps of concrete, the burned-out cars and the wrecked buses. To my right the Avenue was empty. Anyone who ventured there was shot immediately. I lay down on the balcony and slept for a few minutes, but was wakened by a wild volley of shots. Twenty soldiers were walking down the road in a group towards the crowd, firing up at the buildings. Wang peered over the balcony and a bullet cracked close to him. He glanced at me, shocked for a moment, then laughed. The firing became heavier. I looked over now and saw why: two helicopters were approaching from the east, and the soldiers wanted everyone to keep their heads down.

I watched through binoculars as the helicopters landed, one after the other. It wasn't very sensible, but I had to see what was happening. We were several hundred yards away, too far to be able to identify the men who got out, but there were long lines of soldiers on parade to greet them. Maybe it was Li Peng or Yang Shangkun. Maybe it was Deng Xiaoping himself. They walked over to a heap of white plaster where the statue of the Goddess of Democracy had stood. Soon smoke began rising from the northern part of the Square. It came from burning tents – maybe from burning bodies too. The smoke drifted eastwards with the wind and joined the smoke from an ambulance in the middle of the road which had crashed and caught fire.

There was another burst of fire, and directly below me a woman fell to the ground. Three men came running over, bent double, and put her on the back of a flatbed trishaw. The driver pedalled off fast, hoping to get out of range as quick as he could. Another body, covered with blood, was driven past. One leg seemed to be missing. At the crossroads to my left a small crowd gathered round a car and pulled out a policeman. His hat and uniform were pulled off him roughly and heaped on top of the car. In the end they let him go, still in his underclothes.

We had heard that security policemen were manning the door of the hotel and searching everyone who came in or left. Somehow the cassettes we had shot all through the night had to be taken to our main office, where they would be edited and copies sent to Tokyo and Hong Kong by plane for satelliting to London. There was no point in hanging about any longer. I put the cassettes in my socks: I couldn't think of anywhere more sensible. As I walked down the vast corridors of the Beijing the cassettes clanked and I could only walk slowly. Ahead of me as I came out of the lift was a group of security policemen in plain clothes by the door. They were searching someone who was trying to leave.

I walked towards them. To have stopped would have looked suspicious. I could smell the stale sweat of a long and difficult night on myself. The floors were highly polished and the hall echoed to the sound of the cassettes clanking. It was both ludicrous and nerve-racking, and there was a distinct temptation to laugh. I made my way around the kiosk in the middle of the hallway where they sold carved jade and ivory. Everything was arranged as tidily as if there had been no massacre. There was just the empty area between the kiosk and the main door now, and the security policemen were starting to turn their heads to look at me. At that instant there was a loud and prolonged burst of firing outside. The security policemen crowded round the glass doors to see what had happened. I pushed my way through, excusing myself politely. They didn't look at me. I got a little way down the ramp then pulled the cassettes out of my socks and ran for it. The pictures of the massacre would be seen after all.

PART III
BERLIN – BREAKING OUT

6
THE CLAUSTROPHOBIC STATE

*With some satisfaction, but without self-congratulation or arrogance, we can
state clearly today that we have created a society which in spite of increasing
productivity is free from mass unemployment. . . We have, fortunately, no
drugs mafia and no trade in babies, as they do in the Federal Republic. With
us, the protection of society goes hand in hand with the improvement of
material values.*

ERICH HONECKER on the 40th anniversary of the founding of the
German Democratic Republic, October 1989

There was no escaping it. It seemed to block the end of every side street.
Old tram lines appeared to run directly at it, sometimes swerving away
at the last moment, sometimes not. Its bland grey neatness made it
hateful. If it had merely cut Berlin into two along a straight line it might
have been less offensive. Instead it jinked its way through the city along
the haphazard line of occupation, so you could find it to your left when
you expected it to be in front of you, and travelling along the road beside
you when you thought you had left it far behind. And always, on the
other side, there were tantalizing glimpses of a place where, for all its
faults, they did things better, quicker, more sensibly; and there was real
money. Perhaps it wasn't freedom they had on the other side, so much
as greater scope. But from the shabby eastern side, to all except the
Marxists it looked like freedom.

The Berlin Wall defined the German Democratic Republic in two
senses. It provided its outline, dividing the city of Berlin itself and
followed the frontier of the state from Plauen in the south to the
Lübecker Bucht in the north. It also defined it in a topological sense.
The Wall was a metaphor for a country held prisoner. While the
western part of Germany had grown and developed, the eastern part
behind its Wall had wizened and atrophied. It was not unsuccessful
when compared to other parts of the Soviet bloc, but it had never
persuaded a majority of its citizens that it was as good a place to live as
the Federal Republic just over the Wall. They felt the ennui of the
long-term inmate.

Once I drove for much of the day from East Berlin to the south-west

of the state, near the West German border. The countryside was grey
and featureless, the weather was cold. I was tired of the jolting from the
pockmarked roads and the slow progress through the ugly, rebuilt
towns. As we came closer to the West German border there was
evidence of the huge population of Soviet soldiers: nearly 400,000 of
them altogether in the GDR. Untranslated signs in Russian warned the
occupying forces of the need to slow down, or the approach of another
of their installations. Crude trucks and jeeps with Russian lettering on
them lurched out of side roads, leaving a heavy cloud of unassimilated
oil-fumes in the air. My companion had said little to me during the
journey. She was depressed.

At the beginning, as we drove south-westwards out of East Berlin,
she had sought to make things clear.

'I am your translator. I shall translate to the best of my ability. But
please: don't bother to tell me how wonderful things are in the West. I
am very happy with my life here in the GDR. My husband has a good
job and we have many benefits you in the West don't have. So don't try
to convert me. You will only be wasting your time.'

We were close to Halberstadt. It was starting to get dark, although it
wasn't yet 5 o'clock. People were huddled in their drab clothes, heads to
the wind. The car rumbled on the uneven surface, shaking us both from
side to side. The great blocks of workers' flats on the outskirts of the city
closed in around us. It seemed to trigger something inside her.

'God, I hate this country. For years now I've talked it over with my
husband: how can we get out? I have to keep quiet about it because I'm
in a sensitive job, but he's talking about it openly now. I think if we stay
here much longer it'll drive him mad. We both feel so trapped.'

To her and to the millions who felt as she did there were endless
galling reminders of captivity: the West German television programmes which people in two-thirds of the GDR could watch (at one
time Young Communists went around turning the aerials on houses
away from the direction of the Federal Republic); the advertisements
for the state airline, Interflug ('Fly to Europe, Africa, Asia, the
Americas', when it was clear the Europe meant the Soviet bloc, Africa
meant Angola and Ethiopia, Asia meant North Korea, Vietnam and
China, and the Americas meant Cuba and Nicaragua); the carefully
phrased letters from relatives across the Wall; and above all the sight of
the West German flag flying on the old Reichstag and the other tall
buildings, so tantalizingly close on the other side of the Wall. For years
at a time people would become obsessed with plans for getting out.

A third of a million people, most of them retired or handicapped, did
so legally between the construction of the Wall in 1961 and its breaching

at the end of 1989. Year after year the figure for those who escaped was the same: five thousand, more or less. Of those, most made their way through less well-guarded countries: Hungary and Czechoslovakia in particular. The official GDR figures show that eighty people died in trying to cross the Wall illegally. Another 104 died at other points in the frontier between East and West Germany. The first was Rudolf Urban, aged forty-seven, who died of his injuries after abseiling from a house on the eastern side six days after the Wall was built. The last was Chris Gueffroy, who was twenty-one. He was shot as he tried to make his way across on 6 February 1989: only nine months before the Wall was opened. Eight East German frontier guards were shot from the West during clashes of different kinds, often when they were themselves trying to kill escapers. Twenty West German citizens were abducted and taken across to the other side of the Wall.

The Museum at Checkpoint Charlie, on the western side of the Friedrichstrasse crossing, contained dozens of examples of ingenious methods of escape, from a home-made light aircraft to a submarine and an elaborate pulley system. Tunnels were dug, buses and trucks tried to burst through the barriers, people hid in tiny compartments in cars. In one way or another, since the German Democratic Republic was founded in 1949 more than three million people, a sixth of its population, had become refugees in the West. Half were under twenty-five years of age.

There was a kind of counter-tunnelling going on from the eastern side. The GDR's intelligence organization was effective and well funded. Over the years there were dozens of cases of the penetration of the Federal government and its agencies. The East Germans specialized in the entrapment of secretaries in early middle age who held sensitive jobs. They also recruited the head of West German counter-intelligence and the chief personal assistant to Chancellor Willy Brandt. The counter-intelligence chief defected; Willy Brandt resigned. If you were lucky, you could sometimes hear the East German intelligence service broadcasting instructions to its innumerable agents in the West. The timing and the frequency were both apparently random. No doubt each broadcast contained details of the next one, but none of the Allied agencies was able to crack the code that was used. Any VHF radio could pick up the messages. They lasted for a few minutes at a time, and consisted simply of a series of digits read out by a man or a woman in a flat, mechanical, toneless voice: '*Sieben. Eins. Null. Null. Zwei. Neun. Sieben. Acht. Drei. Sechs. Vier. . .*'

Perhaps because the East German security service, the *Staats-sicherheit*, knew how easy it was to penetrate the West, its own suspicion of every servant of the state was a settled habit of mind.

A friend of mine, Klaus N., served for many years in the diplomatic service of the GDR. He is now in his late forties, a handsome, intelligent man with a precisely cut beard and a slight stoop: his only concession to the passing years. He calls it 'my weird career', and for a citizen of an Eastern bloc country, where the senior jobs were allocated and directed with care from above, he certainly chopped and changed considerably. Even now, he's unwilling to have everything he did made known.

Klaus was cut out for university, but went into the army first; he voluntarily had to join it, he says wryly. Not long after, conscription was introduced because the system of obliging young men to become soldiers voluntarily was not working. After the army, while he was still at university, he became restless. Someone steered him towards the youth organization which sent people to work in the Third World. A lot of idealistic people went in for it. He was selected, and went to West Africa. It was not easy: there was a coup, and things were dangerous. He came back after a year and finished his degree course at university. By returning, he passed a test. He had been given a passport, he had spent a week in Egypt on the way out, and since Swissair had evacuated all the Europeans from the West African capital he had been taken to Zurich. In spite of all these opportunities to defect, he still came back to the GDR. He was trustworthy.

When he graduated, Klaus was called in and told what career had been assigned to him. It was to be the Foreign Ministry, the best job possible. He did several years at another Eastern European capital, and then went to a Western one. His ambassador, a decent and honest man, talked Klaus into joining the Communist Party, the SED. It was relatively democratic, highly motivated, and its members were well educated. There was a good deal of earnest discussion at the lower levels, and the members were by no means simply careerists. But at the middle levels, where the members had hopes of a political career, most of these things stopped. You became afraid of criticism, of putting a foot wrong. You followed the Party line.

At first, none of this was clear to Klaus. He was given the opportunity of teaching courses in political instruction at the embassy, and was allocated a special office. They hoped to buy you that way, he says now. But Klaus wasn't easy to buy, if only because he believed in the freedom of conscience which he still thought every Party member possessed. He began using the works of the semi-dissident economist and philosopher Rudolf Bahro in his classes. Gradually he realized two things: first, that someone in the class was reporting on him to his superiors; second, that his superiors disapproved very strongly of his use of Bahro. They also wanted to know how he managed to get hold of the works of an author who was banned in the GDR.

They were right to be concerned. He had obtained them from a Swiss couple he met while he was based in Western Europe. Klaus and his wife became close friends with them, and they took holidays together in Hungary. It was strictly forbidden. Someone in as sensitive a job as Klaus should have declared the contact with the Swiss couple in the first place. From the moment he decided not to do so, he put himself outside the system.

The arrangements for their annual meeting had to be made very carefully. Writing was too dangerous: the letters would be opened. He used to use a public telephone in East Berlin and pretend he was a West Berliner who had come across to the East for the day. He would introduce himself as Hans, and say how much he was looking forward to seeing the Swiss couple in the South of France, on such and such a date. The South of France meant the resort they always went to on Lake Balaton in Hungary. The real date was a day and a month later than he said, so the Swiss couple knew 15 July meant 16 August.

Why did I always come back after these holidays? Because my family was here, I suppose. We were scared our parents would suffer if we left. And my daughter, when she was older, had to stay behind. We couldn't get a passport for her as well as for us, and anyway she wanted to be with her own friends. If we'd got to the West from Hungary she would never have been able to join us, and she'd have been thrown out of university. She used to say, 'If you get the chance, go ahead: I'll join you later.' I would have done it, but my wife said no. In a way, I think that led to the break-up of our marriage, later on. It was hard to forget how different things would have been if she hadn't refused to come with me. But anyway we decided to stay on.

Even so, the *Staatssicherheit*, known as the Stasi, had their eye on him. He had, as a matter of course, to return his passport after each trip. Before they would give him a new one, they would come round and ask questions of the neighbours: Does Klaus N. often come home late? Does he get mail from Western countries? Have you ever seen him in a Western car? Do he and his wife have expensive clothes? Once when he and his wife were away from home for a few days he returned to find that their flat had been searched. It had been done very methodically, and almost everything was put back exactly as it had been left. The next time they went away he pasted a couple of hairs on the door jamb. They were gone when he returned, and the books and magazines showed signs of having been examined. The Stasi were looking for insights into the way he thought.

At first I was really afraid. It was terrible, to feel you were being watched and suspected. But slowly, over the years, I found I was shedding the fear. It didn't happen suddenly, but I stopped caring. Maybe it was because they didn't do anything to me, I don't know. Anyway, I started to make sarcastic jokes about the system, about Honecker, about the GDR as a whole. I didn't really notice I was doing it, but my boss at the Foreign Ministry called me in and told me. By that stage I didn't really care, even about the job.

When I went to see friends of mine, really close friends, they would always turn the radio up in case the place was bugged. In this country of ours, it took a long time to make friends. You watched people very carefully if you thought you liked them. You had to see if they were trustworthy. But when you did finally make friends, that was it: you gave yourself away totally, and they did the same to you. In a way, you had to. It was a kind of insurance policy for each of you, though no one would ever put it that way.

The Stasi was probably the most effective security police force in the Soviet bloc apart from the KGB. Its constant, unremitting war against West Germany's counter-espionage organization gave it a degree of experience which none of the other satellite countries could match. The Stasi trained several secret police agencies in the Third World. It was widely believed to have approached two out of every three students at East German universities, though most claimed they rejected the thought of working for it. By the time I talked to Klaus the Stasi had effectively ceased to exist for three months. Even so, he found it a difficult subject to speak about.

We just called the Stasi 'they'. But it was better not to mention the subject. No good comes of discussing it, I assure you. I think one friend of mine worked for it, but of course I never asked him. I was always very careful what I said to him, and yet I liked him all the same. I suppose that's hard to understand. There were other names for the Stasi. Sometimes in the Foreign Ministry we called it the firm. That was a kind of joke. And then with my friends it was fashionable to call it the Konsum, after the Consumers' Co-operative. We knew where its headquarters were in Berlin, but not its other buildings. I realize now how many it had, all over the place. And there was one very strange department in the Foreign Ministry. Its doors were always locked. I knew the faces of one or two of the people who worked there, but I never found out exactly what they did. Officially it was called 'Department Number 1'. It wasn't listed in our internal telephone directory.

It became obvious to Klaus that the Foreign Ministry was dissatisfied with him. The episode with Rudolf Bahro's books had been a black mark against him, and the sarcastic jokes made it worse. But the beginning of the end came when he tried to leave. A friend had offered him a job with Interflug, and he was keen to accept. But you couldn't escape that easily from a state assignment, as his head of department told him.

'Of course you can leave. But there are three ways of doing it, and only one is any good for you. You can give us notice, we can give you notice, or it can be mutual. I promise you, unless it's mutual you won't find another job anywhere.'

Klaus told him he'd been offered another job. The head of department merely smiled.

'I promise you,' he said.

Klaus went back to Interflug, but somehow the offer wasn't there any more. No one wanted to employ a person who did not have the confidence of the Foreign Ministry; especially an airline, which would provide a thousand opportunities of escaping the country. By now, though, his days at the Foreign Ministry were numbered anyway. In 1984 the second of the three options was exercised. He was asked to leave. Klaus N. was unreliable material. It took another friend weeks to cut through the red tape and obtain a job for him which was probably well below his qualifications. This was based in East Berlin, and there was no possibility whatever of travelling. The Berlin Wall closed him in: though in his case it was built of opinion, suspicion, reputation. It was just as unsurmountable as concrete and barbed wire.

*

On 15 June 1961, at the height of the outflow of GDR citizens to the West, the President of the Council of State, Walter Ulbricht, gave a press conference. There had been rumours for some days that the East German authorities were planning to stem the flow by erecting some kind of wall to block the open crossings to West Berlin. Inevitably, someone put the question to Ulbricht. It may be that the press conference was called in order that this should happen.

> If I understand your question, there are people in West Germany who want us to mobilize the building workers of the GDR in order to construct a wall. I am not aware of any such intention. The building workers of our capital city are chiefly engaged in housing schemes, and their efforts are fully employed for that purpose.

He spoke nothing but the literal truth. Two months later, on 13 August 1961, soldiers of the GDR started work on a wall and a barbed wire fence along the line of the Soviet sector of Berlin. Building workers were scarcely involved. Ulbricht's denial, which had seemed so categorical, helped to confuse the Western powers, and when the construction work began it took everyone by surprise. People gathered to protest on the Western side. To the East, old ladies, little children, men and women jumped from the buildings along the line of the new wall and were caught in canvas sheets held out by rescuers. The youngest was a boy of six, the eldest a woman of seventy-seven. Four others were killed.

The man who was given responsibility for the operation to build the Wall was a grey eminence in a grey regime: Ulbricht's amanuensis, Erich Honecker. Honecker was not a native of the territory of what was to become East Germany. He was born in 1912 in the industrial town of Wiebelskirchen in the Saarland, on the French border. His family was actively involved in left-wing politics, and Honecker himself became an enthusiastic Communist. He was arrested in 1935 by the Gestapo and spent ten years in prison. In the post-war period he worked his way up slowly until he caught the eye of the top leadership. Ulbricht used him for some of the most difficult and distasteful tasks the East German state carried out in the 1960s.

Chief among them was the building of the Wall. The idea, according to Khrushchev's memoirs, came from Moscow. Khrushchev is however as disingenuous about the plan as Ulbricht was:

> We'd long since decided that free passage in and out of Berlin was nothing more than a loophole for capitalist intelligence services, allowing them to collect information on the location of our troops. The only way to close the loopholes was to close the border. . . At one point I asked our ambassador in the GDR, Pervukhin, to send me a map of West Berlin. We deliberated on our tactics and set a certain date and hour when the border control would go into effect. We decided to erect anti-tank barriers and barricades. We also planned to use our own troops to guard the border, although the front line would consist of German soldiers. Our own men would be a few metres behind them, so that the West could easily see that Soviet troops were backing up the German troops. We wanted to give the impression that the whole operation was being carried out by the Germans in co-operation with their Soviet allies.

And so Erich Honecker, who had started life as an apprentice roofer, became a master-builder. He was in direct personal charge of the structural planning, the military preparations, the intense security which surrounded the building work, the propaganda campaign which prepared the way for it and which justified it afterwards. The official description of it, 'the Anti-Fascist Protective Wall', was his invention. The extraordinary success of a project as vast as this, which took the

West almost entirely by surprise, was his. So was the decision to shoot anyone who tried to escape to the West by getting over the Wall. The Four-Power Agreement continued in force after the Wall was built, and military personnel from each of the four exercised the right to travel throughout the entire city. Khrushchev's memoirs claim that he took advantage of this to have himself driven incognito around West Berlin, to see what it was like. He didn't get out of the car.

In 1968 there was another difficult job for Erich Honecker. When the reforms of the Prague Spring began, he became characteristically the most outspoken critic of Czechoslovakia in the East German Politburo. Ulbricht gave him personal control of the operation when East German troops joined the Soviet army in the invasion of Czechoslovakia. Soon his position was sufficiently strong for him to begin challenging the power of the man whose faithful servant he had been. By the middle of 1970 Honecker was pressing Ulbricht to resign. The following year Moscow openly joined in the pressure. Ulbricht fell. The amanuensis had become the master.

But there was more to Erich Honecker than unrelenting greyness and unquestioning devotion to the wishes of Moscow. There were times, as he reached his seventies, when the Federal government in Bonn thought he might be preparing some unlooked-for move towards the West. He had already shown signs of a curious desire to be popular in his own country. By the early 1980s young people in the GDR were becoming seriously disaffected. A West German rock star, Udo Lindenberg, a man with a powerful talent for public relations, scented this. After a series of heavily publicized letters Lindenberg travelled to East Berlin, made Honecker's acquaintance, and made him a present of a leather bomber jacket.

They made a strange couple as they stood side by side for the cameras: the septuagenarian in leather and the rock star with his peaked cap, their arms around each other. Who was using the other more was hard to say. Lindenberg certainly regarded it as a daring and amusing public relations gambit, though privately he maintains that Honecker had a surprisingly pleasant side to him. Soon Lindenberg wrote a song to commemorate the unlikely friendship:

Ich geh' über sieben Berge
Und über sieben Brücke
Und hupf noch kurz durchs Minenfeld
Und dann bin ich auch schon da
In der jungen Welt
Und dann komm ich ganz rasant
Mit einem Trabant

In die Hauptstadt eingefahrn
Und da hat Erich dann die Lederjacket an.
Es war enimal ein Generalsekretär
Der liebte den Rock 'n' roll so sehr
Gitarren statt Knarren
Und locker
So wie ein Rocker. . .

(I go over seven hills and over seven bridges, and hop quickly through the minefields, and then I'm there, in the young world. And then in a Trabant I come in pretty fast and drive into the capital, and there is Erich wearing the leather jacket.

There was once a general secretary who really loved rock 'n' roll, and guitars instead of guns, and was cool, just like a rocker. . .)

Far from trying to forget what his Politburo colleagues must have seen as an unfortunate lapse, Honecker made an arrangement to meet Lindenberg when he made his much-heralded visit to West Germany in September 1987. There again they posed for the cameras, their arms round one another. The publicity did Lindenberg no harm at all. What it did for Honecker is less clear. He met Franz-Josef Strauss, the right-wing Christian Social Union leader, in Munich and came away with promises of extra trade and technological help for East Germany. He paid homage at the birthplace of his fellow-Saarlander, Karl Marx, in Trier.

Above all, he went to the Honecker family house in Wiebelskirchen to see his sister, who still lived there, and picked a much-photographed apple from a tree in the garden. At the time, it all seemed to be the preliminary to some further step towards better relations with the Federal Republic. There was speculation in the West German press that Honecker might go on and do something spectacular: even, some newspapers and magazines suggested, knock down his own Wall.

But the one thing no one seriously expected was some move towards German reunification. When Franz-Josef Strauss talked of it during their meeting, Honecker smiled and shook his head, and waved his hand as though refusing another cup of coffee. Reunification was the one unthinkable concept. The Politburo in East Berlin had felt obliged to strip the words from the GDR's national anthem because they could be interpreted as referring to Germany as a single, undivided entity. Nobody had come up with an alternative, unexceptionable version, so whenever it was played in East Germany, it was merely a wordless tune; and although it was played countless times during Honecker's visit to the Federal Republic, no one sang the words, even if anybody had been able to remember them.

But it was clear that Honecker wanted a new relationship with Bonn, if only to attract more investment and more direct aid from it. That was obtained. As for anything deeper, the moment passed. Neither the brief flirtation with West Germany nor the hint that an unconventional elderly rocker lurked under the boring grey suit had come to anything. No one suspected it at the time, but this was to be the GDR's last opportunity of negotiating a place for itself as a separate entity within the Federal Republic. From now on, the reunification of Germany could come about only with the collapse of the GDR as an independent state. As the wordless anthem was played for the last time and Erich Honecker left West Germany for home, however, he seemed as much in command as ever. The GDR, one felt, would certainly last him out. There was no reason to imagine it would not outlast his successors as well.

> He wasn't a man who could inspire you, no. But he wasn't unpleasant in any way. I suppose you would say he was just rather ordinary in many respects.

The speaker was one of Honecker's personal interpreters: a staid woman in her late forties, formal and polite, with a man's white shirt and a dark grey skirt. She wore no make-up. Her English was almost perfect: English English, rather than American English. She used just enough colloquialisms to demonstrate her mastery of the language, but not so many that you would call her English slangy. Far from it: it was as neatly presented, as clean of improprieties, as she was.

> He had a strange personality. He was, for instance, very impersonal. I suppose he must have known his secretaries and bodyguards on a personal basis, but not me and not the other interpreters. We were simply adjuncts as far as he was concerned. The most personal remark I ever heard him make was when he was waiting for some distinguished guest to arrive; I can't remember who. I'd been working for him that morning, and I took my place beside him again.
> 'Oh, it's you again,' he said. That was all.
> He was a very poor public speaker. He would stumble over the easiest words in his prepared scripts. You felt embarrassed to listen to him – sympathetic, even. And yet in private he was totally different. He had an extremely sharp mind. And he could even make jokes. Little jokes, not like your politicians make, perhaps, but he wasn't always one hundred per cent serious. Once, I remember, the foreign minister of the Netherlands paid him a visit, and Honecker suddenly produced an old piece of paper from his pocket and put in on the table.
> 'Am I still a citizen of your country, or has this expired?'
> It was an identity card he had carried when he was on the run from Germany, and was working on the Rhine barges. So you see, he could be quite relaxed, and even human.

But after his downfall Honecker's way of life was regarded as deeply corrupt. His fleet of Mercedes limousines went on show, and television cameras were conducted round his hunting-lodges and those of his Politburo colleagues. To Western eyes they were pleasant enough, if badly furnished. To the eyes of those who were restricted to cramped flats and Trabant cars for which they had to wait ten years, such luxury was indecent.

One afternoon after the great political change I drove out of East Berlin to the north, to the resort of Wandlitz where the Politburo had a complex of dachas. The road was one of Hitler's autobahns, scarcely changed since it was built in the late 1930s. There were two lanes only on each side, and a narrow strip of unprotected grass between the two carriageways. The barriers dated from the 1930s too. A spur road, especially built to enable members of the Politburo to reach their country houses with speed and comfort, branched off the autobahn. I was to look out for the chimney of a power-plant among the woods. I saw it, and turned off into a short approach road. A rather seedy green-painted wall like a smaller version of the Berlin Wall ran right around the estate.

It was a fine Sunday afternoon and a lot of people were there. About forty cars were parked in front of the gates to the Wandlitz compound: big, expensive, electronically operated gates, with a guardhouse to keep out the unauthorized and apartment blocks outside the grounds where servants and security guards lived. Even they were a great deal better than the places where most East Germans lived. The crowd around the gate thought so too. A harassed man in plain clothes was trying to calm the crowd down.

'I'm sorry, it's simply not possible,' he said politely. 'The whole place is now being converted and there's a lot of building material around. It wouldn't be safe to let you in.'

'Converted to what, exactly?' The question came from a balding man in his late thirties with a beer belly. He had his arm round an attractive girl in a tight dress.

The plain clothes detective pointed to a brass plate which had been newly attached to the gate post. 'Rehabilitation Sanatorium', it said.

'And who's going to be allowed to come here? More politicians?'

Everyone laughed. The detective was still flustered.

'People from this area. If they're ill.'

'Show us. We want to see. After all, it belongs to us.'

The argument began to go round in circles. The small crowd became heated again, shouting, gesticulating, pushing towards the gate. Eventually an older, rather better educated man calmed them down.

'Suppose you describe to us what's inside.'

That was greeted by an immediate shout of assent.

There were, it seemed, twenty or so houses in the complex. Each was set apart from the others, with gardens and woodland in between. We all stared down the long road that led directly into a thick forest of pine trees. From here you could see nothing. There was also an entertainment complex, with a cinema, barbecue pits, and a separate theatre. The health centre contained a big gymnasium, an Olympic-sized swimming pool, and mineral baths.

'Bastards,' said someone.

Several people nodded in agreement. They began to drift away. The detective was relieved.

'Now it belongs to the people,' he said sententiously.

No one asked him what his function had been before Wandlitz came into the people's possession.

'Were you,' I asked Honecker's translator, 'very aware of the high living of the Party leaders?'

We certainly knew about Wandlitz. A lot of people did. But I personally never went there, and I had no real idea what it contained. I thought it was just dachas or hunting-lodges in the forest. When I went with him on official visits abroad, I would always fly on his plane. Then, I must admit, I saw quite a lot of luxury. I mean, the aircraft was always a Soviet-built one, but absolutely everything inside was from the West. The seats, the toilets, the little kitchen, everything right down to the last can of beer. All the alcohol, all the food was from the West. And I knew from his office that he and everyone else had Western television sets, not those awful Russian ones, that always exploded and went wrong. And of course he always had West German cars – big Mercedes and so on. So I was aware of the privileges these people gave themselves, but somehow you felt it was natural. You know, their life-style is different from ours, and so it seemed acceptable to me that they should have things that worked properly and looked good. After all, they were representing the country. But all these hunting estates and houses, that's something different. And of course the special shops. We knew about them vaguely, and people didn't like the idea much, but it was mostly just rumour. I never saw one myself. If I had known the extent of the corruption, I would have been very angry. Most people would have been. It was extraordinary, unforgivable.

She shook her head virtuously and compressed her lips. And yet I had the impression that her anger about corruption was a little synthetic. I experienced the same feeling time and again in the GDR in the days after the Wall was breached and the Communist Party collapsed. The leadership lived well, but there were no real signs of the gross abuse of power that took place in Romania. Corruption means more than good living in the midst of relative shortages. But the people of the GDR were simply turning the rhetoric of Marxism-Leninism back on the people who had preached it for decades.

The East Germans were not like the Poles, the Czechs or the Hungarians: at some level of their political consciousness they had been prepared to accept the Socialist Unity Party, the Sozialistische Einheitspartei Deutschlands or SED, at its own assessment of itself. There was a certain idealism at the base of the Party which simply never existed to any serious degree in the other countries of the Soviet bloc, except in the Soviet Union itself. That idealism was affronted by the relatively minor revelations about hunting lodges, Scotch whisky and cans of West German beer on the leaders' aircraft.

But the people who might have kept the SED in power had moved away from it in disgust long before. In a fast food restaurant on the Unter den Linden in East Berlin I queued with a writer, Wolf H., to collect my solyanka soup and a nondescript salad. The restaurant looked Western, but the system was unquestionably Soviet-bloc. We queued while the cashiers went slowly through each person's order. Our food grew cold. Other people who had ordered fewer dishes pushed into the queue ahead of us. We had to share a table with a couple of others.

Wolf was a thoughtful, shy man with a neatly cut beard and a tidy appearance. I was surprised to find how quickly he became emotional when we talked about the past.

> My parents were very anti-Communist, so I suppose I reacted against them and became an idealistic Communist. I was testing them. It looked on the outside like a political choice on my part, but maybe it was simply a psychological one. I was very sympathetic to what was happening in Czechoslovakia in the mid-60s. Dubcek was very popular here. And then, of course, it was all over, and we found that our army had taken part in the whole military involvement there. It was a great, great shock to us – to me – to find out that we had done that. Terrible. Terrible.

I glanced at him as we sat side by side. He was in tears. Worse, he was embarrassed that I should see him and that the young couple sitting opposite should be watching him stolidly as he rubbed his eyes with his neat white handkerchief. He went back to his food more as a cover for his emotions than because he was hungry.

> But I stayed with the Party. By 1973 it looked as though things were really going to change here. It wouldn't be like Czechoslovakia under Dubcek, maybe, but there was a real chance that this society would slowly open up to

the West. For the next few years there was more cultural freedom, at least in spells. And then in 1976 there was the whole business with Wolf Biermann.

The young couple had gone by now, but even so he dropped his voice slightly at the mention of the name. Wolf Biermann was a songwriter whose bitter, sharp, ironic songs had often touched the Party leaders on the raw. In 1976 he was on a tour of West Germany when it was announced that he would not be allowed to return to the GDR and that his passport was being rescinded.

> There was uproar among us members of the Writers' Union. Some were expelled, though I wasn't one of them. Maybe I didn't protest with the necessary amount of courage. But it was terrible. And after that only the hack writers stayed with the Party. You couldn't support them after that. It was the final split. In my opinion it was the blow from which socialism in our country never recovered. That was the beginning of everything. And in some ways, for people like me, it was the end of everything too.

He looked out of the window at the people hurrying past in the sunlit Unter den Linden. The SED had collapsed, elections were coming, the reunification of Germany would not be long delayed. But the things for which he had fallen out with his parents had come to nothing. He wasn't going to weep again, though there was just as good reason to do so.

*

The political situation in East Germany began to deteriorate in 1985. The reasons varied. The economy was weaker, and people were becoming increasingly concerned about ecological problems, following the example of the West German Greens. Small demonstrations about specific problems became commonplace. From 1987 onwards the Stasi had orders to crack down on illegal demonstrations. In 1987, for instance, small groups of a dozen or more would form in the pedestrian precinct in the centre of Leipzig to demand the right to emigrate. The Stasi would charge at them and beat them up in front of the crowds. There was increasing intolerance in cultural matters, so that more and more writers like Wolf H. found it impossible to get their books published in the GDR, and had to send them to West Germany. That was illegal, and created more trouble for them. The authorities found petty ways of getting back at them. The novelist Stefan Heym, who had fled to the United States after Hitler came to power and then returned to East Germany in 1952 as a matter of personal conviction, was charged with currency offences. He had been forced to smuggle his work to the West for publication.

But by the end of 1987 the government was trying to temper its new

ferocity towards outright dissenters by being more lenient to those who
wanted to travel abroad. This was disastrous from the government's point
of view, and from then on things began to disintegrate. The reason was
simple: up to that point it had become reluctantly accepted that no one
could leave. It was a condition of life in the GDR. Now the authorities
made it possible for people with close relatives in the West to visit them.
The system was cumbersome. To obtain permission to visit your uncle
you had to show four different birth certificates: yours, your uncle's, your
father's or mother's, and their father's. But it breached the prison walls.
From now on there were two different groups in society, a small one which
could travel abroad and a much larger one which could not. The larger one
became increasingly angry and vociferous.

So the government widened the rules. Now you could visit not just
your parents, children, uncles and aunts, but cousins as well: even
distant cousins. The result was that something like half the population
was eligible to go to the West, while the remainder became more bitter
still. And those who went and came back were bitter too, realizing now
the full extent to which they and their part of Germany had fallen
behind by comparison with the West. At this stage, halfway through
1988, it was clear that the process was out of control.

The carrot was laid aside once more in favour of the stick. The Stasi
became more restrictive. The police had orders to be more aggressive to
those who came to apply for a passport. But ordinary people were
becoming more aggressive as well. There seemed to be only one topic of
conversation everywhere – who was allowed to visit the West and who
was not. The grounds on which people were turned down seemed to be
increasingly absurd: the writing on the necessary birth certificates was
illegible, the names in question were too common for the police to be
certain the relationship was genuine.

But if the right to travel preoccupied most people, the opposition
activists were increasingly concerned with the wider issues of the
citizen's relationship to the state and the way the country was run. Ever
since the 1960s opposition organizations had been in operation, often
under the umbrella of the Evangelical church. To all intents and
purposes they were human rights organizations, but because of
pressure from the authorities they had to concentrate on ecological
questions. This was not by any means a cover; it was a useful indirect
method of striking at the issues that mattered. These 'green' groups met
in Protestant churches, even though many of the people who attended
were radicals with little interest in religion. That had the effect of
pushing the Evangelical church itself further towards radicalism. And
the protests became increasingly courageous.

Most radicals date the rise to significance of political activism in the GDR to the Rosa Luxemburg demonstration of January 1988 in East Berlin. The idea of holding it came from the new groups which had been springing up, and it found little favour with more established opposition figures. When it became known that demonstrators demanding the right to travel to the West would be taking part, many of the older activists decided to stay away. Their line had always been that they were citizens of the GDR who wanted normal human rights. Many of those who turned out to commemorate the murders of Rosa Luxemburg and Karl Liebknecht, founders of the German Communist Party, regarded themselves as Germans *tout court*. So at the demonstration about half the placards read 'We Want The Right To Leave', while the others carried the best-known quotation from Rosa Luxemburg's writings: 'Freedom is the freedom to think differently.'

The police beat both persuasions with equal vigour. The leading figures – the artist Bärbel Bohley, her boyfriend Werner Fischer, and Stefan Krawschech, a song-writer and poet – were arrested. The police gave them the option of staying in prison or leaving the GDR. Bärbel Bohley decided to stay. When news of the choice offered to her leaked out, her supporters rallied in Leipzig in surprising numbers. Four thousand people demonstrated against the suggestion that she should leave the country.

Nevertheless she decided that the time for such demonstrations was not ripe, so she made a compromise with the authorities: she would leave the GDR for six months, if they would undertake to allow her back at the end of that time. She went to England, where she worked quietly as an artist, avoiding controversy. Six months later she was not stopped when she returned to the GDR. For her supporters in the small opposition groups it had been a valuable experience. They became more assertive, and even though the demonstrations which followed were consistently broken up by the police, those who took part in them became increasingly brave. Larger umbrella groupings slowly grew: Democracy Now and Democratic Awakening, and then, on 11 September 1989, the largest and most important of all, the New Forum.

As the local elections of May 1989 drew closer, it was clear that the old fear of authority was fading. During the campaign people became more hostile to the state security apparatus, more critical of the government. It became common for groups to hold election meetings in church halls rather than public places. The issues were discussed in an open way, and radical criticisms were voiced. Soon they began to be heard at larger open meetings, regardless of who might be there taking notes. In a number of towns and cities throughout the GDR citizens' committees were formed to monitor the conduct of the forthcoming elections. The government dismissed them as 'illegal groupings'.

In Leipzig, the seat of opposition, the Stasi received orders to use all necessary force to re-establish the position. They staged dozens of raids on the flats and lodgings of students, often in the early hours of the morning, demanding to see people's identity documents. One student put a placard reading 'Free Elections' in his window. The night before the poll the Stasi broke into his house, beat him up, threw him downstairs and took him to the police station where he was again beaten up. The following morning, badly bruised, he was allowed to go free. The offending placard was destroyed.

The election duly took place in an atmosphere of heightened suspicion and hostility, and the count began. The citizens' committees which had been set up right across the GDR scrutinized the count at the local polling-stations with great care, and for the most part ensured that the results were accurate. But the system demanded that the votes should then be taken to district electoral offices for the overall result. Here the counting was done behind closed doors. Documents discovered after the fall of the government showed that in most cases the local Party secretary and the local head of the Stasi manipulated the district returns. When the results were made public there was uproar. They bore little relation to the results as checked at the local polling stations. Allegations of electoral fraud came pouring in. The government dismissed them as groundless and inspired by the Western media as part of a concerted attempt to damage the state. Of the many complaints addressed to the State Prosecutor by individuals, not a single one was upheld.

In the days after the local elections groups formed spontaneously to discuss the situation. In Berlin a group of about four hundred people met in one of the city's grander Protestant churches to formulate a letter to the Council of State asking for an official investigation into the conduct of the elections. As the group left the church to go to the Council of State building with the letter, Stasi buses and trucks were waiting outside. The security police set about them with sticks and truncheons, and dragged them into the buses where they were beaten up.

The case of a seventeen-year-old girl, Helga M., was typical. She was kept in prison and interrogated all night long. She was not allowed to sit down. A bright light was shone in her face. Her interrogators tried hard to make her confess that she had been told by Westerners to take part in the protest. They asked her time and again to act as an informer in the group. She and everyone else who refused to give in were fined. Helga, who earned 200 Marks a month as an apprentice, was fined 300 Marks.

She refused to pay. Then followed a series of appointments at the police station. Each time the Stasi threatened to take action against her. In the end nothing was done.

On 10 September the new government in Hungary, still composed of Communist Party members but post-Communist in its attitudes, announced it was opening its borders with Austria. The fortifications had already been removed. The barbed wire was rolled up along the full length of the frontier. An enterprising metal-working company bought it and proceeded to turn it into thousands of little mounted trophies ('A Piece of the Iron Curtain'). President Bush was presented with one during his visit to Budapest in July. From the GDR there was an exodus on the scale of 1961, a haemorrhage of population which came to threaten its economic and social existence. On that day alone 6,000 East Germans crossed into Hungary, and another 13,000 were to leave before the GDR closed the border on 3 October. The route was long and circuitous, but people drove their Wartburg and Trabant cars through Czechoslovakia to Hungary, for which no exit visas were required, and then on to the West. They received every assistance from the border guards.

The refugees were free to drive through Austria into West Germany by way of Bavaria. Camps were set up on the Bavarian border to look after the refugees. Special supplies of two-stroke petrol were sent to ensure that the Trabants could make the journey. The new arrivals quickly spread out all over West Germany. Most of them were young couples in their twenties and thirties, who found work quickly.

Like the oxwagons of the Voortrekkers, the symbol of this exodus became the Trabant: small, ugly boxes of insecure metal, painted in a limited range of colours (six, according to the manufacturers, though you only saw yellow, rust red, grey and blue), designed in the early 1960s and never changed. It took the average East German ten years of waiting to take delivery of a Trabant. When it came, it had to be made to last. Its design was primitive: low, poorly sprung seats, a single dial for speed and kilometrage and petrol, a gear-shift on the steering column shaped like the horn of a bull. For the lower gears it was easier to reach through the steering wheel than to grasp it from the outside.

The speedometer went up to 120 kilometres per hour, but its maximum practical speed was about eighty-five. You could hear it coming from some way off, its engine buzzing and spluttering angrily. The two-stroke engine was too dirty for West German exhaust emission standards, and an exception had to be made for them. As for fuel, the big petrol companies were encouraged by the West German government to set up pumps with two-stroke fuel near the points of entry for the refugees and their cars. The Germans called them 'Trabis', and at first they were wildly popular. As the weeks and months passed their slowness and exhaust fumes were the cause of growing irritation to the impatient, fastidious Westerners.

★

For most of the period of the exodus Erich Honecker was seriously ill, following his collapse at the Warsaw Pact summit in Bucharest. He played little part in the making of decisions. The government swung from ferocity to weakness and back again. Everyone knew the fortieth anniversary of the founding of the state, on 7 October, would be a critical moment. Once again Leipzig saw the biggest demonstrations. For a number of years there were peace services in the Protestant churches there every Monday, after which the congregation would go in procession to the pedestrian precinct in the old town carrying candles. Now human rights organizations and radical groups joined in.

The GDR had been one of the few countries to congratulate the leadership of Deng Xiaoping, Yang Shangkun and Li Peng after it had shot down the demonstrators in Tiananmen Square and Chang'an Avenue. There seemed to be a real possibility that the growing demonstrations in Leipzig might be dealt with in similar fashion. The nerve of the government was now in question.

There were signs of growing discontent everywhere. People were no longer as scared of the authorities as they had been. The tension was building up. The Interior Ministry's record of threats received in different parts of the country showed a remarkable increase over normal times:

Anonymous telephone call to the regional office of the SED in Marienberg, 09.35, 4.10.89: 'Your place is going to be blown skyhigh, you miserable rabble.'

Anonymous telephone call to Lichtenberg railway station, 23.50, 4.10.89: 'Here's a birthday present for Erich Honecker: bombs have been planted at Lichtenberg and Schönefeld stations. It's going to be a lot of fun. They're set to go off at two o'clock.'

Anonymous telephone call to the Volkspolizei station in Coswig, 10.00, 5.10.89: 'You arse-lickers, you ought to know that your place is going to be blown up today.'

Anonymous telephone call to the central warehouse in Dresden, 10.30, 5.10.89: 'Three ejector-seats available, deadline 11.15.'

Anonymous letter received by the *Ostseezeitung* newspaper in Rostock, 6.10.89: '40th anniversary of the GDR. . .On 6 October, 16.00, attacks on the *Ostseezeitung* and the Dierkow market. We want freedom. Death to Honecker. We mean it!'

Anonymous telephone call to the regional office of the Staatssicherheit in Freiburg, 11.57, 6.10.89: 'Write this down: We're going to blast the presidential platform in Berlin tomorrow. Message ends.'

Nothing happened, of course; anonymous calls rarely come to anything. But the guest of honour at the celebrations on 7 October exploded a device of his own. Mikhail Gorbachev allowed it to be known he had warned Erich Honecker that Soviet troops would not be available for use against demonstrators in the GDR. Speculation that he was encouraging the younger and more liberal members of the Politburo to overthrow Honecker grew when he said, 'Life punishes those who hold back.' That evening there were demonstrations in Berlin, Dresden, Magdeburg, Leipzig, Plauen, Karl-Marx-Stadt, Potsdam and Arnstadt. The Stasi broke up most of them with great brutality.

But it was on the following day, in Leipzig, that the great test came. Leipzig, where the Lutheran churches had given great support to the demonstrators, was pre-eminent in the campaign for reform and democracy. Early in the morning of 8 October the Stasi went from factory to factory and office to office, warning people that they shouldn't take part in the big demonstration which was planned for that afternoon. Schools closed early. So did many of the shops. The centre of the city was unnaturally quiet all day. No trains came in to the main railway station. The station had been put to another use: it became the headquarters of a large military force.

The opposition groups later established with some precision what happened that day. They found that the military and the Stasi had orders to open fire on the demonstrators if there was no alternative way of stopping them. The Tiananmen option, which Honecker had praised in June, was available in Leipzig. Several thousand troops were deployed. Units took up position on every street corner, and tanks and armoured personnel carriers were drawn up at all the main intersections. On the rooftops near the station marksmen were positioned. Some were equipped with machine guns. The army had arranged trailers and trucks to carry the wounded to selected barns and sheds on farms outside the city. Everything was ready.

If the troops had opened fire, as in China, it might have worked. A show of overwhelming strength could have stopped the demonstrations and saved the political life of Erich Honecker, just as it stopped the demonstrations in Tiananmen Square and saved Deng Xiaoping. Equally it could have brought about Honecker's downfall even more quickly, and might have led to civil disorder throughout the country. The gamble was simply too great to take. Honecker and Egon Krenz, the Politburo member responsible for security, had created this formidable military build-up. Now, as 70,000 people gathered in the centre of Leipzig, the decision had to be taken on what to do about the situation.

Egon Krenz later claimed the credit for having deterred Honecker from giving the order to open fire. But he was himself fighting for political acceptance in the aftermath of Honecker's fall, and his evidence cannot necessarily be taken at face value. The indications are that the army, and perhaps even the Stasi lacked the will to carry out its orders. That being the case, it was easier to convince the politicians and soldiers who were part of the chain of command that it would be disastrous to shoot down the demonstrators. Almost certainly, the real credit should go to a small number of SED Party leaders in Leipzig itself. And there is evidence that Soviet officials got wind of the possibility that a massacre was being planned and warned against it.

The demonstrators marched through the streets, and the soldiers watched them go. The marksmen peered down from their positions on the roof tops. The trucks and makeshift ambulances stayed where they were drawn up. The barns outside the city remained empty. The opposition had faced down the threat. From now on it was clear that whatever the Stasi might do with clubs and tear gas, no one who appeared on the streets faced the risk of being shot dead. The government was on the run. Nine days later, on 18 October, Erich Honecker resigned as Party leader and was replaced by Egon Krenz. Five out of a Politburo of eighteen were purged within two weeks.

Nearly 200,000 people had crossed into the West, half of them illegally, during the first ten months of 1989. Soon a massive new exodus of East Germans began when Czechoslovakia opened its borders to them on 3 November. On 7 November the entire government resigned. The following day the Politburo itself resigned. Krenz was re-elected Party leader, Hans Modrow was proposed as prime minister. In Moscow, the Soviet leadership shrugged its collective shoulders. It became known in the West as the 'Sinatra Doctrine': let them do it their way.

'It's their business,' said Gennadi Gerasimov, the foreign ministry spokesman.

The SED was on its own. The Wall, which had shored it up for so long, had become the instrument of its destruction.

7
TUMBLING DOWN

Why did you not take this down 20 years ago?

Graffiti on Eastern side of Berlin Wall, January 1990

It was a pleasant enough flat, though the rooms were small. From the window you could see the Reichstag, the Brandenburg Gate and the empty site between the inner and outer Wall where Hitler's Führer-bunker had once been. It was the kind of property which would command big money when Berlin was eventually united. The present occupant was finding it difficult to pay the absurdly low rent which the East German authorities were still charging.

'I have a wardrobe full of expensive suits,' he said. 'Before long I may have to eat them.'

His attractive Russian wife smiled at him and stroked his thin grey hair affectionately. He began to smile too, but he was a worried man. All round us were the accoutrements of a prosperous existence: bottles of Scotch, books from the West, an expensive hi-fi set, some good records and tapes. And now he had nothing except these things, and no means of earning a living. He had not been trained for that. I felt as though I were in the apartment of a Romanov prince after the 1917 Revolution. But this was no minor royalty. Günter Schabowski had been the general secretary of the Communist SED in East Berlin and a member of the Politburo: one of the most powerful men in East Germany.

Erich Honecker had been overthrown and was in disgrace, the SED had been thoroughly reorganized and had changed its name to the PDS – the Party for Democratic Socialism. All the old figures like Schabowski and Egon Krenz had been thrown out of the Party by early December. Krenz had become a wealthy man. He had sold his story to the right-wing tabloid *Bild* in West Germany for a fee which he insisted was not as high as 1.5 million Deutschemarks. Günter Schabowski refused to do that kind of thing. But he was hoping to earn some money from writing his own account of the collapse of Marxism-Leninism in the GDR.

I had come to see him to ask about one single episode in the chain of events which brought about the SED's downfall. Time and again people in East Berlin had spoken about the miraculous way in which the opening of the Berlin Wall had been announced to the world on the night of 9 November 1989. In East Germany this had now taken on something of the supernatural aura of the Angel of Mons or the leaning Virgin of Albert. Everyone who watched the moment on television had different versions of it. Some said an East German radio correspondent had come up and handed him a piece of paper, which he had then read out. Others said the paper was brought in by a messenger whom no one recognized.

'If you find out how that announcement came about,' a minor government official said to me, 'you must tell everyone. It's the great mystery of our time.'

'There was something very strange about it, I know that,' said a Marxist historian. 'No one has been able to explain it satisfactorily. I'm positive that the Politburo didn't intend it to come out like this.'

Some senior figures in the opposition, whose lives and careers had been radically changed as a result of the announcement, seemed to regard it almost as an occult intervention in Germany's affairs.

'It was a miracle,' said one senior CDU official in East Berlin. 'We still don't know who wrote that small piece of paper which ordered the Wall to come down. It was read out in a most extraordinary way at the end of a press conference. It created such amazement. Even the man who read it out was amazed.'

The man who read it out was Günter Schabowski. I had come to his flat to find out if it really was the Finger of God which had placed the piece of paper in front of him. It took him a long time to decide whether to tell me. He had, he said, refused to talk to everyone else. There was silence. His wife made tea in the kitchen. His pet parrot squawked. The lift clattered into life outside his front door. Finally an innate courtesy overcame him, even though he felt he might be lowering the value of his own exclusive account of the Miracle of the Wall. He decided to talk.

At the time, Schabowski was the Central Committee's secretary for the media as well as being a member of the Politburo. He had a reputation as a straight and honest man. He wasn't scared to go onto the streets after the fall of Honecker and argue out the unpopular policies of the SED with ordinary people. Shortly before 7 p.m. on the evening of 9 November he gave a press conference to announce the latest decisions of the Council of Ministers. Much of it dealt with the new philosophy of the Party. It was now accepted, he said, that the GDR was a pluralist society. There were details about the forthcoming Party conference.

Schabowski came to the end of these announcements. There was an awkward pause. The 300 journalists who were sitting there became restless. He whispered something to the man next to him, and shuffled his papers. The man next to him leaned over. A piece of paper appeared in Schabowski's hand. He read from it slowly and hesitantly.

> This will be interesting for you: today the decision was taken to make it possible for all citizens to leave the country through the official border crossing points. All citizens of the GDR can now be issued with visas for the purposes of travel or visiting relatives in the West. This order is to take effect at once.

Everyone started talking. A correspondent from GDR radio stood up and asked for more details. Schabowski had used the expression *'unverzüglich'* ('at once', 'immediately'); when precisely did that mean? Schabowski gave no clear answer. He was still holding onto the piece of paper. A crowd of journalists gathered round him, trying to find out further details. How soon was *'unverzüglich'*? Schabowski was confused and tired.

'It just means straightaway,' he said.

The art of politics is to create the illusion of competence. An illusionist who admits to letting the doves escape from his inside pockets is an illusionist who has given up all hope of a return booking. Sitting in his flat overlooking the Brandenburg Gate, Günter Schabowski was at first unwilling to admit to any confusion in announcing the breaching of the Wall.

'I finished giving my information about the Central Committee business, and then I turned to the next item on the agenda.'

I pressed him. Finally he admitted it. The mysterious piece of paper, the note which had been passed to him by some superhuman agency, written with the pen of an angel, was the typed-up note of the decision which the Politburo had reached that afternoon. It had been on top of his sheaf of papers when he came into the press conference. Somehow it became mixed up with the rest. So instead of reading it first he had to go through Any Other Business, in the hope of coming across it later. He discovered it at the bottom of the pile. End of miracle.

The decision had been taken by the full Politburo a few hours before on the afternoon of 9 November. It was an acknowledgement of the anger building up in East German society over the inequity of the rules governing permission to visit the West.

> The fact that some were allowed to go and some weren't was silly and Kafkaesque. It demanded a solution. but it had to be done quickly. We didn't have time to think about it carefully. We had to make our draft programme public fast, and that had to be in it. There was already the draft

of a special law on the subject in existence, and so we in the Politburo decided to instruct the government to take some of the points from this draft. It had to be written in a way people could understand. We didn't want it to be in a kind of india-rubber language which could be stretched in one way or the other. We wanted to make it quite clear: if you want to go to the West, you can go. Full stop. There would have to be some transitional measures, because most people didn't have passports. But our aim was to have a system like you do in the West, whereby if you have a passport, you can leave the country.

I was unwilling to interrupt the flow, in case he decided that he'd told me more than enough already. But it was important to know whether the members of the Politburo understood the significance of what they were doing. Had anyone, for instance, suggested at the meeting that this was really the end of the Wall, and might well be the end of Communist government in the GDR – the end, indeed, of the GDR itself?

No one realized. No one said anything like that. No one really thought about the result. We knew we had to take this step. As for its leading to the end of the GDR, none of us expected that at all. And I have to say that none of the opposition groups in the country expected it either. We hoped, quite simply, that this measure would create a better GDR, more open to human rights and so on. We thought the Wall was stable, I must say.

In its way, then, it was a kind of miracle. Without the suddenness of the announcement, the impact of the opening of the Wall would have been less. Without the great outflow of surprise and delight at the Berlin Wall, the tidal wave which swept across Czechoslovakia might not have happened as it did. And without the suddenness of the revolution in Czechoslovakia, people in Romania might not have been emboldened to come out and challenge Ceausescu.

The nuclear reaction required a powerful detonating explosion. That had been provided by Günter Schabowski. Now he sat in his small but disturbingly expensive flat overlooking the Wall which he had helped to demolish, wondering how he was going to make a living. His papers had been mixed up by the finger of history.

The first news that people could pass freely to the West was broadcast on an East German television news bulletin at 7.30 that evening. The pictures of the celebrated press conference by Schabowski were broadcast, but there was little explanation. Immediately the switchboard of the television station was swamped with callers trying to find out more. The director of news ordered that Schabowski's announcement should be repeated at regular intervals through the evening. By now, too, it was being reported on West German television. People in East Berlin were switching backwards and forwards, watching the coverage.

The message was relayed to the West German Chancellor, Helmut Kohl, who was on an official visit to Poland. A few minutes later he was stopped by a West German television reporter as he arrived for a formal dinner. Kohl was not a man to match great occasions with inspired sentiments. His concern was with the outflow of East Germans to the West:

> The solution cannot be for many people to come to West Germany. Living conditions should be improved in East Germany, so they stay there. It's in our interests that they should stay.

In Berlin itself, people were starting to head out onto the streets to see what was going on for themselves. Schabowski's slightly vague expression, that people would be able to obtain exist visas *unverzüglich*, immediately or at once, seemed unlikely to mean that anyone could cross that night. In a society inured to waiting for everything from officialdom, it was hard to think that police stations would issue the necessary piece of paper so quickly. At the Invalidenstrasse crossing, a little to the north of the Brandenburg Gate, the first East Germans to arrive there at around nine o'clock were told by the officer in charge that they would need a stamp in their identity cards. This, he said, could be obtained only from their local police station. They went away, disappointed.

About a mile further north at the Bornholmerstrasse crossing-point, the situation was altogether different. Shortly before 9.30 a couple in their late thirties decided to test out the system. They walked through to the glass-fronted booth where the border guard sat. He gave them a smile and said they could go through without a visa. He promised them that there would be no problem as long as the same back through the same check-point that night. Several journalists saw them coming through to the western side, but they were so matter-of-fact about it all that it seemed as though they were Westerners returning. No one stopped them to ask them questions.

Erich Knorr, an engineer in his mid-forties, had been out late that evening in East Berlin, seeing friends. His wife had left him a few months before, and his daughter was at university. His flat was cold and uninviting as he let himself in. Automatically, he went over to turn on the television. The sound of voices made things seem a little less lonely. He was still not used to living by himself. It was around 10.30, and the station he had switched on, SFB in West Berlin, was showing a discussion programme of some kind. Knorr was making a cup of coffee when he caught the words, 'And now we're going over to our reporter at the Invalidenstrasse crossing-point.'

Idly, thinking there might have been some shooting incident, he wandered back into the sitting room. The reporter was talking excitedly in front of a crowd of a few dozen people. As he spoke a young man came running up out of the darkness and shouted at the camera, 'They've opened the check-point in the Bornholmerstrasse!' Erich Knorr knew now that the unthinkable had happened. He lived close to the Bornholmerstrasse, in the Schönhauserallee. He rang a girl he knew to see if she wanted to come with him to the West, but she said she was too tired, and didn't believe it anyway.

He left his coffee untasted on the table and set off. Out in the street he broke into a run. As he turned into the road that led to the crossing-point he ran into crowds of people heading in the same direction. There were people of all ages, many with young children who had been wakened up so the whole family could experience this extraordinary moment. Knorr was unencumbered by wife or family. For the first time in weeks, being on his own was an advantage. He pushed through to the front.

He could see the check-point now. They were letting people through very slowly, checking their identity. A big crowd had built up. From time to time there was chanting:

'Take the Wall down! Take the Wall down!'

There was no anger, but there was real impatience at the slowness of it all.

Then the border guards came pouring out of the building, about a dozen of them, and Erich thought there was going to be trouble. He'd worked his way almost through to the front by now, and he was afraid that if they charged he might be injured. But the guards ignored the crowd. They fanned out in front of the post and started shifting the heavy blocks of concrete that lay across the street to prevent cars from passing through more than one at a time. The gates opened. An officer made a gesture with his hand, like a doorman at an hotel. There were no more formalities: the way to the West lay open. Everyone cheered and shouted and sang, and they surged forward, ten abreast.

At that moment, where the road passes over two Stadtbahn lines, one serving the East and the other the West, a couple of trains happened to come along at the same time. As they passed the Bornholmer crossing they both stopped and hooted their horns, while the passengers waved and blew kisses. Erich Knorr was shouting and weeping with the rest of them now, and when he reached the other side of the Wall people came running out of the houses and flats on the West and offered them things: cups of coffee, glasses of champagne, flowers, and West German Marks. Erich saw someone throwing a handful of useless Ostmarks, the non-convertible currency of the East, into the air. The little notes were picked up by the mild November wind and fluttered over the heads of the crowd. Everyone cheered to see them go.

> I can't tell you what it meant to us. All these years we'd been bottled up in our little part of Germany, second-class citizens that nobody wanted, in a country most of us didn't really want to be in. I'd been a prisoner, and suddenly I wasn't a prisoner any longer. I could have shouted and sung and waved my arms. I couldn't stop smiling. A girl came up and gave me a kiss, and I thought I was really in heaven.

A crowd control van belonging to the West Berlin police drove up. Someone made an announcement:

> Everyone should stay calm. No need to get excited. Buses are coming to take you to the Ku'damm.

The crowd cheered. Erich didn't want to wait for the bus. He took the U-bahn to the Kurfürstendamm. The city authorities had just decided that it should be free, since most of the people using it would be unable to pay.

> I got out at the Ku'damm station and walked out into the street. The lights just seemed so bright, and there was so much money about. I felt like some country cousin, shabby and poor and innocent, somehow. It was a little too much for me, the emotion and everything. I'd been planning to wander round the shops and see what there was to buy. But suddenly I didn't feel like that any more. I just walked down to the Gedächtniskirche [the bombed church which has been left unrestored as a memorial] and stood there looking at it in the darkness. The last time I'd seen it was 12 August 1961, the day before they built that accursed Wall. I was nineteen years old then, and now I was forty-eight. I'd never been allowed to see the West in all that time. I was too sad to do any more rejoicing. I just went back to my flat and went to bed. But it was a wonderful memory, all the same.

A British student, Sean Salsarola, was in West Berlin when he heard the news on an East German radio station. He ran to Checkpoint Charlie and made his way into the East at around nine o'clock. Almost everyone at that point was heading in the opposite direction, but Sean had a plan. He headed for the Grand Hotel farther down the Friedrichstrasse, an expensive place on Western lines where most of the foreign television crews stayed. In the lobby he spotted a cameraman and sound recordist. It was Ingo Prosser and Mark McCauley, who had filmed the massacre in Tiananmen Square with me. They were working that night with one of my colleagues, Brian Hanrahan, and Sean's knowledge of East Berlin was invaluable to them as they filmed their remarkable pictures of the night's events.

Elsewhere, the night was loud with singing, cheering and chanting. At Checkpoint Charlie people were singing, suitably enough, the song 'Wilkommen, welcome, bienvenu' – from the musical *Cabaret*. An elderly woman came through in slippers and nightclothes, with a coat over the top, explaining that her daughter had telephoned her from the West and said, 'Mama, Mama, you can come to West Berlin to see us.' So there she was. A young waiter had just come through a check-point from the East when a middle-aged West Berliner came up to him and put a 50 Mark note in his hand.

'Go and buy yourself a beer. There'll never be another day like this.'

A West Berlin teacher took advantage of the open border to drive into the East to see some friends. Then they all headed back.

'The border guards stopped me as I came through. "Have you got anything to declare?" "No," I said, "only four Easterners".'

At the Sonnenallee crossing, which was also crowded with people, a group of young people from the West clambered on to the roof of an East German watch tower. A few hours before they might have been shot dead for attempting it. Now the officer in charge just stood and smiled indulgently at them.

'Be careful you don't fall down,' he said.

A little farther along the border a group of people struggled to raise the barrier across the road.

'This is crazy,' said an officer; 'we haven't opened that for years. It's completely rusted up.'

Policemen from East and West gathered in the middle of the street, talking to each other for the first time.

People crammed the Ku'damm all night long. The air was filled with the sound of car horns, and the long lines of Trabants and Wartburgs filled it with something else as well: the blue clouds of their unrestricted exhaust gas. The Ku'damm stank, but nobody cared.

Joe's Biersalon in the Ku'damm was the place where a lot of Easterners congregated. Joe had fled from the East himself in 1961.

'Tonight,' he announced, 'anyone can pay in Ostmarks.'

He lost heavily on the exchange, of course. But he probably lost more over the distinctive beer glasses from his bar. Dozens disappeared as souvenirs.

'*Mensch, bin ick denn hier uff'm anderen Planeten?*' someone asked, in a heavy Berlin accent: 'Hey, man, am I on another planet?'

But it was the Wall itself which was the great magnet. As the crowds gathered, the boldest spirits started to test the extent of the East German government's commitment to the new era. Where the Wall starts to bulge out in a semi-circle to take in the area round the Brandenburg Gate, two young men in their early twenties vaulted over the low railings and stood beside it. In the arc lights on the western side the wild graffiti – pleas, accusations, and endless names of people and places – stood out like coloured clouds around their heads. One made a stirrup of his hands and launched the other upwards. Fingers scrabbled until he found a purchase. He got to his knees, then stood, then raised his arms over his head, fists clenched. The crowd roared. A new Germany and a new Europe, for good or ill, was being born.

*

It took me hours to get to Berlin after the announcement that the Wall was to be opened. I had been in Poland, covering Chancellor Kohl's visit, and I had to fight my way on crowded planes across Central Europe. When I arrived, the party was still going on. Trabants were everywhere, crammed with laughing, singing, shouting people. Groups wandered along the streets, half-a-dozen abreast, arm in arm. The road that leads to the Brandenburg Gate on the western side, the Street of 17 June, was crammed with cars and people, eight or nine lanes across. The lights of several dozen television organizations were directed on to the Wall. More faintly they illuminated the Gate which rose above it surmounted by the Quadriga, an unreal green in the floodlights, Victory's back towards us as she faced down the Unter den Linden in what had the previous day been hostile territory.

It was then that I saw a sight which I, as a latecomer to the festivities, had never thought to see. Hundreds of people were standing, sitting, squatting, dancing on top of the Wall. Some held sparklers, and waved them in neat childish circles or described outlines with them in the cold night air. There was singing: '*Geh'n wir mal rüber, die Mauer ist weg*' [We're going over, the Wall's gone] and '*Krenz, wir schlagen Dir die Tür an*' [Krenz, we're knocking on your door].

I had a lot to do, to prepare myself for a live broadcast, but I could not help looking round all the time at the unthinkable sight: something which had been the symbol of division and cruelty for nearly three decades had become a symbol of sheer delight I remembered all the times I'd been here in the past: times of tension between the Germanies, times when political leaders came to make their ritual condemnations of a division of Europe and of Germany with which they were thoroughly content. I looked up at the watch-towers from which everyone who came close to the Wall was once photographed as an obscure form of intimidation. Now the guards were leaning out and a number of them joining in the singing. The following morning they would be clambering around on top of the Wall as well, grinning at the western side which was no longer forbidden fruit for them.

I duly stood in front of the Brandenburg Gate in the television lights and answered questions about an exciting present and an unknowable future. Halfway through a reply, as I was speaking to one of the largest television audiences for any news programme in British history, the satellite link with London was accidentally cut. It was an absurd and humiliating moment. I slunk away from the camera position feeling deeply depressed. And then I looked across at the Wall and saw how trivial it was to worry, on a night of such unparalleled pleasure for so many people. My colleagues, all of them good friends of mine, walked with me along the line of the Wall in the direction of the Potsdamerplatz. It was a dirt path through woods and bushes, which had been the centre of government in Berlin. Hitler's Chancellery and his bunker had once lain on the other side of the Wall. But the destruction of April and May 1945 and the tourniquet of the Wall itself, had turned the heart of the city back to its origins, like the Forum in Rome, overgrown and haunted by wild animals.

Now, though, the crowds moved along the pathway so thickly that it was hard for us to keep together. And all the way along there was the sound of hammering. People were beating at the Wall with pickaxes and chisels by the light of candles, anxious to demonstrate their mastery over something which had mastered them so long. Great shadows were thrown across the face of the Wall as the picks were raised. The shuddering of steel against concrete jarred onlookers as well as the would-be demolishers. But their persistence was paying off. They crashed away at the joins between the slabs of concrete and made holes like wounds, so that in some places you could peer through into the wide no-man's-land beyond. There, one of the busiest intersections in pre-war Germany, the Potsdamerplatz itself, had been transformed into an open strip of land nearly a quarter of a mile wide between the eastern and western sections of the Wall, planted with great arc-lights to detect escapes.

As the hammering went on, there was an eerie echo which seemed more than just an echo; and when the man with the pickaxe on the western side paused to ease his aching muscles the sound continued from the other side. A roar of delight broke out as everyone realised the

Wall was under attack at the same place from the eastern side as well. At last another wound was opened by alternate strokes from East and West; and by the light of candles and torches a hand came through the small gap, and the man with the pickaxe on our side shook it. At such a time, genuine miracles seemed to be taking place.

We wandered back to the Street of 17 June. The vans selling Wurst were doing good business. So were the stalls where they were pouring out steaming cups of Glühwein. As the steam rose it took on the blueish colour of the television lights focused on the Brandenburg Gate. From a girl with an excited face and high voice I bought an early copy of the following morning's *Bild* newspaper, crude, raw, nationalistic. There was the picture in colour of the crowds standing on the Wall at the Gate, a hazy version of the real thing which was bright and sharp in front of me in the chilly night air. *'Deutschland umarmt sich'*, it said: 'Germany embraces itself'. And in larger letters underneath, *'Einigkeit und Recht und Freiheit'*, words from the national anthem: unity and right and freedom. All round the front page was a border of black, red and gold, the national colours of a Germany which was suddenly becoming much bigger and more powerful.

★

The following days were unforgettable. I went to Glienicke Bridge, where the far south-eastern spur of West Berlin reaches out towards Potsdam. I had last been there in February 1986 when the Soviet dissident Anatoly Shcharansky was released in exchange for East German spies held by West Germany. Then it had been white and frozen, and the iron bridge with its red flags fluttering at the other end had seemed like the gateway to another world. Shcharansky's tiny figure appeared from a Russian car which had stopped on the centre of the bridge. He was escorted over to an American vehicle and driven away. The East German spies, a bus-load of them, were changed over to another bus. Soon it began to get dark. Over the snow-covered bridge a light came on and illuminated the red flag. It was like every Cold War spy novel ever written.

Now Glienicke Bridge was just another way across a river. Bus services from East and West put it back on their schedules after 28 years, and this time they were delivering shoppers, not spies. Children bounded around their parents in the unseasonably warm air. The sunshine lit up the faces of people who had once stared across the bridge and could now walk across it at will. The East German border guards smiled and banged their gloved hands together and scarcely bothered to look at the identity documents which each person obediently tendered.

We filmed down by the waterside. An East German patrol boat spotted our television camera. A few days before its job had been to search the cold waters for any sign of people swimming across, and shoot them if necessary. Now it staged a little display for us, speeding past and turning suddenly so the spray rose up in an arc and made rainbows in the afternoon sunshine. A flock of wild ducks exploded protestingly into the air as the patrol boat passed them, wheeled overhead, and eased themselves down onto a quieter stretch of water. We went back to the bridge and watched the lines of people heading eastwards across it. They were carrying the shopping they had bought with their own hard-currency savings and with the 100 Marks which Bonn gave them as a celebratory gift. A dog-end of quotation from a Shakespeare comedy floated across my mind: 'You happy winners all.'

*

No country, perhaps, has come out of a major war and behaved as well and as modestly as West Germany since 1945. It has rejected its twentieth-century history almost in its entirety. For much of the forty-five years after Hitler the most frequent complaint of its neighbours and allies was that it failed to translate its economic power into military or political power: not a complaint levelled at Germany previously. Bonn became the quiet capital of a state that was pre-eminently modest. Diplomats and foreign correspondents who were assigned there would groan inwardly at the worthy boredom that lay ahead of them.

Now, within a few November days and nights that had all changed. Helmut Kohl, the bumbling Chancellor whose clumsiness had got him into all sorts of problems in the past, suddenly became the modern Bismarck. He was unifying Germany. People who had paid little attention to the Federal Republic in the past paid attention to it now. Tadeusz Mazowiecki, the Polish prime minister who had been a Solidarity journalist, remarked that repressed hopes were springing into life. It was true; but so were many repressed fears.

Chancellor Kohl had first arrived at Warsaw airport on the afternoon of 9 November – the day the Wall was breached. He was followed down the aircraft steps by dozens of German businessmen, each with a briefcase bulging with plans and agreements. Over the next few days they fanned out across Poland, signing agreements and partnership deals. My colleagues and I followed them round. We were interested in the scope of Germany's new involvement in its old economic hinterland in Central Europe.

In an elderly office block of the Stalinist period in Warsaw the workmen were in. They were nailing down carpets, replacing bits of damaged woodwork, putting in new electric wiring. The Foreign Investment Agency of the Polish government was being set up at speed. The head of it, Zdzislaw Skakuj, sat in the only office they had completed. A little brass model of a ship was on his desk, and he played with it from time to time. He was a marine engineer by training, not a businessman, but he had a plain, straightforward manner, and had been chosen because of his ability to negotiate a contract. His job now was to negotiate contracts with countries that wanted to put money into Poland. Chief among them, by a long way, was the Federal Republic of Germany. Of 600 schemes, West Germany was responsible for 248, the United States for 36, Britain for 30 and France for 22.

> I am pleased as a government servant to see this, but as a Pole I am not so pleased. As a government servant I am worried that a reunited Germany will absorb more German money and attention than the rest of Eastern Europe; as a Pole I hope it does. But then, as a Pole I hope that a reunited Germany doesn't become so rich and powerful that it dominates us again. We have had a long history together, and now we need money urgently. It is my job to get that money from anywhere, but to be honest with you I would be happier if it came from other countries as well as Germany. In 1939 we needed help from Britain and France against the Germans. Now we are not against them, but I think we need your support just as much. You know, it's funny: when they invaded Poland in 1939 I was eight years old. A German soldier fired his gun at me. Now they're here again. And this time we want them, and it's my job to make sure that even more of them come.

The possibility that a united Germany would have a united Berlin as its capital raised the question of the sea-port that would serve it. In the past, the sea-port of Berlin was Stettin. Now, as Szczecin, it belongs to Poland. Soon after the collapse of Communist rule in Poland, the West German embassy sounded out the new foreign minister on the possibility that Szczecin might be turned into a free port. A Polish government official had precisely the same divided views on this as Zdzislaw Skakuj had about German investment.

> If Szczecin were to be a free port serving Berlin, that would mean tremendous growth for the entire area. At the moment it's quite depressed. But think: the growth in trade would have a big effect on the agriculture of the region, because it would have to feed the city and it would be easier to export food from there. The farmers badly need new machinery, and the banks, foreign and Polish, would lend them the money. It would be a good investment. We could see a period of tremendous transformation, and this would spread out from Szczecin all along the Baltic coast, and right down to the German border. And then perhaps our children will say to us,

'Whatever happened to Poland?' Because it'll be swallowed up completely. It'll cease to exist. We'll be wealthy, but we'll be working for somebody else.

The shifting of international boundaries, the movement of hard-working Germans farther and farther eastwards, the savage wars of conquest mean that across a swathe of two or three hundred miles from the Baltic coast to the Black Sea there have been colonies of Germans since the twelfth century; sometimes earlier. All the large towns and some of the villages have two names, one German and one Slavic. The immigrants suffered and made others suffer. Germans in Czecho-slovakia and Germans in Danzig and Stettin were a contributory cause of the Second World War. After 1945 they were forced out as cruelly as their own government had forced others out in the past.

With the memory of the breaching of the Berlin Wall still strong, Helmut Kohl came back to Poland to complete his official visit. When his host, Mr Mazowiecki, invited him to give formal, public recognition to the Oder-Neisse line dividing East Germany and Poland, he declined. His foreign minister, Hans-Dietrich Genscher, spoke of the border as fixed; but Genscher was a Free Democrat, and his party had nothing to gain from the far right. Kohl had a considerable amount to gain by heeding the nationalist voices. He went to Silesia in the south-west of Poland to meet the submerged colony of Germans which once dominated the area.

It was strange to see them. In the pleasant towns and prosperous villages which seemed to an outsider to be entirely Polish, they surfaced as though the previous forty-five years had never been. They were survivors from a terrible upheaval, coming out into the open for the first time. People with names whose Polish spelling could not hide a German pronunciation came out to cheer and wave the German colours. Karel Szulc, who called himself Karl Schultz on everything except official documents, said his family had lived in the area for 400 years. He happened to be a Communist, and identified with Poland rather than with either part of Germany.

> The Germans regarded us as Poles, the Poles regarded us as Germans. This area was hit badly when the Russians invaded, because they identified us as Germans. I spoke German before I spoke Polish. Now I'm bilingual. My father was taken by the Russians and put to work in a coal-mine in Siberia. Then at the end of the War, when hundreds of thousands of Germans were forced to leave, we stayed. Quite a few others managed to as well. At that time, by comparison with Germany, Poland was a land of plenty.
>
> But then they forced collectivization on us, and they began to repress us.

They destroyed all the old German monuments, all German libraries, even German books. For two or three years after the War, when we wrote the word 'German' we had to write it with a small 'g'. I was given the task of collecting all the German books from my school and taking them to be pulped. Each day I used to look at them carefully as I carried them along, and decided which to keep. I hid them behind the big cupboard in our kitchen.

I ran for election to the Polish Sejm a few years ago. When I went to canvass in a shoe factory a woman said, How dare you run for the Sejm? You're a German. But I still got 18 per cent of the vote. Things are much better nowadays. That's why I'm a loyal Pole. But even so there are local authorities which don't allow German libraries or schools. And for years anyone with a German name who applied for a passport to go abroad would automatically lose his job. But I see some things from the Polish point of view. All this reunification is very worrying.

When Helmut Kohl appeared at one rally in Silesia, a German brass band welcomed him and there was German beer. Everything and everyone was decked out in black, red and gold. '*Helmut, Du Bist Auch Unser Kanzler*', one banner read: Helmut, you are our Chancellor too. They were no longer ashamed to admit their Germanness. Kohl, in a speech, appealed for a new start, where Poles and Germans could learn from their history. Some Poles were deeply offended by the hint that Germans should forgive Poles just as Poles should forgive Germans.

*

In a grim auditorium in an outer suburb of Warsaw, a man climbed onto the stage and called for quiet. The two hundred or so people milling round stopped to listen.

'It's no use trying to make your claims without filing in the proper forms,' he said. 'You collect them down at the other end of the hall. Then you can come up this end again and ask us for help.'

The acoustics were bad, and many of the people gathered there were hard of hearing. All of them had a claim on the government of Germany for their treatment during the Second World War. There were survivors from Auschwitz and Ravensbrück, former workers from slave labour camps, prisoners of war, men and women whose houses and families had been destroyed. I spoke to one woman who was arrested with her husband after only a few weeks of marriage. They were sent to separate camps, and he died almost immediately.

'He was such a sweet boy,' said this old, stout woman in a woollen hat and scuffed brown boots. She still wore a wedding ring, and forty-eight years afterwards the tears brimmed over just as readily in her vague blue eyes.

Yet the survivors were cheerful enough, pushing forward eagerly in the hope that after so long they might at last be about to receive compensation. They had been deprived of their rightful payment by Soviet sharp practice. The Allied Powers agreed at the end of the War that West Germany should recompense those in Western countries for the crimes of the Nazis, while East Germany would pay those in the Eastern bloc. The money was collected by the Soviet authorities and never redistributed. Now the West Germans were taking on this burden as well.

'What do you think about the Germans?' I asked them.

'I used to be very bitter about them,' one attractive, middle-class woman said.

She had been at Ravensbrück, and had never been able to bear a child as a result of the injuries she received there.

'But I am a Christian, and I realized at last that I had to forgive. I am glad that they are here. We need all the economic help we can get.'

An older woman, poorer and with a face marked by the years of unhappiness and struggle, moved across when she heard that:

> I saw them on television, singing that national anthem of theirs beside the Berlin Wall, and I knew we were in for trouble. Poor Poland: we can't get our land back from the Russians, and now the Germans will start demanding Silesia back from us. I remember 1939. You wait: it's all going to start again.

*

A PanAm jet too off from Tegel airport in West Berlin and flew noisily over the city, linking it to the real world. It passed over the Unter den Linden to the West, banking steeply. I walked through Marx-Engels Platz, talking to a former Communist in his mid-thirties, and watched it go. To people on this side of the Wall, it must once have been a galling sight: a reminder of their imprisonment. Now, in March 1990, they were free to pass through to the real world themselves, though the non-convertibility of their currency was another, subtler form of imprisonment. I had been away for most of the five months since the Wall was breached. In that time there had been a change of mood.

My companion was loudly dressed: red shirt, orange scarf knotted round his neck, black trousers. All his energy, his enthusiasm and the intensity of his inner life, seemed to have gone into his appearance.

> We lost our chance of self-government here when the SED collapsed. Krenz should have said 'I've kicked out Honecker and taken his place,' but he didn't. He should have said, 'I'm only a transitional figure. I'm going to

abolish the Politburo, I'm going to reconstruct the Party, I'm going to hold free parliamentary elections.' And he should have said, 'Yes, we admit it, the local elections were manipulated. I'm going to clear up the whole mess.' But he didn't do any of that. He just tried to play politics like all the others. He gambled it away.

The former Party member and I headed across Marx-Engels Platz in the direction of the old Party headquarters. It was Sunday, and people were out in their thousands, thronging the streets, lying on the grass, laughing and joking, altogether unlike the old GDR way of behaving. The date was 18 March: the day of East Germany's first free elections. But the former Party member wasn't entering into the atmosphere of it all. His strong American-German accent echoed out over the pleasantness of the scene.

You hear people saying all the time now that reunification couldn't be worse than what we had in the past. Well, that's probably true. I hate the stupid bastards for what they did to this country, the way they fucked it over. But all that euphoria from last November has gone.

He gestured at the scene in front of us, taking in the picnicking families, the dancing children, the entwined couples.

What you see here, this is all because it's a nice day and people are doing something they haven't done for, what is it, fifty-seven years here: they've voted for the party they want to vote for. Great, that's great. But we all know that we're being taken over here, and that's not a nice feeling. We used to have lousy jobs with no real money attached to them, but at least we held on to them for the whole of our working lives. Now the West Germans are going to come in and say, 'What is this shit-heap, man? We're closing it down, and fast.' And then nobody's going to be looking out for us. And they're going to come round to the chicken coops where we live, that we're paying peanuts for, and they're going to say, 'You wanna go on living here? That'll be two thousand Marks a month.' And if you don't pay, you're out on your ass. This is going to be a poor country. Only it won't be a country any more. It'll just be the part of Germany that doesn't do so good.

He had a point. Details were emerging all the time of the terrible backwardness of the place. A man lounging by the Wartburg production line said on television that his pay was still what it had been thirty years before, and his methods of working were the same as they'd been thirty years before as well. An environmentalist stood in an open field and pointed to an evil green liquid bubbling up in the middle of a brackish pool of water. It was the chemical outflow from a fertilizer plant which had sprung a leak and was poisoning the entire area. In the

Harz mountains the trees had been so damaged by acid rain and other forms of pollution that the bird population had fallen drastically. The field-mice who were the natural prey of hawks, owls and eagles were living and breeding almost without hindrance. Now they were beginning to constitute a plague of biblical proportions. A gynaecologist explained why she hadn't been able to set up in private practice in a provincial town outside Berlin. First, she hadn't been able to find two rooms together, so she could have a waiting room and an examination room. Second, the water supply in the town contained so much nitrate that it wasn't safe to treat patients there anyway.

The area around the town of Bitterfeld is perhaps the dirtiest in Europe. Your clothes are grimy after an hour or so; your hands and face have a film of oily dirt on them. There are pesticide factories, aluminium-smelting plants, ten lignite-burning power plants, a dye-making factory. Five employees of one of the pesticide factories have died of cancer within four years. Carbon disulphide escaping from the machinery in a plant that spins cellulose fibres has been measured at concentrations ninety times the danger limit. It can cause brain damage. Farmers outside Bitterfeld find it hard to get their animals to breed. Children in the town are more than twice as likely to contract respiratory diseases than children elsewhere. Their bone growth is retarded. A West German study found that life expectancy in Bitterfeld is five years shorter than average for men and eight years shorter for women.

West German television devoted hours of discussion to the question of the GDR's industrial and economic position. On one programme a Frankfurt banker was pessimistic about the short-term effects of reunification.

> They're at least thirty years behind us. I find it funny to listen to the British and the French and the Poles worrying that our new Germany is going to be a super-power. I think it'll take us at least ten years to get the GDR up to our standard, and it's going to cost a great deal of money. Maybe at the end of that time we'll be rich again, but in the meantime it's going to be like taking out a mortgage on a really expensive second home. Only this home has sixteen million people in it, all demanding our money.

But on this Sunday, halfway through March 1990, it wasn't at all clear what the shape of the GDR's future would be, or what precisely people were voting for. Chancellor Kohl, having given the impression that the two Germanies would be re-united in a matter of months, now seemed prepared to put it off until 1992 or even later. The Soviet Union, Britain, France and the United States were all relieved. The pleasure for most East Germans seemed to lie, not so much in thinking about the future, as in taking part in the act of voting. The last genuinely free election in this part of Germany was in 1933, when the Nazis were voted into power. You had to be older than the former mayor of Berlin and former Federal Chancellor, Willy Brandt, to have voted in that election; and he was now seventy-six.

I had expected the former Communist Party headquarters to be a gloomy place on a day like this. Not so. It had purged itself of the old Party bosses, and changed its name. It had two popular leaders, Gregor Gysi and the ex-prime minister Hans Modrow, both of them widely respected by non-Communists. The old Communist Party building was ugly and lowering: Nazi architecture, Stalinist overtones. But today it was transformed. All across the frontage the former comrades had hung canvases spray-painted with the kind of art you found on the Berlin Wall: heavy pictograms of defiance and confusion and colour. Where Marx and Engels, Ulbricht and Honecker had once hung, there were big portraits of Gysi and Modrow, also in spray-paint style. German rap music blared from the man-sized loudspeakers on either side of the main doors:

This is the Party that can solve your problems,
Solve the problems of ev-ry-one.

Thousands of people lay on the grass and listened. A girl was walking round, wrapped in an East German flag. Another flag was being used as a tablecloth by a group of teenagers who were eating sandwiches. There was a stream hundreds strong going into the building.

The workers and peasants to whom the German Democratic Republic was dedicated would never have come here in the past. Now they were flooding in to see what it was like. Everything was open. Most people, carrying little paper flags with the East German insignia of hammer and compasses on them, were content to hang around the ground floor. That was where the bands were, and the restaurant with a jokey quotation from Marx over the place where you could buy cheap sausages and potato salad: '*Der Mensch sollte nicht mit Kohl vorlieb-nehmen, wenn er edleres Gemüse erhalten kann.*' ('A person shouldn't make do with cabbage if he can get nobler vegetables.') The joke lay in the German word for cabbage: Kohl. There were other jokes too: 'We don't want to be Kohlonized' and simply 'Germoney'. This was the last ditch stand of East German nationalism, and it was remarkably lively and enthusiastic.

I went upstairs. The corridors were empty. The rooms were small, and they still had names from the old SED days on the door: secretary for agitation and propaganda, secretaries for the economy, secretary for inter-German relations. They were all empty. Many of them had newly issued pictures of a smiling Lenin on the wall, with a sticker that said 'Look up – the future's good!' Some even had that rarer phenomenon, a smiling Karl Marx. One door had a brass plate on it from the old, unreconstructed days of Honecker: 'Problems of Peace and Socialism'. The room, when I opened the door, proved to be entirely empty, its walls bare from ceiling to floor. It smelled of dust and stored newspapers. There were no answers to the old problem.

*

The Wall divided Berlin into unequal portions. Most of the grand buildings in the old city centre fell into the East. The West was essentially suburban. The Unter den Linden is a severe North European imitation of Rome, lined with temples in dark grey granite. In the winter, in the rain, after dark, it is gloomy and foreboding. This Sunday, in the sunshine, it was delightful. Four West Berliners coursed along the road on roller-skates. Two exquisites, also from the West, posed by a bench near the Grand Hotel. One wore an apricot-coloured jacket in crushed velvet. The other wore a black leather jerkin and thigh-high black boots. A dog like an Irish wolfhound lay beside them in the sunshine. Compared with such extroverts the East Berliners were dowdier and more sensible, but they may have enjoyed themselves at least as much. A little admiring group had gathered round a couple of West German motor-cycles, parked on the pavement. The owners affected not to notice them, and talked loudly to one another about speeds and manoeuvrability. A group of far right-wingers from West Berlin pushed their way through the easy-going crowds. Their heads were shaven and they wore heavy boots. On their T-shirts it said in English, 'Have A Nice Day – Or Else' and 'Sid Vicious Was Innocent But Sick.'

Outside one of the more sombre buildings along the Unter den Linden, the memorial to the victims of Fascism and Militarism, a crowd had gathered round the two unfortunate soldiers on guard duty there. They wore the flattish helmets of the GDR army, and despite the warmth of the spring day they were in great-coats and boots. They held their rifles balanced on the palms of their hands, taking all the weight of them on their outstretched arms. It was a part of the Prussian drill, like goose-stepping, designed to show that soldiers can endure any physical trial because they are essentially fighting machines. The Prussians exported the drill to imperial Russia in the eighteenth century, and the

Soviet Union imposed it on its allies after 1945. Outside the Memorial to Fascism, Prussian drill had come back home.

A boy on crutches eased his broken ankle forward until he stood beside one of the soldiers; then he handed one of his crutches to a friend, who went and stood on the other side of the soldier. Together, they shouldered arms with them while their friends laughed and took photographs. A few months previously they would all have been arrested. Now, the policeman on duty simply smiled indulgently, while the soldier himself frowned for the photographer and tried to look military. Inside the building, a small granite temple, a flame burned in a faceted cube of yellowish glass, like a new type of cooking stove at an Ideal Home exhibition. A little old man stood beside it in a belted raincoat, boots and a red crash helmet. Somehow he looked military as well. He was a little cracked.

'I am a Communist, and I remain a Communist,' he told a small crowd of teenagers.

They giggled with embarrassment and began to melt away. He saluted the flame and turned to face me. He hadn't shaved for some time, and hair grew irregularly around his face.

'He's just a loony,' someone said.

A fussy statue of Frederick the Great dominates the avenue. Elsewhere, East Berlin is an ugly collection of post-War glass and concrete: the kind of place where the engineers took care of the architecture to save money. But the Unter den Linden has been reconstructed much as it was. It is boastful and unlovable, like Wilhelmine Germany. Even the great Protestant cathedral, which the Communist authorities never finished restoring, carries a verse about victory on its frontage:

Unser Glaube Ist Der Sieg Der Die Welt Überwunden Hat
[Our faith is the victory which has overcome the world].

The Marxist-Leninists did much the same with quotations from their scriptures. I thought of Bonn, comfortable, small, bourgeois, unpretentious, and contrasted it with all this. If a country's capital is an expression of its personality, then a united Germany would be inheriting an unpleasant personality indeed when it moved back into its old quarters. There was something about the Unter den Linden which encouraged noise and agression.

Now there were posters on every wall, beckoning voters to one part or another of the political spectrum. There were obscure personal shafts:

'Anyone who played the *BLOCKflöte* (recorder) in Honecker's orchestra cannot play first fiddle in a democracy.'

'The CDU has been partners with the SED since 1949. The honourable alternative is to vote SPD.'

'Don't Worry, Vote Gysi!'

'The future has a new name. . .' (but unfortunately someone had covered it up).

'We're fighting for every millimetre: The Greens.'

'Modrow – the best reason for voting PDS' (but they had to print the full version of the SED's new name alongside it).

'To all tenants: now at last you can choose – between higher rents and getting notice to quit! Vote for your tenants' rights coalition, CDU-FDP-CSU' (the government coalition in the Federal Republic).

'The left you have. You don't want the right. Vote for a strong centre – the Union of Free Democrats.'

'Hello! Do you remember 1914? Was there anyone who wasn't inspired by the Kaiser and his war for the Fatherland?

'And 1918?

'Do you remember 1933, and the huge jubilation for the new Chancellor with no opposition?

'And 1945?

'And today there's a headlong rush for "unity" at any price.

'So vote with awareness and conscience, so that tomorrow you won't have to crawl away and hide.'

But the voters did vote for unity after all. That night, at an ugly glass and concrete social centre, the CDU celebrated its relative victory. There was Country and Western music in German, and a curious mixture of the smart and the rough in the crowd. A blonde woman in an expensive leather suit edged her way past a group of youths in T-shirts, and watched as one laughed and swept his hand across the table, knocking several glasses to the ground. The others cheered.

The chairman of the CDU in East Germany, Lothar de Maiziere, announced to the crowd that they were winning 49 per cent of the vote, compared with 22 per cent for the Social Democrats and 16 per cent for the former Communists of the PDS. It hadn't mattered that the CDU had been a meek and silent part of the Communist coalition in East Germany for decades, nor that one of its leaders was discovered shortly before the election to have been a security police informant. A vote for the CDU was a vote for union with West Germany as soon as possible.

It was, in its way, an aspiration: if you vote to join a rich country, perhaps you will become rich too. Chancellor Kohl gave them the impression, which was later denied, that the East German Ostmark would be converted to West German Marks at a rate of 1:1. A vote for the CDU was a vote for maintaining savings, pensions and incomes at a decent level. Later, Kohl was obliged to promise that there would be a 1:1 exchange for the majority of private savings. There was something else about the election. Time and again during the campaign I had had the impression that voters and candidates were just doing what they thought people did in democracies. They were acting out a role rather than doing something that was natural to them. It wasn't surprising: nothing came naturally in the GDR except obeying orders. And now there were no orders to obey, only economic imperatives.

The next morning I went back to the Wall. Once it had been the central metaphor for the GDR, just as a booming economy had been the central metaphor for the Federal Republic. There was the constant murmuring of hammers, as people on the western side chipped away at the spray-painted surface and loosened pieces to sell or keep as mementoes. There is no hammering on the eastern side, partly because there was less spray-paint. But there was some. The unthinkable had happened: if people were free to write on the eastern side of the Berlin Wall, the East really was free at last. On the other side the slogans had been painted thick and deep for decades. Here they were new:

The Wall Has Fallen, The Others Will Follow
1990: Gorby's Year
East or West, Down With The Nazi-Pest
FUCK TO DENG
28 Years Are Enough

Someone had painted a life-sized doorway on the Wall, with the door slightly ajar. Elsewhere there was the familiar joke:

Last One Out Turn Off The Lights

In Berlin there was more to the joke than there usually is. The East German army was simply melting away. According to one estimate, 40 per cent of its effective force had crossed into the Federal Republic by March 1990. The evidence lay beside Checkpoint Charlie. The stalls still sold neat little packets with pieces of the Wall in them (five Marks for a small one, ten for a larger), and hired out hammers and chisels so you could break off your own pieces. But now they had a new stock in trade: army hats. In places they were piled up, eight lines wide and six or seven deep: light blue fur hats of the Soviet army, darker ones from the East German army, hats of border guards, officers' hats, peaked caps, even the occasional Stasi hat. East German great-coats hung from the branches of the trees overhead, as if the revolution had been hanging Communists. There were shoulder flashes and cap badges, belts and gaiters and water bottles, and a tank commander's leather helmet. That was being sold by an Egyptian, whose piles of hats were the largest and most expensive. He said:

> I saw a man come through from the East in civilian clothes, carrying a big bag. He pulled everything out. It was all his uniform, even the boots. And a lot of documents about the tank, with his orders and everything. I laid it all out to sell, and five minutes later two men in civilian clothes, they looked like officers, one with a British accent and the other an American, bought all the papers. I've sold most of the uniform now. It's rare. The tank commander just carried on walking after I gave him the money. He won't be back.

A little later I was talking to another stall-holder, a West German expert in GDR militaria. His trestle table was covered with East German medals and badges.

> You see them all come past here: not just Easterners, but Poles and Russians. Most of them are going to the West illegally, and they stop off to get a little money for the journey. We don't pay them much. Directly the Wall comes down and Germany is reunited, no one will want these things except a few collectors like me. The tourist trade will be gone.

He picked up a cheapjack medal in imitation bronze and dangled it for me to look at. '*Für Treue Dienst*', it said: for faithful service.

'Cheap shit. But it's worth a little to a collector.'

A man came uncertainly towards us, from the direction of East Berlin. His hand was in his pocket. He was in his mid-forties, with a tired, worried face.

'I've heard you buy things,' he said. 'Are these of any interest?'

He said it as though he expected to be rebuffed.

'Yeah, I'm interested. These aren't bad.'

The East German smiled. He was a dignified man in his way, tall and straight. One of the medals had a double X on its ribbon of black, red and gold. I asked him what it was for.

'Twenty years' service in the army of a country that doesn't exist any longer, that's what it's for. Twenty years of my life wasted.'

The dealer gave him twenty Marks. He looked at the notes and smiled at me.

'I'm going to use this to buy some real coffee, ground from coffee-beans, to take back to my wife in the East. It's her birthday. So you see, maybe twenty years of my life have a value after all.'

He made his way towards the shops further down Friedrichstrasse. I bought the medal. *'Für den Schutz der Arbeiter und Bauern'*, it says on the reverse: for the protection of the workers and peasants. It's as unconvincing, as gimcrack, as the State which issued it. I have it in my hand as I write, but what I remember when I look at it is the bitterness as its owner said, 'Twenty years of my life wasted.'

PART IV

PRAGUE – NOT A
WINDOW DAMAGED

8
LARGO DESOLATO

Grandpa, don't be sad. We never take any notice when our teachers say what a bad man you are. I always leave the classroom and the teachers never say anything. I know that you're good.

ALEXANDER DUBCEK'S GRANDDAUGHTER, 1988

The sequence is as clear to me now as when it happened: taking a corner wide, seeing the words outside a newsagent's shop, stopping, running in to buy a paper. 'Russian Tanks In Prague'. Tears were running down my face before I had paid for the news I had never thought to hear. Prague was our revolution: peaceful, witty, decent, a poke in the eye for the old super-power systems that ran the world. Socialism with a human face seemed to mean something then. It had been purely, pointlessly, unforgivably smashed.

'Don't forget us,' a voice said on Prague Radio in the last minutes before it was captured. 'Remember us, even when our resistance has finished, and the rest of the world has found other things to think about.'

Nowadays, the television pictures of it don't tell you much. Tanks ramming into trams, an officer standing in a turret pointing, people shouting or kicking the armour, soldiers listening stolidly to earnest arguments. They're in black and white, as foggy and imprecise as the pictures of Hungary in 1956 or Berlin in 1933 or the Somme in 1916: decaying beyond rescue, as though reality were made of nitrate like old film. The events are grey and fixed, just another piece of impacted history. No sense now that they could have been completely different if a single element of the equation had been changed. For those of us who saw something of ourselves in the reforms of the Prague Spring in 1968, it would always seem as though some irreparable damage was done at the instant of greatest hope, like Vronsky's horse breaking its back at the most important fence.

It was thirteen years after the Soviet invasion that I first thought of visiting Prague. The Czechoslovak ambassador in London offered me a colourless liqueur which he took out of a safe. He proceeded to get mildly drunk on it. Then he approved my visa application.

'Normally we are very cautious about BBC. Frankly speaking, we don't like. But maybe this time you don't do bad things. Or maybe you say you don't.'

He laughed, and nudged me, and emptied his glass again. I smiled soberly. The smell from the glass was enough for me. Some days earlier I had had an interminable lunch with the press attaché, who had probed my reasons for wanting to go to Czechoslovakia. I had no reasons: I just wanted to see what had happened to the country since 1968. I explained this as tactfully as I could. There were long silences. A clock ticked heavily. I chewed away at meat wrapped in cabbage.

'Frankly speaking . . .'

It was a familiar phrase: Soviet bloc officialdom's way of introducing an unpleasant note.

'. . . we find that there is an unhealthy interest in the West about the wrong kind of things in our country. We have many things to be proud about. The past is over. We have forgotten the past. Only you have not forgotten the past. You will find this if we agree to allow you to go to our country.'

A silent waitress took away the remains of the cabbage. The clock ticked on. There seemed nothing more to say. Perhaps, I reflected, he was right. Thirteen years is a long time. A country can't stay frozen in time that long.

But when I walked through the streets of Prague a week or so later, I found it could. It was dark. The cobbles of the old town were wet from the early spring rain. An occasional bicycle hissed along in the silence. My footsteps echoed off the walls on either side, and my shadow moved jerkily along the cobblestones ahead. The walls were freer of graffiti than those of any city I had ever known. I saw a café with its windows misted over with condensation. I expected to find a kind of private jollity here at least. But it was quiet. People sat alone or in pairs, not saying much, taking an occasional sip of beer, paying silently, leaving.

In the Old Town Square the churches and public buildings were mostly barricaded with wood for repairs. It was a place of startling beauty, as grand a piazza as you could find in Europe. It was almost entirely empty at 10 o'clock at night: no cars, no bicycles, no footfalls, no sound. In the middle was the statue of Jan Hus, caught in the agony of his martyrdom, his train of fellow saints and martyrs with him, his mouth open in a silent scream of pain. It was the fate of the Czech people to be silenced.

The independence which the Czech people lost in one carelessly fought battle at the White Mountain in 1620 took 298 years to regain. It was then taken away by Hitler at Chamberlain's earnest instigation twenty years afterwards. Since then, there were three anxious years before the Communists seized power in 1948, and a few months of free thought and free expression in 1968. Fewer than twenty-four years of national independence in 370 years. People in the West explained it all in terms of a literary stereotype: the Good Soldier Schweik, who kept his head down, filled his belly, and wasn't much interested in the nobler things of life. No one mentioned the stranger fictions of Karel Capek, or Janacek's opera *The Diary of One Who Disappeared*. Those things didn't fit the explanation.

I walked around the Castle which Kafka had used as his symbol of disturbing, overseeing power. The defenestrations which were part of the beginning of the Thirty Years' War took place there, and the battle of the White Mountain was the result. It wasn't possible to see the window from which Jan Masaryk, the independent foreign minister, was defenestrated in 1948 by the Communists. An examination of the case in 1968, when such examinations were briefly possible, turned up a document which said that traces of excrement and the scratch-marks of fingernails had been found on the window soon after Masaryk had fallen to his death. The Cathedral was dark and quiet, except for a few elderly women. In the precincts, a bird gave a strange harsh, whistling cry. I had never been in a more silent city.

For a time, after the tanks of the Warsaw Pact invaded Czechoslovakia, there had seemed to be a faint possibility that the reforms of the Prague Spring would continue. Dubcek, though taken to Moscow in chains, returned as General Secretary of the Communist Party still. President Svoboda was still Czechoslovakia's head of state. His very name meant 'freedom'. Together, Dubcek and Svoboda promised that nothing would change. But everything changed. Early in 1969 Dubcek was dismissed and sent to Turkey as ambassador. He was a virtual prisoner in his own embassy. Svoboda died shortly after being replaced by Moscow's nominee, Gustav Husak, having failed to prevent the new men from overturning virtually every change that had been made during the Prague Spring.

Then began the purges. Throughout the Prague Spring the secret police, the Statni Bezpecnost or StB, had continued to operate for their old masters, not their new ones. Photographs existed of everyone who had spoken at every important public meeting throughout the period of the Prague Spring. Large numbers of people in the crowds had been photographed too, and notes taken of everything that was said. All this had been carefully collated.

The tribunals began to sift through the StB's material. Every member of the government, the civil service, the management of factories and businesses, was investigated to see what line he or she had taken during the Prague Spring. It was a long and careful business, carried out with the obsessive attention to detail of a new Inquisition. As with the Inquisition, the purpose was not to rescue the individual soul of the heretic but to preserve the integrity of the faith. Active supporters of the heresy were dismissed. Usually they could find only menial jobs. The applications of young men and women applying for places at universities were examined with the same care. No active supporter of the reform movement was accepted.

The caretakers, roadsweepers, stokers and maintenance men of Czechoslovakia were the best educated in the world. Distinguished academics, senior civil servants, leading journalists, economists tended furnaces, washed steps, cleaned out lavatories. The men and women who took their jobs in the Party and the government and the economic life of the country were often less well-educated. The looking-glass world was well represented in Czechoslovakia.

There could be no let-up in the tight control, not just of the Party but of the group which headed the Party – the group which took power in 1968 and 1969. Gustav Husak, Milos Jakes and the others remembered the last months of the old Party leader, Antonin Novotny, in 1967, and how the hope of greater liberalization had split the Party and forced even the liberals to go much farther than they intended. Husak and the others knew that if there were the least easing up, they would be swept away.

At an institute which employed translators the management had instructions to persuade more people to join the Communist Party. Each of the translators was called in, one after the other, as one of them told me later.

I was so nervous when I walked in that I could feel my legs shaking. I could see they had my file in front of them. They must have known that I was quite active at the time of the Prague Spring. But I had worked out carefully what I was going to say beforehand. So when the deputy director asked me 'What is your social attitude?' I knew what to say. The others who had gone in in front of me had been taken by surprise and they'd just stammered and hadn't been able to answer anything. But I'd found out from them that that was what he'd say. So when he asked me that I just said, quite politely, 'Could you be more specific?'

Then he was the one who was stammering, because he hadn't thought out really what he meant. So he said to me, 'Well, are you going to join the Communist Party or not?' and I just said 'No I'm not'. After that no one said anything for a bit. Then they said they'd be in touch with me. I went out of the room absolutely certain that I'd lost my job. But they needed qualified translators so much that they couldn't get rid of me.

That incident took place, not in the aftermath of 1968, but in 1989. It was difficult for the Party to generate any enthusiasm or activity even among its own members. Three days after the fifteenth anniversary of the invasion, the Party newspaper *Rude Pravo* complained on 24 August 1983:

It is a serious matter that our Party members live in near-anonymity. They cannot be formally rebuked for this, because they pay their membership dues, regularly attend Party meetings, and take part in agit-prop sessions. However, they have nothing to say on serious matters under discussion, they never raise their hands, and they never speak their mind. They never oppose others, but they never fight for their Party.

Like Winston Smith in *1984*, Czechoslovakia had undergone a kind of lobotomy. People had been given the opportunity to express their political feelings in 1968, and they had suffered for it. It was rare to find anyone, whether a Party member of not, who was prepared to make the same mistake again. A Czech who worked with my colleagues and me in Prague in 1983 found it awakened painful memories.

I hear you saying the kind of things we used to think about saying in '68. Sometimes we did say them, but only towards the end. And ever since I've not even thought about it. And now I hear you making funny remarks about Husak or the police or your own people, and I think, 'That's just the sort of jokes we used to make.' But no one makes them now. It's not even that if we did, we'd get into trouble. Probably we wouldn't. But you need to be in the right frame of mind to make jokes about things or be irreverent, and we just aren't in that kind of frame of mind. I don't even see the people I knew in '68 now. I wouldn't want to, somehow. It would just remind me of the way things used to be, just for a bit. What's the point of that? We'll never be like that again. So it'd only be raising a lot of memories.

The authorities demanded quiescence and offered in return a decent material standard of living. The shops were well stocked with food, and in the Tuzex stores it was usually possible to find the sort of consumer goods which were rare elsewhere in the Soviet bloc: microwave ovens, compact disc players, video cassette recorders. Any Saturday and Sunday in the summer people would head out of the cities to the dachas which the authorities made available in large numbers. It was a sleepwalker's existence. You concentrated on the small circle of your friends and family, and ignored the outside world.

*

I went to Czechoslovakia again in May 1983. As part of the Soviet Union's so-called 'peace offensive' the Czechoslovak authorities were holding a conference of peace organizations: The World Assembly for Peace and Life, Against Nuclear War. It was mostly a propaganda show against NATO's plans to install medium-range nuclear weapons in Europe. There was little evidence of new thinking about it. Nevertheless, for various peace groups in Western Europe it offered a platform for a more complex approach to peace and security on the European continent.

The British Campaign for Nuclear Disarmament had a strong interest, not simply in doing away with nuclear weapons, but also in the relationship between the state and the citizen. It had established links with the opposition group Charter 77. Charter 77 wasn't formally pacifist. Many of its senior members seemed to support the Western alliance's view of the Soviet Union. But it too was concerned with questions of disarmament and especially the rights of the citizen. CND decided to be represented at the Prague conference but it instructed its two representatives to discuss the issues with Charter 77 as well.

I decided to go back to Czechoslovakia and report on these three elements: the peace conference itself, the CND mission, and Charter 77. I also wanted to make a film about the problems of the Christian church in Czechoslovakia.

The ten days my colleagues and I spent there were some of the most intense and productive of my life. That short period saw the first genuine stirrings of widespread opposition to the government since 1968. We were well prepared. An Englishman, Gerald Turner, had gone on ahead of us to make contact on our behalf with various people within Charter 77. There was nothing, as far as the authorities knew, to connect him with us. Charter 77's office in London, run by Jan Kavan, a man with a strong instinct for underground activities, had also been working to help us with contacts. Finally, Keston College, which studies the persecution of the churches under Communism, had given us a list of people to see and interview.

Preparations on this scale were necessary. The Czechoslovak authorities were effective at repressing opposition. The assignment was a difficult one. I assumed that when it was completed I would not be allowed back into Czechoslovakia. That made things easier. There would be no temptation to pull our punches.

We had one big advantage. CST, the Czechoslovak television authority, had given an undertaking to the Western European television organization Eurovision, which oversees the interests of its members at big international occasions, that there would be no interference with the reports which Western journalists would be sending by satellite or land-line from its studios. The one problem we would not have to worry about was censorship.

The conference authorities had assigned us to a charmless hotel which had once been reasonably grand, but whose four-star status history was rapidly stripping away. A couple of dusty display cases in the lobby contained examples of Bohemian glass and of Czech heavy engineering. The lobby was also equipped with video cameras on fixed mounts to keep an eye on the hotel guests. By the door, in two rump-sprung plastic armchairs, sat two large men who usually kept their hats on. Following Wagner and Somerset Maugham's secret agent Ashenden I thought of them as Fasolt and Fafner. They were my first definite sighting of the StB. Behind the reception desk was a remarkably beautiful woman in her late twenties. Her name was Anna.

The authorities had tried to avoid any difficulties by ordering known dissidents to leave Prague for the period of the peace conference, when so many foreign journalists would be in town. Some had been placed under preventive arrest. We were unclear precisely who was at liberty and who was not; so that night I set out with the producer, an energetic American called Tom Roberts, to make contact with Charter 77. We smiled politely at Fafner and Fasolt and headed off in an antique hired Skoda to the old centre of the city. We parked discreetly, and walked by a roundabout route to the flat of Anna Sabatova, a leading figure in the opposition. Her husband, Peter Uhl, had just been sentenced to a long term of imprisonment.

The building looked as if it had been condemned. The street door yawned open on a single serviceable hinge. Inside, there was no light at all. There was a mass of twisted pipes on the floor, and the throat-catching smell of cats.

'It can't be here,' I hissed. And then we knew it must be. One of our contacts in London had told us that it was the least likely place on earth for someone to live.

The cats and the pipes became less of a problem as we climbed the once grand staircase. It was impossible to see where we were going. The steps crumbled under our feet. On the second landing we stopped in front of a heavy door with a thin frame of light seeping out around it. I fumbled and found a bell.

Noise and brightness rushed out at us. A pleasant-looking man in his early forties stood silhouetted in the doorway. I knew him at once, even from his outline. I had spent a good deal of time looking at photographs in London. Jiri Dienstbier had once been the star foreign corres-pondent of Czech Radio. After 1968 he was lucky to get a job as a janitor. He had been expecting us. He turned and called out something to the people inside the flat. There were a great many of them, packed into a small space. It was a party for all the opposition people who hadn't been arrested or forced out of town. There was a lot of laughter, and a lot of noise. Music was playing.

The playwright Vaclav Havel was talking to Jiri Hajek, the foreign minister in Alexander Dubcek's government. Others whose faces I recognized were standing by the bookshelves, sitting on the bed, half-lying on the floor. Anna Sabatova, a pleasant, dark-haired woman in her late twenties, forced her way through the crowd with a tray of glasses. There was beer and white wine and coffee, and people reached across to take a new glass and replace it with an old one without interrupting their conversation. The music came from a guitarist in the corner. An older couple, perhaps in their sixties, were holding hands and smiling. People smiled at us too, and nodded as though we belonged there. I began to feel we did. Deeper into the room I could see the two delegates from British CND. Their contacts, like ours, had begun early.

The walls were covered with books in at least three languages. Propped up against them on the shelves were photographs: too many to count, or to take in. Dozens of small black and white faces looked out at us, smiling or serious, usually formal. These were absent friends: the people who had paid the price of their convictions. The signatories of Charter 77 were in prison, under house arrest, in exile. In a country where the great majority chose to keep their heads down, these were the exceptions. The people in the room around me all faced the imminent, hourly possibility of police harassment and arrest. Many of them already knew what it was like to be in prison. Just about all of them had found their careers terminated. By any normal measure of judgement, they were failures, outcasts, wastrels: at some time or another, the authorities had called them all these things and more.

Yet this flat was the only place in Czechoslovakia where I came across a genuine sense of liberty. It hit me, just as the rush of warm air and light and sound had hit me when we stood in the cold, smelly darkness outside the front door. These people had made a deliberate choice between keeping quiet, and behaving like free men and women. I spoke to the sister of one of the people in the little photographs: a man who had already been in prison for four different periods because he refused to stop advocating religious freedom. Why did he keep on, I asked?

'Because he is a free man, and wants to live in a free society.'

She smiled as she said it, as though it was the most obvious point which scarcely needed to be made.

It was another of the antitheses, the paradoxes, which autocracy had imposed upon real life: the only men and women who were really free were those who were prepared to give up their freedom. Those who stayed silent in order to remain physically free were prisoners. I looked around me. People were laughing and joking, or talking with a real passion. Laughter and passion were things which the regime had effectively stamped out in the world outside the warmth of this room. The people here could be deprived of these things at any moment, on the whim of a secret policeman. There must have been an added sweetness to be here, knowing that.

Weakness is strength, I thought, imprisonment is freedom, insecurity is comfort. In the months and years which followed, I remembered the atmosphere in that flat every time I read that someone else who had been at the party was arrested, tried, sentenced, deprived of everything the régime thought was valuable and worthwhile. 'I'm afraid I never could understand them,' said a friend of mine after the revolution. 'They seemed pointlessly quixotic to me. I wasn't going to risk everything just to join them. And yet now they're running things! Perhaps they were the clever ones after all.'

Another paradox: stupidity is cleverness. Or rather, since no one at the party was there out of long-term calculation, the cleverness of the people like my friend who stayed out of trouble turned out not to be so clever in the long run.

Charter 77 was a complex group of intelligent people. It had no leader. No one even dominated its discussions. But Vaclav Havel was the guiding spirit. When I saw him at the party he had been released from prison only four months before. He had been freed early from a sentence of four and a half years on the grounds of ill-health. For the Czechoslovak state to gaol one of its best brains and finest writers matched the tone of his plays and writings – *Largo Desolato* for instance, with its countervailent streak of humour. Havel's was the humour of absurdity, the ludicrousness of the human condition rather than its more genial forms. The stage directions of his play *Temptation*, first published in the West in 1986, are as follows:

> The music thunders, the stage is completely obscured by smoke. As far as technically possible, the smoke invades the auditorium. After a while the music stops, the auditorium lights come on, and the audience sees that the curtain has come down in the meantime. There is a short silence, then music is heard again – this time softly and the most banal muzak. If the smoke, or the play itself, has not driven the last spectator out of the theatre, and if there is anyone left to applaud, the first to take a bow will be a fireman in uniform, with a helmet on his head and holding a fire extinguisher.

But Havel was a serious man. He would sit and talk, without gesticulation, quietly and reasonably, frowning as he spoke, watching the other person's face for signs of meaning, picking up the words in order to work out the wider implication of what was being said. He had a kind of long-distance courage, not the short-term kind. He would endure everything that was thrown at him and outlast his enemies, but he wouldn't flare up and charge straight at them. In his letters to his wife, written in prison, he listed his own characteristics:

> I mean my courtesy, my extravagant politeness, my timidity, my tendency to embarrass easily, my anxiety, my frequently inappropriate thoughtfulness, my respect for those in authority and my apprehensiveness in dealing with them, etc. In a way all these qualities derive from my instinctive lack of self-confidence and my continuing uncertainty as to whether I am accepted by those around me . . .

One of my favourite pictures from Czechoslovakia now is a poster of Vaclav Havel soon after he became president in 1989. He is sitting down, wearing a sweater, smiling an amused, gap-toothed smile, his left hand raised as if to say, 'Neither you nor I can entirely believe this is happening'. But he did not seem like that when I first saw him. Then, he faced the prospect of constant harassment and arrest, and Czechoslovakia seemed darker than it had ever been. There was no sign that change would ever come; and to be a clearly identifiable figure, obliged to speak out continually, was a serious task. He looked tired and pale and nervous, and rarely smiled.

At the party, a full-scale meeting was arranged between CND and Charter 77. Since houses were watched and rooms were bugged, it was decided to hold it outside. Someone suggested the large public park in Prague 6, a suburb on the edge of the city. But in a system like Czechoslovakia's, no arrangement like that could remain secret for long. The StB came to hear of it. By the time the two CND delegates turned up at the park for the rendezvous, it was already full of StB men and women. There were also a dozen or so Western journalists, and three television crews, all there with the knowledge and approval of Charter 77.

It swiftly turned into absurdity, the prevailing spirit. While the journalists circled round, the park benches were mostly taken up by young men in leather jackets. Each had a plastic carrier bag or a leather holdall beside him on the seat. As the people who were being monitored walked past, each young man would turn his bag, keeping it pointed towards them. In the woods there were other men in leather jackets. Some had two-way radios. There was an StB television camera crew, equipped with the latest in home-movie gear. We filmed them and they filmed us. Only we seemed to find it funny. There was even a security agent up a tree.

When the meeting finished, an impromptu press conference began in the middle of the park. Documents were handed out, interviews recorded, questions asked.

'What you're doing is illegal,' shouted a stocky, unlikeable figure in his fifties who had come striding over when the press conference was at its height.

He wore dark glasses. At some point in the past he had suffered badly from acne. He ordered us to disperse. If we didn't, we would be arrested.

'Bullshit,' retorted a journalist from a Dutch magazine specializing in dissident causes.

There was a pause, and he was taken off into the bushes by the StB and given a working over.

'No one is going to do anything serious against us as long as we stay together,' said the calm voice of Vaclav Havel. He was a veteran of dozens of such incidents, and it was plain that he was right.

The Dutch journalist emerged from the bushes. His glasses were broken and he had a cut lip, but no other obvious injuries. He was brushing the leaves off himself.

'I must ask all the television cameramen to give me their cassettes, and all the photographers to give me their exposed film.'

The acne-scarred man in dark glasses was immediately surrounded by protesting journalists. My cameraman colleague took advantage of the noise and confusion to slip me one of the two cassettes he had shot. I hid it under my jacket. There was no opportunity to switch the other cassette for an empty one. We gave it up to the StB man, while I held the other cassette under my arm.

The retreat began. There were a couple of dozen of us, and at least fifty StB men. There was also a sprinkling of StB women officers. They followed us down the long straight pathway to the park exit, a body of large, healthy people in their twenties and thirties, clever-looking or doltish, scruffy or well turned out. We, on the other hand, did not look so good. I walked with Jiri Hajek, the former foreign minister, whose acidulous and witty English I enjoyed listening to, and an elderly former spokeswoman of Charter 77 who suffered from dropsy. The three of us gradually fell behind the rest of our group, since Hajek was in his seventies and the elderly lady could walk only very slowly, leaning on my arm.

Behind us I could hear the men and women of the StB talking about us and laughing. My companions didn't notice. They were arguing about why Dubcek had lost control of his revolution. They spoke English out of politeness to me. I walked along at this artificially slow pace, thinking how proud I was to be in the company of a bent old man and an old lady with bad legs who had turned out for reasons the healthy young men and women behind us couldn't comprehend. They took our names and passport details at the exit to the park.

'Hajek, Jiri, diplomatist,' the old man said with a caustic pride.

It proved to be a busy day. That afternoon we were tipped off that a small demonstration would be taking place at the statue of St Wenceslas in the square named after him. The statue had been the centrepiece of most of the main gatherings during the Prague Spring and afterwards. But in the years since 1969 very little had happened there. A guard of StB men was always on duty, hanging around at the exit to the underpass and sitting on the raised stone flowerbeds, their shoulder-bags ready to register anyone who looked as though they might cause trouble.

By now, the unusual presence of so many foreign journalists for the peace conference had emboldened some students who felt strongly about the political situation. These were not members of Charter 77: theirs was a much more instinctive opposition. Some had scarcely heard of Charter 77. As we waited at the base of the statue for something to happen, it was plain the StB was expecting something too. There were extra numbers of young men sitting around idly, their bags over their shoulders.

We waited in the hot sunshine. The pavements were thronged with people in summer clothes, glancing idly across to see what could have attracted the interest of a foreign television camera team. The island in the middle of the avenue – for Wenceslas Square is not a square at all, but a long avenue which runs southwards, downhill, in the direction of the Vltava River and the old town – was left mostly to us, and to the StB.

There was sudden movement. Two young men ran forward, pulling out a flag. One was seized immediately. The other, still grasping the flag, hopped nimbly over the chains at the base of the statue and held out the Czechoslovak tricolour for a brief moment. Then two things happened. He was tackled and hustled away, and a young StB man sprang across and smashed his fist into the lens of our camera. The picture went blank. Within half a minute the cameraman had recovered himself and was filming the aftermath. The StB man who had attacked him was being calmed down by his colleagues. No one tried to confiscate our tape. The word had gone out that we were to be left alone.

That evening I went to the television station to send our edited report on the day's events to London by satellite. The pictures we had managed to save from the meeting in the park were good: the secret policemen, in particular, looked splendid lurking in the foliage. The pictures of the brief demonstration at the statue showed the StB clearly, and the moment when the fist collided with the camera lens was unforgettable. We had the first openly filmed television coverage of a Charter 77 meeting, and we had some telling material of the activities and habits of the security police. Such things had never before been satellited from Czechoslovak Television, and in spite of the undertaking it had given I was nervous as I walked into the studio building with our picture editor.

The CST's senior management was expecting trouble. A small delegation of top men was already there. They didn't introduce themselves.

'We hope you are not planning to transmit anything that is bad,' said one of them.

I assured him that we had only the best possible pictures, and I was very pleased with them. They looked at each other.

In the darkness of the control room, the pictures began to run. There was a little chorus of outrage and complaint. Vaclav Havel's face, the StB in the park, and the attack on our camera each produced a greater degree of anger.

'Switch that off!' the most senior man shouted, as the pictures ran again for recording in London.

He pointed a stubby finer at the monitors where Vaclav Havel was being pushed about by the security police. I reminded him of CST's undertaking to permit all foreign broadcasts to go through unhindered. Briefly, he consulted with the others. No one told the technicians to pull the plugs. The pictures continued to run. The executive turned and wrenched open the creaking studio door. It slammed shut behind him.

An elderly studio cleaner had stood aside to let him pass. Then he began sweeping again. From time to time he looked up at the television monitors. Now they were filled with the distorted features of the secret policeman who was running up to attack the camera. The screen went black. Then the last sequence began: some demonstrators sang a hymn by Comenius. It had been written after the battle of the White Mountain, and said that one day the Czech people would govern themselves in freedom again.

It was very quiet indeed when that ended. Someone turned on the overhead lights. Several of the leading figures from CST were still there.

'Disgraceful,' one of them said.

'You have betrayed the honourable profession of journalism,' said another.

I walked out while they were speaking. As I passed the elderly studio cleaner, he reached out and touched my arm, discreetly. A moment later I looked back from the doorway. The bosses were still gesticulating. The old man was sweeping the floor, his head bowed. The moment had passed.

*

Over the next few days we made the most of our opportunities. We interviewed both Vaclav Havel and Jiri Dienstbier at considerable length, and broadcast what they said from CST's studios. We covered the peace conference, but only intermittently. It had no serious new ideas. We assembled the materials for our documentary on religious persecution in Czechoslovakia.

Officially, there was no religious persecution. I interviewed the head of the government secretariat for Church Affairs, Vladimir Janku, who denied that the government controlled the religious activities of the churches in any way. Priests and ministers of religion had to be licensed by the state. According to Janku that was simply in order to ensure they received a decent wage. The ministry paid them. In reality, the licensing system was a way of winding down the church. The number of masses a priest could say was strictly limited. He was not permitted to teach. Because of a long-running dispute with the Catholic hierarchy, no new bishops had been allowed to fill the empty sees for years.

The result was that new and informal religious groupings were forming. We went to a Protestant church hall where a congregation of a hundred worshipped. The majority were Catholics, but the service was ecumenical. They sang 'Kyrie eleison', and knelt before a Cross at the end of the hall. People read out short prepared addresses instead of sermons. There were no priests, so there was no need for the service to be authorized by the ministry. The official atheism had created a spiritual need which the formal church, policed by the government's tame organization of priests, Pacem in Terris, could not satisfy.

Absurdities abounded. Because all songs which were performed publicly had to be passed by a censor, the Christmas carols broadcast on radio or television were exclusively about shepherds abiding in the fields and keeping watch, and going to lowly cattle sheds. Why they went there, and what they saw when they were arrived, were censored.

The unofficial church was the religious equivalent of the opposition movement. It was linked to Charter 77 by people like Father Vaclav Maly, who was a member of both the political and religious groupings. Another was Vaclav Benda, a poet, mathematician and prominent Catholic layman. He had just been released at the end of a four-year prison sentence. The StB had stationed men at the entrance to his block of flats during the period of the peace conference so that the foreign journalists who were in town would not be able to speak to him. We had made our prior arrangements, however. We spirited him out into a waiting car, and drove him to the country. In a clearing among the birch trees we interviewed him about the way he had been treated.

It had, he said, been very difficult. He had been regarded as an ordinary criminal, and that was hard enough. But the worst thing was that he had been continually offered the opportunity to get out of gaol and leave the country. All we had to do was sign a statement to say he had broken the law. Benda was a strange, witty man, with hunched shoulders and glasses that did not fit properly on his nose. As we walked through the wood he looked at me, his glasses glinting in the afternoon sunshine. If there had been a law covering what he had done, he said, he might have been tempted to sign. But the security police themselves couldn't think what law he might have broken. That made it a lot easier, he said. The glasses glinted again. He was laughing.

After the successful operation with Vaclav Benda, we tried the same technique with a young Jesuit priest, Fr Josef Kordik. He had recently received a six-month suspended prison sentence for working as a priest without a government licence. By speaking to us he was running a considerable risk. We sat hunched up together in a car, while the cameraman filmed the interview through the open window.

Young believers, in particular, are dissatisfied with what they are being offered. Priests are screened, and as soon as one proves his quality he is moved to some small country parish where he can't do very much, or else his licence is revoked, or he's gaoled. The believers are unsatisfied. That's why they go to those who help to resolve their problems and talk about the kind of things that matter to them. The priests who get their money from the state and are worried about the security police can't do it. But there are always some priests who are prepared to serve people, and to live in accordance with their faith. They're the ones who are fulfilling their mission, which is simply to follow the gospels.

The authorities were becoming steadily more upset by us. Our rooms were searched when we went out. My car was followed at night time, and it was sometimes hard to shake off the pursuers. We found and covered up the microphones in our hotel rooms, but the StB knew what we were doing. Each night we sent the results of our day's work back to London from CST. Once, to stave off imminent deportation, I agreed to a government suggestion that we should interview the official in charge of the peace conference. It turned out to be an ambush. When we arrived we found his office had been converted into a temporary television studio; not for us, but for a full two-camera outside broadcast unit belonging to CST. The lights were switched on, the cameras followed our progress through the room. There was no interview. It was a surprise programme, going out live, and our professional misdeeds were the subject of it. According to the man who conducted the show, I had singlehandedly set back the cause of understanding between our two nations. My colleagues and I relaxed and laughed in order to make the cutaways more difficult. They used them anyway.

We were heroes then, even in our hotel. People brought in little anonymous gifts for us. A flower lay beside my pillow. In the restaurant the old, cantankerous waitress beamed at us over breakfast and gave us things which had been off the menu before. She warned us about the men sitting at the next table. They had shoulder bags which were pointing in our direction.

But we had to leave the country within two days. I went for a last walk, alone and at night, along the Charles Bridge: perhaps the most beautiful bridge in the world. The statues along it stood out against the clear night sky. The spires of the old town and the towers of Hradcany Castle were dark geometrical shapes, farther off. The Vltava River roared and hissed beneath me. There seemed to be no chance that I would be allowed back here. The Czechoslovak authorities were famous for their vindictiveness. It was hardly likely that the government would change, or the system soften. I took a last look up at the statue of St Nicholas of Tolentino, whose curious halo was silhouetted against the sky. The golden apple in the hand of the child he was carrying glinted faintly. It was very quiet. I turned and headed back.

*

In London two more ambushes awaited me. The Czechoslovak embassy invited me to what seemed to be a small drinks party. I was the only guest. The chilly figure who had once talked to me about my visa over lunch read out a prepared statement about my professional shortcomings in Czechoslovakia. He didn't offer me a drink. He didn't even offer me a chair. I wouldn't have accepted either anyway. I had, the prepared statement said, fabricated untruths about the religious situation in Czechoslovakia. I walked out before the reading ended.

The second ambush came on my birthday: a lonely affair that year, spent in the office. The mail brought a card posted in West Germany. It turned out to be from Anna, the beautiful receptionist from the hotel in Prague. During my time there, she and I had smiled at each other and made a couple of jokes; nothing more. But she had taken our passports when we arrived, so she would have known my date of birth. I spent the rest of the day writing a reply which would encourage her to write again, but wouldn't look bad if this was the Czechoslovak government's way of paying me back for spoiling the Assembly for Peace. I drafted it as cautiously as a lawyer. Entrapment, as everyone knows, is the favoured tactic of secret policemen. But of course there was always another faint possibility . . . Men approaching forty are more given to self-flattery than most.

Her tone soon became startlingly warm. I was the only man who could understand her private thoughts, it seemed; life without me was dreary. And so on. Her letters in which her thoughts were contained were always sent to me at the BBC, and were always posted in West Germany or in Switzerland. Since the BBC was high on the list of organizations which the Czechoslovak government disliked, letters addressed to it were liable to be intercepted. She could have asked visiting German or Swiss businessmen to take her letters and post them when they got home. That's what I told myself. Then one day I had something from her with a GDR postmark. The chances that a letter would get through to the BBC from East Germany were no greater than those of one from Prague. I liked it even less when I read the letter inside. It spoke about sending me some special photographs. Photographs of what?

Soon after, a man with a Central European accent telephoned. He was insinuating and familiar. He wanted to know where he could send the photographs. I gave him the address. Presumably he knew it anyway.

'What sort of business are you in?' I asked, to embarrass him.

There was a pause.

'Import/export,' he said.

I laughed, and he rang off, annoyed.

The photographs arrived. They were of Anna on her own, and they weren't subtle. She was fully clothed. Sometimes she leaned forward, bosom first. Sometimes she lay on a bed, a copy of *Playboy* beside her. It was a secret policeman's notion of erotic promise. Some lip-licking secret policeman, no doubt, had put this package together. I was annoyed that he should have expected to hook me by something so lacking in finesse. I rang a man who rang a man who rang MI5.

'I say,' said the man from MI5 a couple of days later. 'She's quite something, isn't she?'

She was. But she, or the secret policeman, had made a mistake. In the accompanying letter she had written, 'I'm sorry this is so bad but I took it myself.' A magnifying glass revealed the reflection in a glass lampshade of the real photographer, hunched professionally over a tripod. Patiently, the MI5 man explained to me about agents of influence: people whom intelligence organizations could manoeuvre into some embarrassing lapse. She had been talking about taking a holiday in Yugoslavia soon, with the hint that I should join her. Maybe, the MI5 man said, an incident would be engineered there which the StB could use against me. After that I might be asked to deliver a package to someone, or make a favourable reference in a broadcast to some policy of the Czechoslovak government. No doubt our side was busy doing something similar.

Later I was told that the over-familiar import/export man had been of some interest to MI5. When I rang his number, it seemed he'd left the country in a hurry. Others had gone with him. After that, of course, there were no more letters. I missed them. Few of us are proof against the hint of sexual flattery, even when we know it is synthetic.

*

The World Assembly for Peace and Life was a big success for Charter 77. In the West it had usually been lumped together with other dissident movements within the Soviet bloc: comparable in intellectual terms with the loose groupings inside the Soviet Union, perhaps. It was very different. It was a forum not simply for ideas but for policies. Through its outlets in the Western world, like Jan Kavan's Palach Press in London, it issued position papers on a range of subjects to do with government. At the time of the World Assembly there were Charter 77 papers on the nature and moral value of nuclear deterrence; the value and practicability of non-violent resistance; the role of nuclear power and its dangers; the relationship between the Warsaw Pact and NATO. Some members of Charter 77 were pacifists; others believed the very existence of pacifism and the call for nuclear deterrence in the West were a betrayal of the people of Central and Eastern Europe. When the two men from British CND sat in the park in Prague 6 or at a table in Anna Sabatova's kitchen and debated the issues of nuclear weapons with some of the Charter 77 people, they found there were some profound differences between the views held on each side.

Charter 77 concentrated much of its efforts on formulating proposals on environmental questions and ways of introducing an enterprise culture. Much of that was Vaclav Havel's influence. Without him, Charter 77 might simply have been a discussion group. He helped to turn it into something akin to a policy institute. By comparison the Czechoslovak Communist Party and the government it controlled produced nothing serious in the way of ideas. Bright newcomers in government soon realized that was the last thing that was wanted.

It ceased to be possible to keep Charter 77 and its policy-making process quiet. During the revolution in East Germany in November 1989 Vaclav Havel wrote an article for the samizdat magazine *Lidove Noviny*, in which he talked of the greater intellectual space which he and his colleagues now enjoyed:

> The independent initiatives and independent culture have long since left the confines of the parallel world, cut off by stout walls from the life of society as a whole; in short, we are no longer shut up in a ghetto. At the same time, however, there is still nothing here even vaguely resembling a normal political culture that we might be part of. There is no natural and naturally public self-structuring of society, there is no real public life, and the experience of free citizenship is neither something taken for granted nor widespread. As a consequence, although the independent initiatives are far more what they were until just recently, they are not (nor can they be) what so many people would like them to be, and what many people already take them to be – an automatic political opposition with all that it entails from charismatic, professional leaders to concrete, realistic political pro-grammes.
>
>   This entirely transient situation, in which we are no longer what we were, yet at the same time are not yet and cannot be (and often don't even want to be) what we are clearly supposed to be, is slightly unnerving, slightly chaotic, and above all extremely demanding. . . Nobody has any comprehensive recipe for a solution and nor have I, of course.

But his suggestions, which he goes on to list, end with the element he considers the most important of all: the moral aspect.

> It had always been my conviction, and one I still hold to, that the origin of all the symptoms of crisis surrounding us is society's moral crisis, and that none of our crises – from the economic and political to the ecological – can be solved unless we solve that moral crisis.

Even as Havel was writing those words, the revolutionary process that would project him, ready or not, into the political leadership of the country, was already beginning. In the same article he talked about the hope for a clearing in darkness of the forest:

> I am not saying that we have reached that clearing already, I just think that we are beginning to see a glimmer of light and we sense that it is already on the horizon.

By the time the article was published, Czechoslovakia had entered the clearing.

9
THE WINTER FLOWERING

Exactly two years ago, I wrote an editorial for the first issue of Lidové Noviny. *At its very beginning I confessed that we were afraid that our project was a Utopia and that we would not be able to cope with it. If, at that time, someone had told me that, two years later, I would be writing a few lines to say goodbye to the samizdat era of* Lidové Noviny, *I would have thought that he lacked a sense of humour to be able to joke so clumsily. Now it is here: our next issue will be regularly printed . . . Goodbye samizdat* Lidové Noviny, *goodbye conspiracy, goodbye interrogations! Welcome printing house, welcome new readers, welcome freedom!*

VACLAV HAVEL, writing in the newly legalized
Lidové Noviny, 13 December 1989

There had always been something questionable about the events of 17 November – the night when the revolution in Czechoslovakia began. On the face of it, it seemed simple enough. There was a demonstration, the police attacked with considerable savagery, the rumour spread that someone had been killed. Even though it turned out to be false, the peaceable Czechs and Slovaks were enraged. They came out onto the streets in their thousands, then in their tens of thousands, and finally in their hundreds of thousands. The Communist government fell. The men and women who had kept the faith for twenty-one years took over. It was one of the most satisfying moments of modern history.

As far as it goes, the outline is correct. But there was always a niggling question about the origin of the rumour about the phantom death. Even at the time people thought it was a little too convenient. A month or so later the people who had formed the new government were saying that the secret police, the StB, was involved in some way. The government of President Havel appointed a ten-man parliamentary commission to investigate the events of 17 November.

At the end of May 1990 I was asked to write the narration for a television documentary for the BBC about the revolution in Czechoslovakia. The investigative work and the filming had all been done by the time I became involved with the project. The researcher was a small, pleasant, dark-haired woman called Zuzana Blüh, who had been a student leader in the Prague Spring before going into exile in London, and was soon to become head of the Czech news agency. We arranged that she should give me a full briefing about the documentary over lunch at the Chelsea Arts Club in London.

As I drove her there, she started telling me the story. At first I was angry: it seemed to be the worst kind of Central European conspiracy theory. The Czechoslovak revolution had been planned by the KGB, probably with Mikhail Gorbachev's knowledge, and was carried out by the StB. I sat in the sunshine at the Club, looking into my cider and wondering how I could get out of the project.

Slowly Zuzana Blüh's torrent of words began to wear down my resistance. She had interviewed most of the people involved. I flicked through the pile of transcripts she kept handing me: ministers of the new government talking about StB infiltration, Havel himself speaking of the influence of the KGB, former StB men giving details of the operation itself. Finally she produced a dog-eared sheaf of papers. It was a photocopy of the report which the Parliamentary Commission had produced, containing the full details of what Zuzana Blüh had been trying to tell me. The conspiracy theory had turned into a documented account of a real conspiracy.

The findings of the Commission may be summed up as follows. Towards the end of 1988 a small group of prominent Party figures, together with General Alois Lorenc, the head of the StB, the Czechoslovak counterpart of the KGB, met in secret. Unlike their superiors, they were all supporters of Mr Gorbachev's policies. They drew up a paper which concluded that the leadership of Milos Jakes and Miroslav Stepan lacked popular support and could not survive long. Sooner or later, it said, the Party would have to come to terms with the opposition. The paper made two recommendations: first, the old leadership should be ousted (it spoke of 'personnel changes among top officials whom the rank-and-file members do not trust'); second, there should be a new offensive to infiltrate the dissident movement. Thus the way would be open for a moderate, Gorbachevian leadership to negotiate with a divided and weakened opposition. According to a leading Commission member, Dr Milan Hulik,

> There is no doubt that the leading personality of the whole operation of which I am speaking was General Lorenc. . . The contacts between Lorenc and KGB officials which have been discovered couldn't, in my opinion, point to any other conclusion, than a KGB connivance with the whole action, in its preparation, or a direct KGB initiative.

General Lorenc undertook the task of infiltrating the various opposition groups. The plan, codenamed 'Operation Wedge', was highly successful. However, removing Jakes and Stepan from the leadership proved much more difficult. By the middle of 1989, as Poland and Hungary began the process of emancipation from Soviet influence and East Germany showed signs of internal collapse, the conspirators decided they had to act. Their operation was scheduled for 17 November, the fiftieth anniversary of the shooting by German troops of a Czech student, Jan Opletal.

The plan called for the simulation of the death of a student at the hands of the riot police. The conspirators calculated that this echo of the Nazi past would arouse such public anger that Jakes and Stepan would be forced out of office. Here, perhaps, the story appears to veer off into melodrama, yet the Commission's information comes from someone who might be expected to know: the StB officer who played the part of the corpse. Lieutenant Ludek Zifcak had infiltrated the student leadership as part of Operation Wedge. When the demonstrators gathered at Jan Opletal's grave in Vysehrad cemetery on the afternoon of 17 November, Zifcak's was one of the voices advocating a march on the city centre; and when the crowd marched along the embankment beside the Vltava, he led them up Narodni Street towards Wenceslas Square.

The police had turned Narodni Street into a carefully planned trap from which there was no exit. In the attack on the demonstrators there were 561 casualties and the one faked death. In the violence and confusion Lt Zifcak fell to the ground and his body was covered with a blanket. An unmarked ambulance took him away. Rumours of the death spread quickly. A woman who later disappeared, Drahomira Drazska, went to the distinguished Catholic layman and Charter 77 signatory, Vaclav Benda, whom I had once interviewed in a forest outside Prague, and told him the dead man was Martin Smid from the Faculty of Mathematics and Physics at the university, a friend of hers since childhood. Benda told his close associate in Charter 77, Petr Uhl, who ran an information service for foreign journalists. Uhl told the BBC and the Voice of America.

There were two Martin Smids studying at the Faculty. One was away at the time. The other had been at the demonstration, but went on television to show that he was uninjured. The police arrested Uhl for spreading false rumours. But by now the anger of tens of thousands of ordinary people had been aroused. The demonstrations grew by the day, until Jakes and Stepan were forced to resign.

The Parliamentary Committee established that on the night of the 17 November demonstration General Lorenc dined at an StB safe house in

Talichova Street in the northern suburbs of the city with General Teslenko, the KGB's head of station in Prague, and with the deputy chairman of the KGB, General Viktor Grushko, who had flown in from Moscow three days before. Their meal was interrupted by twenty-five telephone calls. At the end Lorenc and Grushko drove to the StB's operational headquarters, where they spent much of the night. The next morning Grushko returned to Moscow. The Commission believed that the Soviet leadership was involved in the conspiracy: Grushko's immediate superior was General Kryuchkov, a member of Gorbachev's Politburo.

The twin objectives of the conspiracy had now been achieved – Jakes had gone, the opposition was penetrated – but it soon became clear that the plot was based on a central miscalculation. Its authors had assumed that the people of Czechoslovakia would be satisfied with a return to the reform Communism of 1968. They had chosen as their candidate for the new Party leadership one of the most respected men from the Prague Spring: Zdenek Mlynar, a leading figure in Dubcek's Central Committee. He was purged in 1969, had signed Charter 77 and lived in exile in Vienna. He was also a friend of Mikhail Gorbachev: they had studied law together in Moscow. Mlynar paid a brief visit to Prague on 27 November, during which he met a member of the Czechoslovak Party leadership, Rudolf Hegenbart, who was one of the conspirators, and two members of the Soviet Central Committee. One of them was the official responsible for inter-Party relations between the Soviet Union and Czechoslovakia.

At this point the plot simply collapsed. Mlynar had no interest in leading the Communist Party, from which he had resigned years before. He agreed to fly to Moscow and saw Gorbachev, but did not change his mind. The people of Czechoslovakia wanted nothing to do with reform Communism. Vaclav Havel and Civic Forum were swept into government on an immense wave of public enthusiasm, the beneficiaries of an unlikely plot by their worst enemies. The regime which had turned playwrights into labourers, Byzantine scholars into road-sweepers and foreign correspondents into stokers had now managed to turn a living secret policeman into a dead martyr and an inert nation into a risen people.

*

I watched events unfold in Prague with some nervousness. Since I was persona non grata in Czechoslovakia, my name would be on the banned list at every border crossing into the country. My only hope of getting in was to wait until things were starting to collapse and the border guards no longer cared who came in. Three days passed after the violence of 17

November; I couldn't bear to wait any longer. We flew in from Frankfurt, with the neatness of Bohemia under snow stretching out below the aircraft. There was ice on the runway at Prague airport, and I slipped on it. Not a good omen. A couple of bulky North Koreans pushed ahead of me in the queue for passport control. I breathed the garlic in their wake, and waited my turn. The immigration guard who sat in his wooden box was a stolid figure. He had a red medal ribbon and a faintly Hitlerian moustache. He ran his finger down a list, and stopped at a name and a number. He looked up at me, then back at the list. He shifted my passport slightly. Then, from below the level of the counter, there came the noise of a wooden stamp on paper. I was through.

There was thick ice the colour of gunmetal on the roads, and we jolted between that and the tramlines. But the afternoon sun was shining, and I had to stop myself telling my companions how good it was to be back. After six years I remembered with great clarity the gloomy blocks of flats and the names on the destination-boards of the red trams. Then we were through the cordon of ugliness that had been laid down in the socialist 1950s and were through to the city as it had always been. The spires glinted over the Vltava. The scaffolding had gone from the best of the buildings. The city of jewellers and craftsmen was returning to its glories. We drove to the hotel where Kafka had once taken his daily coffee – a newly decorated place now, with a top-hatted porter, a good deal of brass and mahogany, and direct-dial telephones – but all I wanted to do was to get into the streets and follow the crowds.

It reminded me immediately of a European Tiananmen. People in their hundreds were flowing along Jindriska Street towards Wenceslas Square. I felt I saw the same expressions as I had in Chang'an Avenue, six months before: interest, pleasure and a fundamental disbelief that these things could really be happening. Everyone was wearing something with the national colours, blue, white, red on it: laces no wider than bits of string, ribbons, scarves. Flags trailed over shoulders. An occasional placard was held at the port so it was impossible to read. The stodgy, solid faces of the Czechs, with their wide Slavic cheekbones and tip-tilted noses, were alive with emotions that were still new to them. The sharpness of the cold made their faces red and their eyes sharp, and their breath flared from them like bubbles in a cartoon strip, so you almost felt you could read the words they were saying.

This was a march of the young. It seemed that no one who was heading down the side street towards the Square was more than 35 years old, and that no one who was moving against the current, moving away from the Square, was less than 35. People who had been through it all before were reluctant to invest so much emotional energy in anything again. Near me I saw a girl who must have been about 18 holding on to her boyfriend's arm, jumping and turning in the air so that sometimes she faced him and sometimes she faced the direction in which they were going. They were both beaming, delighted to be with each other and to be taking part in something so enthralling. As they vanished in the headwaters of the crowd he put his arm round her shoulders and held her so tightly her feet must have left the ground again.

In the growing darkness of that late November afternoon there was a kind of winter flowering. The bare branches were putting out blossom. Barren lives were uniting around a purpose. The empty streets were filling up. The walls of the city which had once been preternaturally free of graffiti were now covered with hastily produced handbills. One, a quotation from Marx, was in a marvellous approximation of English:

'Weapons Uses The One, Who Losted All Ideas'.

Others were more functional:

'Demonstration Friday 24th! Important! Do not miss!'
'Students to the Square, 5.00!'
'Democracy Now!!!! We Won't Wait!!!!!!'
'R E S I G N ! ! !'

Soon that last word, '*demisi*' in Czech, would be on every wall and on everyone's lips. But not yet. People might hope the government and the Party would resign, but they seemed not to believe it could happen this soon, this easily. It was reasonable to assume the state apparatus would put up more of a fight. But there was something else that reminded me of Tiananmen Square. A few policemen stood around, with no orders to stop the flood of people taking over the streets and stopping all the traffic, and quite unable to do so. The looks on their faces, baffled, resigned, apologetic, were very much those of the police on Chang'an Avenue. They were surrounded by people who no longer cared very much about the old rules and the old sanctions.

The crowds made surprisingly little noise: just the purposeful tread of leather and rubber along Jindriska Street. But the sound from Wenceslas Square was becoming audible: a rustling, busy, interested sound, such as you might dub on to a silent film to give it verisimilitude. There was nothing angry or violent about it, and there were no ranting speeches rising over the top of it. I could just see a section of the Square ahead of me, packed from side to side with heads, like caviar in a jar. There the flags and placards and banners were waving, catching the cold evening breeze and lit up by the big spotlights that the television organizations had erected. Great clouds of breath hung over the crowds, caught in the beams of light. As they came closer, the people in

Jindriska Street quickened their pace and their heads rose as they craned to see how many others were there already. The numbers had been getting greater as people slowly lost their fears and allied themselves with the demand for political change. Soon they would no longer be demonstrators, political activists, risk-takers: they would be incontestably the voice of the nation, commanding change and no longer asking for it.

It was an unforgettable moment, turning the corner from Jindriska Street into Wenceslas Square. It was 1968 again, but this time there would be no tanks. In our naïvety we had thought the Prague Spring would succeed because so many people wanted it. Now, seeing the size of the crowds and that quiet thoughtful intensity, I understood that it was going to succeed because there was no force, Czech or foreign, which was prepared to stop it. I worked my way up the hill through the crowds with my head lowered so that no one should see the tears. Around the edges of the Square were the little shrines of candles, warm in the November cold, to commemorate the people who had been injured in the demonstration of 17 November and all the victims of forty years of Communism. Women were kneeling there, tending the candles, lighting new ones, their faces golden in the light like de la Tour paintings: thoughtful, unpassionate, determined.

I came at last to the statue of the King, tatty now with posters and banners. '*Se Stávkou!*' decorated a noble who guarded one corner of the plinth; *Nechceme Vládu Jedné Strany!*' decorated a bishop; '*Přestaňte se bat!*' a monk. Under the hooves of Wenceslas' horse, right on the front of the stone base of the statue, facing down the hill of Wenceslas Square at the sea of faces, was a photograph of Alexander Dubcek as he was when the crowds were here before.

They chanted for Dubcek and for freedom, '*Svoboda*', just as they had before. And they also chanted for the rumpled, mild-looking playwright who had not given up when times were bad: 'Havel! Havel!' They held up the keys to their cars and houses and jangled them. At first it was a reference to the cap and bells of a court jester, meaning 'those idiots in government'. Soon it came to mean 'time for the final curtain'. There was a whole range of chants, most of which rhymed in Czech:

'See how big the crowds are, Gustav! (to Husak).
'Your time has come, Milos, now!' (to his successor, Jakes).
'*Rude Pravo* lied, when it said this was a small crowd!'
'Today the whole of Prague, tomorrow the whole country!'
'Dubcek! Dubcek!'
'Freedom! Freedom!'
'Havel! Havel!'

In the growing darkness, a woman began to sing over the microphones. It was Marta Kubisova, a singer who had been banned since the late 1960s. Her voice echoed off the vast frontage of the National Museum at the head of the Square, filling this huge area. I knew the tune, but couldn't quite place it. Then I remembered the hymn by Comenius, and the television executive in the dark of the studio saying 'Disgraceful', six years before.

> May disputes and envy fade,
> May the governing of your affairs
> Come back at last to you,
> My nation.

Now my eyes were no longer the only ones with tears in them.

*

That night I had to introduce the reports of my various colleagues from Wenceslas Square for the first time. It was necessary to get a little higher than the surrounding crowds. That involved Havelian absurdity, standing on the big concrete tubs which in spring would be planted with flowers but were now merely frozen mud. I said my pieces to the camera, which were duly satellited to London.

The big demonstration was long since over, but a crowd of several hundred had gathered to watch the curious spectacle of a man standing on a concrete tub talking to a camera. At the end, when I signed off with the words 'BBC News' there was an embarrassingly enthusiastic round of applause. The BBC's Czechoslovak service had been a lifeline to large numbers of people during the difficult years. There was, however, one man in his fifties, perhaps a Communist Party member, who wasn't appreciative. It was a sign of the general moderation that people let him speak. His English was good.

'Who invited you here to interfere in Czechoslovakia's internal affairs?'

I wouldn't normally have chosen to score points off a lone heckler, but in these circumstances something needed defending.

'In Britain foreign reporters are free to come and comment on our affairs without being accused of interfering. That is because we are a free country. Soon, I hope, Czechoslovakia will be a free country too.'

It was cheap enough, but there was a much louder round of applause then. I couldn't prevent myself from bowing to them from my concrete flower tub. People wished me a happy and successful stay and asked if I really thought Czechoslovakia would soon be free. Their eagerness was more affecting than a greater self-assurance would have been. After twenty-two years of waiting, a few days of self-expression were not yet enough to instil a real sense confidence.

There was still an instinctive nervousness. The following day, probably talking too loudly, I was reassuring a Czech friend of mine as we walked to the Magic Lantern Theatre that there was nothing really to fear now. The Russians wouldn't intervene. The Communist government had no real strength. It was natural to be nervous, but when the moment came, people would find the necessary courage to complete the task. A middle-aged man in an expensive hat and coat had been walking in front of us, his head turned slightly so that he could listen. He slowed down so that we came level with him.

'I agree with you entirely,' he said, and hurried off. For him the moment of courage had not altogether arrived.

A hundred yards further, I read out a sign on the wall that said 'Dubcek President'. A woman in her late thirties nodded and smiled, then walked away as the man had, as though it were still dangerous to express opinions.

*

It was not that Charter 77 was so good at organizing opposition; it was that the government was so bad at holding on to power. Jakes and his colleagues had reached the point where he could no longer respond with force to the open challenge on the streets. He lacked the guts to do it, and there was no political room for manoeuvre, nothing he could offer the crowds short of his own resignation. And so he responded with apathy. The system began to tear like rotted cloth. Once the 'massacre' of 17 November had taken place, the initiative lay solely with the opposition. All that was required now was a structure to exercise the power which the street demonstrations were making available.

Charter 77 was better at producing ideas than creating structures. Its careful preparatory work on policy-making hadn't been matched by any formal organization. And so it was left to individual members to suggest what ought to happen next. On the morning of Saturday 18 November a leading activist, Jan Urban, turned up at the flat of a former spokesman of Charter 77, Milos Hajek, to talk over the extraordinary new situation that had been created by the senseless violence of the night before. Charter spokesmen and women were elected, three at a time, for a year. All through the period of maximum persecution it had been unwise to set up a proper leadership system, and nobody much liked the idea even when the persecution eased up.

Urban is a pleasant, witty man, good-looking with prematurely greying hair. He had taught Byzantine studies at university before being thrown out of his job. Now, as he and Hajek and another friend chatted about their need for an organization, Hajek suggested that they ought to set up a forum which could gather together all the various opposition groups. The New Forum in East Germany had proved highly effective, and this would be a similar system. Urban agreed, and said they ought to get it started right away. They decided that Hajek should go the rounds of the various independent groups to get their support, while Urban himself went round to Vaclav Havel's flat to see what he thought.

There were half a dozen people at Havel's flat, and they all liked the idea. The flat was a good place to be, since all sorts of people were continually turning up there to talk over the situation. Havel undertook to call a leading member of the Socialist Party, Jan Skoda, to interest him in the idea of a forum. The Socialists had always been little more than a stooge organization which joined the Communists in government at a time when Stalin had insisted that each of the satellites should be governed by a coalition, in order to make Communist rule seem more acceptable. Now, though, the Socialists were showing signs of independence. Nevertheless Skoda refused to join the forum.

At some point that afternoon – no one seems able to remember quite how it happened – someone suggested that it should be called *Občanske Fórum*: the Civic Forum. It was as good a name as any, and it stuck. The next evening, 19 November, the thing was formally agreed at a meeting in the Actor's Studio off Wenceslas Square. Civic Forum had taken less than twenty-four hours to organize, from the moment it had been suggested.

Jan Urban had other problems now. That evening his flat was surrounded by security policemen. He had to escape across the rooftops, and spent the next four days in hiding. Several others weren't so fortunate, and were arrested. It was no time to be out of circulation. The night of the 19th, Urban was at the Wolkers Theatre when the police arrived. The actors helped to smuggle him away.

Before Urban went, Sasa Vondra suggested that they should establish their permanent headquarters in a theatre, and the Magic Lantern was proposed. Everyone agreed. Actors as a group had been as strongly behind the revolution as students, so any theatre would provide a ready-made group of supporters. There were, as Urban found, other uses. A theatre was a good place to hide in, or escape from. They would need a stage and plenty of seating for the press conferences they would hold. The entire experience was turning into the theatre of revolution, with its audience on the streets. There was more than a little element of the theatre of the absurd. And it had a playwright as one of its foremost actors.

The Magic Lantern is in a gloomy arcade near the lower end of Wenceslas Square. From the moment the Civic Forum took it over and hung its sign, complete with the logo of a smiling face, across the entrance, the arcade was always filled with crowds of would-be helpers, activists, foreign journalists, and curious onlookers. It was difficult for most people to get through the narrow doors, though the affection which almost everyone had for the BBC meant that my colleagues and I could always get in when we wanted.

Inside, there were constant knots of people discussing things, and rooms filled with tobacco smoke where Havel and the others were working out their tactics. It was sometimes hard to avoid being drawn into the decision-making discussions themselves. Actors, academics, rock stars and artists were the leading figures. Talk counts for a great deal in every revolution; here, perhaps, the quality of the talk was better than average, but the politics of gesture were still important.

Havel was proposed as president of the Forum on Monday 20 November by another leading activist, Michal Horacek – but only, he insisted, as a joke. Urban and several of the others disliked the idea; they thought Havel should be like Lech Walesa, and devolve power to others rather than exercise it himself. Finally they agreed that someone should do the job on an interim basis, and it might as well be Havel.

On Tuesday 21st the Communist Party leadership stirred itself for almost the last time and moved 1,100 members of the People's Militia, the Party's volunteer force, from Western Bohemia to Prague. They were equipped as riot police. But they were distinctly unwilling to take action. When they were ordered to move in to the University and throw out the revolutionary students who had established themselves there, they refused. These are our children, some of the Militiamen were quoted as saying. Once again, I was reminded of Tiananmen Square, and the soldiers who were sent in to clear it of students. This time, though, there were to be no military units who would obey the orders the rest refused. The only massacre in Czechoslovakia was the one that didn't kill anybody.

By Wednesday 22nd another of the useful accidents which marked the course of the revolution took place. The Socialist Party, one of whose senior figures, Skoda, had come to the first meeting of the Civic Forum, decided the time was right to distance itself from the government of which it was a nominal part. The decision wasn't a particularly noble one: but it played its part. Vojtech Hueber, the senior editorial writer of the Socialist Party newspaper, *Svobodné Slovo*, was instructed to draft an article critical of the 'massacre' and calling for national understanding and the establishment of certain basic freedoms. Hueber, a vast man who smoked several packs of cigarettes a day, said complacently afterwards that many people felt he had made the revolution happen.

Svobodné Slovo was abysmally badly produced, on ancient machinery and using poor quality newsprint. It wasn't the eloquence of Hueber's writing that brought about the important effect, it was the fact that a semi-official newspaper was saying these things. Time and again people told me that when they knew that *Svobodné Slovo* was suggesting reforms, it seemed reasonable (by which, perhaps, they meant safe) to join in the demonstrations themselves.

The Socialists helped the cause in a more practical way. The *Svobodné Slovo* offices were in a building halfway up Wenceslas Square, on the south-western side. The balconies of the building were ideal for addressing the crowd, and soon the Socialists lent them to the Civic Forum. Thanks to this tactical switch of loyalties, the crowds were turning out in ever larger numbers, and there was now a clear, organized focus for the demonstrations, equipped with amplification.

But one man had not entirely given up the hope of reversing the situation. Miroslav Stepan, the aggressive and corrupt leading secretary of the Prague City Communist Party, went to a working-class district of the city, Prague 9, to seek help from the workers at the vast CDK factory there and try to rally support against the reformers. He was given a hearing.

'There's no country on earth where fifteen-year-old kids can lecture adults on what they should do,' he said.

The workers took offence.

'Who's calling us fifteen-year-old kids?' they chanted back at him.

'You don't understand . . . You've got me wrong,' Stepan shouted. But they were whistling and booing so much by now that he had to stop. If he had turned up there a couple of days earlier, the workers might possibly have passed a resolution supporting him and the government. They certainly wouldn't have booed him. But it was the fate of the Communists to be a little too late in everything they did. And once Stepan, the toughest-minded member of the hierarchy, realized that the game was up there was no one else left to play.

By this time Civic Forum was giving nightly press conferences at the Magic Lantern: confused, creative occasions where unexpected things happened and people would hurry on stage and make announcements, like messengers in a Shakespearian history play.

'And we've just had information that the Praesidium of the Union of Journalists has resigned, and has been replaced by a new leadership.'

(Sustained applause: not many foreign correspondents here were objective as between Civic Forum and the régime.)

The proceedings were usually conducted by Fr Vaclav Maly, a saintly figure with a round, boyish, ungrown-up face who was nevertheless 40 years old and had endured imprisonment for his determination to go on celebrating mass illegally. He had been beaten up and cruelly assaulted by the security police in the past. Now he maintained a gentle control over the inchoate, crowded sessions at the Magic Lantern.

Beside him on the stage was a pre-1968 economics professor, Rita Klimova: stocky, red-cheeked, noisy, with iron-grey hair that looked as though it was woven out of wire. She came back from a trip to Hungary, where she had been trying to get printing equipment to smuggle into Czechoslovakia, and turned up at Vaclav Havel's flat to find that the first press conference of the revolution was taking place. She immediately began translating into English, and carried on the job when the press conferences moved to their grander premises at the Magic Lantern. Mrs Klimova's raw, gravelly New York accent cut through the equally raw atmosphere of cigarette smoke which hung over the stage and the stalls of the theatre, cutting off bores in mid-flow and re-establishing some kind of order.

One thing was still lacking from the reformers' point of view: the presence of the man whose face and name were on every leaflet and every poster. The previous night Alexander Dubcek had addressed a vast crowd in the Slovak capital Bratislava, where his own political career had begun, and where he had lived in internal exile since 1969. That Friday afternoon he came to Prague.

For us to get into the Socialist Party building was not easy, even with the BBC's name. But there were always people who were prepared to help, and to give us the necessary accreditation for the right places in the building. Outside in the Square the crowd had been building up for several hours. We took our position in the office that led onto the balcony. At first we were the only television crew there. But on some lower floor a large group of cameramen and photographers was waiting, and some at least of them fought their way into the room itself. These scenes are rarely edifying, and the patience of the Civic Forum broke. They threw everyone out, except for Czechoslovak Television, whose pictures would be seen by everyone in the country that evening. We too began to leave, but the Civic Forum people were gratifyingly annoyed by this.

'*Not* the BBC,' said the head of the organization in an exasperated voice, as though it were stupid of us to regard ourselves as being only on a par with American, German and French television.

I found myself becoming increasingly nervous as the time came for Dubcek to arrive. This was something I had never hoped to see: the Magic Lantern of the Czechoslovak revolution was perhaps creating the illusion of it all. Things did not behave with this attractive symmetry. For the man of 1968 to be the man of 1989, and for me to be there to see it, seemed inherently unlikely. I remembered the newspaper placard: Russian Tanks in Prague.

Dubcek seemed older than his 68 years. Vaclav Havel shepherded him in, as gentle as a son with a frail father. The lights from our cameras affected his eyes, which were rheumy and weak. I thought at first that he was too old for this moment: that it had come too late. But it wasn't so.

I stayed inside the room as he and Havel climbed out onto the balcony, together with Fr Maly, the skilful moderator at these rallies. I could see Dubcek's slender, bent, elderly figure with the absurd nose and the thin hair outlined against the great mass of blue, white and red flags and the upturned faces. The roar and the physical warmth of the crowd were stunning, and they infused the old man with a strength he hadn't seemed to possess a few minutes earlier. He straightened, and gripped the microphone, and said the words which he, too, must have found unthinkable, unhoped for:

'Dear people of Prague, I am glad to be among you after so long a time.'

His thin voice was drowned in the roar and upsurge of warmth from people who perhaps had only heard from others about the vast public meetings of 1968.

Much of what he said was predictable enough. He spoke of the mutual need of the Czech lands and Slovakia to work together in the renaissance of the country, and the importance of ensuring that the People's Militia served the interests of the people. There were times when he seemed to ramble, and the ideas were not following each other coherently. And then, like the twenty wasted years, the incoherence lifted and the ideas and the words shone through with a clarity that silenced that huge sea of listening, eager, hungry faces.

The light was here before. Why should it be dark again? We had the morning. We must act now as though the light has come once more.

They called out 'Freedom!' then, with such intensity and certainty that you felt nothing would separate them from it ever again. His face was lit by the arc lights and by the sheer pleasure of people who had thought they would never see him again. And when he finished, the crowd chanted 'Stay healthy!', which is a Czech toast. It was as sublime a moment as I hope to see.

That night, at the Magic Lantern, Alexander Dubcek was giving a slow, fragile press conference where the questions were as restrained as the answers, when Vaclav Havel, who had been protecting him as carefully as a son, bounded up and announced in the most Shakespearian fashion of all the news that Milos Jakes, the Communist Party leader, had resigned, together with other leading Party officials. One could only sit there and marvel at the timing, as Havel in his shirtsleeves embraced the older man and people in the audience stood and applauded.

On Saturday 25th the ninety-year-old Roman Catholic primate, Cardinal Tomasek, held a mass in St Vitus' Cathedral in which he called for people to be moderate in their political demands. He enjoined on them the virtues of St Agnes, daughter of the king of Bohemia, who made peace between her brother Vaclav I ('King Wenceslas') and his son, Premysl II. The mass was televised, and was watched by people all over the country. But in the square outside the Cathedral thousands of people had waited since the early hours of a freezing morning to attend the mass. Coaches had brought them in from the farthest reaches of Slovakia. These were mostly the devout of the countryside, a world away from the active, well-informed Czechs who filled Wenceslas Square every afternoon between four and five o'clock. Now, as they sang their hymns and waited for their Cardinal, it was plain that these quiet, undemonstrative people felt their moment had come as well. That afternoon a vast demonstration of more than half a million people took place at Letna Park. Wenceslas Square was now too small for the crowds which were turning out. Dubcek and Havel spoke. So did Ladislav Adamec, the Communist prime minister. He was booed and hissed, but the Civic Forum wanted to build him up as someone they could negotiate with.

★

On the Friday night when Dubcek made his speech in Wenceslas Square, it was only the fourth item on the television news in Prague. Jakes' resignation, a report about coal production and the news of a sporting success for the country came before it. The government might be abandoning every position it had occupied, the leaders of the Party might be resigning, the system might be in a state of collapse, but the television service, the faithful watchdog of the Communist Party, remained on guard because no one had called it off. On Monday 27th I went with a camera team to the studios of CST. Civic Forum had called a two-hour strike to demonstrate the uncontested scope of its control over the country. It was due to start shortly.

No one was in charge at the television station. The harassed people at the reception desk called for help to numbers which didn't answer. A week or so before we would have been thrown out for trying to bring a television camera into the headquarters of the television service. Now, no one in authority wanted to notice. The strike committee was pleased to see us, though. They were planning the route they would take to Wenceslas Square, the slogans they should chant, the length of time they would stay away from work, the names of those who would keep a limited news service operating.

'It is essential for people to be told what is going on,' someone said to me earnestly. 'News, information, is central to a democracy.'

They had been fighting the management for days about the coverage of the events in Wenceslas Square. After a series of mass meetings the management had agreed to allow longer reports and more pictures. It was a hard battle. You could tell from watching television each night who was winning. The place the political crisis occupied in the running order of the news bulletins and the length of time given to it were the clues.

The banner the strikers were to carry was unfurled for inspection. There was general enthusiasm for it, though someone asked if the word *Demisi* – resign – should not be more prominent. When they had finished I asked the head of the strike committee if the editor of television news would give us an interview.

'For the BBC, yes.'

'But he doesn't like the BBC. And if he remembers me, he won't like me either.'

The editor of television news was the man who had stood in the dark transmission room at CST seven years before and demanded that our report of Vaclav Havel and Charter 77 should be taken off the air.

'If we tell him to, he'll want to do it.'

It was true. The managers were afraid for their jobs. The head of international relations came down to see us first, and writhed in his chair while I interviewed him. The situation was extremely difficult, he said. Mistakes had been made in the past. There was no doubt about what was worrying him. They had been among the most faithful of the *ancien régime*'s servants. And the *ancien régime* had made its opponents suffer. The memory of all the writers who were stoking furnaces and the academics who were sweeping the stairs of offices must have been in the minds of the faithful servants. Now, perhaps, it would be their turn.

The singing and chanting faded into the distance, and the red, white and blue flags were scarcely discernible in the thick industrial air. The strikers had gone. The only people left in the television station were the journalists who had been appointed to do their democratic duty, and a small clutch of management figures with no one left to manage.

A young reporter with a leather tie and a way of ducking his head respectfully like a shopwalker in a Victorian department store showed us up to the office of the editor of television news.

'He's a very fair man, very popular,' said the reporter. An important qualification for any reporter in CST under the old régime was a willingness to lick people's boots. Suddenly there was a disturbing selection of boots to lick.

'I've met him before,' I said.

But if the editor of television news remembered me, he didn't show it. He was sitting at his desk when we were ushered in. His deputy hovered in the middle of the room, reading out items of information off bits of paper. The editor wasn't listening. He was gazing out of the window in the direction his staff had taken. Absently, he held the telephone receiver against his chin, as though he couldn't remember who he'd been going to call. He looked like a man who was thinking about his future.

He was wearing the uniform of the senior Eastern European official: baggy suit with overlong sleeves, fatly knotted blue and silver tie, rubber-soled black shoes. A faint odour of nervousness emanated from him. As our interview began he moved about a good deal in his seat, using the stubby hands I had last seen waving angrily at my report on the television monitors. He wanted to persuade me of his good intentions. The past was the past: his instructions had been wrong. He could accept that now. He should have allowed his own reporters to interview Hajek, Dubcek or Havel during his thirteen years in the job. Now, said the editor of television news, he realized his mistake. He pulled at the knot in his tie and looked at me as though I might act as a character witness.

'Privately I was always a liberal. I always wanted to broadcast more objective news.'

It should have been a moment of sapid pleasure. I tried to summon up the memory of the hectoring, the insults, the ambush of the live television programme, seven years before. Instead, it was distasteful to watch a man of seniority asking a quietus of someone he had forgotten having wronged. Perhaps he was thinking of all the people who had lost their jobs over the years: Jiri Dienstbier, his former colleague in broadcasting, for one. He was still a stoker at a factory. There would soon be plenty of jobs going as stokers and caretakers.

I stood with Jiri Dienstbier in Wenceslas Square a few days later in the early morning sunlight, interviewing him about the collapse of the government and the extraordinary change of fortune which would soon make him his country's foreign minister. To get him to the interview we had to send a chauffeured car to his factory. He had been on a night-shift, and although he was spending his days in negotiating and planning at the Magic Lantern Theatre, the factory had not yet been able to find a replacement for him. So he continued doing both jobs for the time being. The absurdity of it, like the absurdity of everything, amused him. He used to say he almost enjoyed his job. He didn't have to work too hard, and he got four days off a week for his real job. Dienstbier was a much sunnier, less angst-ridden figure than Vaclav Havel. His harsh voice cracked with amusement in the morning sunlight, as people stopped to see who it was that was being interviewed by foreign television, and smiled if they recognized him. Not many did. He had been a non-person for twenty years.

'You've had a difficult time,' I said to him. 'Your family has suffered; you haven't always been able to get proper medical treatment for your children. It must be a temptation to treat the people who were responsible for all that in the same way?'

'We're trying to build a new society here,' he answered. 'You can't build it on vengeance.'

Our interview ended there. But he carried on for a minute or two after the camera had been switched off.

'I mean it, you know. Just to be standing here, knowing what's happened, is enough for me. Why should I need to get revenge on anyone?'

He looked round at the sunlit, wintry morning, the streets empty of secret policemen, the feeling of relief and pleasure that everyone seemed to feel. A few yards up the street someone had painted some words in English on the back of a newspaper stand: 'It's Over – Czechs Are Free!'

'That's our revenge.'

*

Every day now brought further ironies, further resonances from the past. On 28 November the head of the government secretariat for Church Affairs, Vladimir Janku, who had assured me in an interview six years before that the state did not control the religious activities of the churches, announced that draft laws were being prepared to end state control over them. Elections were announced. Civic Forum was given free air time on radio and television. The government called on the Federal Assembly to re-evaluate the Soviet invasion of 1968. Since the People's Congress of the Soviet Union had condemned the invasion a few days before, there seemed little point.

The collapse of Communist government was happening so quickly that for two or three days at the end of November the Civic Forum was obliged to support what remained of the Communist leadership and prevent them from resigning. In particular, the Forum took a conscious decision to represent the stand-in Communist prime minister, Ladislav Adamec, as a sympathetic figure with whom it could work. The Forum leaders had to have a negotiating partner. They did not want uncontrolled demonstrations demanding ever more concessions from the Communists. And the Party had to order the security police, the StB, to cease its activities and remain in its offices until it could be disbanded.

The negotiations with the government had been based on the Round Table principle, following the Polish example. On 5 December Civic Forum had what was called 'a turbulent but constructive' session with Adamec to discuss the make-up of a new federal government. Jan Urban was sitting with several Forum people in the basement of the Magic Lantern Theatre when the government rang to ask the Forum to name its candidate for the presidency within twenty-four hours. Soon after, as the government's crisis worsened, another call came: the name of the new president would be needed within an hour. It was a subject no one had previously had time to consider.

'I suppose it had better be Vaclav,' Urban said.

The others agreed.

'In that case I'd better go and tell him.'

The Czech writer and journalist Karel Kyncl, who now lives in England, once wrote that Vaclav Havel had the necessary intellectual and moral qualities to fit him for the post of President of the Czechoslovak Republic. At the time, Havel was annoyed. Now it seemed natural. On the day of the inauguration he laughed and joked with Jiri Dienstbier, the new foreign minister ('Mr Minister Won't Have To Look After The Central Heating Any More', said a newspaper headline; the factory had finally found a replacement). Still, Havel was clearly nervous, and kept fiddling with the waistband of his trousers. And in the Cathedral for a mass to mark the installation of Czechoslovakia's first non-Communist president since Eduard Benes, Havel's wife Olga had to nudge him when it was time for him to kneel down. 'I am constantly aware of the ridiculousness and absurdity of my situation,' he said in a television interview.

*

I returned to Prague briefly on the day when the security police, the StB, was formally abolished. It was 1 February, and the sun shone. I didn't bother to try to see President Havel and Foreign Minister Dienstbier: they had no time now to see passing foreigners. There were pleasant stories that Havel rode the long corridors of Hradcany Castle on a scooter, like a schoolboy. I walked down Wenceslas Square, where even now there was a small demonstration around the statue, and headed towards the old town. Everywhere there were pictures of the new president looking statesmanlike and uncomfortable, or relaxed and friendly, as though he might indeed have a scooter hidden away somewhere.

It was a school holiday, because the new minister had decided that teachers had had a difficult time and deserved a break. On Charles Bridge there were crowds of children of different ages, shepherded by parents or wandering around on their own. Seagulls hovered over the Vltava and caught the bread people threw into the air. St Nicholas of Tolentino's halo was outlined against the sky. St Francis Xavier, birdshit on nose, was held up on the shoulders of smiling Indians and Chinese. Somebody, possibly St Agnes herself, played with a baby of black stone holding a pomegranate. It still said *'Demisi'* on the walls of the gatehouse at the end of the bridge.

Above the city, where the statue of Stalin with its buttons the size of loaves once stood, someone had erected a liberty bell. *'Havel na Hrad'* said the older posters in the windows; Havel to the Castle, the seat of the presidency. *'Havel na Hrad ě'* said the later ones triumphantly; 'Havel IS at the Castle.' 'If only this had happened in 1968,' a friend of mine said; 'I've wasted my whole life waiting for it.'

There was one last thing I had to do. I took a taxi to the hotel where I had once stayed. I wanted to see an old friend. I walked through the familiar double doors with a certain apprehension. Inside there was a lot of varnished wood and ugly copperwork. The windows rattled in the February wind. It had gone down in the world. Now it had been colonized by visitors from the farther reaches of Moravia and Slovakia. Round the bar was a group of Communist Third Worlders. History had stripped the establishment of its star-rating. But it was a great deal livelier than when I had last been here, seven years before. The showcases which had once been full of dusty Bohemian glassware and the marvels of Czechoslovak heavy engineering now contained jewellery and perfume. President Husak no longer stared gloomily from his picture like an undertaker. I didn't even mind the canned music. In the old days it was so quiet your shoes creaked on the hard floor.

Better still, the hotel had dismantled the surveillance cameras which once kept an automatic eye on all the exits. And the two bulky secret policemen, Fafner and Fasolt, were gone from their seats by the door.

From today they were out of a job. The StB's personnel files were being inspected to see who might be suitable for ordinary police work. I walked over to the counter. A guest was arguing about his bill with the receptionist. This was the difficult part.

I was a little surprised to see her there. Seven years is a long time to be in one job, even in Czechoslovakia. She was still as beautiful as she had been in the photographs she once sent to try to entrap me. The years had merely made her look more vulnerable, less disdainful. Her hair was blonder now. There was an ambiguous ring with a green stone on the third finger of her long left hand. Perhaps it was to fend off tiresome guests. The complainant paid up and left. It was my turn.

'*Prosím?*'

She didn't recognize me. Under her clear gaze my prepared phrases evaporated. I just said my name, and the BBC's. She looked away for a moment, in the direction where there had once been a remote camera. Then the gaze came slowly back to me. Her cheeks went a delicate pink. She made a sound like a murmured cough, turned, and headed away from the desk fast. The varnished door slammed shut with the unconvincing sound cheap wood makes. It did not reopen. I was left there, alone.

The door stayed closed for some minutes. I could hear the faint sound of talking behind it: a well-modulated, low voice, an excellent thing in women, and a harsher, higher one. Then the door opened and shut. A squat blonde figure in her fifties emerged. Her bust was vast and cunningly cantilevered. She pointed this marvel of Czechoslovak heavy engineering in my direction.

'*Prosím?*'

'Is Anna there?'

'Sorry, is not here.'

'When will she be back?'

'*Prosím?*'

I gave up. No one stonewalls better than a hotel receptionist trained under Marxism-Leninism. I walked out, unwatched by remote television cameras, unfollowed by secret policemen, into the streets of a city which was still enjoying the feeling of having liberated itself from such things. People looked relaxed and happy. They even apologized now if they got in each other's way. Forty-two years of surveillance, tale-telling and entrapment had come to an end. Anna's job with the secret police was over. From now on, she needn't write to foreign guests any more. Unless, of course, she chose to.

PART V
BUCHAREST –
A DARKER REVOLUTION

10

HEART OF DARKNESS

God preserve me from those who want what's best for me
from the nice guys
always cheerfully ready to inform on me
from the priest with a tape recorder under his vestment
from the blanket you can't get under without saying good evening
from the dictators caught in the chords of the harp
from those angry with their own people
now when winter's coming
we have neither tall walls
nor geese on the Capitoline
only great provisions of tolerance and fear

'Cold Comfort' by MIRCEA DINESCU
(translated by Andrea Deletant and Brenda Walker)

It was April 1989. No one was predicting revolution in the Communist bloc, least of all in Romania. We were about to enter a brutal world. A line of cars with sad, nervous people sitting in them had formed in front of us. There were old Yugos with Belgrade number-plates, a couple of small trucks carrying produce of some kind, and a Volkswagen minibus from Holland with a large family on board. As we drove up, the Dutch family was having a difficult time. The Romanian customs officers were examining everything: the mattresses, the boxes of muesli, the baby's feeding bottle. They dug into the oranges with their thumbs. They searched the three-year-old child till she screamed. They prised out the panelling of the van and poked rods into the fuel tank.

Perhaps they thought a young couple like this were religious missionaries, trying to smuggle Bibles into Romania. Perhaps they just did it for the exercise. I went over to the mother of the children to see if there was anything I could do. They were driving through Europe from Amsterdam to Turkey. No one had told them that Romania would be this brutal.

We knew, though. There were four of us: Tira Shubart, who was to be my producer on this trip; a BBC cameraman, Steve Morris, who had been a personal friend of mine for several years, and his girlfriend

Lynne Kemp. Lynne worked for the BBC too, but as an administrator. She had bravely volunteered to come with us. Two couples seemed a little more likely than any other grouping. We were pretending to be on holiday. In fact we intended to make a documentary on the human rights abuses in Romania. Our visas came from the Romanian embassy in Paris; the London embassy would have guessed what we were planning to do. We had rented a large blue Mercedes from a car-hire desk at Belgrade airport. The tired, grey man behind the counter tried to dissuade us.

'Why you want go there? Is crazy place. No gas. Everywhere cops. We hired car there before, everybody die. Big smash. Yugoslavia is nice. You drive in Yugoslavia.'

It would certainly have been pleasanter, but we had work to do. We had equipped ourselves with emergency rations and a small, efficient Video-8 camera of virtually professional standard.

'We've always wanted to see Romania,' I said, trying to act in character. 'We're interested in Dracula.' I touched a couple of imaginary fangs hanging over my bottom lip as I said it.

'They have Dracula now,' he replied glumly. 'His name, Ceausescu.'

I laughed obediently and began signing the forms.

In his way he was right. The government of Nicolae Ceausescu, which had been assiduously courted in the 1970s and later by politicians who should have known better, was responsible for the worst dictatorship in Europe. For a time it had been useful to the West, which believed Ceausescu's independent policies were turning Romania into a Trojan horse within the Warsaw Pact. He had kept his links with Israel and China, when the rest of the Soviet bloc had severed theirs. He advocated the reduction of short-range nuclear weapons in Europe and ways of relaxing tension between the two power groupings. But directly Mikhail Gorbachev became General Secretary of the Soviet Communist Party in March 1985, Ceausescu's usefulness to the West dropped away. Now, with the exception of a nuclear-free zone in the Balkans, Gorbachev was proposing everything Ceausescu had advocated, at a far more influential and effective level.

Ceausescu's regime had a dreadful human rights record. For its size, Romania had the highest number of secret policemen in the entire Soviet bloc: the Securitate had almost 100,000 full-time members. One third of the population, it was said, were informers. Every Romanian who talked to a foreigner was required to report the conversation to the Securitate within twenty-four hours. Securitate officers had powers to enter people's houses under any number of pretexts and confiscate 'illegal' possessions. The Illicit Goods Law of 1974 declared the ownership of rare metals and precious stones a state monopoly; to keep your family heirlooms when the Securitate raided your house was therefore a near-impossibility. Everything had to be registered with the police: fruit trees, vineyards, farm animals, typewriters. A typewriter, indeed, was a potential engine of sedition. A sample of the typeface from every machine in the country was kept on file by the police, so that samizdat literature and anonymous letters could be traced. Duplicators were forbidden by law. A supposed shortage of paper meant that writers were not allowed to publish more than one book a year. The single exception was the most prolific author in the country. Ceausescu's collected writings and speeches, in 27 volumes, were entitled *On The Way Of Building Up The Multilaterally-Developed Socialist Society*. Every volume was a bestseller.

Ceausescu himself had become a parody of a dictator. The newspapers, radio and television were mostly devoted to his and his family's doings. His English-bred Labrador dogs, two of them presents from the Queen, lived far better than most ordinary Romanians. They had their own limousines, which drove down the centre lane in the main streets of Bucharest just like their master's, and they were fed on the finest lean steak. They had the honorary title of 'Comrade', and government ministers were expected to address them that way. It was a familiar and not very funny joke that Ceausescu, Caligula-like, was thinking of giving them seats in the Senate.

In 1978 the Queen had been obliged by the British government of James Callaghan and his foreign secretary, David Owen, to invite Ceausescu to Buckingham Palace. She was both amused and annoyed by his assumption that his rooms were bugged. He would gather all his ministers around him each morning and go for a walk in the gardens of the Palace in order to avoid the microphones which he characteristically assumed were everywhere. President Giscard d'Estaing of France had warned Buckingham Palace that during Ceausescu's visit to the Elysée his men had ripped off the valuable wallpaper in the rooms where he had stayed in their search for microphones. One of Ceausescu's obsessions was that his enemies (and in particular the Soviet Union) might try to give him cancer by secreting a radioactive isotope near him. His predecessor, Gheorghiu-Dej, had died of cancer which both he and Ceausescu ascribed to a radioactive door handle. There was always someone with a Geiger counter in Ceausescu's entourage.

Yet Western politicians of all persuasions were prepared to overlook his increasing megalomania and the unpleasantness of the government he controlled because they felt he represented an independent voice within the Warsaw Pact. Right-wing politicians courted him because they felt they were helping to weaken the Soviet bloc. Politicians on the left praised him because they believed doing so would ease the confrontation between the super-powers. Sometimes it was hard to know who was praising Ceausescu more.

> As the result of the unconditional acceptances of the [past] abuses of the legal system, Ceausescu has declared that steps must be taken to ensure that such injustices can never occur in the future. The importance of democracy is therefore being increasingly stressed and whilst the standards set for loyalty to the Romanian State are high there is no question of rigging trials as occurred in the past. Democracy in Romania must be based on complete acceptance of what is legal. Interference by anyone, no matter how important, is unacceptable in Ceausescu's view.

That was the British left-wing Labour MP, Stan Newens, writing in 1972.

> I was impressed by the personality of President Ceausescu . . . Romania is making sustained efforts for consolidating peace and understanding, in particular by means of numerous direct contacts leading to the development of bilateral collaboration.

That was Margaret Thatcher, after meeting Ceausescu on his visit to Britain in 1978.

The former American president, Richard Nixon, praised Ceausescu in similar terms. As late as 1988, a little over a year before the people Ceausescu ruled drove him out of office, Lord Wilson of Rievaulx, who as Harold Wilson had been Britain's prime minister in the 1960s and 1970s, sent him a telegram which read: 'You have raised the Romanian nation to a unique role in the world.'

Some Western journalists helped Ceausescu indulge in a form of vanity publishing: favourable biographies and histories of Romania were usually bought in large quantities by the Romanian government. *A Concise History of Romania*, edited by Andrew McKenzie and published in London in 1985 reads:

> It is obvious to me as a visitor to Romania for 17 years that conditions have greatly improved there and the régime is more relaxed than it was . . . There are no long queues for food . . . Ceausescu still remains a popular figure.

Pergamon Press, owned by the former Labour MP and owner of the *Mirror* group of newspapers, Robert Maxwell, who died in questionable circumstances in November 1991, published collections of writings and speeches of most leaders of the old Warsaw Pact countries. They generally contain a short, uncritical biography at the start and an interview conducted by Robert Maxwell at the end. In the volume on Ceausescu, published in 1983, Maxwell takes up the question of the Romanian leader's personal standing with his people:

> Dear Mr President, you have been holding the highest political and state office in Romania for almost 18 years, a fact for which we warmly congratulate you. What has – in your opinion – made you so popular with the Romanians?

Ceausescu's answer to this fearless question takes up an entire page. Taxed about this later, Maxwell replied engagingly, 'Haven't you ever made a mistake?'

Ceausescu's wild extravagance made Romania's economic situation far worse. He decided to build a boulevard through Bucharest longer than the Champs-Elysées, lined with shops and mansions. At the head of it there was to be a presidential palace larger than Buckingham Palace. It was to contain a thousand rooms. These plans cost more than a billion US dollars, though much of the labour was done by the army. Ceausescu also wanted to link Bucharest with the Danube by canal. Since they were separated by 50 miles of land, that would cost hundreds of millions more. His declaration that he would pay off Romania's foreign debt by the middle of 1989 meant a disturbing degree of belt-tightening in a country which had been kept short of food and consumer goods since at least the early 1970s.

Romania was once called the bread-basket of the Balkans. By the end of the 1980s it exported 90 per cent of its food produce. Eggs became a form of currency, changing hands perhaps a dozen times before they were actually eaten. Westerners who stayed in the foreign currency hotels of Bucharest in the dead of winter were unnerved to find ordinary Romanians watching hungrily through the street-level windows of the dining room while they ate. Local citizens had to plan their day around the food queues, which started before dawn. Peasant women often had to make journeys of 30 miles to buy meat. In the province of Transylvania, rationing was intensified to five eggs, a kilo of flour, a kilo of sugar and a kilo of cheese per person per month. Conditions were a little easier in Bucharest. But for the country as a whole the rationing was worse during the accelerated repayment of the debt than it had been during the Second World War.

There was a pattern to Ceausescu's decision, the debt repayment included. The initial idea was grandiose, and would have been rejected out of hand by political leaders who were less imperious and less sure of their position. But with Ceausescu there were scarcely any policies, no matter how ferocious their effects, which he could not force on to the country. The so-called 'systematization' of the rural areas, for instance, was something only a Stalin or a Mao Zedong had tried to introduce before him. Its origins lay, as Mao's reorganization of the countryside had, in a desire to reduce the very real disparities of wealth and opportunity between country and town. The intention was to turn the Romanian peasant into a New Socialist Man along Stalinist or Maoist lines. As early as 1967 Ceausescu announced a policy of 'homogenization' between the two, and the first projects were begun in 1979. Poor villages would be demolished and their inhabitants rehoused in 'agro-industrial centres'; 558 villages were selected for the process.

It was deeply unpopular. Even the Communist Party bureaucracy opposed it, and local Party secretaries used every available tactic to delay its implementation. Various Western journalists claimed to have seen or filmed the process of 'systematization', particularly in Transylvania where it became mixed up with the issue of ethnic Hungarian opposition to Ceausescu. In the end only five villages, all in the Bucharest area and all on Ceausescu's route to one of his country houses, were seriously affected. Even so the policy was crazy, and only hubris prevented Ceausescu from realizing how dangerous it was to combine a concerted attack on the values of a largely agrarian society with a savage lowering of living standards.

*

When our turn came at the customs post on the Yugoslav-Romanian border, we had already been waiting two hours. The Dutch couple had finally been allowed to go on their way, their minibus leaving the noise of children's crying hanging behind it in the air as heavy as exhaust gas. The customs men were rude and aggressive.

'Out here. Everything out.'

We piled our suitcases on to raised stone platforms beside the road. They looked like altars with our offerings on them. The things we had brought with us had been carefully chosen; we didn't want to raise suspicions about our plans at the very start. They examined every book, every tape cassette, every item of equipment and clothing and food we had brought. They questioned us about our plans, and they looked in every compartment of our hired Mercedes.

'Bibles? You have Bibles?'

We had no Bibles.

By the time they had finished with us, and we had changed the necessary amount of hard currency into Romanian *lei* and bought our petrol coupons, it was late in the afternoon. We headed through the Transylvanian countryside. It was lush, but poorly farmed and poverty-stricken. Children in ragged clothes ran into the streets to watch our car pass. Old men sat hunched over the skinny horses that pulled their carts. There was little farm machinery: this was a country where most jobs were done by hand. The level of advancement was more like that of East Africa than Europe. And yet you could tell from the style of the houses in the villages we passed through that this had once been part of the Austro-Hungarian empire. Those single-storeyed, expansive cottages with their plastered walls, and the doorways that always looked a little too grand for the rest of the building, could have come from anywhere within a 500-mile radius. Since the days of the Habsburgs, Romania had fallen on hard times.

As the daylight faded, we could see further evidence of that. The lights that appeared in the cottage windows as we passed were few in number, and brownish-yellow in colour. Electricity was so strictly rationed in Romania that people could afford only to use a single 40-watt bulb per dwelling. Officials came every month to check that no one was exceeding the limit. We drove on through the dusk, our headlights bright on the unlit, uncared-for roads. The occasional cart was still on the road, but we saw very few cars. Petrol, oil, tyres and spares were hard to come by. Life in the countryside was returning to the nineteenth century.

We had decided to spend the night in the town of Deva. To my ears, it had an attractively Roman sound to it, like so many towns in Romania: Maximin, Caracal, Turnu Severin. It turned out to be deeply unattractive. The streets were almost entirely dark, except in the centre. Our headlights illuminated quotation after quotation from President Ceausescu on placards by the side of the road. In the centre of Deva the placards were huge, and the great man smiled out from them at the inhabitants. The slogans were changed throughout the whole of Romania every few weeks. Each stressed some new aspect of his character and policy. This month's special slogan was in praise of Ceausescu's courage.

CEAUSESCU EROISM!
ROMANIA COMUNISM!

His heroism lay partly in his long struggle for Romania's independence from the Soviet Union, which had begun in 1964 when he came to power. In the centre of the town was the biggest portrait of him we had yet seen: smiling benignly out into the darkness of this obscure corner of his empire. He visited the place occasionally, because he had a villa not far from Deva. He had a villa not far from almost everywhere in Romania.

The hotel where we were planning to stay proved to be another example of Communist civic brutalism. It was concrete, and our headlights, as we swung in to park in front of it, lit up the orange panels under every window. The girl behind the counter was genuinely shocked to see four foreigners standing there and demanding rooms for the night. There was a nervous conversation with someone in a rear office before we were allocated a couple of double rooms.

Dinner was unappetizing: a piece of unnamed meat, some grey potatoes, a slice or two of beetroot. It was a great deal better than the townsfolk of Deva were eating that night. Afterwards we went for a walk. On our way out of the hotel we passed a contingent of policemen standing at the door. A heavy-set elderly officer with quantities of silver braid and a blue band round his uniform hat stood aside politely to let us pass. Nine months later I discovered that a hat with a blue band was part of the uniform of the Securitate.

We were not gone long. The streets were too dark and too uneven to walk along with any ease, and there was nothing whatever to see. When we came back the man in the Securitate hat was examining the forms we had filled in. Our passports were in a pile beside him. He looked up as we came in, and so did the men who were with him. No one showed any sign of embarrassment. The Securitate had no need to apologize for anything it did, and since it was everywhere, there was no reason for its men to hide. We wished him good night, and he answered pleasantly enough in Romanian.

'*Bona sera.*'

The next day they started following us. There was a car behind us when we went sightseeing. When we filmed the grey streets, the empty shops, the buses and taxis which ran on tanks of methane gas fixed to their roofs, we were carefully observed. We went into a butcher's shop. It was empty. The trays in the glass-topped display stands contained nothing but dried bloodstains from the time when meat had last been on sale. The two shop attendants in their white coats leaned against the counter, bored and surly. On the wall, hanging from meat hooks, were a dozen pig's feet; the Romanians called them 'patriots', because they were the only part of the animal that didn't leave the country.

In a nearby market there was nothing for sale but strings of garlic, unhealthy small lettuces and radishes. A group of people had gathered round a small truck. A man was selling a live sheep, and the by-standers were struggling as much as it was. At last someone bought it and hurried off, the sheep baa-ing under his arm. We were filming the rows of sickly radishes when a young man came barging into us.

'Securitate,' he warned in a whisper, and ran on.

There was no time to get away. Within a minute we were arrested and marched off to the police station. At this stage the Securitate still believed that we were tourists, but Steve Morris, the cameraman, was obliged to show everything he had filmed to the interrogating officer. At the end they let us go. There was no warning, and no apology either.

We left Deva and headed eastwards. From now on there was always a small Dacia car in our rear-view mirror. It stopped when we stopped, and turned when we turned. From time to time, as we moved from one Securitate district to another, the car would change; but there would always be two men inside it. Sometimes it would drop behind so far that we thought the following was all in our imagination. Once, when the road behind us was empty, we stopped for a picnic. Unintentionally, we had parked a little way round a blind curve in the road. After fifteen minutes or so a Dacia came round the bend very fast. For an instant its occupants looked at us in shock, but they were obliged by the rules of the game to continue driving. At the next town they were waiting for us by a fork in the road, their heads ducked down so we shouldn't see them.

Yet even secret policemen are only civil servants. At five o'clock each evening the Dacia would drop away from our rear-view mirror and we would be alone. They knew roughly where we were heading, and would leave it to the staff of whichever hotel we chose to ring the local Securitate office when we arrived. At the once-magnificent Hotel Continental in Cluj the receptionist picked up the telephone as we were going upstairs to our suites (four vast, Germanically furnished rooms for a few pounds per night). The Securitate in Cluj was particularly nervous. The British ambassador had been manhandled there when he tried to see the most famous of all the Romanian dissidents, Doina Cornea, at her house in the city. Now a group of four British people had turned up in a town which had almost no visitors from the West.

Our plan was not to see Doina Cornea, who was too well guarded, but a woman and her daughter who had contacts with a dissident movement in Britain. We had been told they were both courageous and reliable and would be glad to speak to us. That night we went out for a walk, then drove through the pouring rain in the direction of the suburb where the women lived. We were so badly lost and turned back on ourselves so frequently, that we were certain no one was following us; though it was possible that a radio beacon had been fixed to our car. We stopped a little way from the large complex of flats, and Tira and I left Lynne and Steve and headed off into the rain and the darkness.

I carried the video-camera with which we hoped to record an interview with the two women. Tira had with her the most valuable of presents: a large packet of coffee and some Kent cigarettes, the effective currency in Ceausescu's Romania. We wandered in the muddy darkness around the blocks of flats for some time, shrinking into the shadows whenever someone came along. It took a long time to find the right block. We opened the creaking door with great care, and walked up the stairs to the second floor.

The moment the two women caught sight of us standing in their doorway I knew we should never have come. The look of despair and fear on their faces was terrible. For us, the worst that could happen was a beating up and a quick expulsion. For them it could mean house arrest, even imprisonment. They hustled us inside. The flat was dark, except for the flickering of a black and white television screen. Ceausescu and his wife were, inevitably, the subject of the programme. Each night they were the subject of the majority of programmes shown by Romanian television. Here at least they were peforming a useful service by illuminating the room.

The older woman was too hospitable to let us go without offering us something. By the flickering light of the Ceausescus she poured us a glass of plum brandy. Her hands shook so much that some of it dripped onto the sleeve of my jacket. The younger woman was angry with us.

'It's very dangerous for us that you should be here. Why did you do this?'

She was small and dark, and completely absorbed in her sense of injustice. The older woman, who was now in her seventies, seemed to wander between fear and a *haut bourgeois* appreciation of the wealthy, dashing figure in the Romanian opposition in London who had given us their names and address.

'I remember him from before the War. His family and ours were friendly. He was splendid in those days.'

At times her mind seemed to wander away, so that she was no longer in the dismal world of modern Romania. There were a few expensive objects around the room: a little silver, some good china. But the flat was fusty and old, and there was a sour smell of old cooking from the kitchen. I guessed that the older woman looked after the house while her daughter worked in an office. From the television I caught the repeated murmur 'Tovarich Nicolae Ceausescu'. The older woman came back from the days before the War and turned down the sound irritably.

'Terrible little man. We have to put up with this every night. It's too much.'

After that we spoke in whispers, crouched together in the light of the Great Dictator. If their neighbours heard us they might inform the Securitate. I felt obliged to ask the younger woman if she would record an interview with me. She refused vehemently. She was still angry with us and with her mother's friend in London for having given us their address. She plainly did not believe me when I said we had not been followed there. The myth of the Securitate's omnicompetence was unbreakable. But as we sipped our plum brandy she slowly confirmed the stories we had heard in the West: that women of child-bearing age, like her, were obliged to submit to a monthly gynaecological examination at their factories or offices.

Ceausescu's government had declared that it was every woman's duty to bear children for Romania. Until the target of five children per woman was reached, anyone who used contraceptives or had an abortion was guilty of an act of treachery. Legal abortion for anything except strict medical reasons had been abolished in 1966. The penalty for an illegal abortion was a prison sentence. The result was that when an illegal abortion went wrong no one would dare to ask for help. The doctors who carried out the gynaecological examinations were turned into agents of the Securitate. As we sat there in the dark flat listening to the woman talk, she explained that the doctor who came to her office was a kind man who would probably not report anything he found. But she, and everyone else, loathed the intrusion that the policy represented.

Once she had begun to attack the system she found it hard to stop. The shortages of food, the disappearance of imported fruit, the problems of travelling from one city to another to see her friends, the difficulties of getting to work when the buses were halted by shortages of petrol and methane gas, the lack of medicines for her mother who was often sick: resentfully, she poured out her feelings. Old people received less medical care and fewer rations than younger ones, because they were less productive. She gestured towards the television set, where Nicolae Ceausescu was still making a silent, impassioned speech.

'It's all because of him. Just one man. And her, of course.'

Elena Ceausescu stood beside her husband on the platform as he spoke, nodding from time to time and looking out at the audience from under her black eyebrows. The younger woman told us all the familiar stories about Elena's illiteracy and the vanity which obliged universities and institutions to award her a continuous flow of honorary doctorates and degrees – in engineering, chemistry, philosophy, medicine.

We drank the last of the plum brandy. The older woman had reverted to the pre-War years, and to her memories of the man in London who had said she and her daughter were as brave as lions and completely loyal.

'He was always so handsome and well-dressed.'

She held my hand with a dry intensity. She was back in the days of King Michael again.

'Thank you for coming and enlivening our evening.'

Affected by her courtliness and by the guilt I felt, I kissed her hand.

Her daughter showed us out in silence. She hustled us out past the dirty kitchen, with its pots piled in the sink. She put her finger on her lips and shook her head to show that any sound was dangerous, and that we must leave silently. The cheap, thin door which was their only protection against the absurd nightmare of Ceausescu's Romania closed behind us. We walked down in the darkness towards the rain and mud. The stairs smelled of urine.

The next morning the four of us pretended to be tourists. We filmed the windows of a bookshop where all thirty-one volumes of Ceausescu's writings and speeches (except those which had sold out) were on display. We filmed in the empty food shops, and the queues drawn up in front of them. We were walking through the main square when a man in civilian clothes addressed us in good English.

'I must ask you to come with me and answer some questions.'

Three uniformed policemen were close behind him. We did as we were told. On our walk I found the English-speaker a pleasant enough companion. He wouldn't talk about the reason for our arrest, but he told us a little about the history of Cluj and was proud of his command of colloquial English, which he had learned, he said, without leaving Romania. I assumed he was an interpreter. He led us to an ugly modern building. Inside, the corridors were empty and echoing. There were notices on the walls about firearms and the need for vigilance.

BE ON THE ALERT! PROTECT COMMUNISM!!

We were shown into a room with a thickly padded door. Four chairs had been drawn up, waiting for us, in front of a desk. A large relief map of Romania hung on the wall, and a calendar with a photograph of the Carpathian mountains in spring. It could have been the office of an insurance agent, except for the padded door. To my surprise, the man I had thought was an interpreter sat down at the desk and looked at us sternly. He ignored the rest of us and spoke to Tira.

'I think, Miss Shubart, that you are not just an ordinary tourist. I think you are a producer for the BBC programme *Newsnight*.'

It was clear what had happened. When we had seen the elderly woman and her daughter the previous evening, Tira had done the talking at first. She hadn't introduced me at any point. She had told them which programme we were working for, and she had explained she was the producer. Obviously the younger woman had spent a sleepless night worrying that the Securitate knew about our visit there. That morning she must have gone to the police. The law said that anyone who had come into contact with a foreigner must report the full details to the police within twenty-four hours. She had simply been obeying the law.

Our interrogator didn't shout or bang the table. He was urbane and unthreatening. He simply asked us for our passports, and left the room. For three of us, being held by secret policemen was not a new experience. It is always disturbing, but the secret is to remain calm and, if possible, be the master of the situation. Tira and I played chess. We had brought a small travelling set with us in the knowledge that we might spend some time as prisoners. I was impressed by Lynne Kemp's coolness. She was the one member of the team to whom this kind of thing was not part of everyday life. She and Steve Morris talked quietly together. None of us discussed what had happened.

Enough time passed to send a computer request for information to Bucharest and receive a reply. It was no great consolation to think that the computer system had been installed for the Securitate by a British firm, Ferranti. The pleasant English-speaker returned.

'Mr Simpson. Why didn't you tell me you had visited our country before, and had met some of my colleagues?'

I was genuinely taken aback. I had indeed been to Romania before, in 1978, but had thought it best to say nothing about that trip, since I had been there as an officially accredited television reporter. I didn't remember meeting the Securitate.

'You were arrested in Galati, it seems, for doing what I assume you were doing here: filming without permission, Mr Simpson.'

He shook his head in mock sorrow at my misdeeds. I remembered now: the military installations, the Soviet emplacement across the river, the frog-marching to a police station, the ritual of taking my passport details. I had managed to talk my way out of trouble ('We were filming your famous blue Danube') and my colleagues had managed to hold on to the pictures they had shot; but the details had obviously remained on my file ever since.

Now, the pleasant officer and his colleagues spent the length of an entire chess game examining our video cassette, and in the end they kept it. Fortunately we had others that they did not see. Then the officer told us we could go.

'I suggest you do what you said you had come to our country for. Go and be tourists!'

His joviality was fake, but we were glad to take advantage of it.

I bore him no ill will. When the revolution came, nine months later, I asked a cameraman friend of mine who was going to Cluj to find out what had happened to him. He had apparently slipped away when the crowd attacked the building where we had been held. They burned it and took away the files. For a time the revolutionaries considered sending me my file. Then they realized what every new government realizes: that intelligence is the life-blood of an administration. No file arrived.

As for the woman who had reported us to the Securitate, it was impossible to blame her. Only a handful of Romanians had the moral courage to speak out against the conditions Ceausescu imposed on them. Once they had put their heads above the parapet they could expect to be badly treated. Most people were prepared to put up with the unrelenting hardships of everyday life in silence rather than endure that. She could not have known that we would be allowed to go free; but a régime like Ceausescu's induces and rewards selfishness and inaction. Later, maybe, she was embarrassed at what she had done. But in the spring of 1989 there was no reason whatever to suppose that Ceausescu wife would be overthrown before the end of the year. At that time, the régime looked as though it would last for ever.

Some days later we arrived in Bucharest. Here, the Securitate did not break off at five o'clock in the evening. Nor did they stint themselves in terms of numbers. When we drove around the city, we counted at least five Dacias with us at any one time. They crossed our path from side streets and trailed us from the front in the most sophisticated way. Sometimes, as the Dacias sliced their way back and forth before and behind it was like a car chase from a Keystone comedy. When we went for a walk twenty recognizable Securitate men and women trailed us: not counting those who were stationed permanently at the main crossing-point near our hotel, or the fake black market currency dealers who offered us good rates of exchange in order to entrap us.

We checked in at the vast and gloomy InterContinental Hotel. It was almost empty. Everyone from the fat, phonily jolly doorman to the more sinister people behind the desk looked at us appraisingly. Tourists did not stay at the InterContinental; there were, in any case, almost no tourists now. We had plainly not come to negotiate a business deal. They assigned us two rooms, separated by a third, on the twelfth floor. Later, when the few non-Securitate people on the staff were able to talk freely, they told us that the listeners would have been placed in the intervening room. There were microphones in the telephone handsets and in the electricity plugs. In the various hotel restaurants the Securitate stationed people near us with listening devices hidden in bags, of the kind the StB used in Czechoslovakia. One unfortunate night the four of us were dining in the main hotel restaurant when a big, blonde Romanian woman who had been living in London recognized me from the television screen. She stood up at her table and called out my name. The conversation everywhere was hushed. Heads turned to look at me.

'Afraid not,' I said in English as convincingly as I could.

There was no real reason now to deny it, but I felt I had to stay with our cover story, in which I was a lecturer in history from Magdalene College, Cambridge.

'A lot of people confuse us,' I added lamely.

She sat down again, embarrassed and uncertain. Every now and then I caught her looking across at me, frowning.

You could see the extraordinary transformation of Bucharest from our hotel bedroom. Dominating everything was the immense House of the Republic, which in true looking-glass fashion was not being built for the republic at all, but for the Ceausescus.

'It's like White House and Kremlin together,' said the bellboy who brought up our luggage. He looked at us slyly. The bellboys were not generally Securitate agents. I gave him a sizeable tip in German Marks, but said nothing.

Cranes towered across the skyline, from south to north, ending at the half-finished House of the Republic. They marked the track which the Boulevard of the Victory of Socialism had carved through the attractive old city of Bucharest. Churches, monasteries, mansions, terraces of houses, shops, had all been devoured in its passage. Once, after an international outcry about the destruction, Ceausescu ordered that a small Orthodox church should be moved to the side rather than knocked down. His propaganda people filmed it and sent the pictures round the world. The church was placed on rollers and slowly eased out of the path of the oncoming Boulevard. When it settled it was too badly damaged to survive; Ceausescu's pictures didn't show that.

We walked down one afternoon to film the Boulevard and the enormous palace at its end. At first sight it was surprisingly pleasant. The style of the buildings was along the lines of the new romantic architecture in the West: pillars, pilasters, scrolls, balconies, columns, balustrades, decoration everywhere. There was much stress on Roman motifs, to flatter the questionable belief of Romanians that they are the direct descendants of the legionaries who were settled in the area under the Severan emperors. Ceausescu had always maintained that the Romans were imperialists, and that the true Romanians were the disposed tribesmen who fought a long guerrilla war against them; but presumably the tribesmen had no architectural style worth copying.

Along the centre of the Avenue, down which only the vehicles associated with the Ceausescu family could drive, was a line of fountains. They were empty, and no water rose from them. Indeed, it was doubtful whether any ever would. The pressure was too weak for it to happen naturally, and there was no provision in the budget for a pumping station. It was fortunate for the engineer in charge that there was a revolution before the moment of truth arrived. Each fountain was differently decorated, with motifs deriving from the sea, from sport, from everyday life. They were crumbling already.

The entire project was built for show. The buildings which were supposedly of white stone were in fact of rendered cinder-blocks, shoddily rammed together. The pavements which appeared to be of coloured marble had merely been stained. Already, before a single occupant had moved in, the stain had begun to run. Some of the apartments, intended for members of good standing in the Communist Party and for Securitate officers and their families, turned out to lack running water, window frames, and sometimes doors and floors. Ceausescu's imperial Roman capital was as phoney as the set of a Hollywood epic.

At the head of the Avenue rose the vast, elegant, absurdly expensive House of the Republic: Ceausescu's greatest monument to himself in white marble. Only Romanian materials were used, and the best craftsmen and architects in the country were employed on its construction. Ceausescu was obsessed with the project. In 1989, the year of his death, he paid 99 visits to it, examining the smallest details. He told the men and women in charge of the work that they should remember it was to last for five hundred or a thousand years. For all its folly, it is a magnificent building, far better constructed than the shops and blocks of flats along the Boulevard. The Ceausescus were influenced in their choice of furnishings by their stay with the Queen in 1978. The president's office, uncompleted during his lifetime, is more than a hundred feet long, with a huge patterned carpet. A little man with skilfully built-up shoes, he needed imposing circumstances to seem imposing himself.

There was almost no limit to the flattery poured over Ceausescu by his courtiers, and by the press, radio and television. The epithets which were applied to him in the years immediately before the revolution were embarrassingly florid, and sometimes reached the level of ersatz religion. This is a small selection, culled from the newspapers, from television and from official documents:

The great architect
The banner
The builder of everything good and just in the country
The celestial body
The creator of the epoch of unprecedented renewal
The credo, spur and luminary
The defender of the present and future
The demiurge
Our destiny
The flag of our national pride
The living fire
The polyvalent genius
Our secular god
The new morning star
The leader ('*Conducator*')
The navigator
A nimbus of victory
Our Prince Charming
A saint, a saviour, a scion
The sun
The source of living water
Our warm spring
Our tall standard
A titan
This treasure of wisdom and charisma
The zodiac

It was a Sunday afternoon. In the watery sunshine we wandered around in front of the palace which was being built for Romania's Prince Charming. The vast square, laid out for massive ceremonies of state which would never take place, was cold and empty. Most people seemed to avoid it, as though it was a place of ill omen. They have Dracula now, I remembered the car hire man in Belgrade saying; his name, Ceausescu. We wandered back along the Boulevard, looking in the empty shop windows, stopping every now and then when Steve Morris saw a shot he wanted.

Tira noticed them first.

'I don't like to tell you, but there's a group of seven men over there who are taking a big interest in us.'

They were tough-looking, and they made no secret of the fact that they were following us. When we stopped, they stopped. When we wandered on, so did they. It was distinctly worrying. There were enough of them to beat us up, smash the camera and take the cassette on which our day's work had been recorded. There were no comforting crowds around for us to use as shelter: just a vast, empty avenue the width of a football pitch and the length of half the city. All we could do was to wander on. There were enough empty windows down the Boulevard to give us plenty of time. An elderly man accosted us in English, and we guessed immediately that he had been sent to provide the thugs with some pretext to intervene and attack us.

Everyone stayed remarkably calm. I felt badly about having involved Lynne in this, but she stood up to it all splendidly. We ignored the old man, and eventually he wandered off. The seven came closer. They looked as though they meant business. They spread out on either side of us, three on the left, four on the right. We tried to walk slowly and chat about everyday things, but it was difficult. For some reason they didn't move in and take us in the empty Boulevard. We led them past the big unworkable fountains at the first main crossroads, and towards the old main avenue which was crowded with Sunday strollers. We didn't vary our slow pace. They were near enough now for us to be able to speak to them, but we were careful not to give them any chance to pick a fight with us. Steve was holding the camera under his arm.

We felt a little safer at first when we headed into the crowds. Soon, though, three of the seven dropped behind us. Two walked alongside us to the left and two to the right. They were well positioned to move in, knock us down and grab the camera. The crowds would have done nothing to stop them, if they had shouted the single word 'Securitate'. We gave the camera to Lynne to hold, and Tira walked a little behind her while Steven and I bunched in closely on either side of her. That left each of us with both hands free to use against the thugs. They were older than the usual run of Securitate agents, and they looked rougher. A couple of them could have been boxers. All were dressed in dirty old clothes. We moved along the street in a little huddle, like a rugby scrum.

As we approached another main crossing and waited for the lights to change they came very close: so close I could smell the sweat on the man beside me. The InterContinental was in sight, a couple of hundred yards away. It was now or never. Full of the ferocity which only real fear produces, I turned and glowered at the thugs who were standing close beside me. They whispered together and I said to the others, 'This is it. Watch out.'

But it wasn't. They moved apart from us as we crossed the road. By the time we had reached the other side, they had melted away. Maybe they simply wanted to give us a warning – though in a country where western ambassadors could be beaten up with impunity there was no reason why they should spare four illicit television people. Perhaps it was simply that our defensive tactics would have caused them too much trouble and attracted too much attention.

They mostly left us alone after that. We left the InterContinental at seven o'clock one morning, having laid a careful trail of disinformation to indicate that we were leaving later. We had the satisfaction of seeing the Securitate men lounging in the lobby jump up in nervous surprise as we left. It was a long drive to the border, and the Dacias which had trailed us out of Bucharest soon peeled off and were not replaced. For the first time in days, we were travelling alone. We headed down to the border crossing of Turnu Severin, on the Iron Gates of the Danube. Across the gorge lay Yugoslavia and freedom.

We ate one last unpleasant meal in an hotel. People sidled up to us even in the lavatories, asking us to change money. Here on the border it is possible they were genuine. We lined up to leave the country. Only now did we realize why the Securitate hadn't bothered to follow us down there: the border guards had been warned to take everything off us. We redistributed our video and audio cassettes. Tira carried one in her pants and one down her blouse. I tried to disguise a video cassette as a piano concerto by Bartók. We sat in the sun and waited. The border guards were leaving us till last.

When they searched us they left nothing unexamined. They gave us the treatment the Dutch couple had had. The inside panels of the Mercedes were opened with screwdrivers. Men lay on boards and wheeled themselves under our car to see that nothing had been attached to the underside. We must have been a disappointment to them, with our lack of ingenuity. A large female border guard enjoyed finding Tira's hidden cache of tapes. They searched each of us with the same thoroughness, and laid out their trophies on a table. I counted them up quickly. One video tape was missing. They had failed to look in the least clever of our hiding-places – my shaving gear.

They took it all away: the cassettes, the film from our stills cameras, my notes. They were gone for a long time. A pleasant enough English speaker came out eventually. We could reclaim our cassettes tomorrow. When we said as politely as possible that we were not prepared to wait, he said they would post them to us in England. My irritation boiled over. We wouldn't, I said, leave without the tapes. We would stay where we were until they gave them back to us. He shrugged, and walked away.

The shift changed. New men who spoke English came on. Some were pleasant, some not. Other cars arrived and were thoroughly checked, though not as thoroughly as our. A group of three men arrived in a Dacia car from the centre of town. They looked like Securitate. They glanced at us from time to time through the window of the office. It was late in the afternoon when one of the customs men came out to see us. They had finished with our material. We could take it and go.

Perhaps they were amused at our relief. We drove across the bridge which separated Romania from Yugoslavia as the sun was going down. The gorge through which the Danube flowed was extraordinarily beautiful in the red and golden light. Hills shaded off into the distance, blue and violet and indigo. The river ran red in the sunset. When we were properly in Yugoslavia Steve stopped and played one of the returned tapes on the camera, looking at it through the view-finder. He spooled on a little way, stopped, and played it again. He swore.

'They've wiped it.'

We took turns to look through the view-finder ourselves. The picture was there, but there were lines through it. Sometimes they were broad, sometimes narrow. The Securitate men had put each of our video cassettes through a bulk eraser. The only one that we knew was not affected was the cassette they had failed to find in my luggage. But since the hiding-place had been so obvious, I had put the least valuable of our material there. We drove through the rest of the sunset and into the ensuing darkness in a mood of quiet depression.

And yet, as it turned out, the Securiate's bulk eraser was too weak to destroy most of our pictures. Our documentary was shown, more or less as we had planned it. That was a considerable victory – but I assumed I wouldn't see Romania again for years.

11
THE INSTANT OF VULNERABILITY

I must express my high feelings of gratitude and appreciation towards you, Comrade Nicolae Ceausescu, hero of the nation. The Romanians never had a greater thought than following you.

CHRISTIANA STOIAN, industrial worker, speaking
at the 14th Party Congress in Bucharest, 23 November 1989

The Great Dictator stood on his balcony and surveyed his people. This was familiar territory for him: he had spoken from here hundreds of times before. In his black astrakhan hat and his coat with the matching astrakhan collar he looked very presidential. You couldn't see that he was standing on a box to make him look taller. Beside him were his wife Elena and assorted courtiers and his personal head of security, Neagoe, a large man in a fedora hat. Ceausescu looked out over the obedient ranks of his supporters in the Square below. All were carrying the right banners, all were chanting the right slogans. Everything was under control. Soon a few words from General Neagoe would help to change the course of Romanian history.

Normally the Square was large, silent and menacing. The Securitate patrolled it constantly. It had been carved out of the elegant buildings surrounding the royal palace in the 1930s, so King Carol II's men could open fire on crowds of would-be revolutionaries. The best modern guidebook describes it as 'waiting for a coup'; but the régime which Nicolae Ceausescu had run since 1964 was coup-proof. It was, in its way, a text-book example of a Marxist-Leninist state. There was no area inside the system where ideas hostile to the ruling orthodoxy could be sown and grow in secret. 'Scientific Socialism,' he had told his congress on 20 November, 'is in absolutely no danger.' They had applauded him to the echo, given him more than forty standing ovations, and re-elected him President for a further five years. The autocracies of Central and Eastern Europe might be collapsing all round its borders, but Romania itself was safe for dictatorship.

Then in mid-December in Timisoara, a city in Transylvania with a big Hungarian-speaking population, a trivial enough incident took place. The Securitate came to arrest a Hungarian-speaking Protestant pastor, Laszlo Tokes, for speaking to the Western media. Many of his parishioners, themselves Hungarian-speakers, gathered round the house to protect him. They drove off the Securitate. The temperature rose. In the days that followed, it ceased to be a religious or language dispute. Ethnic Romanians joined in. It became an uprising against the government. The tanks were summoned and many people died, but the troops were beaten off. Now the Army's loyalty was in question. A little local incident had turned into the only really serious threat that Ceausescu had faced in twenty-six years.

He was not given the full facts about the Timisoara rebellion. The Securitate kept some of the worst details from him, fearing that it would be blamed for having allowed the incident to get out of hand; unless, like the StB in Czechoslovakia, it was involved in a plot to get rid of another conservative leader. Either way, the President had no real idea of the intensity of feeling or the spread of the uprising against him. He probably never found out, even later. His response was to call a public meeting in the Square. He would address it, and people would listen as they always did. No one dared to tell him otherwise now. One or two of his advisers tried to suggest that something else, a television appearance perhaps, might be better. Ceausescu waved their anxieties away.

The Securitate sent its men to the factories and offices of Bucharest, instructing people to turn out. Every factory had to provide fifty people to go to the Square. Those who failed to turn up were threatened with the sack. Loyal Party members were to take up their positions in front; the rest of the Square would be filled with ordinary people. The Securitate would be out in force, standing in the crowd. It would be all right. It always was.

If the weather hadn't been so mild there might have been no revolution in Romania; but in the pleasant winter sunshine most people decided that they would, after all, go to the Square and listen. The size of the crowd was important. It helped give anonymity to everyone there. The Securitate had to spread out to cover the whole area.

The front few rows were solidly loyalist. They held up long red banners that spoke of Socialist progress and Ceausescu's heroism. Above their heads bobbed photographs of Ceausescu from the early 1960s, dark-haired and pleasant-featured, which were still the official issue. They clapped in unison, in the way he liked. Romanian Television showed the rally live. That turned out to be a considerable error of judgement.

Ceausescu began talking. Each time he paused there was more clapping in unison. He waved back, in a way that may have been intended to be modest but merely looked imperious. He was still thanking the Bucharest Party Committee for organizing the rally when something altogether new happened, something Ceausescu had never heard in his life before. Part of the crowd was booing him. It began as a low groan, but quickly grew louder and higher. Over and above the groaning was another, sharper sound. People were whistling as well.

It was a total surprise. He had been reading in his hoarse, old man's voice, his eyes on the sheet of paper in front of him. As the sound of the booing gradually penetrated to him he looked over to his right, where it was loudest. But he went on pumping out the bland words for a little, much more slowly now, not thinking what they meant but trying to think instead about the booing. At last the words faded away altogether, and he stopped. His mouth was a little open. It was a laughable and shocking moment: a tyrant coming face to face with the hatred of his people, Macbeth watching the wood begin to move. Even the television camera shook, as the cameraman's arm trembled at the thought of what might happen to him for recording this terrible event.

Ceausescu put up his right hand. He was trying to order the crowd to be silent, but it looked as though he were warding off the noise of the booing and what it meant. One of the group of ministers to Ceausescu's right must have offered some advice, off-mike, because he waved angrily as if to say, 'Don't be stupid'. An official photographer ran across the back of the balcony, from left to right of the television screen. It was not to get a better picture; he was there as a court photographer to capture another triumph for Ceausescu. He must have been trying to escape. Then from the right of the screen the head of the President's personal bodyguard, General Neagoe, came into shot, walking swiftly towards Ceausescu. He paused behind him for an instant, and the microphones picked up his voice and boomed it out over the Square:

'They're getting in.'

The general headed for the big glass double doors behind Ceausescu, holding his coat open as though he had a gun in a shoulder holster and would soon pull it out. Elena Ceausescu's thin, harsh voice was also picked up on the microphone:

'Stay calm, please.'

Her instincts were right and Neagoe's were wrong: unless, indeed, he was part of a plot. The crowd wasn't getting in. The booing was simply the reaction of people expressing their real feelings after years of repression. At that point someone at the television station took a decision, and cut the transmission. The picture disappeared. The screen went red: it showed a caption which said, with patent untruth, '*Transmisiune Directa*': live transmission.

In the Square, standing in the crowd almost directly in front of the balcony, was a young taxi driver, Adrian Donea, sharp-witted and handsome in a Latin way. He had been drawn there by curiosity, and by his utter hatred for Ceausescu. He hadn't expected anything like this, but he knew that he, like most people in Romania, was getting to the point where anything was better than continuing with things as they were. The anonymity of the crowd made it easier to join in the booing.

> Everybody's yelling and screaming, and they've all got their heads like this [he shielded his face with the lapel of his coat] because the Securitate used to film you in the Square. And at that moment we had the feeling and the sensation that maybe we win. We can see they're scared, and in that moment we see we can do something and that we're really a force.

That, certainly, was true. The shaken dictator, the nervous body-guard, the wobbling camera, the screen that went red, and above all the sound of booing, all had an extraordinary effect throughout the entire country. It seemed impossible that with such immense power over the lives of his subjects Ceausescu could be threatened. Yet the evidence was transmitted live to every home and every factory where the television was switched on. He was vulnerable after all.

The moment quickly passed. When it became obvious that the crowd wasn't breaking into the Central Committee building and the rally was continuing, the television director cut back to the President. Ceausescu was continuing with his prepared speech as though nothing had happened, warning about the consequences of the rioting in Timisoara. The crowd, as seen by the camera on the balcony, continued to wave the banners and the out-of-date portraits. Elena Ceausescu, tough and resourceful as ever, led the applause. But it was too late.

Over the years, the ferocity of Ceausescu's repression had knocked most of the resistance out of people. Paraschiva Cornelescu, the widow of a man who died during the revolution, was typical.

> I was afraid of everyone I didn't know. If you said something you shouldn't they could arrest you, they could beat you, they could kill you. They could do anything to you.

It was an attitude the Securitate naturally encouraged. Plotting to overthrow the state, gathering together in opposition groups, planning any form of resistance were all impossible. There were only two ways of challenging the régime. One was the way of individual conscience, by giving interviews critical of Ceausescu to foreign journalists. The other was a simple spontaneous rebellion on the streets by people who felt they had nothing more to lose. It had happened two years before in the city of Brasov, and had been put down with great brutality.

Marian Cornelescu, Paraschiva's husband, worked in an abattoir. He was a rough sort of man, unfaithful to his wife, fond of drink, sometimes violent. When we interviewed her a few days after the revolution she looked old and haggard, though she was still in her twenties. Money and food were scarce. They received occasional unappetizing joints from the abattoir, but otherwise they fed their four young children on bread and the 'patriot's' pig's trotter. Paraschiva scarcely saw her husband. In order for them to have enough to live on she had to work night-shifts, six days a week. Her sister did the shopping for them; and because she would have to be at work for a ten-hour shift at 6.30 a.m. she usually had to get up and start queuing at around 2.30. Such conditions drove even the most docile people to think of ways of breaking out, of finishing once and for all with such a system, if only the opportunity arose. Now Paraschiva's husband felt the moment had arrived.

> He was a simple worker, but he wanted revenge in some way. He wanted revenge for the conditions he had to live in. He shouted out loud for his family back at home, who couldn't shout. He told me he was going to fight for the children, and if he died he would die for the children – for the way we lived, with no food or rations.

There were thousands of people on the streets that afternoon and evening with the same sense of burning grievance. They realized that Ceausescu's régime was momentarily weakened and might just be overthrown if they stayed together and kept their nerve. At first they just hung about in the streets, not certain what to do. There were a few thousand of them, mostly people who had been at the rally in the Square and had drifted away in disgust as Ceausescu continued to harangue the crowd. People with banners and portraits who had been his trusted supporters were walking out on him. That had never happened before. They chanted, 'We want free elections.' But another chant, which one or two of the sharper and more far-seeing demonstrators started up and the rest took on, was: 'Don't leave the streets.'

The uniformed men who were out with riot shields and helmets seemed uncertain what to do. They looked like ordinary soldiers, but a closer inspection showed that they were Securitate troops. The Securitate was not simply composed of men and women who tapped telephones and followed suspects in unmarked cars. It was an organization run on military lines and it had its own soldiers, well trained and equipped, to deal with internal unrest. Their uniforms were almost identical to the army's, but the Securitate had a slightly different insignia on the lapels of their uniforms and boots with different straps. Ceausescu had always mistrusted the regular Army, suspecting that it might one day stage a coup against him. He had built up the Securitate to act as a parallel force.

If the Securitate troops had charged the crowd they might have broken it up; but they waited a little too long. Soon the extraordinary spectacle on television, when the live broadcast was interrupted, brought many more people out. They knew that Ceausescu's power was being seriously challenged, and they came from all over the city to join in. It was turning into a full-scale rebellion.

At nightfall the Securitate at last received clear instructions. Ceausescu and his advisers could think of nothing better than the tactics which had already failed in Timisoara: they sent in the troops, and ordered them to shoot to kill. The crowds hauled cars into the middle of the main avenue, Boulevard Nicolae Balcescu, and set fire to them. The street fighting became general. However, the demonstrators had no means of countering the bullets of the Securitate troops except with stones, Molotov cocktails and the sheer weight of numbers. If they stayed on the streets – and people were still shouting the slogan – then they could take advantage of the darkness and hope to beat down the Securitate's resistance. An amateur television cameraman filmed a young boy creeping up to a Securitate vehicle and setting fire to it while they were shooting at the demonstrators. It began to get dangerous for the Securitate.

By dawn on Friday 22 December the extraordinary outcome was clear. The crowds were marching up and down the main avenue, chanting and singing, and the Securitate troops had melted away. Everyone knew they hadn't gone for good, but it was an essential victory at that early stage. It showed the power of numbers and determination. The key now lay with the Army. So far the soldiers and their officers had taken no part in the fighting. Some were in their barracks, others had been ordered on to the streets, but they had neither supported the Securitate troops nor taken the side of the demonstrators.

As the morning wore on, Ceausescu and the men around him in the Central Committee building became more and more angered by the Army's refusal to fire on the crowd. Ceausescu believed it was the fault of his defence minister, General Vasili Milea, for refusing to pass on his orders. At about ten o'clock members of Ceausescu's bodyguard took Milea upstairs to his office and shot him. At eleven there was a statement on Romanian television. Milea, it said, was a traitor and had committed suicide.

For the second time television played a part in the developing revolution. The announcement infuriated the Army, which had regarded Milea with considerable respect. Many ordinary soldiers and some of their officers began to go over to the revolutionaries.

Ceausescu made one last effort to save the situation. A helicopter had landed on the roof to take him away, but he insisted on going out on to the balcony again and trying to address the crowd through a loud-hailer. It was a disaster. There was no control over the people in the Square. The plainclothes Securitate men were starting to make themselves scarce. The crowd hurled stones and pieces of wood at Ceausescu, and his bodyguards bundled him back into the building. Now everything was lost. His ministers and bodyguards screamed at him to escape. A helicopter was waiting on the roof to take him off. They ran over to the lift.

By this stage the crowd were breaking into the building. Adrian Donea was one of them. They forced open one of the three great doors and got through into the lobby.

> I forced in the main entrance with some other guys, and we take the weapons of several people. They just put their hands up and say, 'OK, we can't shoot the people, so if you need some guns here they are.' They put the guns down and run upstairs. So these were the first weapons we've taken. We try to go upstairs to see who's inside and who's firing. So a group of us who have some weapons just run up the stairs.

There were soldiers at the top of the grand staircase who put up more of a fight. When they had been forced back by the gunfire of the newly-armed insurgents they took refuge among the marble columns and down the corridors at the side. As Adrian Donea and the others charged up the stairs the entrance to Ceausescu's office lay ahead of them, across another vast lobby. The marble walls were pockmarked with bullets from the fierce fighting. They charged across the empty lobby, disregarding the fire from the soldiers in the passageways on either side. Donea and the others burst through the doors and found themselves in the ante-room. That was the way on to the balcony. They ran out, waving flags and shouting. The crowd in the Square below erupted with joy to see them. There was no organization. Anyone who wanted to leave the buildings was allowed to do so. Afterwards the revolutionaries realized that they had allowed many senior Securitate officers to go.

What none of the insurgents knew was that Ceausescu was still in the lift, only a few feet away from them. The electricity had been cut off in the gunfire and the lift had jammed. He was rescued only by luck. The waiting helicopter pilot, Lt-Col. Vasile Malutanu, was a heavily-built humourless man of forty-six who had landed there half an hour before. There were other helicopters on the roof, to take everyone off and act as decoys, but Malutanu's French-built Ecureuil was the main presidential helicopter.

> The rotor blades were turning, and we could hear the angry shout of the crowd. My colleagues and I were terrified. Our mission was secret. The Army high command had just given me orders to go and find the President, but I had no idea what the situation was. The revolutionaries had managed to block the lift which was carrying Ceausescu, his wife, Emil Bobu [the prime minister], Manea Manescu [deputy prime minister] and two bodyguards from the Securitate. We had to force open the doors of the lift to get them out.

Ceausescu and his party of six stumbled across to Malutanu's helicopter at about the time that the first members of the crowd reached the roof. For a moment the crowd was disorientated. Some of them stayed to wave to the people in the Square. Others headed over to the helicopters, but they were too late.

The five helicopters took off, each heading in a different direction. The time was ten minutes past twelve noon. Inside the Ecureuil people were so jammed together that someone had to sit on Ceausescu's knee. Elena was in tears. Her husband was pale and at a loss to understand the position. They kept on changing their minds about where they wanted to go, but eventually they decided to make for their lakeside palace of Snagov, 20 miles north of Bucharest.

Below them the crowds in the Square were singing their victory song. It was the same football supporters' chant that Solidarity sang in Poland.

> *Olé, olé, olé, olé*
> *Ceausescu unde e?*
> (Where is Ceausescu?)
> *Olé, olé, olé, olé*
> *Ceausescu nu mai e!*
> (There's no more Ceausescu!)

It had been an almost entirely peaceful revolution. The tyrant had been forced out of power, not with guns and tanks but by the sheer force of mass anger. By standing their ground the people of Romania, in whose name everything had been done and yet who had never received the slightest benefit from it, had overthrown the most ruthless dictatorship in modern Europe. Timisoara aside, it had taken two days. What no one at this stage foresaw was the savagery of the counter-revolution.

*

An hour or so after Ceausescu had escaped from Bucharest I came face to face with a man I recognized at Belgrade airport. He was sitting behind the car hire desk, and eight months before he had rented me the car in which four of us drove around Romania. There were four of us this time, too: Tira Shubart, who was once again working as producer; and a two-man camera crew. Bob Prabhu was born in Aden of Indian parents. I had worked with him before. In Chile in 1988 he had been the sound recordist with Steve Morris, who had worked with me as cameraman on the previous foray into Romania. At various times during our Chile trip Bob and Steve had been tear-gassed, knocked off their feet with high-pressure water hoses loaded with sewage, and threatened with truncheons and shotguns. In all this they had behaved with exemplary bravery and cheerfulness.

Now Bob had been promoted to cameraman himself. In his quiet way he was extremely ambitious. He would volunteer for anything: even a trip to a revolution over Christmas. Cameramen tend to fall into two categories: those who look like cameramen, with medallions clinking in their chest hair and jeans tucked into high leather boots, and those who look like bank managers. Bob Prabhu looked like a bank manager. He wore a suit and a pair of spectacles. In my experience they are the ones who keep the camera steady and don't make an excuse and leave when the trouble begins.

His sound-recordist was Paul Francis, who was in his early twenties and had come from a more sedentary department. This was only his second foreign expedition as sound-recordist. The first had been to Strasbourg for a European Community summit: a rather different proposition. But he was resourceful, and good company. Altogether I couldn't imagine a better group of people with whom to spend a busy Christmas.

The man at the car hire desk didn't remember me. He made the same joke about Ceausescu and Dracula and rented me the same dark blue Mercedes. It was in perfect running order, he said, which would have meant that a great deal of work had been done on it in eight months. As we were leaving, a pleasant-faced Frenchman came over and asked me if I had a map of Romania which he could photo-copy. He was a reporter for the Paris magazine *VSD*, Jerome Fritel. There is an instinctive desire in those of us who work in a highly competitive business to keep our advantages to ourselves. Fortunately I ignored it. As a Francophile, I can rarely resist showing off my French. I even stood him a drink. To have drawn him into our group at this early stage was one of the luckier things I did during the Romanian revolution.

The Mercedes was only big enough for Bob and Paul and their camera gear. Tira and I accepted the offer of a Belgrade taxi driver to go with us to Bucharest. He wanted fifteen hundred US dollars; it was a large amount of money, but we needed a car and a driver and had little practical alternative. He agreed to find a second driver for Bob and Paul as well. The deal was struck. We set off for the border in the dark winter afternoon, the French reporter and his photographer colleague, Marc Simon, following in their hired car. As we drove we listened to Belgrade radio. The driver translated as best he could: there was fighting in various Romanian cities, particularly Timisoara, Sibiu and Bucharest itself. I was impatient to get on, but somehow we went slower and slower. At one point we stopped at the driver's house, while his wife hung round his neck and begged him not to go.

We arrived at the Romanian border. It was a different world from the last time. Several of the customs men had been there when we passed through in April. This time they told us the border was open and they wouldn't need to search our gear. They were free, they said, though they didn't seem too certain about it. The captain in charge of the post breathed heavy alcoholic fumes on me and said he had the commander of the Timisoara Securitate locked away, and what did I think he should do about it? I explained that it was in his best interests to let us film this man, but the captain was too frightened for that. He swayed away and sank into noisy sleep on a couch in the office where we had to buy our petrol coupons for the journey.

The Yugoslav drivers, thoroughly frightened by what they had heard on the radio, then refused to cross the border. This was a serious problem: there simply wasn't enough room in the familiar blue Mercedes for four of us plus the gear. I was still shouting at the Yugoslavs and refusing to pay them the thousand dollars they demanded, when Jerome came up.

'It is our duty to take you and Tira with us,' he said.

I could scarcely speak. The relationship between French and Anglo-Saxon journalists is, alas, rarely good; and the relationship between television cameramen and stills photographers, especially French ones, is usually poisonous. We crammed into the back of their car, still marvelling, and drove off in convoy into the darkness of Romania. None of us knew what lay ahead. We had been warned that the Securitate were staging ambushes along the main roads. Our headlamps were the only source of light in a black landscape. The only guides were a fitful white line down the middle of the road and the spectral trees on either side, their trunks painted white.

We braked sharply. Three men stood motionless in our headlights, not even blinking. They formed a weird tableau in the dark. I assumed they were part of a Securitate roadblock and braced myself for a bullet. Nothing happened. They held flags over their heads and their hands, grasping the wooden staffs, remained intertwined. There was something strange about the flags: the Communist emblem in the centre had been roughly hacked out of them. These were not Securitate men, they were revolutionaries. The three unsmiling peasants, their lined faces as white as the painted tree trunks in the headlights, had heard that the mutilated flag was the symbol of their revolution. Word had radiated out from Bucharest until it had reached even this obscure place, 400 miles away. They did not speak to us. They merely watched us uncomprehendingly as we circled around them, filming. We climbed back into our cars and drove off, leaving them still standing there in the darkness.

In the nearby villages, unlit except for the statutory 40-watt light bulb per dwelling, people turned out to cheer us and dance in the light of our camera. The young had never seen artificial light so strong. They were singing the song I had last heard in Gdansk at a Solidarity rally, and before that on the Champs-Elysées when Francois Mitterrand was re-elected:

Olé, olé, olé, olé . . .

At 10 p.m. we reached Deta. They were out in the streets with candles here. The local Party boss was on the balcony of his headquarters, a small-town Ceausescu pledging everlasting loyalty to the revolution. The candles lit up the faces of the crowd. They were thoughtful and determined faces, like the ones we'd seen earlier on the road, the faces of people who had been pushed to the limit of endurance, and weren't going to lose their one chance of smashing the system which had ground them down for years.

Then at a word the crowd was kneeling, praying for the dead of Timisoara. Soon there would be more dead, in every city in the country. The bulky figure of the Party boss in his warm overcoat knelt too, uncomfortable and unpractised. Behind him, inside the office, the television was starting to show pictures of the Great Dictator's son, Nicu, captured and in handcuffs. That made kneeling easier for the Party boss.

In the street they got to their feet again, and cheered and sang. A small group came running in with flaming torches. There was a wildness about them now, the wildness of newly released prisoners. The world was a different place, and they wanted to show they were alive in it. For a moment or two I wondered whether there might be violence, but it swiftly turned from the violence of action to the violence of feeling. Three policemen who had been onlookers were mobbed and, for no good reason, raised on the shoulders of the crowd as though they were responsible for everyone's change of fortune. Wild eyes rolled in the torchlight, long yellow teeth flashed. You felt they would have worshipped or destroyed anything in the moment. Instead they went back to singing the only revolutionary song they knew:

Olé, olé, olé, olé,
Ceausescu nu mai e!

We drove on. Timisoara, when we got there at eleven o'clock, was in total darkness and the crowds in the street were hysterical. Groups of people would emerge from the shadows, demand to see our accreditation and wave us through to the next batch of guardians of the street, often only ten yards farther on. Soon our natural irritability took over, and we drove on at speed, ignoring the protests. The phenomenon of the self-appointed roadblock was something we quickly grew used to in Bucharest itself. So was the phenomenon of the mass delusion.

'No lights! No lights! The Air Force is threatening to bomb Timisoara!'

At first it seemed plausible, and we weaved an uneasy way without lights through the dark, littered streets. But the plausibility ebbed away. Why should the Air Force bomb Timisoara at night, when there was no armed resistance? What difference would the headlights of two cars make anyway? We switched our lights back on. So did Bob and Paul in the car behind. People shouted, but took no action. We became a force as powerful as the delusion.

'The water is poisoned! The Securitate have poisoned the water!'

I was less impressed by that. I remembered the Islamic insurgents in Tehran in 1979 saying the same thing during the Iranian Revolution. Certain ideas appeal forcibly to the self-dramatizing mind of the revolutionary, and it is useful to be able to discriminate between genuine danger and mere paranoia. We drove fast and angrily through Timisoara and were glad to leave its hallucinations behind. The serious action lay ahead in Bucharest.

For people who hadn't slept much during the previous twenty-four hours it was a long and difficult drive. Once both our cars swung wide round a bend and hit sheet ice. The crew's car rammed a grass bank and stuck there. We had no means of towing it off. It was 3 a.m. and there hadn't been another vehicle on the road for an hour. Before there was time to rail at our bad fortune an immense Soviet-built truck thundered towards us. We flagged it down, and the driver produced a great length of wire cable and tugged the other car free in a single roar of his engine. Then he climbed back into his cab, a tubby man with a barrel chest who wore nothing but a T-shirt on a cold night like this. He drove off into the darkness, his passenger seat covered with chocolate and packets of American cigarettes. He was as bewildered as if he had been stopped by Good King Wenceslas.

*

At first, the focus of the revolution in Bucharest was the Central Committee building. Directly Adrian Donea and the others had fought their way into Ceausescu's office – the room whose ante-room led out on to the balcony – they took it over as their headquarters. None of them knew each other. They had been brought together by their impetuosity and their courage. They were an unlikely bunch of people: among them an ordinary soldier who could scarcely write, a cinema stunt man, a sculptor, a couple of would-be politicians, a 'hostess' from the InterContinental Hotel, a witty and worldly-wise sociologist who was hoping to write an account of the group dynamics of creating a revolution, and Adrian Donea who had started his career as a designer but had switched to driving a taxi because there was more money in it. He tried to create order in all the noise and excitement.

> I said, We've got to do something sensible here. If we don't, forget it. We've got to clean up all this shit for a start. This was inside Ceausescu's office. Everything to do with running the country was here. I mean, just looking round on the shelves and desks we found papers about how much gold was dug up and how much food was sold to other countries. This kind of thing was top secret, and we were just passing the papers backwards and forwards and looking at them.

They gathered round the table in the middle of the room to talk it over. Everybody was still shouting at once. There was no order of any kind. A video camera recorded the confusion. One man with a louder voice than the rest banged his fist on the table:

> We've got to organize ourselves here. And another point is to check at the television station. If we don't organize, there are people outside who'll crush us.

But the danger at that point lay not so much from being crushed as from being squeezed out. The Army was extremely anxious to take over the revolution in its early stages and restore order. Several days later I spoke to one of the ordinary soldiers who was involved at that early stage. His friends giggled and joked when I tried to talk to them, but he took the whole thing very seriously:

> I first found out that the Army had gone over to the side of the people by listening to the radio. Our commanders ordered us to go into action. We were the very first soldiers to take up position here at the Central Committee building. I was very moved when the people embraced us and chanted The Army is with us! You are our sons, our brothers. You must help us!

Once the soldiers had taken up their positions the generals started arriving. In the heat of a revolution people are extraordinarily generous, and their emotions are easily touched. As the generals made their way through the vast crowd in the Square no one seemed to recall that they had stood by the previous night and watched the Securitate shoot down the demonstrators, nor that they had waited to see who was winning before they joined in. In those early hours there was a distinct feeling of helplessness in the crowds, and even among the people who had taken over inside the Central Committee building. No one knew how a country should be run. They were grateful to find that the Army was prepared to help them.

The generals made their way through the shattered door and up the marble stairs. When they appeared on the balcony there was a shout of joy from the people below.

'The first imperative,' said the senior general, 'is to restore order.'

The crowd cheered him to the echo. The atmosphere was catching. One of the generals gave the Victory sign, except that his lack of familiarity with such things led him to make it the wrong way round. No one cared.

'The Army is with us!' they chanted.

All over Bucharest now there were scenes of wild rejoicing. People danced down the streets a dozen or more abreast. Trucks roared up and down the boulevards, crowded with people waving flags with the centre cut out. Church bells rang for the first time in years. Everywhere you could hear the chanted syllables:

'*Li-ber-ta-te! Li-ber-ta-te!*'

Liberty came to different people in different ways. The poet Mircea Dinescu had been under house arrest since March, after he gave an interview to the French newspaper *Libération* in which he criticized Ceausescu's policies. He was guarded by eighteen Securitate men in three shifts, so that there were always six of them outside his house. No one could come to visit him. His life was made intolerable by their presence.

> At lunchtime a neighbour came and told me that the Securitate guards had run away from my front gate. I came out on to the streets and looked around. For the first time the road was empty of Securitate. A friend came running towards me with his arms raised, saying the Ceausescus had fled. I walked into the boulevard, where I saw hundreds of thousands of people led by an armoured personnel carrier. Someone recognized me [Dinescu had been the presenter of a television show before his house arrest] and stopped me. He shouted, 'It's Mircea Dinescu, the poet! He's alive!' Then they lifted me up, put a flag in my hands, stuck me on to the APC and drove me to the television station.

The television station was the alternative centre of power in the revolution. Dinescu found that an interim government was starting to take shape there.

> I was amazed when I arrived. All the soldiers who were on duty seemed to know me, and they all cheered. I waved to them and they let me in. The cameras were going full blast, and everyone was talking and making speeches. I had some statements to make too, so I made them, but there were quite a lot of generals there who weren't interested in poets, so after a bit I thought I'd go home again. Even so I couldn't resist watching it all on television when I got there, and when they announced the result of the voting for the members of the new National Salvation Front I was elected anyway: which just shows the power of poetry.

Dinescu was a remarkably fiery character in his mid-thirties, almost artificially Latin, his hands describing splendid arcs in the air as he spoke and his poet's eye in a fine frenzy rolling. In a way, the generals were right; he wasn't really suitable material for a government. His wife, a quiet and attractive woman some years younger than he, said as an aside that the only job she would agree to his taking was Minister for the Opposition. Too much agreement seemed to unsettle him, and he would begin to put alternative points of view. Sometimes they would be the opposite of the point he had previously been making:

> For years we were pretending to be socialist when we were really fascist. Now we're pretending to be democratic when we're really – something else.

Another man who was swept up by the revolution was Dumitru Mazilu, a former ambassador to the United Nations. Mazilu was a tough-looking figure with silver hair and a forceful manner which somehow overlaid a slightly sentimental approach to the revolution. He was inclined to tears when he reflected on what he had been through: not, perhaps, surprisingly. He had once been a crony of Ceausescu's, but he had formulated a statement condemning the human rights abuses in Romania.

> I informed Ceausescu that I had no choice. I preferred to be killed rather than stay silent, but I had a duty to tell the truth to the world. So that is what I did.

He was in prison at the time of the revolution, and in the early hours of Friday 22 December the Securitate came to take him away. He was dressed only in his pyjamas and dressing-gown, and was certain he was going to be executed. He stayed in the car with its Securitate man for most of the night. They drove around the city until it grew light, the Securitate man saying nothing and Mazilu believing all the time that he would soon be shot. They went back to his home and then someone came for him with a car again, and drove him around once more. By this time he had the strong impression that the Securitate agent with him was trying to use him to get himself out of trouble. Eventually the agent let Mazilu out of the car and drove off. It was late in the afternoon. Someone took him round to the Central Committee building, where he was recognized and welcomed, and taken on to the balcony for everyone to see. He was still wearing his pyjamas and dressing-gown.

When I interviewed him a few days later he thrust his hand suddenly into his inside pocket and produced a dog-eared piece of paper.

> In prison I prepared our programme of revolution. This is now official. All ten points of our programme were accepted by my colleagues and by the people in the Square. I read this text before the people in the Square, and the people applauded and said OK – this is our programme. And that's how it was agreed.

Politics were to be fairly poisonous in post-Ceausescu Romania, however. The change in Mazilu's fortunes did not last. His enemies discovered files which showed that he had had links with the Securitate. Most people in his position would have had similar links, but it was enough to destroy his new political career. He was forced to resign.

Everything was done haphazardly, even the creation of the new government – the National Salvation Front. In the first few hours after the flight of Ceausescu, when they had time to take stock of the position, the revolutionaries in the Central Committee building began to discuss who should form the new government. None of them was a politician. Nor, as Adrian Donea admitted, did they have much knowledge of politics.

There were just a few names of guys we knew, but we couldn't know if they'd be good or bad. So after a bit I said, 'Maybe we should just go for some of the guys that were with Ceausescu, only not the bad ones.' Everybody agrees to that. I think of a name or two, the others think of a couple. I go out on to the balcony and say, 'What about so-and-so?' and at first they all say 'Boo!' and whistle. So then I go out again. What about Iliescu? Well, maybe they don't remember much about Iliescu, but anyway they say 'Great, yes' and they all cheer. So that was how Romania gets its new president.

To Adrian Donea fell the honour of announcing the news about the fate of the of the old president. A telex clattered through to the Central Committee machine at 4.25 that afternoon. Someone handed it to Adrian as he stood near the microphones on the balcony where Ceausescu himself had stood for the last time only a few hours before.

I will now read a telex to you: 'THE COMRADE AND THE COMRADESS HAVE BEEN ARRESTED AT TERGOVISTE.' So your good friend Ceausescu could even now be on his way to Bucharest.

The crowd in the Square went crazy. They danced and sang and threw hats in the air and kissed each other. Now, at last, the régime was finished. The dynasty had fallen.

At the moment I was announcing that from the balcony everybody was terribly happy, because we thought, That's it – now we've won. It was important because he started the tyranny and the tyranny stops with his capture. The symbolism was very important.

It wasn't to be as easy as Adrian Donea thought. The Ceausescus might be prisoners, but the Securitate had not given up. It had just been regrouping. A number of Securitate snipers, men of Ceausescu's own bodyguard, had taken up positions in different buildings around the centre of the city. In particular they had congregated in the block of flats where they lived opposite the Central Committee building, and in the various wings of the old royal palace. As darkness fell they opened fire on the dense mass of people who had packed into the Square to celebrate the revolution.

According to one of the legends which sprang up, Ceausescu's bodyguards were selected as orphans and brought up to be ferociously loyal to him alone. None of this was true. The loyalty was unquestioning, but Ceausescu secured it by supplying the bodyguards with all the goods that were otherwise unobtainable in Ceausescu's Romania, and by ensuring that they were so hated that they had no alternative but to fight for their lives. There was even a strategy behind it: in the event of a coup against Ceausescu they were to create such instability that Ceausescu could be rescued and reinstated.

In the shooting which began that Friday night hundreds died, among them Marian Cornelescu, the abattoir worker who had joined the demonstrations because he couldn't stand the poverty he and his family were suffering. He was shot in the forehead and died instantly.

*

We reached Bucharest at dawn on Saturday. The sky to the east was a brilliant carmine and glinted on the armour of the tanks that were heading into town with us, their barrels pointing at the rising sun. The Army, having declared for the revolution, was rumbling in to protect it. It was a curious sensation for me to find myself on the same side as the tanks. In Iran, in Afghanistan, in Tiananmen Square, the military had been the enemy. Now the squealing and grating of the tank tracks was a comfort, and the stench of oil and exhaust a guarantee of safety. We drove alongside them while Bob filmed from the other car and Marc, the French photographer, leant out of the window, the noise of his camera's motor-drive swamped by the ferocious racket of the tracks on asphalt and cobblestones, and the tank crews waving and giving Victory signs, flattered by the attention.

There is nothing more disorientating than to find yourself in the middle of a civil war without knowing what is going on. Ordinary people are no guide. They have little idea themselves, and mostly want to get away from the firing. We left our cars in the Boulevard Nicolae Balcescu, near the entrance to the University Metro station. Ahead of us was the InterContinental Hotel. I headed off with the others, shouting at Tira to get the vehicles into the car park and telephone London to make a satellite booking for our report. It took her more than an hour, under fire, to drive the hundred yards to the hotel. Not many other people would have attempted it. We shouted our goodbyes to Jerome and Marc, and thereafter saw them from time to time in the heat of the battle, usually a little way ahead of us.

People screamed at us, grabbing our sleeves, shouting instructions and warnings.

'Come this way, gentleman!'

'Keep down, keep down, keep down. Is much periculoso!'

'I show you where is fighting. I English speak good.'

'No, not by there! Is dying!'

There was the nasty snap of sniper bullets close by, near enough to be heard over the general racket. Two Air Force jets screamed over the buildings. Submachine-guns hammered away somewhere. There was the occasional terrible crash of a tank-mounted gun slamming heavy bullets into stonework or brick. Over the rooftop pillars of grey and white smoke were going up, but it was hard to work out exactly where they were. I was in an agony of haste and uncertainty, afraid the battle would die away before we could track it down.

There was a time before Afghanistan, the Gulf War, Lebanon, Rhodesia, Angola, Northern Ireland and the rest, when I would have run in the opposite direction if I had heard firing. The passing years have changed that, if only by teaching me that the noise is nothing: all that matters is avoiding the path of the bullet. The vast majority of people present at a fire-fight survive it unscathed; the knack lies in being among them. But you need experience to realize that, and it takes a little time to become habituated to a street battle – to realize that if you step out into this street, in spite of the racket around you, you will be perfectly safe; while if you put your head round that corner you could have problems. It isn't courage that's required, it's good hearing and an eye for angles of fire. It soon became obvious that the guide whose offer of help we accepted was unwilling to take us too close to what was happening. We described wide circles round the fighting, edging away when it came too close.

There was a great deal of shooting going on. We ran through the empty streets and Paul linked up his sound-gear with Bob's camera as they ran. Every trace of tiredness fell away from us. At moments like this every nerve and synapse seems to crackle with tension and energy. We ran down a couple of side streets, following our guide. The firing was more urgent. Neither of my previous visits to Bucharest had brought me round here, behind the University. Now we were coming across more people, sheltering in doorways, huddled together in dead ground, talking nervously, looking round at us, waving at us to get down or take cover.

The familiar pungent smell of explosive and bullets came to me. There was another smell too, sweetish and corrupt: twice that day I saw piles of human excrement on the pavement. People were so frightened by the shooting that they lost control of themselves. And yet they wouldn't go away. They were determined to stand their ground and see for themselves the downfall of the Ceausescu régime. Our guide was losing his nerve by now, but we ran down an arcade and saw an armoured personnel carrier at the end of it. Soldiers were using it for cover and firing up at a building half opposite. Someone in the building was firing back. They were bullet marks on the APC's armour, and one of the tyres had been punctured by a volley of shots.

A bullet slammed against the APC and I shrank down against the cold metal of its side. I looked across at Bob and Paul: they were still standing up and filming a soldier who was firing at the fifth-floor window of a block of flats opposite. Bob was so close to him that the cartridge cases ejected by the man's Kalashnikov were hitting his camera and his head as they spun out. That mild head with its friendly spectacles looked very vulnerable. Guiltily, I left my place of refuge and held my arm over Bob to protect him. The cartridge cases were burning hot.

The racket was immense in the archway, and the view was limited. We decided to retrace our steps and come out lower down the same street, where we could get a clearer picture of the battle. There were people in every doorway, looking up. Soldiers were sighting along their rifles at the fifth-floor windows. A few civilians had guns too, mostly revolvers and pistols. The street was empty all down one side, where the sniper had been firing. There were bullet holes in some of the windows, and a viscous patch of blood on the ground where some passer-by had been hit. The snipers moved around as much as they could, heading on to another hiding-place each time they were spotted and pinned down.

Later we followed the track of a couple of Securitate snipers. They had made their way across the rooftops and smashed their way into a glass-enclosed passage between two flats at the top of a building. They had been able to command two busy streets from there, and for a few minutes they blazed away. When the Army finally pinpointed their positions they melted away. We were given a good description of them: in their mid-twenties, unremarkable in every way, dressed in civilian clothes. They carried their guns, broken down, in holdalls. Once they were in the street they mixed in with the crowds and moved on to the next vantage-point.

There was angry shouting. The crowd, suddenly careless of the bullets, surged across towards a group of soldiers. They were bringing in a captured sniper. It is always strange to see your enemy face to face, and at first the crowd was content simply to look at him. He was completely unremarkable, a pale young man in pale clothes with his arms raised. The soldiers prodded him along with their rifles. Then the crowd moved in. They screamed at him and beat him with their fists. He crossed his arms over his head to defend himself against them.

By now some people were pushing in between him and the soldiers guarding him, and he might well have been beaten to death. One of the soldiers poked his rifle in the air and fired a couple of rounds. It frightened everyone, and for a moment or two they held back. It was enough time for the soldiers to group more tightly round their prisoner and pull him into the side door of a building. The crowd milled around, unsatisfied. Inside, the soldiers searched him. When they found his Securitate identification one of them put a bullet through the back of his head. They could have left the job to the crowd outside.

We realized from the sound of heavy firing and the columns of smoke billowing up into the air that the fighting where we were had only been a sideshow. Our guide re-materialized, full of warnings, and led us by some circuitous route through a park. It was almost empty, but it was more dangerous than going through the streets: the bullets cracked across the open spaces, and the only shelter was provided by trees. The park was almost empty. We made our way across, trying not to duck, our voices sounding artificially loud away from the streets and the crowds.

A group of about twenty people came towards us, brandishing a large Romanian flag with a ragged hole in the centre. They were terrified by the noise of guns and the angry sound of bullets passing just over our heads, but although they were doubled up to offer as small a target as possible they too were determined to be in at the death. They said they were going to march to the Central Committee building and offer their support. I think it was then that I realized the revolution was bound to succeed. Ordinary people had been so goaded by want and repression that they were prepared to make any sacrifice to finish the job.

Bob Prabhu had found a piece of green curtaining somewhere, and he covered his camera with it. Cameras and sound equipment always present an attractive target to men with guns. Either they know what they are and want to destroy them anyway, or they think they're some form of weapon. The curtain, being made of some synthetic material, kept slithering off and revealing parts of the camera, like a silk dress on the shoulders of a drunken girl. Paul had nothing with which to cover his sound gear. He carried it down by his side.

By chance we had come to the back of a building near the Square which was occupied by the Securitate. The Army, it seemed, hadn't yet realized it. In this kind of warfare the Securitate had every advantage. There was a network of tunnels under the Square which meant the snipers could move around between the big government buildings with ease. Later, when a BBC team went into the tunnels, they found they were equipped with tanks of fresh water, refrigerators full of food, air purification plants and thick steel doors. There were several miles of them, some of which led simply to a blank wall set with rungs for climbing. Overhead were the concrete foundations of a street, and beside the rungs there would be a box containing a small pneumatic drill so that anyone trapped there could blast his way out.

Against this planning and subtlety the Army was clumsy and ill-prepared. Its strength lay in its fire-power. As we made our way up towards the Square this fire-power was being used to the full. There must have been forty or more tanks there, each with its heavy machine-gun trained on a building where snipers were thought to be. The racket as they all fired at once was unbearable. Soldiers ran towards the tanks, bent double. A car had just crashed against a lamp post, its driver shot by a sniper, the passenger killed by the impact. Blood and glass lay on the pavement.

Women brought bread and bottled water out to the soldiers. One threw his head back and up-ended the bottle, letting the water flow out over his face and chin. Then he straightened up, grinning, and offered me the bottle. I drank greedily from it. The soldiers were hot and nervous, with no clear orders about what they should be doing. The Army, weak and poorly trained, was anxious to demonstrate the extent of its new allegiance to the people. And so it used its overwhelming strength to hammer away at the grand buildings in the centre of the city, regardless of the damage it was doing. The noise and the damage were an end in themselves, the outward and visible sign of an inward and guilty desire to make up for its failure to side with the popular cause earlier. The Army was demonstrating its fitness to carry on serving the people. A few buildings destroyed were less important than the construction of a new public trust in its loyalty.

At one point later in the day I was so angered by the wanton destruction of the University Library, opposite the old royal palace, that I ran up to a tank commander and ordered him to stop firing. It seemed to me that the shape of the lead-covered dome was a tempting target for him, and he was simply firing for fun. He took no notice of me, of course. The building was already on fire, and most of the priceless collection of books and manuscripts was destroyed.

All round us the Army was using hundreds of thousands of rounds of ammunition to reply to a few dozen well-aimed shots from men who were agile, well-trained and highly motivated. They knew that if they were caught they would be killed, and that their only real hope of survival was the restoration of Ceausescu. By now the greatest danger came from the Army, not the Securitate. There was no need for Bob to cover his camera with the green curtaining any more, and he threw it away.

A group of Romanian commandos appeared out of a side street and ran up the steep incline of the avenue, crouching as they ran.

'I'm going with them,' Bob shouted, and he and Paul ran off while I followed clumsily after them. The noise of gunfire was tremendous, and at this stage it wasn't obvious to us that the shooting was mostly being done by the Army. We thought we were in the middle of a major gun battle. When so much ammunition is being unloaded into the air, no one is safe. We took cover and filmed the commandos taking up their positions. Bob's glasses gleamed with enthusiasm as he looked round the camera for the next shot. Paul showed no anxiety as the machine-guns crashed and chattered beside him.

We went inside a block of flats with a group of soldiers who had heard that there was a sniper on one of the upper floors. Standing in the hallway was a deeply impressive piratical figure with a naked Army bayonet stuck in his belt. I got talking with him. It turned out that he was working as interpreter for a British friend of mine, Rory Peck, a freelance cameraman whom we had hired to get into Romania separately, and who had managed to get the first pictures of the fighting in Bucharest on to British television the previous night. I had worked with Rory earlier in the year in Afghanistan, and knew him to be a remarkably brave operator.

'Where's Rory now?' I asked.

The bayonet-wearer nodded across the road.

'In there.'

I looked. The building he meant was on fire at several points.

'You mean he's outside there?'

'Not outside. Inside.'

It was true. Rory had managed to get into the building while the snipers were still there, and it caught fire and burned while he was filming the firemen. His main complaint afterwards was about losing the breathing-apparatus someone had given him. He'd wanted it for his collection.

I went off to the Athénée Palace hotel, on one side of the Square, to make a telephone report to London for our lunchtime news bulletin. It was difficult to get in. The Athénée Palace, always one of the more sinister hotels in Eastern Europe, was a base for Securitate gunmen. They had apparently left a cache of guns and ammunition in one of the rooms and had been firing out at the crowd from the upper floors. By the time I got there they had probably moved on, but the tanks were firing away at the hotel and I had to wait for a brief lull before I could get in. I had been there the previous April with Tira, Steve Morris and Lynne. It was then, as it always had been, a natural home for spies and dubious people of all kinds. In the bar it had been difficult to avoid them. They put their bags on the tables and turned them to us as we spoke.

The bar was badly smashed now, and so was the main reception area. There was broken glass on the desk.

'Very difficult here,' said a greasy man behind the counter. He polished the surface with an old piece of grimy cloth absently. I remembered him from before: hostile, suspicious, unhelpful. Anyone who worked in this place must have been a Securitate agent.

'From BBC? I am very good listener of BBC. Always hearing.'

Anxious to show how things had changed, he took the phone from me and shouted over the noise of the tanks to the woman on the switchboard. It worked. Within a couple of minutes I was talking to my colleagues in London. Perhaps she, too, wanted to prove her new attachment to democracy.

It was a long and very expensive call. I recorded a report on the scene outside the windows of the hotel, looking at the tanks and flinching at the noise of firing as I spoke. Finally I hung up. The greasy man behind the counter had been listening to everything I said. I suppose it was partly force of habit.

'What you think will happen here?'

This was something I quickly became used to: people with a past to hide often asked you for your opinion so they could agree with it and ingratiate themselves with you. I was more interested in him and in the hotel. He told me a little, guardedly, about the Securitate gunmen upstairs. There had been three of them. I had the impression he knew them. They had no guns when they arrived, he said.

'What will you do now?' I asked.

He grinned at me slyly.

'I carry on. Everybody needs people for hotel.'

His instinct was right. I saw him several days later, after the hotel had been cleaned up. He seemed to be in charge of things. He scarcely spoke to me.

I met the crew back at the InterContinental. They had given the tapes of what they had shot to Tira, who had gone off to the television station with a Romanian, Dan, whom she had encountered after we had left her in the street battle. Dan spoke some English, and was chivalrous enough to go with her to see that she was safe. I was worried, knowing there was fighting there. I knew she had arrived safely because my colleagues in London had spoken to her and seen Bob's and Rory's pictures. But I had to wait several hours until she came back.

She and Dan had had serious difficulties in getting through. Snipers had taken over several of the houses round the television station, and the Army was involved in its usual heavy demolition work trying to get them out. Tira and Dan came to the front of the station, where there was an open stretch of about 200 yards to cross. The Army and the snipers were firing across this ground at each other. The soldiers on duty had refused to let them go, but she knew there were only a few minutes to go before our satellite booking began. Eventually she and Dan pushed the soldiers aside and set off at a run, with a soldier floundering unwillingly after them as escort. They made it while our satellite was still up. But they were lucky.

By no means all the Western television teams behaved as well as Bob, Paul and Tira. One group made their way to the television station and never left it again, leaving others to do the dangerous work on the streets. Elsewhere a British reporter and cameraman were so nervous they decamped altogether, leaving their sound-recordist behind. An American camera crew landed at Bucharest airport, abandoned their equipment and took the same plane back to where they'd come from. Many newspaper and radio correspondents scarcely set foot outside their hotels while the fighting was going on. It proved, admittedly, to be a dangerous time for journalists. Five were killed altogether. The Mercedes in which a Belgian photographer had been shot dead was parked outside the InerContinental Hotel for several days. It served us as a memento mori.

12
THE FLIGHT OF THE MACBETHS

What you're saying is a calumny. When this is over I'll have you put on trial.
NICOLAE CEAUSESCU after being found guilty of murder and
corruption, 25 December 1989

By Christmas morning the fighting in Bucharest was over. The revolution was accomplished, the counter-revolution defeated. It had taken three days. The Square was a depressing sight. Tanks and armoured personnel carriers were skewed around in the middle of the Square. Exhausted soldiers lay on them in a muddle of uniforms. I saw one soldier in his regulation Lincoln green felt jacket with a black homburg hat on his head. An old woman was using the branch of a fir tree to brush away the accumulated rubbish: brick-dust, bits of stonework, official papers thrown out in the first excitement of the Central Committee's capture, cartridge cases, human excrement. The dome of the University Library was a smoking skeleton, the windows blackened by fire. The ground below was covered with black ashes from the books that had burned. I kicked my way through bits of decorative leadwork in the shape of oakleaves which had fallen from the roof of the library: a bitter autumn.

Every frontage in the Square had been splattered by purposeful gunfire. The old Royal Palace was a terrible sight, the grand rooms a mess of charred beams and burned furniture. The firemen had been here, and our feet squelched deeply into the wet carpeting. This was where the last Warsaw Pact summit had been held. Now in a relatively untouched side office a television set which no one had bothered to turn off was broadcasting the endless arguments of the National Salvation Front: the only sound in an entirely empty building.

Fire was still licking the walls and roof of the block of flats opposite the Central Committee. It was the only place where the damage was easy to forgive. These were the flats where the senior officers of the Securitate lived, and they had been built with the thought of possible counter-subversion in mind. The windows of the expensive shops which had sold chocolate and jewellery had been smashed by rifle fire. An elderly vigilante with a blue, red and gold arm-band was busy tying a long length of pink plastic string around the nearby lamp posts. It meant that passers-by had to keep their distance from the windows and the goods inside them. This was two days after the windows had been broken, and nothing inside had been looted. The revolutionaries were mostly hungry and poor, but they weren't thieves.

It was the first Christmas many of them had been permitted to celebrate. This was a society where even Father Christmas had been forbidden. Now there were decorations everywhere, and people were still dragging Christmas trees home that evening. On television one of the announcers who had been on duty for two days made an announcement.

You may notice something different about our studio set today. First, we have a new flag. You can see it behind me: just our country's old blue, yellow and red. Secondly, we have some new decorations.

The camera tilted down to show the table in front of him. On it was a bowl filled with Christmas ornaments. They were just the usual balls of coloured glass, and in any television studio in Western Europe that day they would have been part of the fixtures. In Romania they were revolutionary, and people's eyes filled with tears to see them.

That afternoon I was walking with an English-speaking Romanian past a food shop near the InterContinental. The new government had ordered that the goods held in the special Securitate and Party stores should be distributed to the ordinary shops. There was a pile of oranges in the window of this shop as a result. Two boys of around twelve were looking at them. I asked the translator what they were saying.

'They are trying to decide if they are things you play with or things you eat.'

These children had never even heard of oranges.

In the Square people had been camping out all night round fires of rubbish. At first they had sung their new revolutionary songs and cheered the singing of others at other camp fires. They cooked whatever food they had been able to find and called out to us to sit down with them and share it. It was like the field of some great battle after the fighting was over. Dark outlined shapes in blankets and makeshift uniforms crouched close to the fires. Suddenly, terrifyingly, there was a wild burst of shooting. It came from a wing of the Central Committee building nearby. There was the waspish sound of bullets hitting stone and winging overhead. In the panic people flung themselves to the ground or ran through the camp fires looking for safety.

We went cautiously over to look through the windows. The shots had mostly been fired in the main downstairs room, through the ceiling. The soldiers had discovered a small group of Securitate men hiding out in the room above. They were captured and taken away for questioning. Questioning, I was told privately later, consisted of searching them for Securitate documents. Those who had them were taken down to the cellars and shot in the back of the head. Their bodies were taken away in trucks before dawn each day. So were the bodies of the Ceausescus' black labradors which had had the misfortune to be discovered upstairs in the Central Committee building. Their bodies were so riddled with bullets that two men had to lift each one.

There was a kind of revolutionary insanity in the air. The Securitate could be anywhere. Sudden myths swept the Square; some we'd heard before. Two of Ceausescu's doubles had been sighted; Colonel Gadaffi had sent in troops to support the counter-revolutionaries; Ceausescu had escaped and was in China/Iran/East Germany/Albania; Securitate paratroopers had been dropped on Timisoara; all the drinking water throughout Romania had been poisoned and only bottled water was safe. The sound and sensation of crushing plastic water bottles underfoot, or kicking them to one side, is as strongly associated in my mind with the Square in Bucharest as treading on bits of broken glass and bamboo was with Tiananmen Square.

The myths could be heavily self-defeating. On Christmas Eve we had filmed at a block of flats in the Boulevard Nicolae Balcescu. A group of Securitate gunmen had used it as a base for firing down the main artery of Bucharest. Someone who lived in the flats told the group of revolutionaries gathered round the entrance that there were Arab students living there. That immediately tied in with another of the myths: that Palestinians and North Koreans undergoing training in Romania were responsible for much of the sniping in the streets. It was true that the Securitate trained the PLO and other groups; but there was no evidence they were involved in the fighting.

After a certain amount of firing and some unpleasant work creeping through the cellars and up the stairs of the block of flats at the back, which we filmed, the revolutionaries found the flat where the Securitate sniper had been hiding. It was empty. A few minutes later a man in a fur hat slipped out of a side entrance and got calmly into his car. It refused to start. He was spotted, and pulled out. The crowd treated him roughly. Someone punched him in the face. Then they discovered a pistol on him. He remained perfectly calm, though his eyes moved quickly round the circle of faces, searching out the people he had to convince. When they looked through his pockets they couldn't find any Securitate documents. Things became more relaxed. He explained coolly that he was an ordinary policeman, off duty, and that he had kept his gun with him to help in the search for Securitate snipers.

The crowd liked that. They'd also got it firmly into their heads that they were looking for Arabs. He gave them some advice about where to search in the building, then said he'd better be getting along. They clapped him on the back and went back with him to his car. It still wouldn't start, so they helped to push it. As they waved him off I said to one of the self-appointed commanders of the revolutionary group that they'd let the real Securitate sniper get away. He laughed.

'I think you're right. But you've seen these people. How could I change their minds?'

Normally in revolutions the supporters of the *ancien régime* do their best to escape. Not the Securitate. What heightened the atmosphere of paranoia in Romania was that during those first days the Securitate really were everywhere. The cameraman Rory Peck was filming from his balcony at the InterContinental when he heard the crack of an automatic rifle close by. He looked to his right, just in time to see the barrel of a Kalashnikov being withdrawn from sight a few balconies away. A day or so later the leading British academic authority on Romania, Dr Dennis Deletant of London University, was assigned to the room the Securitate sniper had used. He always wondered, he said mildly, whether the Securitate man might come back at some point.

In the leaden greyness of Christmas morning we made our way towards the Square. A man was collecting money for candles for a little pavement shrine to the dead. I gave him a low-denomination note. A woman bustled up and shook her finger.

'No, no, gentleman! Is gypsy! Holds money for itself!'

I looked back. True, the man had the dark features of a gypsy, but gypsies had to live too. I tried to point this out, but the woman went away clucking her impatience at the stupidity of the rich.

It was bitterly cold. Outside the Central Committee building a hundred or more people were queuing for a free hand-out of bread and a watery light brown soup. There were problems. Each person who received a ration began wolfing it down then and there. Behind them the queue bunched up and the process was slowed. Those who were waiting shouted angrily, but they seemed listless and unthreatening. The eaters moved a little, their eyes moving warily over the rims of their metal bowls. They didn't stop eating. Above their heads the skeleton of the University Library dome still smoked in the cold dull air. There were new camp-fires this morning in the ashes of the ones from the previous night. Cheerful, ugly, unshaven men wrapped in the eviscerated national flag gave us Victory signs, and when we gave the same sign back they chuckled and nudged each other like schoolchildren.

*

Someone had pinned a hand-drawn picture of Ceausescu as Dracula on the door of the Central Committee building. It had the letters 'PCR' for 'Romanian Communist Party' in its eyes and red ink for blood on its fangs. There were in fact three doors, side by side, but only the right-hand one was now in use. Adrian Donea and the others forced their way in through this door three days earlier, and it had been the only entrance ever since. Once only the Ceausescus and a handful of their most favoured courtiers came in this way. Now there was a stream of common soldiers and roughly dressed revolutionaries passing through. We had to wait and argue our case for getting in with an Army colonel, his eyes red with fatigue. He lost his temper fast, and so did I; over the previous few days I had probably had less sleep than he had.

No foreigners of any kind had been allowed in before, but somehow the red eyes took on a weaker look and he stood to one side. Like everyone else he listened to the Romanian service of the BBC. Inside everything was dirt and chaos. There were streaks of blood on the marble floors and clusters of bullet holes in the doors. Helmets and greatcoats were piled up along the walls of a corridor. Heroically bandaged figures emerged from makeshift surgeries where state secretaries had once worked. The Winter Palace in Petrograd must have been something like this.

Going up the main staircase was a perilous business. The soldiers on guard at the foot of the stairs bellowed up to the soldiers on guard at the first landing (who were in full view of us).

'Three men coming up with camera gear!'

We walked nervously up to the first landing. The guards had orders to shoot anyone who didn't match the description. I was carrying no television gear but felt obliged to go first.

'Three men coming up with camera gear!'

The message was shouted by the men on the first landing to the men at the top of the stairs, who couldn't see us. We turned and went up the next flight. The guards there were lying behind a barricade composed of imitation Second Empire furniture and rolled up carpets. Their rifles pointed at us as we moved up the stairs towards them. I tried smiling. There was no answering smile in the eyes behind the rifle-sights.

Other soldiers in fantastical uniforms, with Christmas decorations on their caps and ribbons of the national colour woven into their epaulettes and buttonholes, talked to nurses who were waiting to go on duty. We stood at the top of the stairs, on the main corridor, looking at the damage everywhere. There was still a reek of gunfire, scorched material and damaged marble. Someone had written JOS TIRANUL!! – Down with the tyrant! – on an undamaged section of marble. The grand door beside the inscription opened. For a moment there was the sound of shouting. It was cut off by the closing of the door.

A blonde girl in a black dress and a long black astrakhan coat a little like Ceausescu's stood there and looked at us curiously. She was the hostess from the InterContinental who had been in the first wave of the Revolution on Friday. Her eyes were black and empty, and she laughed foolishly when I told her who we were.

'Oh, you English,' she said, as though I had tried to persuade her of some pointless untruth.

It was a relief to find someone who could understand me and who didn't have a gun. I explained what we were interested in filming.

'Oh, indeed?' she said, her eyes as empty as ever.

I tried asking her some questions. She had just been thrown out of the Central Committee. They'd accused her of selling secrets to the Securitate. Since she must have worked for the Securitate when she was at the InterContinental this wasn't entirely surprising, but she seemed outraged. Her English had a strange affected quality, as though she had learned it from old films. She leaned against the marble like a torch-singer.

'Sorry to say it, but this place is shit, dahling. Shit. I come in here with ideals, eye-dee-alls, dahling. Then I find out they are just little dirty crooks like all the others.'

She swept off down the staircase, caring nothing for the guards who shouted out that one woman was descending. It seemed to me extraordinary that the insurgents had allowed her to stay for so long; but I came to realize later that in the early phases of a revolution everyone accepts everyone else at face value. It is what you do that is important, not who you are. If you act in a revolutionary way you can be one of the revolution's leaders.

There was Christmas tinsel on the handle of the door of Ceausescu's office. No one stopped me turning it. We found ourselves in an anteroom. There was a lot of shouting: men and women arguing about who was to say what to the crowd from the balcony. Furniture had been pushed to the walls. All the drawers in the desks had been forced. While we waited for someone to take us into the main office I opened a couple. There was a copy of the newspaper *Lumea* from another and nastier world. It was dated 4 May 1989, and the front page had a large photograph of Ceausescu waving from the balcony that lay outside these very windows. The headline read:

MANIFESTARE PATRIOTICA A UNITATII INTEGRII
NATIUNI IN JURUL PARTIDULUI COMUNIST ROMAN,
AL SECRETARULUI SAU GENERAL, TOVARASUL NICOLAE
CEAUSESCU.

Romanian, someone said, is like a mixture of dog Latin and Esperanto.

Ceausescu's office was constructed along the lines of a football pitch. Until a few days before he had sat at the enormous desk in the far corner while his ministers stood in the circular pattern in the middle of the carpet and called over their business to him. Now there was even more calling of business. The air was thick with rank tobacco smoke and the staleness of three days' shouting. Every member of the extraordinary group which had taken over the office seemed to sport a weapon. The crew had taken command of the admiral's cabin. Wild emotions swayed them. Points were emphasized with revolvers or Kalashnikovs.

The cinema stuntman who had been in the first rush on Friday morning whispered hoarsely, his voice wrecked by political argument. A private soldier, later promoted to sergeant-major for being the first Army man to go over to the revolutionaries, strutted around in an assortment of uniforms. He wore three cartridge belts, all well-stocked with bullets. A girl of eighteen sat at the desk in the corner hammering away at an antique typewriter, trying to catch up with the flow of orders and invocations to the people. She wore the peaked cap of an army officer and an army tunic over her dress.

Then there was no more shouting. A mildly satanic figure with a coat over his shoulders and a fur hat on his head was making a point. The others seemed to recognize his quality and listened in silence. When he had finished the shouting resumed.

There was no doubt about it: power had slipped away from these people. It had shifted irrevocably to the television station, where the National Salvation Front was also, as here, in permanent session. Yet the Central Committee group was the conscience of the revolution. This was also the heart of the powerfully anti-Communist emotions which had welled up and overthrown Ceausescu. Most of the influential people in the Front, by contrast, were former Communists themselves. The people in the Central Committee represented a genuine principle in the new Romania; it would become more important as the weeks and months went past.

Still, they had no staying-power. The loudest voice won the

argument. At the moment that belonged to a sculptor. He was sniffing out treason. There were, it was true, Securitate men still at large inside the maze of tunnels under the Central Committee building. It was also true that a team of special agents had been detailed to infiltrate the revolutionaries in case of a coup: they had found orders to that effect in Ceausescu's safe, complete with photographs of the men concerned.

The sculptor exhibited the symptoms of paranoiac psychosis. Another man, a portrait painter, suggested going into Ceausescu's private apartments, which were reached by a door at the far end of the office. These apartments contained both treasure and safes which hadn't yet been opened. The sculptor became manic with rage. He jammed his revolver against the portrait painter's head and threatened to kill him there and then. Only a Securitate agent would want to get into the private apartment, he said. He forced the painter to lie face down on the floor, hands behind his head, and screamed insults at him and orders at everyone else. It is disturbing, to say the least, to be in the presence of a madman with a gun; no one disagreed with him.

At last, though, the sculptor relented. Then he wept, and begged us not to use the pictures which Bob had filmed of the incident. I countered by asking if we could film inside Ceausescu's apartments. I hadn't realized that anything so important might lie behind the door at the back of the room. It took on the interest of the entrance to Tutankhamen's burial chamber. The sculptor's eyes glittered, but he agreed to consider it.

In the end it was Adrian Donea, one of only two or three entirely sensible people in the room, who insisted that we should be allowed in.

'This guy is crazy,' he said. 'But he's got a gun. We have to wait till he gets quieter.'

There was another incident before he did so. I had to leave the building and return to our hotel for more camera batteries and more tapes, but before I went the cinema stuntman and someone else had been identified as Securitate infiltrators. I last saw them standing in their underpants with their arms in the air. When I returned the sculptor had been led away and the cinema stuntman was giving the orders.

Things were a great deal easier after that, but there was always an undercurrent of violence at the Central Committee building. Even so, when it condemned the National Salvation Front, the Front had to listen. Dumitru Mazilu, the deputy President whom Adrian Donea and the others had appointed, swept energetically into Ceausescu's office. The revolutionaries gathered round him as he sat down at the table. At first Adrian explained their anxieties: the Front had too many

Communists in it, and not enough ordinary workers. It was out of touch. Mazilu listened, then leant forward to reply.

It was a signal to everyone else to interrupt him. A man with a voice so hoarse he seemed only to be able to speak by holding his throat hissed at him. Someone read from the Front's newspaper, then spat on it. The word '*fascista*' emerged from a babble of angry noise. An army officer whom I'd come to know looked at me and shook his head, loosening the revolver in his belt meaningfully. A weightlifter, as huge and glowering as the villain in a Charlie Chaplin short, moved threateningly across, his head brushing the Christmas decorations. Somebody ran in and shouted out that chemical weapons had just been discovered downstairs. No one took the slightest notice.

Mazilu listened to the storm about him, refusing to be offended, his finger-tips together. At last he said he would make them an offer. Everyone went quiet. The representatives of the Central Committee group should, he said, act as observers and special advisers to the Front. Some should be attached to the ministries. Adrian, he said, selecting the one really able man there, should advise on the planning for the forthcoming elections. He should also oversee the police.

There was an explosion of applause. The weightlifter clapped his hands over his head, louder than all. They cheered when Mazilu announced that everyone who had taken part in the capture of the Central Committee would be entitled to a special certificate.

*

We had heard stories of the fabulous wealth of the Ceausescus. Now, as we stood outside the door to their apartments we felt a growing excitement.

'Everything in there is made of gold,' someone said. 'It is richer than anything you have ever seen.'

But it wasn't. It was a sad place. The curtains were unlined, so that the pale morning sun shone through them, and so skimpy they failed to reach the lower edges of the windows. The carpets were thin and stained. The rooms were dark and narrow, and overlooked by the Securitate flats opposite. The door handles seemed to be made of gold, but Paul Francis examined them and said they were just brass. There was a tacky feel to everything. The dining table had an imitation gold call-button to summon the servants, but the electrical cord was attached to the leg of the table with adhesive tape.

In these small, dark, dispiriting rooms the Ceausescus had lived their private lives. They had palaces everywhere, but this was where they spent their time together. Yet it had nothing of them in it. The books had apparently been chosen by committee: political studies in French, the autobiographies of de Gaulle and Churchill, several books by Richard Nixon. None of them showed any sign of having been read. The pictures were purloined from the National Gallery nearby: the Ceausescus did the opposite of the great philanthropists, hanging the originals on their own walls and sending copies to the Gallery. There was expensive, unattractive silver which had apparently been confiscated from wealthy families when Romania became Communist. I imagined the Ceausescus hunched over the silver plates, swallowing down the game which Nicolae shot in industrial quantities, ringing the imitation gold bell for the servants to bring them more.

Their apartment was furnished from gifts, as though from a vast international wedding-list. Everything had a label: malachite ashtrays from the President of Mongolia, carved wooden heads from the President of Ethiopia, knick-knacks in jade and ivory from the President of China. The Ceausescus were international scroungers, travelling a shrinking world exchanging objects taken from the Romanian people for objects taken from other subject nations. Near his bed stood a toy tank. It had no label. It may have been the only thing Ceausescu had bought himself.

There had been stories of diamante high-heels in Elena's wardrobes elsewhere, but in the flat there was nothing but sensible clothing, and not too much of it. Ceausescu's wardrobe held a selection of the light-coloured suits which he seemed to have designed himself, the jackets with four buttons and high collars, the trousers wide-bottomed. The 1960s were the years when his reputation was high, and in fashion terms he never outlived them. The imperial couple's bed was meagre, with a simple headboard. Every high-street furniture store in the West sells one like it. The sheets on which they had spent their last night of power were striped in candy-pink, and some joker had laid out Ceausescu's brown silk pyjamas on them as though he were still in them. We filmed it all. But everyone was getting nervous; there was always the chance that the crazy sculptor might come back and threaten our guides with death.

Earlier he had discovered some of my belongings and confiscated them at gunpoint. They included several pictures I had been given of the Ceausescus at play. Now I asked for them back, but no one knew where they had gone. Instead, someone brought out another album – there seemed to be dozens – and took some pictures out of it for me. We were preparing to leave when one of the guards, an older man whom I hadn't noticed before, drew me into the Ceausescus' bathroom and closed the door. It was unnerving: the room was particularly small. He sat down on the fluffy yellow lavatory seat and produced a large box containing all sorts of objects made of gold. From it he selected a fountain pen and handed it to me.

I looked at it: he told me, in a kind of English, that it came from the British Labour Party. He had, he said, seen the label attached to it. It was a large, bulbous Mont Blanc, worth about £200. When I handed it back to him he insisted, with nods and waves of his hand, that I should keep it, but put it in my pocket out of sight. Later, back in England, the Labour Party said it had no knowledge of having given a fountain pen to Ceausescu. It was an object around which untruths seemed to gather. When I telexed an article from Bucharest to a London newspaper about the incident, I called it, feebly, a Venus pencil: by that stage the free and easy atmosphere of the early revolution had changed and several of the guards had been accused of pilfering. I wasn't certain if anyone in Bucharest might be reading the telexes.

That evening Rory Peck and I took our material to the television station. Getting there was easy: one simply had to flag down a car in the Boulevard Nicolae Balcescu. Self-appointed guardians of the peace had organized so many roadblocks in those first days that timorous drivers would stop for any authoritative figure. We hailed the first car that passed and asked the driver to take us to the television station. He insisted on stopping whenever he was asked – this being the disadvantage of the system; but there were no taxis and we had no petrol. It was only later that I realized we could go by Metro, and that during the revolution travel was free.

Approaching the television station was harder. Since there had been a considerable amount of fighting there, the soldiers camped around it were inclined to shoot at any movement. Once, when Rory Peck had spent the whole night at the station, someone crept in and murdered seven soldiers who were asleep in a corridor. Now the fighting was over, the trouble was the nervousness of the soldiers. At first we had to run from cover to cover: everyone believed there were still snipers about, and the soldiers demanded it. But when we reached the approach road to the television station we had to walk slowly and carelessly in the middle of the road, as though we had nothing to hide. If they fired over our heads, as they did occasionally, it was a mistake to dive for the side of the road. They regarded that as proof that we were hostile.

The Securitate's target was the National Salvation Front, which was housed in one wing of the television station. The atmosphere at the Front's meetings was saner than anything in the Central Committee building; but the Front was poorly organized, far too large and lacking any sense of proportion. It was half unwieldy Cabinet, half debating chamber. Its members harangued each other at length, especially when their deliberations were being televised. Then and later, when the Front moved to new quarters, it could spend long periods of time on trivia.

Vice-President Dumitru Mazilu: There's a proposal from the Young Revolutionaries to adopt a law renaming that famous and odious so-called Boulevard of the Victory of Socialism [the wide avenue leading to Ceausescu's new palace] the Boulevard of 22 December. I agree.

Mircea Dinescu, poet [rising]: Excuse me, but I'm not sure that this particular avenue, which looks rather unpleasant anyway, should be called '22 December'.

Mazilu [wearily]: Well, that's the proposal.

Dinescu: No, no, the date should certainly be commemorated, but not by that Boulevard. Now I think. . . .

By Christmas night the Romanian television staff hadn't slept in a bed for three nights. They scarcely looked at the Scotch or the fresh fruit we had brought as gifts. One of them, a woman in her fifties, fell asleep while speaking to the co-ordinators of the satellite in Geneva. Those correspondents who had made it to the station, as well as those who had never ventured out of it, fought each other for the limited resources. I wrote my script, which dealt in some detail with the incidents in the Central Committee building and with the Ceausescus' apartment, in a little recording booth beside the control room. Its walls were made of glass. Ten minutes before our satellite to London was due I glanced up and saw the television screen. The Romanian announcer was reading out a statement. Everyone in the control room was standing, silent and shocked. I ran in.

The list of charges for which the Ceausescus were tried – the murder of sixty thousand people, sabotaging the national economy and corruption – had just been read out. The news reader continued:

For these serious crimes committed against the Romanian people and Romania, the accused, Nicolae Ceausescu and Elena Ceausescu, were sentenced to death and confiscation of assets. The sentences were final and were carried out.

The tired men and women of Romanian Television broke into spontaneous applause. One woman danced around the control room, kissing everyone. Most of the rest of us found their reaction deeply unpleasant. But there were only fifteen minutes before our satellite. I threw away most of what I had written, especially the part about the Ceausescu's bad taste; that seemed in bad taste itself. Instead I sketched out a rapid portrait of a man and woman corrupted by absolute power. With a minute to go, I finished, I sat back and looked down. I had written Ceausescu's obituary with his own pen.

★

The heavens themselves blaze forth the death of princes. That night the mild weather which had made the revolution possible came to an end. It froze, then snowed hard. The time for rejoicing was over. There was no more dancing in the streets, no more singing of '*olé, olé, olé, olé*'. Later on Christmas night the television station showed an edited version of the pictures of the Ceausescus' trial, and of their bodies lying in the snow. Birnam Wood had come to Dunsinane. The Macbeths were dead.

People all over the world competed with each other to condemn Ceausescu: even those – especially those – who had encouraged him and praised him and given him presents. No one wanted to think of the ghastly museum in Bucharest which housed the trophies from his good relations with the outside world: with, in pride of place, the insignia of an honorary Knight Grand Cross of the Order of the Bath which the British government had insisted that the Queen should give him (against her will) in the 1978. The museum was shut. A guardian, dimly visible inside, wagged a finger. It must have been a relief to a good many politicians and civil servants who watched their televisions in Western Europe that night that it was impossible to provide pictures of the honours once showered on him. No unfortunate memories were aroused.

The Ceausescus were evil and vicious. An entire nation was imprisoned, went hungry, and lived in the half-light because of them. Yet their lives and deaths weren't small or squalid. Nicolae Ceausescu was a tragic hero along lines that some grand, out of date Shakespearian scholar, some A.C. Bradley, would have recognized. It was the heroic Ceausescu, the man who stood on his balcony and defied the Russians when they invaded Czechoslovakia, whom the Western world praised and rewarded. The museum of his foreign honours was dedicated entirely to the Ceausescu of Act I, the Ceausescu who was prepared to fight for the nation's independence to the last, the Ceausescu whose dark hair and boyish looks appeared on the posters at his rallies, the Ceausescu who wore his 1960s four-buttoned jackets. Characteristically, the world awarded its honours to him around the time of Acts III and IV.

A.C. Bradley would have recognized the single tragic fault that turned noble defiance into savagery: it was Ceausescu's vanity; and the vanity was fed by an assumption that he was invulnerable. The Marxist-Leninist system was his Three Witches:

Be bloody, bold, and resolute; laugh to scorn
The power of man, for none of woman born
Shall harm Macbeth.

As long as the Securitate controlled every place of work and every street and housing estate in the country, Ceausescu could do what he wanted. He could consider pulling down the villages, or reducing living standards to African or Central American levels, or repaying the entire national debt in an absurdly short space of time, because he was immune to opposition. If he looked after the Securitate he was safe; the Securitate were his Murderers, reckless in what they did to spite the world.

And behind him was Elena, grimmer and more clear sighted than he was, more aware of the real situation in the country, of the fact that he was loathed instead of loved, and yet determined to push him on to worse and fiercer crimes. It was she who had eased out their playboy son Nicu, Ceausescu's natural successor. Elena herself planned to succeed Ceausescu. Thinking of those candy-striped sheets, that narrow double bed, it was impossible not to wonder about the nagging accusations that had gone on there.

*

Over the days that followed we and our French colleagues Jerome Fritel and Marc Simon from the magazine *VSD* put in a good deal of work to find out what had happened to the Ceausescus after their heavy-laden helicopter lifted off from the roof of the Central Committee building. Another friend of mine, Peter Jouvenal, who had made his reputation as a combat cameraman in Afghanistan, had joined us in Bucharest. So had Vaughan Smith, a freelance photographer who had also worked in Afghanistan. Peter followed the trail of the Ceausescus for days, meeting and interviewing the people who had come across them on their way to arrest and execution.

The helicopter pilot, Lt.-Col. Vasile Malutanu, explained how he had rescued the Ceausescus and the others in their party from the jammed lift, and flown them the short way to their villa by the lake at Snagov. They arrived at around 12.30. The staff at the villa were appalled to see the helicopter land and the Ceausescus get out. The President and his wife hadn't been there for a long time and the servants thought they would be in serious trouble because nothing was prepared for them. They knew nothing of the morning's events in Bucharest. Snagov had once been one of the Ceausescus' favourite houses. It was a large place, with more than forty rooms. Now everything was shrouded in dust- covers and all the curtains were drawn. The chief of security at the villa, Sergeant-Major Lalescu, heard the helicopter's engines and went out nervously to meet them.

> Elena and Nicolae Ceausescu got out of the helicopter and started running. They ran along the path to the back of the house and went upstairs to their apartment on the first floor. There they went searching through all the cupboards, emptied the drawers and turned over the mattresses. They put everything into two big blue bags. On top, I could see blankets and loaves of bread. I've got no idea what was under them. Then they made a couple of calls.

The first of these calls was to the commander of the military air base at Ototai, where they could catch a plane to take them out of the country. The other was to a Party secretary in the mountains to the north. The sergeant-major's reference to the mattresses is intriguing at first sight. Both Nicolae and his wife had a peasant upbringing, and their parents and grandparents may well have kept their valuables under the mattress. More probably, though, they just pulled the blankets off their beds and disarranged the mattresses in doing so. It took three-quarters of an hour to pack the bags and make the phone-calls. At 1.15 p.m. they hurried out to the waiting helicopter.

By this time the two unwanted passengers, Emil Bobu, the prime minister and his deputy, Manea Manescu, had headed off by car. There was little sentimentality about the entire escapade, and they scarcely said goodbye. So now there were four: the Ceausescus and their two Securitate bodyguards, one of whom, General Neagoe, had been with the President on the balcony the previous day and had said the crowd was getting in.

The pilot, Lt.-Col. Malutanu, had been in radio contact with his superior officers at Ototai.

> They said to me, 'Ceausescu's been on the phone asking for a helicopter escort. We've said no.' When they got back on board, Ceausescu asked me, 'Whose side are you on?'
>
> 'Where are we going?' I said. 'You give the orders.'
>
> We took off at 1330 hours. The bodyguards were very nervous. They kept their machine-pistols pointed at me. On my headphones I could hear my commanding officer saying to me, 'Vasile, listen to the radio – this is the revolution!'

After that, Ceausescu ordered me to cut all radio contact with my base. I wanted to persuade him to let us land so he could be captured, but I was on my own, cut off from the world. I deliberately flew into the range of air traffic control radar so they could track our helicopter.

'Head for Pitesti,' he said.

'I can't. I haven't enough fuel, and we're being tracked. If I don't put down, the anti-aircraft defences will shoot us down.'

It wasn't true, but he didn't have any choice. We landed next to a country road eight miles from Titu, outside a village called Salcutsa. The time was 1.45. Ceausescu didn't want to get out of the helicopter. I pushed him out. One of the bodyguards said: 'I ought to kill you for daring to abandon your President.'

As he was leaving, Ceausescu turned to me and asked, 'Why are you abandoning the cause like this?'

'What cause?' I said.

I took off straight away. I was happy I was still alive.

In a nearby farm, four men were watching the television coverage of the unfolding revolution. One of them was a forestry official.

I looked out of the window and saw the president's helicopter. I immediately jumped into my car with the others and we got there just as Ceausescu and his wife and their two bodyguards were getting out of it. You can imagine how I felt! There I was, a yard or so from the President! One of my colleagues went up to him and asked, 'Is there something we can do for you, Mr President?' He just said that to break the silence. The rest of us were completely tongue-tied. Ceausescu said something, but I couldn't hear what. Elena shouted, 'Everything's fine! Go away! Get out of it!'

At that moment a car drove up. It was a red Dacia. The driver was wearing a black coat and a hat, the typical clothes of a Securitate agent. I was certain that Ceausescu had arranged a rendezvous here. Ceausescu got in the front and his wife and one of the bodyguards got in the back. The other bodyguard took my car. He pointed his gun at one of my friends and made him get in. Then they drove off towards Bucharest. The red Dacia headed in the other direction, towards Titu and Tergoviste.

Then there were three: the Ceausescus and one bodyguard. The bodyguard who commandeered the other car, Ivan Marian, who came from Mrs Ceausescu's home village and had been her private detective for years, had told the Ceausescus he would follow them. In fact he was deserting them. As for the driver of the red Dacia, he wasn't a Securitate man at all but a local doctor, Nicolae Deca. He takes up the story.

During my medical rounds that morning I'd heard on the radio that the dictator had fled. When I got to the hospital everyone was overjoyed and we celebrated the fact that we were now free. I had a strong feeling that I should head home and as I left the hospital I joked 'I'm going to catch Ceausescu.' Some sixth sense told me to get in my car and drive back towards Bucharest. I was looking forward to being alone in the car to think quietly about this new liberty of ours. As I drove along, deep in thought, I suddenly saw a big man by the side of the road. I know his name now: Ivan Marian. He was carrying a walkie-talkie. He ordered me to pull over to the right side of the road.

He shouted, 'You see these two people? We have to drive them to the militia headquarters in Gaesti.' The two people were Nicolae and Elena Ceausescu. Not far away I could see the white helicopter which had brought them from Bucharest. I said, 'All right, I'll drive them.' The Ceausescus slowly, wearily crossed the road. They looked exhausted. Ceausescu climbed into the passenger seat and Elena sat behind me. A heavily-built man got in the car with us. I later found out he was General Neagoe, the head of Ceausescu's bodyguards. He pointed a gun at me. I was confused, because I thought we were going to drive to the militia station to hand in two arrested people. Then Ceausescu asked Neagoe 'Is Marian coming?' Neagoe answered, 'I can't see him.'

Dr Deca, a stout man in his mid-fifties who looked a good ten years older, was extremely scared, but that didn't prevent his making a shrewd assessment of his passengers.

They were completely dumbfounded by the situation they were in. There was disbelief written all over their faces. I think they were terrified and close to despair. They seemed to get smaller and smaller as they sat in the car. We continued down the road, Ceausescu contemplating his situation and me trying to think what to do next. Ceausescu asked me if I knew what had happened. I replied that I had been on duty at the hospital all night and had no idea. He said, 'There was a coup', and lapsed into silence. Later he turned to me and said, 'We're going to organize the resistance. Are you coming with us?' This was an astounding question and I was thrown off balance. I tried to tell him I wasn't young any more, my constitution was frail, I had a family, and so on. I ended up by saying, 'Anyway I'm not even a Party member.' That seemed to come as a real blow to him. He went white and refused to say any more.

All the signs are that Ceausescu thought the Army had seized power. He had always been afraid of that, and had been particularly anxious about Soviet influence over his high command. This dated from the time of his resistance to the Soviet invasion of Czechoslovakia. Later he seems to have believed that Gorbachev was planning to overthrow him. The idea of a mass rebellion by the ordinary people of the country doesn't seem to have occurred to him, then or later.

The doctor, meanwhile, was trying to work out ways of getting rid of his passengers.

When we reached the junction Neagoe ordered me to turn in the direction of Tergoviste rather than Gaesti. Elena had kept her left hand inside her coat and I suspected she was holding a pistol. I knew she was a very good shot. I was beginning to get nervous; sweat was pouring from my forehead. When I glanced at Ceausescu I saw he was in no better shape than I was. Some of my friends said to me later 'You should have driven the car into a tree,' but that way I'd have been the first one to die. My plan was to get rid of them. I decided to pull a trick and told them the carburettor was giving out. I then saw a man I knew washing his car by the side of the road and I pulled up to ask him for help. Neagoe ordered him to get into his car and take the three of them with him. Then he told me to follow. I didn't, of course. The trouble was, a crowd of people surrounded me, saying 'This is the one, he's Securitate.' They wanted to lynch me, but when they saw my identification they accepted my story. I went to the police and told them everything. I said 'You must make sure not to shoot the driver. He's innocent – like me.'

The latest man to be hijacked, Nicolae Petrisor, repaired bicycles for a living.

I recognized the doctor, so when the bodyguard asked me if I'd got petrol I said yes. Then I realised Ceausescu was sitting behind the driver. I panicked, I'm afraid. I shouted out to my wife, 'It's the Ceausescus!' The bodyguard pointed his gun at me and said 'Don't say anything. Just drive.' Ceausescu got in beside me. His wife and the Securitate man got in the back. Throughout the journey Elena Ceausescu held a gun to the back of my neck.

Ceausescu asked me, 'Is there a good place round here where we could hide? A village, maybe?'

I said, 'Everyone knows you're here.'

He reached over and turned on the radio quite loud. The poet Mircea Dinescu was speaking on it. I recognized his voice because I'd seen him on television in the past and I know his way of speaking, very loud. When Ceausescu heard what Dinescu was saying his head slumped forwards onto the dashboard. He stayed like that for a few seconds. Then he said to me, 'Turn it off.'

General Neagoe, the bodyguard, suggested going to a steel works at Tergoviste, because he knew the security people there. When they reached the outskirts of the city Ceausescu said, 'I built them all these factories, and they still hate me.' Elena Ceausescu snorted. She seemed much less surprised by the hatred of the ordinary working-class people of Romania than her husband. Suddenly they came face to face with a group of workers who were on strike. They recognized him and started throwing stones at the car. Petrisor drove down the back streets of Tergoviste. Elena Ceausescu told Nicolae to take off his coat. They hunched down in their seats and hid their faces when they passed anyone.

> He suggested we should head for Ulmi, a village where he took refuge during the War. But Elena made fun of him for that. She said the old woman he'd stayed with was dead and the house was shut up. Half a mile further on, we stopped so the bodyguard could get out and check which way we should go. I was left alone with the Ceausescus. Suddenly some kids spotted us and started shouting to the neighbours. Elena pulled out her gun and shouted, 'Get going!'

Then there were two. The Ceausescus had abandoned their faithful bodyguard, who escaped but was later captured. They tried to take refuge at a nunnery: a considerable irony, given Ceausescu's persecution of the Church. The nuns refused to let them in. They went on to a hotel for Communist Party officials. Ceausescu got out to talk to the porter.

'Can we spend the night here?'

'No. There's no room. Get out of here!'

Finally their driver, Nicolae Petrisor, took matters into his own hands. He turned into the driveway of an agricultural institute on the outskirts of Tergoviste, where he knew the staff. It was 3 p.m.

The director of the institute, Victor Seinescu, was watching television. Just as they arrived the television announcer was saying that there'd been a report that the Ceausescus had been arrested in Tergoviste. Seinescu was delighted to hear it. He had been a member of the Communist Party, but ten years earlier he had been dismissed for political reasons. He was a jaunty character, always making jokes. Perhaps that was why the Party threw him out. Suddenly Petrisor burst into the room and said, 'I've got the Ceausescus outside in my car.'

> I could tell it was true, because he was as white as a sheet. I said, 'Bring them in', and in they came as quietly as you please, without even saying hello. They were terrified. Ceausescu went over to the window and stayed there as though he were waiting for something or someone. He kept looking at his watch all the time, then up at the sky. I got the strong impression he was expecting someone to come and rescue them.
>
> I said, 'What's going on? Why are you here?'
>
> 'Traitors and foreign agents have got together to overthrow me,' said Nicolae.

I tried to lock the door.

'Why do you want to hand me over to the authorities?' he asked.

'So you can be tried by the people, you bastard.' I enjoyed saying that.

'But haven't you had any benefits from the Party?'

'What benefits?' I said.

I got on the phone to my boss and told him what had happened. He told me to hang on until the police got there.

I went into my office, but Elena followed me. I couldn't shake her off. She offered me a lot of money if I'd help them get away somewhere safe.

'I'll really make you somebody if you help us,' she said.

I didn't answer. The police came for them at 3.20.

It was strange that the Ceausescus should have been caught in Tergoviste, since that was where Nicolae had been arrested and imprisoned half a century before. Yet he had an affection for the place. He had even tried to turn it into a second capital, investing considerable amounts of public money there. Now they were taken to the old cavalry school near the railway station, which had become an army barracks. It is a grand building, built in the early years of the century, which fronts onto the main road. There was little security about it; the room in which the Ceausescus were held for the next two days and nights looks out on to the passing traffic, only twenty yards away.

Their arrival threw the base into utter confusion. Lt.-Col. Mares, who was placed in charge of them, did not even know there had been a revolution until he received the order from his commandant. There was a serious problem with security: the five hundred soldiers and forty civilians on the base had to be restricted from leaving, so that the presence of the Ceausescus there would not become known. Even so, the Securitate came to hear of it. The officers at the base began receiving threatening calls. One of them asked who was calling. 'The special troops,' was the answer.

The Ceausescus were difficult prisoners. Their fear quickly left them, and they began hectoring their guards. They were held in the office of the barracks, and slept on iron bedsteads which had already been placed in the room before their arrival. Ceausescu had placed the military on full alert early in the Timisoara crisis, and the beds had been brought in as a result. An officer slept on a third bed, between them, and stayed with them during the day. Captain Stoica was one of the officers chosen for the duty.

Ceausescu came up and stood as close as you're standing to me now. He put out his hand and said, 'I'll give you a million American dollars and any rank in the army you like if you help to get us out of here.' But it never occurred to me to believe that the offer was genuine. I thought that instead of a million dollars I would just get a bullet in the back of the neck. So I said to him, 'Nothing doing.' And Elena, who was sitting over there, said 'Oh, leave him alone.'

Sometimes Ceausescu demanded a car to take him back to Bucharest. He had been badly misled about the danger on the morning of 22 December, he felt. If he had stayed there, he would have been able to cope with the trouble. Now he wanted to go back and speak to the people, either on television or at the Central Committee building itself. He still believed he was the victim of a coup. At one stage a crowd of demonstrators passed along the main road outside the building, chanting '*Olé, olé, olé, olé, Ceausescu nu mai e.*' Ceausescu heard his name and started trying to open the window.

'The people have come to rescue me!' he shouted, not realizing that they were singing 'Ceausescu is no more.'

The officer with him caught him round the waist and threw him onto the bed. Captain Stoica heard the noise from outside and came rushing in with his gun.

'Are you going to kill us?' Elena asked. They both seemed badly frightened.

On Christmas Eve the Securitate troops finally worked out where they were being held, and took up positions in buildings around the base. Soon after darkness fell they opened fire. You can still see the bullet marks on the front and sides of the headquarters building: there are several hundred of them. The Ceausescus were hurried out and put for safety into an armoured personnel carrier, which parked in as sheltered a place as possible. They spent the night there. The following morning they were driven back to the headquarters building and taken to a room beside the one where they had previously been held. It was used as a lecture room. Now the tables and chairs had been arranged to form a rudimentary court, with a dock formed by two desks and chairs in one corner.

In Bucharest a prominent lawyer in his late fifties, Nicu Teodorescu, was spending Christmas morning in the office of the College of Advocates when the phone rang. It was the National Salvation Front, asking for someone to go to Tergoviste to represent the Ceausescus. Teodorescu agreed; it seemed, he said with unconscious humour, like an interesting challenge. It was nearly to cost him his life; that afternoon, as he returned from the trial, his car was ambushed by Securitate agents. Teodorescu was grazed by a bullet which killed the man beside him.

Now, a military escort raced him the 90 miles to Tergoviste. He arrived to find the Ceausescus already sitting in the court room. They still wore the clothes in which they had appeared on the balcony on 22 December. Ceausescu occasionally toyed with his astrakhan hat or threw it on the table to make a point. Elena sat with her hands together, her headscarf on: an ugly old village woman, for all her expensive coat and shoes. There were five judges, all senior army officers in uniform, two prosecutors, a junior to help Teodorescu with the defence and a young officer with a video camera whose job was to record the proceedings but not to show any of the participants except for the defendants themselves. There were to be no witnesses. The couple had been examined by a doctor that morning. He pronounced them fit to stand trial.

Teodorescu told them their only hope was to plead insanity. Not surprisingly, they were deeply insulted. The trial began.

Judge: You stand before the People's Tribunal, the new legal body of the country.

Ceausescu: I do not recognize any tribunal but the Grand National Assembly. A state coup cannot be recognized.

Judge: We try you in accordance with the [word indistinct] of the Council of the National Salvation Front. Accused, please stand up.

Ceausescu: Read the country's Constitution [words indistinct].

Judge: You want us to read the Constitution? We know it better than you, who have never observed it.

Teodorescu: We are here to defend the two accused. Mr Ceausescu, you have the chance to tell us what made you [words indistinct]. The bodies that you are calling in your defence have been wound up in accordance with the wishes of the people.

Ceausescu: I do not recognize you.

Another voice: Although you have been holding a dialogue with the people for the past twenty years, now you are not able to talk with the representatives of the people.

Another voice: [words indistinct] . . . standing in the entrance hall, and in the most luxurious clothes, receiving more fuss than a queen, while speaking in the name of the people, and today you do not want to co-operate with the people.

Prosecutor: Today we have to try Nicolae Ceausescu and Elena Ceausescu, who are guilty of serious crimes against the people, incompatible with human dignity, for the despotic way in which they behaved towards the people. For these crimes we consider these two guilty and ask the tribunal to sentence them to death.

The charges were then read out.

1. The 'genocide' of more than 60,000 victims. (That was the much-inflated figure for the deaths in Timisoara the previous week, and in the rest

of the country during the counter-revolution. Later, when it became clear that the number of deaths was to be measured in hundreds, rather than in thousands or tens of thousands, the figure was hastily reinterpreted to cover all the death attributable to Ceausescu since he came to power.)

2. Organizing armed action against the people and the state.

3. The destruction of public assets, buildings etc.

4. Sabotage of the national economy.

5. Attempting to flee the country with funds of more than a billion dollars, deposited in foreign banks.

Prosecutor: Have you heard this, accused? Please stand up.

Ceausescu: Everything that has been said is a lie. I recognize only the Grand National Assembly. I do not recognize this tribunal.

Prosecutor: You know the disastrous situation that prevailed in the country until 22 December 1989. You are aware of the lack of medicine, of heating. . .

Elena Ceausescu: [words indistinct].

Prosecutor: I am talking now to Nicolae Ceausescu, not to Elena. Who gave the order to the Army to shoot young people in Timisoara? Do you know about the bloodbath in Bucharest, which is still going on? Women and children are being killed by fanatics. Who trained these fanatics? We, the people, or you?

Ceausescu: I am unwilling to answer any questions, but I [indistinct] that nobody has been shot in the Square of the Palace of the Republic.

Second Prosecutor: Who ordered the shooting in Bucharest and in every large town? Who ordered the destruction of establishments built through the efforts of the people. . .? Who made the cream of your society leave this country because of the situation created here? Who paid those mercenaries [a reference to the supposed involvement of Palestinians and North Koreans in the fighting]? Who ordered those mercenaries who are carrying out this bloodbath to come to Romania?

Ceausescu: I will only answer questions in front of the Grand National Assembly.

Prosecutor: Who directs the mercenaries who are carrying out terrorist actions? Elena Ceausescu, doctor, engineer, academician, you usually have a lot to say. Why are you silent now?

Elena Ceausescu: My colleagues will hear you [indistinct].

Prosecutor: Who is stopping you from talking?

Ceausescu: I will speak only in front of the Grand National Assembly and the representatives of the working class. I do not recognise those who lead a coup.

Another voice: The Grand National Assembly has been dismantled. Through the unflinching will of the people we have another body in power, the Council of the National Salvation Front.

Ceausescu: The people will fight against this gang of traitors who, with foreign help, succeeded in this coup.

Another voice: Who are these people fighting throughout the country?

Ceausescu: For their existence, independence and sovereignty. . .

Prosecutor: Do you know that you have been dismissed from your position as head of the Party and President of the country, and that you have lost all your other positions? Are the accused aware of the fact, are they aware that they face trial as two ordinary citizens?

Ceausescu: I am President of the country and supreme commander of the Army. I do not recognize you. You are ordinary citizens and I answer only to the Grand National Assembly. I do not answer those who, with the assistance of foreign organizations, carried out this coup.

Prosecutor: Why did you take these measures of bringing the Romanian people to this state of humiliation today? To export everything that they have produced? Why did you starve this nation that you represented?

Ceausescu: I will not answer your questions, but I will tell you that for the first time a co-operative worker received 200 kg of wheat per person, not per family, but per person. These are lies that you are saying, and you are not patriots.

Prosecutor: [indistinct] systematization, which actually meant the destruction of our villages.

Ceausescu: There has never been such a level of development in the villages as there is today. We have built schools, ensured that there are doctors, ensured that there is everything for a dignified life.

Prosecutor: A last question. Since we are supposed to be equal, all of us, why did we see on television that your daughter was weighing meat from abroad on golden scales? Wasn't the meat from our own country any good. . .?

Elena Ceausescu: How can you say such a thing?

Prosecutor: Nicolae Ceausescu, tell us about the money that was transferred to Swiss banks.

Elena Ceausescu: Proof! Proof!

Ceausescu [putting his hand restrainingly on Elena's arm]: I do not answer the questions of a gang which carried out a coup.

Prosecutor: Nevertheless, if it is proved that there is money in foreign banks in your name, do you agree that it should be brought back to . . . the Romanian state?

Ceausescu: We will discuss [indistinct] with the Grand National Assembly. I will not sign anything. What is this National Salvation Council? It is impossible to set up a body without the state power, without the approval of the Grand National Assembly. As happened hundreds of years ago, people like you will have to answer to the people.

Prosecutor [to Elena]: You, who have always been your husband's primary collaborator, do you know about the events in Timisoara and about the genocide there?

Elena Ceausescu: Come on, what are you talking about. . .?

Prosecutor: As First Deputy Premier of the country, you made decisions together with your husband, you wanted to be informed about everything. So, who gave the order to shoot in Timisoara? What can you say about security activity?

Voices: Who demoted General Milea [the defence minister, shot on 22 December] and accused him of being a traitor? Why did you not try him properly?

Ceausescu: I heard about his betrayal that day. He did not do his duty in making the Army carry out its tasks. . .

Prosecutor [to Elena Ceausescu]: Who paid for the publication of your and your husband's volumes abroad. . .?

Elena Ceausescu: Leave me alone. How can you say such things?

Prosecutor: You have behaved just like you always did. Have you learned nothing today. . .?

Elena Ceausescu: I have fought since I was fourteen years old. How can we betray the people?

Second Prosecutor: For the atrocities committed by these two accused, we ask you to sentence them to death and order the confiscation of their wealth.

Teodorescu: I want you to understand that we, as lawyers, want to defend everybody in accordance with the valid laws. Only a President can ask for the Grand National Assembly to be called, but you are not President any longer. You are ordinary citizens. It is a mistake of the two accused that they still have power and try to act accordingly. . .

Prosecutor: You have killed young people in Timisoara and your security forces were disguised in soldiers' uniforms. You were shooting at hospitals, at the wounded. . .

Elena Ceausescu: Who?

Prosecutor: You say you do not recognize our organisations of the people's power. You do not have to recognize them, Mr Ex-President. King Michael had more dignity than you.

Prosecutor: [asks if the accused wish to say something in their own defence].

Ceausescu: I am not an accused person. I will answer only to the Romanian people. Have you not seen how the people cheered when I went to the factories?

Another voice: Stand up!

Elena Ceausescu [to her husband]: No, dear, we are people. . .

Judge: The sentence is pronounced today, 25 December 1989, in a public gathering.

Ceausescu: I do not recognize [words indistinct]. . .

Judge: This is a final decision.

The end was shabby and terrible. This part of the official video record was suppressed, though a copy of it came into the hands of the French television channel, TF-1. The Ceausescus' hands were tied behind their backs. Elena wept, though when one of the soldiers who tied them up said 'You're in big trouble now,' she snarled at him, 'Go and fuck your mother.' Everyone who heard her was shocked by the words and by the intensity with which she said them. Lt.-Col. Mares led them down the corridor and out into the yard of the barracks. The Ceausescus seemed to have no idea that they were to be executed immediately. On the parade ground, fifty yards away, they could see the helicopter which had brought two members of the National Salvation Front from Bucharest to attend the trial. Assuming that they were to be taken somewhere in it, the Ceausescus headed towards it. Lt.-Col. Mares gently but firmly directed them down another path that led to the yard. They were two old people, nothing more than that now, who had stayed together and retained an affection for each other.

The entire complement of the base, soldiers and civilians, had been drawn up in a large semi-circle to watch. Three private soldiers and a lieutenant stood by a flower bed, their Kalashnikovs by their side. This was the firing-squad. When Elena saw them she said 'Nicolae, is it possible they're going to shoot us, in our own country?' Ceausescu said nothing, but he seemed as frightened as she was. They were marched over and stood against the wall of the building opposite the firing squad, Elena on the left and Ceausescu on the right. Ceausescu shouted, 'Long live a free and independent Romania!' and began singing the Internationale. But he had only sung the first four words when the order to shoot was given. A blast of firing toppled them over. Elena was hit in the head by at least two bullets, and Ceausescu was hit in the chest. Everyone with a gun who was standing nearby joined in the firing, shooting wildly in the general direction of the bodies. Several shots struck the paving stones in front of them. Others hit the window ten feet above the ground. Altogether 120 rounds were fired until Lt.-Col. Mares shouted the order to stop. The television cameraman who had filmed the trial had had some problem with his equipment, and missed everything except the last few seconds of the shooting. The bodies of the Macbeths lay side by side on the ground.

They were taken back to Bucharest by helicopter, and by a ghoulish absurdity their bodies were mislaid that night. It took considerable searching the next morning before they were discovered, hidden under a pile of wood by the soldiers who had brought them back to the capital. They were then taken to a cemetery on the outskirts of the city where they were buried, a hundred metres apart. Two wooden crosses were taken from the military cemetery next door and the names roughly sandpapered off, leaving only the rank, 'Lt. Col. (r)' and the dates 1920-1989 and 1921–1989: almost but not quite their own dates. In the spaces where the original names had been, new ones were painted: 'Popa Dan' for Ceausescu, 'Enescu Vasile' for Elena. Probably by coincidence Popa was the name of the president of the military tribunal which condemned them to death; two months later he committed suicide. As is traditional in Romania someone threw a handful of earth on the coffins. Then boards were placed over the open graves and cemented together.

So the socialist republic of Romania ended in melodrama. Yet even though Ceausescu had died singing the hymn of international socialism, the regime he had led was Marxist-Leninist only in name. It was more like Mussolini's Italy, an expression of the personality of its leader rather than an ideological state. With his death the socialist façade in Romania crumbled away immediately and left scarcely a trace behind it. It had been an affectation, a matter of a few words ('comrade', 'revolution', 'class enemy') and a few props (red flags, stars, a nomenklatura). Apart from them it was a kind of fascism. Later I recalled what a writer and sociologist, a gypsy by birth, had said to me as we walked down the bullet-smashed, bloodstained marble staircase at the Central Committee building.

We Romanians will always suffer as a result of Ceausescu. He made everyone afraid of everybody else, and he made it impossible for any of us to take our own decisions, to think or act for ourselves. Ceausescu is inside every one of us, and we haven't killed him yet. If we had given him a proper trial, we might have dealt with him. Now we can't. That is his revenge on all of us.

PART VI

MOSCOW – EMPIRE'S END

13
WHAT IS TO BE DONE?

The least relaxation of the autocracy would lead to the separation of many provinces, the weakening of the state, and countless disasters to the nation.

Report by Tsar Alexander I's Private Committee, 1825

It was April, 1990. An entire empire in Central and Eastern Europe had evaporated, the Soviet Union was no longer competing for influence in the world and had practically ceased to be a super-power; but in the Moscow Metro nothing had changed. I pushed through the heavy doors of the Prospekt Marksa station and held them open for an old woman in a headscarf. She forced her way through without looking. The odour of the Metro enveloped me: machinery oil, sweat, damp clothing, the sweetish smell which permeates all Soviet institutions. I put a five kopek coin in the slot of the electronic turnstile and passed through.

The escalators were packed with travellers, all silent. People moved steadily upwards at a strange angle, leaning against the gradient two to a step, bulky in their spring clothes. Not far from here the first builders of the Metro discovered Ivan the Terrible's underground city: a maze of tunnels, storehouses and dungeons, laid out in the 1560s as an insurance against invasion. Circumstance changes, purposes remain: the tide of passengers took me past the huge metal door, 18 inches thick, which could shut off the tunnels of the Metro and turn them into shelters in the event of nuclear war.

The platform opened out in front of me: absurd but palatial, with marble pillars and bronze chandeliers. In some stations every arch that leads on to the platforms is decorated with statues of sturdy revolution-aries. In others, the ceiling opens to mosaics or frescoes in which buildings soar, bi-planes loop the loop and parachutists fall gently to earth. The effect on working-class Muscovites on 15 May 1935, when the Metro was opened, must have been something like that of a new cathedral on a mediaeval peasant.

Nikita Khrushchev, chief assistant to Lazar Kaganovich, the minister of transport, was in day-to-day charge of the work. He forced it through at a brutal pace: one metre per shift, which was four times the speed for minimum safety. Hundreds of workers died, and it was still six months behind schedule. Even in the 1930s the Soviet Union was making its bid for parity with the great nations of the earth: nations whose capitals all had underground railways. It was done in the only way Russia, Tsarist or Soviet, has traditionally achieved its aims: through violent, convulsive effort.

I looked down to the end of the platform. An electronic board showed that the last train had left a minute and fifty-two seconds earlier; the next could be expected within thirty-eight seconds. Even at midnight the interval is only five minutes. Lights shone in the darkness of the tunnel. The people on the platform shuffled forward expectantly as the train moved heavily in. Three men shared the driver's cab. A crowd of people pushed their way out through the doors, another of equal size replaced them. The doors closed. The latest train to leave Prospekt Marksa for the Lenin Library station on the Kirovsko-Frunzenskaya Line was under way.

There are nine lines, 200 kilometres of track and 138 stations. Each year seven million passengers are carried and up to three new stations built. The drivers never go on strike, there are no graffiti and there is very little crime. The trains may be noisy, spartan and overheated, and the entire system grossly over-staffed, but it is still what the Metro's unwholesome trio of founders, Stalin, Kaganovich and Khrushchev, planned it to be: the cheapest, most ornate and possibly best underground railway in the world.

What Kaganovich and Khrushchev did with the Metro is what Marxism-Leninism set out to do in the Soviet Union as a whole. It might have been born in suffering and bloodshed, it might be less sophisticated than capitalist systems, but it worked. It served the people, and in 1990 the fare was still what it had been on 15 May 1935: a third of a British penny or half an American cent in real terms. Assuming the cost of a ticket on the London Underground, the New York Subway or the Paris Metro approximates to the truer market price of travel, the Moscow Metro was underpriced by something like 16,000 per cent. Yet for the people of the city the Metro was a stabilizing force in their lives, lending support to the old official assurance that there was no inflation under Socialism. No one appreciated that there would be another, different price for it all.

The Soviet system had its genuine achievements. While after 1945 the great imperial capitals of Western Europe lost their influence, Moscow raised itself to the status of a super-power. It frightened the United States and its allies by its formidable ability to compete in weapons systems. It built up a vast fleet and air force, and an army of five and a quarter million men. It maintained an effective space programme. Each of its grand achievements had the same characteristics as the Metro: intelligent use of resources, simplicity to the point of crudity, an almost total disregard of human life. In the United States the space programme and the military build-up grew out of a vibrant and growing economy. The successes of the Soviet system had to be forced out of the population under conditions of extreme military discipline.

The West tended to see this as a characteristic of Marxism-Leninism. In reality, it was a characteristic of Russia itself. The railway line between Moscow and St Petersburg, begun in 1842 and completed nine years later, was built in much the same fashion as the Moscow Metro. The father of James McNeill Whistler, the artist and founder of the Chelsea Arts Club, was chief technical adviser on the railway, but the driving force in the construction work was a man very like an aristocratic version of Khrushchev.

General Count P. A. Kleinmikhel was a gross, sycophantic, bullying figure, a close friend of Tsar Nicholas I. He was in overall charge of the vast teams of serfs as they dug the earth with shovels or their bare hands: sixty million cubic yards of it. A corps of railway police was appointed to flog or shoot those who failed in their task or revolted against Kleinmikhel's savage discipline. When the railway was opened in 1851 it was the longest in the world, and it had required an enormous effort of will from the very top of the political system.

This same force of will, which had turned the Soviet Union into a super-power, faltered at the end of Leonid Brezhnev's life. Because people were less frightened of the State they were less prepared to obey it. In the 1980s Brezhnev and his three successors had the worst of both worlds: military discipline had ceased to work, but there was none of the benefit which a free market would have provided.

Left to itself, the Russian Soviet Federative Socialist Republic – the largest and most populous in the Soviet Union – would have been a subsistence economy, just as it was under the Tsars. In this respect little changed in the seventy years of Socialism, except that as Moscow was the centre of every planning decision and the heart of the system of distribution, even the halting methods of a subsistence economy could not work properly.

There is the example, as absurd as anything in Gogol, of the cement-making plant and the factory which made plastic bags for cement. The two had been built side by side in a small town about 500 miles from Moscow. Only a chain-link fence separated them, but the plant and the factory were not allowed to trade together. The central planners required the plastic bags to be sent to Moscow, over bad roads and with inadequate transport. The cement factory, while it waited for its share of the bags to be sent all the way back, carried on with production in order to fulfil its norm. Often there was nowhere to store the newly-made cement, so it had to be dumped out in the factory yard. The rain quickly turned it into small hills as hard as rock. As far as the managers of the two factories were concerned it was no great problem: their production targets were met, and it was someone else's job to get the cement and the plastic bags to the customers. Somewhere, though, building work was being totally disrupted, and the ripples duly spread through the economy. Such problems meant that newly-married couples in Moscow could expect to wait up to ten years to be allocated an apartment to themselves. Out in the rain in the factory yard, meanwhile, the hills of undistributed cement continued to grow.

The Metro rattled through its tunnel, southwestwards toward the Lenin Library station. Opposite me sat the usual cross-section of people. An old man in imitation leather coat and cap, with the lined face of a heavy smoker and the eyes of a drinker, stared at nothing. A young woman, tall and thin with colourless blonde hair, read a literary review. An older woman next to her looked away each time I caught her eye. Her cheeks were red and puffy, and there was a long package in her shopping bag – perhaps a toy for a grandchild. An Army officer in uniform with a briefcase and a band like synthetic moleskin round his cap peered at the sports pages of the newspaper a teenaged boy was reading beside him. The boy's maroon and grey anorak was mass-produced but smart, his jeans and running shoes looked new. In the twelve years since I began visiting the Soviet Union regularly, there had been a considerable improvement in the way people dressed.

Not, however, in the way they ate. The consumption of starch, fats and sugar had all gone up. The consumption of green vegetables was as low as ever: probably about the same level as a century ago. This was a matter of habit. But the poor distribution system meant that tea, sugar and some types of meat had all been rationed at some stage during the first few months of 1990. After the December revolution in Bucharest, Romania, which under Ceausescu supplied the Soviet Union with grain, meat and fruit, cut its supplies to almost nothing. The people of Moscow had not faced the rationing of basic foodstuffs since the end of the Second World War. It was a disgrace and a scandal, and people forgot the slow improvements and remembered only the ways in which their lives were poorer and more difficult. The one topic of conversation with everyone was the problem of getting decent food. A senior economics teacher from a secondary school, a man in his mid-forties, explained the economics of food-buying:

I earn four hundred roubles a month. My wife could go to the ordinary Gastronoms [food shops] but she is also a teacher and she has little time to spare for queuing. Also there isn't much that's worth buying, even though it doesn't cost much. So she goes to the private markets. They usually have the things she wants there, but they're very expensive. It'll cost her thirty roubles or more – and all she comes back with is some cabbage, a few tomatoes, a kilo of potatoes, maybe some root vegetables. It doesn't last long, and yet we've run through a quarter of what I earn. We estimate that we spend more than three hundred roubles a month on food. That doesn't leave much for anything else.

At Sheremetyevo airport, on my way back to Moscow from a trip to Leningrad, I accepted an offer of a lift from one of the freelance taxi drivers who operate illegally there. It was past midnight. He drove fast and badly through the heavy rain, jerking the steering wheel as he made his angry points. His car was in bad shape: on a night like this he had to peer through the windscreen, his nose an inch from the glass because the wipers didn't work. We seemed to hit every pothole in the road.

My daytime job is as a tennis coach, but it's so badly paid I have to do something else. I get two hundred roubles a month, and meat costs eighty roubles a kilo at least. I can't afford to live in this country any more. My marriage broke up because I was working all the time, and my wife just found another fellow who had more money. There's a girl now that I teach tennis to – she wants to marry me. She can get a passport to Canada and wants me to go with her. But I've got some standards left. I don't love her, and I don't want to take advantage of her. So she doesn't go because of me, and I don't go because I don't love her.

He laughed at the ludicrousness of it, but his face still had an angry expression as he hunched forward, trying to see where he was going.

'Have you tasted the sausage?' friends asked me. 'It's filthy – quite inedible.'

Sausage was the symbol George Orwell used for the product of the Communist state. I felt obliged to taste it. It was indeed filthy, packed out with gristle and with some strange tasteless white filler. It lacked even the fat which Russians like but which makes most Westerners gag. A thin colourless juice leaked from it as I bit into it. Its flavour was indescribably bad: something only a vulture could appreciate. I had once caught worms by eating Soviet sausage, but this was worse.

There had been bad sausage in the past, and shortages of food too. What was different now was that people were freer than at any time since the early 1920s to discuss the difficulties they were experiencing and to complain about them.

'Talking is the only thing we're free to do now,' a friend of mine said in April 1990. I had gone round to the flat where she and her husband Sasha lived near the city centre. He liked to cook, and was working away in the kitchen. She was educated, liberal-minded, and nothing like as dedicated a Communist as he was.

> In every other way, it's a disaster. Gorbachev does it too: yak-yak-yak, talk-talk-talk, preach-preach-preach. We used to be a country, but now we're a big debating society. And no one does anything. There's no food, no cars, nothing in the shops. What's the point of having money when there's nothing to buy? I tell you honestly, I've come to hate Gorbachev. Sasha still supports him, but for me he's worse than useless. And I'll tell you something else. . .

Her voice dropped in case her husband might hear her as he chopped the vegetables.

> I hate the bloody Communists as well. They've wrecked this country, and they don't have the faintest idea how to put things right.

That view was, I found, entirely representative. Indeed, of the fifty or so people of different backgrounds, ages and attitudes I spoke to, it was the only opinion I heard. No one had a good word for the Communist Party or for Gorbachev.

I got out at the Arbatskaya station. By now I was starting to notice little changes, which would once have been revolutionary. Women were selling flowers in the station, and the blank walls in the ticket hall were plastered with 1990 calendars for sale, four months into the year. Outside in the street crowds gathered round the people whom the Muscovites call *fartsovchiki* and we in Britain once called 'spivs': they were selling T-shirts, a puppy, stockings, little toys, a few sticks of Russian chewing-gum (very unpleasant) or chocolate (almost tasteless). Among them was a young girl selling a new environmentalist newspaper, *Alternativa*. It cost a rouble, compared with a few kopeks for *Izvestiya* or *Moskovskaya Pravda*, but people were thrusting their money at her and seizing the copies, reading them as they walked away. Another woman was selling colour posters of the Tsars. She did not lack for customers either. A letter to a Moscow newspaper that morning said: 'If we had the Tsars still, there would be no economic problem – they knew how to work the market system.'

I walked on to the Arbat, one of the oldest streets in Moscow, where writers and artists have always gathered. For the last few years it has been a pedestrian area, and people come to have their portraits drawn by any of three dozen artists, sitting out in the open on little stools. Not far away there was the braying sound of a man making a speech. I could see the crowd of about fifty which he had attracted, but had to work my way through the outskirts of it to catch a glimpse of the speaker. He was small and middle-aged, with a neatly clipped grey beard the shape of Tsar Nicholas II's and a blue mackintosh cut like factory overalls. He spoke well but hoarsely, and had to stop every now and then to drink from a litre carton of milk by his feet. What he had to say was unedifying:

> The Slavic people of this country have endured many things over the centuries. We have brought enlightenment to many. We have spread our faith and our civilization to peoples who knew nothing of either: savages, indeed, whom we allowed to join with us in the benefits of our society. But it has become necessary to warn of the dangers to the Russian nation which many of these people pose. Some, indeed, have battened on us for centuries. They are just as vindictive now as they have always been, and they hate our civilization worse. Further, they have their own doctrines which we have been obliged to follow. I don't need to tell you about that.

A little ripple of laughter and agreement passed through the crowd: he was talking of Communism, which ever since Marx and Trotsky Russian nationalists have identified with the Jews. As Communism has become more and more unpopular so the blame for its introduction has been placed with increasing firmness on the Jews. A policeman stopped to listen to what was being said, but the speaker was careful not to be specific about anything. He belonged to the organization known as 'Pamyat', or 'Memory', which began as a religious and historical movement dedicated to preserving Russia's past. It soon moved on to overt anti-Semitism. The speaker spoke in a code which was readily understood by his audience. The policeman shook his head and grinned, then moved away. The orator went on making his stiff gestures, his voice braying out across the Arbat. The man beside me spat copiously on the ground and raised his hands high in the air to clap. But it was an old woman with a caved-in, toothless face who clapped the loudest, with an energy that was hard to account for.

> The day of the Russian people's liberation from the diabolical influences of our enemies may not be far off, my friends. You and I will see that day. Those who have imposed upon us in their different ways will have to look to themselves then. We will call many people to account when it comes.

The speaker took another gulp of milk, the crowd clapped and I moved away. The freedom to speak one's mind has been rare in Russia, and when it has been permitted it has always produced ugly results.

I thought of a flat I had visited with a colleague of mine in Moscow in 1978. It had been an unsettling business. The apartment block was watched day and night, as well as being bugged. I had a small amateur camera with me, and (to my colleague's agitation) paused to film the exterior of the building. It was a comfortable place, allocated to members of the Soviet Academy of Sciences, and by Moscow standards the flats were large and desirable. We went up in the ancient lift and I clutched the camera under my arm nervously.

It was Elena Bonner, Andrei Sakharov's wife, who opened the door. Her husband, she said, was lying down in the next room. His heart condition had been troubling him, but he was anxious to see us. When we went in, Sakharov was lying fully dressed on the bed. He was reading an old Penguin detective novel in English, with its familiar green cover. He laid it down and bowed his head politely, then gestured at the ceiling and walls, where the microphones were presumably hidden. He smiled pleasantly, like a country vicar.

'As your English expression has it, everything you say here will be taken down and used in evidence against you.'

I had, I suppose, been expecting an Old Testament prophet along the lines of Alexander Solzhenitsyn. Instead, Sakharov was witty and gentle and decidedly moderate. He showed no signs, then or later, of the Russian intellectual's traditional habit of rejecting limited progress because it falls short of perfection. When Gorbachev came to power Sakharov accepted him for what he was: a distinct improvement on his predecessors, but nothing more. By contrast a wide range of exiles and critics attacked Gorbachev because he was something less than ideal. The best, as so often among Russian thinkers and writers, was the enemy of the merely good. Sakharov suffered his fatal heart attack in 1989 after an angry argument with Gorbachev in the Congress of People's Deputies; but he supported much of what Gorbachev was trying to achieve. Sakharov was essentially a liberal democrat along recognizably Western lines. Solzhenitsyn by contrast was an instinctive supporter of autocracy. His complaint about Communist dictatorship was not that it was dictatorship but that it was Communist.

> Everything depends on what sort of authoritarian order lies in store for us in the future. It is not authoritarianism itself that is intolerable, but the ideological lies that are daily foisted upon us.

That is from Alexander Solzhenitsyn's *Letter to the Soviet Leaders* in 1974. When I first encountered Andrei Sakharov four years later it was impossible to think that he would support any form of authoritarian order. His overriding aim was freedom of thought and expression. He championed the cause of every political prisoner and every dissident, but not simply because they opposed the government; it was because he refused to accept that there was only one given way of thinking and speaking. As my colleague and I talked to him in his flat he moved from his bed after talking to us for a little, and sat in an upright chair. 'I cannot,' he said, 'be interviewed lying down. I shall be like those emperors who preferred to die in the saddle.' Behind him was a bookcase. There was a crucifix on the wall. My colleague asked him about the persecution of the critics of the Soviet system.

> I cannot accept that the Party should dictate to me or to any other citizen what to say. It is my right to consult my own conscience and to speak accordingly. For this reason we – that is to say, the people whom you in the West call the dissident movement – cannot be destroyed, because it exists within us. No doubt they will try to destroy it, but they will not be successful.

While my colleague asked the questions I filmed away, panning shakily off the crucifix and back to Sakharov's face. The knowledge that I was filming it badly worried me much more than the question of how we were going to get the pictures out of the country.

At Sheremetyevo airport a few days later I was stopped just as I was about to board the plane for London. I had passed all the usual security checks with my film of Sakharov undisturbed, but now my name was called over the public address system. I duly reported to the security desk. The man behind it was very polite. He wondered if I would mind placing my briefcase in something on the wall that looked like a microwave oven. It had a large black and yellow radioactive sign on it. There was nothing I could do. My case stayed inside for a minute or so, and then the man handed it back to me with a swift formal bow.

Back in London I told my colleagues that there was little point in developing the film: it was bound to have been wiped. However, the wiping of television pictures is not necessarily easy. An hour later the technicians reported that only the first few feet on the outside of the reel had been affected by the machine at Sheremetyevo, and we duly broadcast the whole of the interview that evening. There was another small victory: the police had been so concerned with my briefcase that they had failed to search me thoroughly. In my astrakhan hat, bought at a Moscow foreign currency shop, I had hidden a piece of thin typing paper which carried a message which Sakharov wanted published in the West.

The Soviet autocracy, like the Tsarist one, managed to range some of the best brains in the country against itself. Throughout the 1970s

Sakharov was the focal point of the entire dissident movement. If there were an arrest he would know about it and would ensure that a campaign was mounted, both in Moscow and in the West, on the prisoner's behalf. If there were a trial he would stand outside the court-room with the small group of demonstrators and observers, regardless of the weather or the brutality of the police. When political prisoners were sent to psychiatric hospitals and locked up with the most violent patients; when they refused to sign undertakings about their future behaviour and were kept short of food or physically maltreated; when they were charged with unspecified crimes against prison discipline days before their release was due, and given further long sentences, Sakharov would hear about it and make sure the outside world was told.

Sometimes he made mistakes. Not all the cases he championed were worthy ones. But he kept the movement alive. The Soviet authorities exiled Solzhenitsyn, but Sakharov, one of the country's leading nuclear scientists, could not be allowed to leave the country. Equally, he was the one man whose arrest would have caused a complete rupture in Soviet relations with the West.

In 1980, however, the government summoned up the courage to exile him to the provincial city of Gorkiy, which was closed to Westerners. He went on hunger-strike there, and the KGB, alarmed by speculation in the West that he might be close to death, made available the pictures of him which it had shot as part of its routine surveillance. At one point the woman doctor who was examining him moved him closer to the hidden camera, so it could film him more effectively. Elena Bonner continued his work in Moscow, drawing Western attention to cases of human rights abuses, until she too was exiled to Gorkiy.

In November 1986 Gorbachev summoned Sakharov and Elena Bonner back to Moscow. A little over a year later, they gave their first officially sponsored news conference. As I took my seat in the auditorium I was nervous about the price Sakharov might have paid for his freedom. Would he now praise the Gorbachev line, the latest and strongest advocate of reform Communism? He did not. His criticisms of the shortcomings of glasnost and perestroika were as sharp and as witty as ever.

But he was a sick man. The hunger strikes and the years of confined existence in Gorkiy had aged him. His jaw was slack, his features sallow, his neck thin and scrawny. A friend reintroduced me to him afterwards and he was polite enough to say he remembered me, though I doubt if he did. When he said goodbye he walked off, leaning slightly on Elena Bonner's arm, his stick in his other hand. I knew I would not see him again, and as I watched him go I thought of the words Maxim

Gorky had once used about Tolstoy: 'While he is alive, no man is altogether an orphan.'

*

During the days of opposition and exile in the 1970s, everything was clear-cut. We in the West knew exactly whose side we were on. People who demanded the right to speak their minds were good, those who tried to silence them were guilty of crimes against human rights and the human conscience. No doubt this was true; but standing in the Arbat some years later, listening to the orator from *Pamyat* make his lightly disguised attacks on the Jews, the rights and wrongs of the issue seemed less clear. Some of the people for whom Sakharov had campaigned turned out to be violent irridentists who wanted independence for their particular part of the Soviet Union at any cost.

Many of the national movements were disturbingly extreme. Even those which were not, like the Lithuanian independence movement, displayed a lack of statesmanship and moderation in their dealings with Moscow. Lithuania's president, Vytautis Landsbergis, was weak and inexperienced in his handling of the national demand for independence in March and April 1990, forcing Gorbachev into heavy-handed imperial actions. A wiser government would not have planned to station customs officials on the Soviet-Lithuanian border, where they achieved nothing sensible but constituted a serious insult to Moscow, nor allow soldiers to desert the Soviet Army and declare their intention to join a Lithuanian one.

After fifty years of often brutal servitude, Lithuanians resented the slightest delay in obtaining their freedom; but their government failed to channel the urgency of their desires in directions which would benefit Lithuania while at the same time making it easier for other nations to move smoothly to their rightful independence. Landsbergis openly called for the break-up of the Soviet Union; as a result Gorbachev was obliged to demonstrate to the Soviet military that no such thing would happen. Reality was often a stranger in the Lithuanian parliament. 'This is a rich country,' one member said. 'In five years we will be as rich as Finland.' It was not Lithuania's fault that half a century of centralized planning had made such optimism absurd.

'Gorbachev = Stalin', said some of the placards in Vilnius, with an equal lack of common sense. Soviet Army commanders had been ordering their men to drive provocatively through the streets of the city, and to take over public buildings with a considerable degree of brutality. It was at least a possibility that the Army was deliberately trying to increase the tension in order to weaken Gorbachev's position. But such subtleties passed the Lithuanians and their government by.

For them there was only one enemy: the Soviet Union as a whole.

It was nevertheless curious to find Western countries sympathizing more with Gorbachev than with the national demands of the small Baltic states which had been cruelly absorbed fifty years earlier by Stalin. The West had benefited greatly from the Gorbachev effect and was anxious that he might be replaced if he appeared now to be weak. It was harder for the Lithuanians, and for those in Estonia and Latvia with similar aspirations, to understand this response. They had watched the West's delight as nation after nation in the old Soviet empire declared its independence. Now that Lithuania was doing what Poland, Hungary, East Germany, Czechoslovakia and Romania had done the West counselled caution or watched largely in silence. There was no upsurge of international outrage when the Soviet Union placed an economic tourniquet on Lithuania. The view was that Lithuania had tried too fast for something that would come anyway if its people were patient.

In Moscow, government officials saw Lithuania as the place where they had to make a stand if they were not to lose the Ukraine as well. That would be an economic and political catastrophe from which Gorbachev would not recover. In April support for the Ukrainian nationalist movement Rukh was strong, especially in Galicia, which had historically been Polish. 'You don't,' said a Ukrainian friend of mine, 'see a single red flag flying there now, only the blue and gold flag of our Ukraine – the blue of the sky and the gold of the corn,' he explained, with the piety of a native son.

As it happened, he was a Jew; and Ukrainians, like Lithuanians, had so powerful a reputation for anti-Semitism during the Second World War that the SS recruited many for concentration-camp work and found them hard-working, brutal and obedient. Why, I asked him, had a Jew become a Ukrainian nationalist?

> In Lvov [the capital of the Western Ukraine] things are different. Rukh isn't like these other groups, Pamyat and so on. It's got some brains. When they found out that in the elections Jews had voted almost 100 per cent for Rukh it changed its whole approach to us. Some of my friends and I had a meeting with the Rukh leadership. They agreed to set up Hebrew lessons, they decided to start demanding the right of emigration for the Jews. And you know what? They asked us for help in distributing their literature in Yiddish. Yiddish. Oh yes, and one other thing. They came round to see us later, and said they'd heard there was a secret Pamyat cell operating in Lvov. They offered us protection if we wanted it.

The thought that Jews might vote for a Ukrainian nationalist movement and that the movement might protect them from violence as a result set him laughing and shaking his head again.

In Russia itself, though, anti-Semitism was growing fast. The Jewish demand for emigration enraged people who would like to get out themselves but lacked the international support the Jewish refuseniks have received.

> People in shops and in the streets say to us, 'When are you going to Israel?' or 'What are you waiting for?' You find swastikas drawn on posters near where you live. They shout at us and our children. The mood is getting uglier: you can feel it.

The anger and extremism in Moscow that April reminded me of Bucharest at the time of the revolution there. I wandered a little farther down the Arbat. Outside the house where Pushkin had lived in 1831 there was the sound of voices raised in anger. I worked my way through the crowd which had gathered round a police jeep and listened.

The police had arrested a woman for some black market offence, and they were about to put her in the back of the jeep when the crowd gathered round. The woman was in her late fifties, her grey hair slipping out from under an old black beret. She was shouting at the three young policemen in front of her. They were red in the face and sweating.

'Get your hands off me, you big idiots! Who do you think you are, anyway?'

She was emboldened by the support of the crowd. No one standing immediately beside the policemen said anything, but from a little further back where it was safe there was a regular barrage of insults.

'Leave her alone, Fascists!'

'What's she done? Nothing!'

'An old lady like her? You ought to be ashamed of yourselves.'

The policemen whispered among themselves. They were rattled, and it was obvious they would never get the jeep through the crowd if they pushed her inside it. There was an atmosphere of real violence in the air.

'Give me your name and address.'

The policemen were backing down. The woman laughed contemptuously and pushed a wisp of grey hair back under her beret.

'You hear that?' she asked the crowd. 'These brave men of ours are going to take my name and address.'

She wrote them with a flourish and watched as the policemen took the paper, then climbed into the jeep and started it up.

For a moment it looked as though even now the crowd would refuse to move. Then someone shuffled a few paces and the rest opened up a path for it. There were shouts as it inched its way through the mass of bodies, the driver anxious not to hurt anyone. Some people beat on the roof with their fists, others kicked the sides and the tyres, but as it reached the fringes of the crowd it speeded up and drove off. For a time the crowd remained, listening to the woman as she reenacted the entire episode. Then, slowly, they drifted off. Nothing serious had taken place, but there was a tension about these people which I had rarely seen in the streets of Moscow – a feeling that they would be happy for an excuse to attack any symbol of the government which had mismanaged things so badly for so long.

Little signs of contempt for the state were everywhere. Among the artists along the Arbat I found a man who painted political portraits on the flattened bark of birch-trees. In fractured English he explained his choice of material.

> Because the birch is the symbol of my country. It is a statement – a statement of my nationality. So I place these people on the background of my country. It is a contrast. Not always a very good contrast.

I bought an oddity from him: a portrait of the four main post-war leaders of the Soviet Union, Stalin, Krushchev, Brezhnev and Gorbachev. None is caricatured, but Gorbachev has been given a halo and a crown, like a modern icon.

'This is how you think of him in the West,' said the artist; and before I could answer he wrenched the picture round in my hand to show me the back, almost angrily. On it he had written in English, 'The cleverness, the honestness and the conscience of our epoch.' It was meant as savage irony.

'Poor Russia,' he said, 'if these are the clever and honest people of our time.'

A little further down the street I came to a shop that sold secondhand goods. In 1978 I had brought a pre-Revolutionary samovar here, but it was damaged and in need of repair. In those days there was little worth having in the shop: china from the 1930s, an occasional inkstand, ugly ornaments from Cuba or Africa made in the 1960s. There were few customers, just a few elderly people looking for small bargains. Those who had family treasures wanted to hold on to them. They had little need for money, and there was still a mild anxiety about showing that you owned things from the period before the Revolution – a hangover, perhaps, from the Stalinist days when there was a real danger of being denounced as bourgeois. For the most part the shop had been empty. Ten years later, when I visited it again, it mostly sold books. At that time it was still hard to find good editions of Russian classics, and people would queue at the bookshops for a new edition of Pushkin or Tolstoy. In April 1990 there were books for sale which would have been impossible to find, and in some cases illegal, a few years before: Solzhenitsyn, Pasternak, Akhmatova, Mandelshtam, Blok. But it was no longer primarily a bookshop. It had become an antique shop.

Icons hung on the walls. Good quality enamelled crosses filled one show-case, Tsarist medals and orders filled another, Bibles a third. There were cavalry sabres and statuettes of nineteenth-century generals and a marble bust of Stalin. At 2,500 roubles (about £160 or $250 at the tourist rate) he fetched a better price than almost anything else in the shop, because of the identity of the sculptor. A crowd jostled at the counter; it was hard to get the attention of the languid, rather beautiful young women behind it. A larger notice over their heads warned foreign visitors that official permission (probably unobtainable) would be required to take most of the goods out of the country.

Behind the impatient crowd of customers and spectators was a line of people with plastic bags and parcels wrapped up in brown paper. They were queuing at the door to the office beside the counter, where a sharp-featured woman opened everything and appraised it, then counted out piles of rust-red ten rouble notes from a box in the drawer beside her. The piles were often large ones: in a country where too much money chases too few goods, the shop could afford to pay good prices and charge even better ones. One man had brought a nineteenth-century telescope complete with folding tripod. A woman had a large Chinese lacquer box. A young man who scarcely seemed out of his teens carried a striking seventeenth-century 'closed' icon which still smelt of incense. The sharp-featured woman appraised each item carefully.

> They bring them here because they need the money to live. There's another aspect to it as well. Things like these icons, the pre-Revolutionary medals and so on, were too difficult to handle some years ago. So people have been storing them up for years. Maybe they would have sold them a long time ago, but they thought it would get them into trouble. Nowadays no one cares. They can bring anything they like here – the only judgement now is whether someone else is likely to buy it.

*

By the spring of 1990 the accelerating failures of the system were engendering strange forms of psychopathia in the Soviet Union. Everything that could be classed as paranormal became highly fashionable. People would pay fifteen roubles to go to healers who claimed extrasensory powers rather than be treated by ordinary medical doctors for nothing. There were long queues, and appointments had to be made days, sometimes weeks, in advance. The prophecies of Vanga, an old, blind woman who told fortunes in Bulgaria, were reported in the newspapers and people studied and discussed them endlessly. In the summer of 1989 she had forecast that there would be serious bloodshed in the Baltic states, and this was interpreted with the usual believers' generosity as a reference to Lithuania's attempt to obtain its independence from the Soviet Union.

Another of Vanga's prophecies had an electrifying effect on large sections of Soviet society. Conditions would get steadily worse there until 1996, she said; then some climactic event would take place which would either make or break the Russian people. If they survived, life would then start to improve. The prophecy created endless speculation, but there were signs that people welcomed the idea that things were approaching a decisive point. 'Vanga makes it all a little easier to bear,' said an otherwise rational, intelligent woman.

A Georgian mystic, Dzhuna Davitashvili, healed people through the laying on of hands. She used to sell photographs of her hands, with magical rays issuing from her fingertips. The rays worked briefly for Leonid Brezhnev in the 1970s, but in 1990 she founded the Dzhuna Corporation to sell an extra-sensory machine which had the same effect as her fingers. Somehow she also obtained the title 'Inventor of the USSR'.

Stranger figures have arisen. There was Anatoly Kashpirovsky, a Ukrainian television hypnotist whose powers were so great that he had to be barred from the air waves and later went to the United States so that he could be studied under clinical conditions. Kashpirovsky began with sessions in a crowded football stadium in Kiev. 'Imagine,' he would say, 'that you are falling asleep.' Hundreds, perhaps thousands of people immediately fell asleep as the television cameras watched. 'Imagine,' he went on, 'that it is a hot summer's day' – it was winter – 'and that you are about to take a swim in a cool river.' They started taking off their clothes. The local television station was scandalized, but Kashpirovsky's reputation was made.

Soon he began giving live hypnotism sessions on national television. He was about fifty, with the alert and energetic appearance of a sportsman, but his dark eyes, deep set, had something alarming about them. When he spoke, his voice was dull and monotonous, and music played quietly in the background. He claimed to be able to heal people through television, and looking straight at the camera he would tell them quietly that their physical disabilities were yielding to his power. 'Listen to me,' he would say, 'I am healing you.'

People wrote in vast numbers to say that their grey hair had turned black, their missing teeth had grown again, their livers and intestines had been cured, the diseases of their children had vanished in an instant. His greatest coup, and one that was not open to question, was to hypnotize a woman in Georgia who was about to have a stomach operation. The television set was placed in the corner of the operating theatre, and sitting in his studio in Kiev Kashpirovsky anaesthetized her at long distance. As the surgeons opened her stomach and the television audience watched, the patient laughed and sang to Kashpirovsky's orders.

After the television authorities became nervous about his powers, he ceased to appear. They were less worried about another exponent of the paranormal, Alan Tchumak, who appeared on Soviet breakfast television. He healed people as well, though less spectacularly: his speciality was children's diseases and sports injuries, but he also claimed to energize his viewers as each new day began. Staring into the camera, Tchumak sent his waves of energy direct to each viewer. Alternatively the waves of energy could be stored in something: a jar of face cream, a bottle of water. A friend of mine living in Leningrad, Irene A., is an educated woman who cannot quite convince herself that all this is simply hokum.

Once I went round to the flat of one of my girlfriends. It was a hot day and I was thirsty. I didn't want to drink the tap-water – it can poison you in Leningrad – so I asked her if she'd got any bottled water. 'Only the stuff that Alan Tchumak energized this morning,' she said. We both laughed, and I drank it. I promise you, I couldn't sleep for two nights, I was so charged up. And I felt great, I didn't suffer from tiredness at all.

A few years ago we'd have laughed our heads off at the very thought that someone might make your teeth grow back or give you energy by talking to you on television. But things are different now. Maybe we need to believe in something outside ourselves, because things have got so bad. We Russians always seem to need something outside ourselves. Nowadays it isn't Marxism any more, so I suppose it's got to be the paranormal.

The echoes of Rasputin and the flight from reality in the last years of imperial Russia seemed strong. But for the man whose task it was to reconcile the absurd distortions of the Soviet economy to the real world there was no easy means of escape. I sat in the auditorium where

Sakharov had once given his news conference on being released from exile in Gorkiy and observed the Soviet Union's deputy prime minister in charge of economic reform as he polished his thick glasses. There was a suitable air of gloom about him. Dr Leonid Abalkin was an academic economist who came to Gorbachev's attention at the time when faith in Arkady Aganbegyan, 'the father of perestroika', was slipping. Unlike Aganbegyan, who was an expansive Armenian, Abalkin was quiet and acerbic, though certainly not without humour. If Aganbegyan seemed like a street trader who had failed to pull off a deal he had promised, Abalkin was more like a scientist engaged on an experiment which would quite possibly explode in his face. Mikhail Gorbachev had already set out the fundamental position in a speech to the Congress of People's Deputies the previous September: 'New methods have not yet taken root, the old ones work no longer.' Abalkin for his part gave the impression of knowing he would fail, but found the experience interesting anyway. At his news conference he tried to explain to the assembled Soviet and Western journalists that change could not come as fast as they or the Soviet people in general seemed to expect.

> It isn't a question of going to sleep under one economic system and waking up under another. It has to be done slowly and in stages. For instance we have to raise prices, but we cannot bring the consumer to his knees. We have to consider whether our system of taxation is adequate. We've talked this over with experts from the West, but they say they cannot solve the problem in its entirety anyway.
>
> Any radical reform needs agreement between the various social forces in the country. We should look for people's understanding, but we have to be firm. We cannot back down in face of disagreement or resentment. At the moment the government gets hundreds of letters, perhaps more, asking all sorts of questions – why is there a shortage of toothbrushes? Why aren't the streets cleaned properly? We are trying to move towards a different kind of society, where we don't have a command economy and where the government isn't responsible for 99 per cent of everything that is done.

A Soviet journalist stood up to ask if the government were not concentrating more on the amount of money available than on the needs of the sick and the elderly. Abalkin came as close to anger as his nature would allow.

> In the old days, whenever we worked out a Five Year Plan each agency of the state would work out how much it needed to carry out its job to the full. In other words the Department of Pensions would calculate the number of old age pensioners in the country and the amount they needed to live

properly. Then it would put in its proposal. Of course, all the other departments and ministries were doing the same thing. As a result they asked for several times as much money as we had. Now the deputies in the Supreme Soviet are appealing on behalf of the people for more money. Well, all I can say is that it's completely impossible to meet all the demands. I may say, I haven't heard anyone in the Supreme Soviet asking how we go about increasing efficiency.

Someone reminded him that he had once said he would not permit the exploitation of man by man to be a part of his economic system. Wearily, he turned his long sallow face towards the questioner.

These things arouse a lot of passions. But nowadays most people believe that we've always had exploitation in the Soviet Union – and that the state exploited people worse than anyone else. Recently one of my colleagues said that anyone who took the fruit of someone else's labour was exploiting them. I think this is a little too simple. Are old age pensioners exploiting the workers?

Inevitably someone asked about a timetable for making the rouble convertible. Was it true it would happen by the summer of 1990?

No one has ever said anything like that. For the past three years people have been asking this question. Everyone agrees that it will be very difficult. The more you know about this subject, the later the date you propose.

Not long afterwards his lecture on the difficulties of entering the real world after seven decades came to an end. He polished his thick spectacles, collected together his papers and walked off the platform. It seemed to me he shook his head a little, recalling the sheer obtuseness of people when you presented them with facts.

*

During my visit to Moscow that April I was hoping to see something of the man whose policies had engendered so many of the changes related in this book. I had encountered Mikhail Gorbachev several times in the past, beginning in December 1984 when he came to London a few months before his election to the General Secretaryship of the Soviet Communist Party. I was introduced to him at a lunch given in his honour at Hampton Court Palace. The intensity of his gaze was extraordinary. It neither questioned you nor checked you out for dishonesty or evasion – it simply absorbed you and everything you said and did for the short time of the meeting. Then it switched to the next person, the next subject. I met him on various occasions after that, usually accompanied by a television crew. He is a man who likes to explain himself. Once, in Yugoslavia, he held up a meeting with the entire Yugoslav government and Party leadership in order to describe in some detail for our camera his anxieties about the regional problems he was experiencing in the Soviet Union. The grey men who governed Yugoslavia looked on irritably as he began with a characteristic joke: 'Show me the country that doesn't have regional problems, and I'll go there.' But even then his eyes were fixed on mine, and he seemed to be searching for my reaction as the phrases were translated one by one. The gaze was as strong when it was directed towards a journalist or a factory worker as it was towards the head of a government.

Now, returning to Moscow, I did catch a brief glimpse of Mikhail Gorbachev. The occasion was the visit of the British Foreign Secretary, Douglas Hurd. A group of Western journalists assembled outside the Spasskiy Gate to the Kremlin and as the bells sounded their strange falling peal on the hour we were ushered in by a side entrance and walked to a late-nineteenth-century building, the office of the Council of Ministers. Here too the corridors had the sweetish smell of Soviet officialdom. The places were long and undecorated. Policemen appeared at doorways, and old cleaning women, the backbone of the entire Soviet system, shuffled from room to room in woollen socks and the felt slippers which Russians call 'Goodbye Youth' shoes. There was little obvious security: the Kremlin had become an easier and more relaxed place than the Palace of Westminster or the White House.

We waited outside a meeting room down an undistinguished back corridor. A Kremlin official watched and listened to us nervously. The doors opened and we were pushed in. The room was large and echoing, but Gorbachev and Hurd sat with their colleagues at a small table in one corner of it. Later, Douglas Hurd said Gorbachev had been his usual enthusiastic and ebullient self, but he looked a good deal older and more tired than when I saw him last, and the lower part of his face seemed slack. Only the eyes were as intense and concentrated as before. He leaned across the table, holding Douglas Hurd's gaze while the interpreter translated their public compliments.

If the problems of coping with a collapsing empire were telling on him, they had not crushed him. The man who asked Margaret Thatcher at length in December 1984 about how Britain had divested herself of her colonies now had personal experience of the process. What he had lost was that indefinable expectation which every new ruler enjoys at first – the feeling that this time things are going to be different. I recalled the stories of how he paid his first visit to Leningrad soon after his election as General Secretary of the Party. When they took him to see a factory on one side of the road he insisted on breaking away from the official programme and seeing the one on the other side, which had been ransacked of equipment in order to make the original one look better. When he was taken to an apartment block he went several floors higher than the pre-arranged flat and saw how people there really lived.

It was splendid, but it also fitted into a precise tradition. Before he became Tsar, the future Alexander II, one day to become the Liberator of the serfs, journeyed round Russia in 1837 making unofficial stops at peasants' huts and convict settlements, to the despair of the officials who had arranged everything for him. Yet even before the serfs were freed Alexander had lost the hope and the expectation of his people. His life passed darkly and gloomily in the belief that nothing more could seriously be done about the immense problems that faced Russia. He died in 1881, the victim of the eighth in a series of assassination attempts against him.

I travelled to Leningrad, where the Democratic Union, an amorphous group of social democrats, religious conservatives and environmentalists, had been elected to a majority of seats on the City Soviet. A new name, that of Anatoly Sobchak, was starting to be heard as a future Soviet leader. In the magnificent eighteenth-century Maria's Palace where the Tsars' ministers once met as a State Council, the newly elected deputies milled around enjoying the experience of arguing politics. A vast plaster plaque of Lenin in profile dominated the chamber, but in the city that was named after him when he died Lenin has ceased to count for very much. I spoke to the head of the Leningrad writers' union, a flamboyant figure with a ponytail and a luxuriant beard and moustache, who was one of the deputies.

> Everything is changing here. Marxism and Leninism don't mean much any more. We have passed that stage. We're moving to a different and more democratic system, in which Leninism had no part to play.

I asked him about the suggestions I had heard, that the name of the city might be changed back to Petrograd.

> Many of my colleagues here would be quite keen on that. To be honest, I wouldn't. I feel that our city's struggle against the Nazis for nine hundred days needs to be remembered, and 'Leningrad' does that. But it could well be 'Petrograd' again; there's a lot of support for it.

The monument to the 900 days stands at the end of Nevsky Prospekt – a tall and ugly spike with socialist-realist figures gathered round it. It replaced a statue to Tsar Alexander I, the victor over Napoleon in 1812. There was a majority on the City Soviet in favour of putting Alexander back in his original place. These people belonged to a group called 'Salvation', which had allied itself with the Greens in order to clean up the city and restore it to its pre-Stalinist beauty.

The deputy from the writers' union was not exaggerating: Leningrad has become a post-Communist city. Over at the Smolny Institute, the former school for young ladies which was taken over by Lenin and Trotsky when they carried out the October Revolution, there was an atmosphere of despair. The Smolny was then the headquarters of the Leningrad Communist Party. A statue of Lenin orating stood in the gardens in front, but otherwise, as with most of the central part of the city, it was much as it was in 1917. Silent Party officials moved up and down the long, gloomy corridors, but after they had gone home for the evening, leaving at a rather earlier time than most Leningrad workers, it was easier to imagine the scene described by John Reed in *Ten Days That Shook The World*:

> The Petrograd Soviet was meeting continuously at Smolny, a centre of storm, delegates falling down asleep on the floor and rising again to take part in the debate, Trotsky, Kamenev, Volodarsky speaking six, eight, twelve hours a day. . .
>
> I went down to room 18 on the first floor where the Bolshevik delegates were holding caucus, a harsh voice steadily booming, the speaker hidden by the crowd: 'The compromisers say that we are isolated. Pay no attention to them. Once it begins they must be dragged along with us, or else lose their following. . .'

Seventy-two years later, the Bolsheviks were indeed isolated. The situation was so stressful that the Party secretary, Boris Gidaspov, suffered a heart attack and yet was back at work within two days. Leningrad had endured corrupt and inefficient local government over the years. This had failed to mend the city's abysmal roads, clean its water or its air, or provide it with proper food supplies. In Leningrad cheese and tea were being rationed for the first time since 1945. Ordinary people, shamed by this, blamed the Communists. The Smolny itself put me in mind of the Central Committee building in Bucharest. It had been that way once, in the days when Trotsky listened to the soldiers dragging their machine-guns along the stone floors of the corridors. Now, it seemed to me, Leningrad was in a pre-revolutionary mood, a mood which would not necessarily break out into violence but which would not allow the situation to return to what it had been.

Effectively, Marxism-Leninism had come to an end in the city where it had first established itself as a governing force.

An earnest, middle-aged man took my arm. He was not in any of the usual senses a revolutionary. He had a good job, he explained, which was reasonably well paid; but he was fired with a sudden political enthusiasm which in Leningrad has taken on a revolutionary form.

> You saw how the red stars were taken off the buildings in Hungary, in Poland, in the GDR and so on. One day soon we'll be taking the red star off the top of the Spasskiy Gate at the Kremlin.

That night I went to an Easter service at the Leningrad seminary where the priests who served the great cathedrals of St Petersburg were once trained. It had been expected that St Isaac's cathedral itself would be opened for Easter, sixty years after it had been turned into a museum under Stalin. At the last minute, however, the dedicated atheist who ran the museum managed to persuade the city authorities that the building would be unsafe. There were other changes too. For the first time since the Revolution the state printing houses had issued Easter cards, while the state television service was broadcasting its first Easter service.

The seminary was another of the splendid early eighteenth-century buildings painted in Leningrad's characteristic chrome yellow. I heard the singing first: the deep voices of men, the high voices of women blending in a seamless, flowing chant which swelled up from time to time then faded again. It was not yet midnight, and they were parading the icons around the outside of the building in solemn procession. The monks were magnificent, their jutting beards and fleshy faces giving them a look of power and virility. Now individual bass voices made themselves heard while all round in the darkness the cheap wax of the red candles, as thin as pencils, cracked and snapped in the hands of the worshippers. The candle-light and the singing graced the faces of the women and dignified those of the men.

I stood in the gallery at the rear of the church and looked down at the waiting congregation. The scarved heads of women bobbed, their hands moving slowly and exaggeratedly as they crossed themselves. They wore scarves lest the sight of a woman's hair arouse the baser passions of the angels, who saw humanity from much the same vantage-point as I in my gallery saw them now. Three young girls, impervious to the tradition, their uncovered hair piled on top of their heads like Tsarist princesses, came in and giggled at the back of the church. Old eyes glinted through spectacles at the glinting icons ranged in front of the congregation. A plump monk watched the progress of a choirboy. The smell of incense was overpowering, and the candles crackled louder than ever. Everywhere, as the congregation thickened in the body of the church below, heads were bowing, hands were crossing – forehead, breast, shoulder, shoulder. A priest laid a cloth over the heads of an unending stream of old women and his finger traced a cross on it as he looked around to see how much longer it would be before the service began.

Over our heads God the Father floated in glory, pointing to heaven and to hell. The faith of the Tsars demands obedience. It is also a dark faith, which in the past encouraged unreason and the pogrom. I remembered Irene A. describing the grip which the paranormal had gained on her and on the people she knew: 'We Russians always seem to need something outside ourselves.' Bells started to peal, incense curled upwards, the chanting swelled, feet shuffled. A further crowd of people pushed in, heads craning, to get a view of the procession of gorgeous figures in white and purple and scarlet which was making its way towards the altar. Over all the other sounds, the bells, the chanting, the chattering, came the rich voice of Father Vladimir, the rector of the seminary:

'Christos Voskres!' – 'Christ is risen!'

And from the congregation rose the response:

'Truly risen!'

But a question remained unanswered: the perennial question, expressed by Chernyshevsky in the title of the radical novel he wrote in the 1860s as a prisoner in the fortress of St Peter and St Paul, a title which Lenin himself later borrowed for his more famous political tract: *What Is To Be Done?*

14
UNDOING THE PAST

The possibility of a coup d'etat with the use of force and rumours of the preparations being made for it had been circulating in Soviet society for many months. Consequently the coup did not come unexpectedly, like a bolt from the blue. In reply to the straight question which was put to me more than once, I had always said that a coup d'etat in the present situation was impossible, that it was doomed to fail, and that only madmen could attempt it.

MIKHAIL SERGEYEVICH GORBACHEV, *The August Coup*, 1991

Through the grey drizzle of a late Moscow summer a column of fifty armoured personnel carriers came weaving through the rush-hour traffic, engines roaring, tracks squealing, bluish smoke puffing out of every exhaust. It was shortly after 9 a.m. on Monday 19 August 1991. They ground their way down Kalinin Prospect, their tracks cutting row upon row of small whitish parallel lines in the road surface, like wave marks on the firm sand of the seashore. The soldiers sat on the upper works of the APCs, gripping the handles and leaning against the angle of turn as the vehicles moved from lane to lane. Their faces were empty of expression. When the column reached the Defence Ministry and the APCs took up positions round it, the soldiers did nothing to clear away the small crowds which gathered to watch them: men and women, white-faced with shock, sometimes weeping. The soldiers sat stolidly on the APCs, looking over the heads of the people round them; the officers seemed embarrassed. They were, one onlooker thought, the least threatening occupying force she had ever seen.

On the radio a couple of hours earlier, an announcer had read out a statement in a light, matter-of-fact voice, as though it were a traffic report:

'As a result of the ill-health of the President, under Article 1277 of the USSR constitution, USSR Vice-President Gennadi Yenayev takes over power. To ensure law and order and to prevent society from moving towards a nationwide catastrophe, a state of emergency is introduced for six months as of 4 o'clock Moscow time on August 19th 1991. The USSR constitution and laws take unconditional precedence across all the territory of the USSR. A State Emergency Committee comprises the first Vice-Chairman of the

USSR Defence Council, Baklanov; the State Security Chairman, Kryuchkov; the USSR Prime Minister, Pavlov; Defence Minister Yazov; and
acting President Yenayev. The decisions of the Committee are binding on
all citizens across the USSR.' That was a statement by the Soviet leadership.

A little later another and much more rambling justification for what had
taken place was broadcast, so critical of the policies of Mikhail
Gorbachev that the story about his illness was plainly a fabrication:

> Fellow countrymen! Citizens of the USSR! In a dark and critical hour for
> the destiny of our country and our peoples, we address you! A mortal
> danger hangs over our homeland! The policy of reform initiated by M.S.
> Gorbachev, conceived as a means to ensure the dynamic development of the
> country and the democratization of the life of its society, have for a number
> of reasons come to a dead end. The original enthusiasm and hope has been
> replaced by lack of belief, apathy and despair. Authority at all levels has lost
> the confidence of the population. . . Malicious mockery of all the
> institutions of the state is being implanted. The country has in effect
> become ungovernable. . .

The breakfast-time programmes on television were replaced by a
mercifully briefer announcement of the emergency. A film of 'Swan
Lake' was shown in its entirety twice.

Some people reacted with despair, others with a sense that was close
to relief: something that had so often been forecast had finally taken
place. 'I lay in bed crying and crying,' said one woman. Another said,
'What is it to do with us? They change things – it doesn't mean that food
gets cheaper.' Now that it was too late, some people were angry with
themselves for not having supported Mikhail Gorbachev more; most of
those who felt strongly about it, however, were angry with him because
they felt he should have foreseen the coup and prevented it. There was
an occasional shout or the waving of a fist from the groups of people the
tanks passed, but no one seemed inclined to resist. 'You can't fight the
army,' a man in his twenties told an American television crew; 'they've
got all the weapons, we've got nothing.'

A British journalist who was out in the streets that morning thought
he detected a feeling that it was all inevitable; that so much freedom of
speech and open criticism of the system was bound to have led to this.
Above all, no one seemed to think that anything could be done about it:
the authorities had decided to take action, and that was that. The
culture of passive acceptance which seven decades of Marxism-
Leninism and the centuries of autocracy had created made it seem at
this stage as though the coup must unquestionably succeed. In Soviet

history, those who controlled the central apparatus of political and military power invariably controlled the state. It seemed there was nothing more to be said. That morning in Kalinin Prospekt, the notion that it might be possible to overturn the coup attempt by a popular uprising simply did not arise.

There was a strong historical parallel. In October 1964 Nikita Khrushchev, the only General Secretary of the CPSU before Gorbachev to have made a serious effort to reform things, was overthrown in a rather similar fashion: he had been on holiday at his villa on the Black Sea coast of Georgia when the Praesidium of which he was head summoned him back to Moscow. A powerful group headed by his protégés Brezhnev and Kosygin, and urged on by the reactionary and unyielding ideologue Suslov, had decided that Khrushchev's policies and eccentricity of character were threatening the stability of the Party and of the Soviet Union. The Central Committee obediently voted him out of office, and it was announced that he had retired 'on health grounds'.

Now Mikhail Gorbachev too had been deprived of power with the same excuse, and a group of conservatives, appointed by Gorbachev, had taken control. The overthrow of Khrushchev showed how easily it could be done: you had simply to take command of the Kremlin's communications system and ensure that the defence minister and the chairman of the KGB were on your side. A few tanks in key positions were desirable, but scarcely essential. In the Soviet Union each organ of power could be expected to remain obedient to the system itself, not to any individual leader nor to any particular policy, and certainly not to the constitution. There had never been an example when the system had failed to obey its instructions. No one, from the new democrats to the men who had organized the coup, seemed to think such a thing could happen now. All that was necessary was to pinch off the old head and replace it with a new one.

Afterwards, a theory took hold that Gorbachev had in some way organized the coup himself, either in order to restore stability or to flush his opponents out into the open. Such ideas were commonplace among ordinary Russians, since conspiracy theories spring up most readily among intelligent people long aware of their powerlessness to control events. A Deputy for the City of Moscow, Boris Kagarlitsky, went so far as to argue that Gorbachev and Boris Yeltsin, the Russian President who led the resistance to the coup, had been in the plot together. An instant book written in the weeks after the events of 19–21 August treated the conspiracy theory with unwarranted respect before coming to an unconfident conclusion: 'In the end, suggestions that Gorbachev consciously connived with the plotters are impossible to prove or disprove.'

As it turned out, the state commission which was set up to investigate the coup announced in its report of February 1992 that the KGB had begun its preparations for the coup as early as the autumn of 1990, and that Gorbachev had no knowledge of their plans. For some months, according to the commission's head, Sergei Stepashin, the KGB flooded Gorbachev's office with hundreds of documents and a good deal of disinformation about the growing lawlessness and collapse of effective government, in the hope that he would agree to introduce martial law. The decision to overthrow him came when it was clear he was not prepared to do so. All the main documents for the coup, such as the declaration of a state of emergency, were drawn up as early as 4 August, two weeks before the coup took place. The timing of the attempt was unconsciously dictated by Gorbachev, in that he agreed that the proposed Union treaty which he had negotiated with the heads of a number of Soviet republics should be signed on 20 August. It had been done in order to give the republics greater autonomy and so defuse some of the bitter racial and territorial disputes which were threatening the stability of the old Soviet Union; but the conservatives, many of whom Gorbachev had been obliged to appoint towards the end of 1990 when the pressure on him from the anti-reformists had been at its strongest, were convinced that loosening the bonds would lead to the total dissolution of the Soviet Union.

Like everyone else, they assumed that the machinery of state would simply operate on their behalf once they had taken over the steering wheel. The videotape of the first interrogation of Dmitri Yazov, removed from the post of defence minister the day before, shows him in uniform, as crude and bearlike as ever, his ten rows of medals still in place. He seems anxious to co-operate with the prosecutor. The date on the videotape is 22.8.91.

> Yazov: There was no conspiracy. Nothing had been organized. We just met the day before it began.
> Interrogator: Saturday 17th?
> Yazov: Yes, the 17th August. . . We felt that Gorbachev was losing his touch as a political leader. He had lost control, or else he was simply burned out. . . We talked about the Union treaty to be signed in two days' time. We were all sure it meant the end of the Soviet Union.

Valentin Pavlov, the Soviet prime minister, was interrogated on 30 August, his absurd podgy figure encased in a maroon shirt; he was slumped in a chair at the prosecutor's table. Pavlov was one of the two or three instigators of the coup. He had already held a meeting of his own with his deputies on the morning of 17th to discuss the dangers, as he saw them, of the Union treaty. He went on to the meeting with Yazov and the others.

> Pavlov: We decided we needed a state of emergency. The economy was disintegrating. We had to avert famine and the collapse of the state.

The man who had planned the coup, and now called the meeting of dissident ministers, was Vladimir Kryuchkov, the chairman of the KGB. The record was later to show that during the two and a half days the coup attempt lasted, he made 200 telephone calls. Yenayev, the titular head of the junta, by contrast made fewer than half a dozen. Kryuchkov had presumably suggested the place where the meeting was to take place on 17 August: a KGB building outside Moscow to the south. After the coup was over he was given his first interrogation on the same day as Yazov. The video shows him as dapper as always, in a dark suit and sombre tie, with a white shirt which looked brand new.

> We wanted to say to him [Gorbachev], 'We have to take steps to stabilize the situation. Those steps may prove unpopular but we have no alternative. We think the people will back our actions.'

Kryuchkov had been receiving detailed reports of Gorbachev's thinking about the Union treaty and the future of the Soviet system for some time. His informant was General Plekhanov of the KGB, who was in charge of the department which provided protection for the leading figures in the Party and the government, and acted as Gorbachev's head of security. Gorbachev himself later revealed that Plekhanov had bugged his telephone and set up microphones in his office and elsewhere. What appears to have convinced Kryuchkov that something would have to be done was the recording of a private conversation between Gorbachev, Boris Yeltsin and Nursultan Nazarbayev, the Party boss of Kazakhstan, on 29 July.

At this meeting the three men had reached agreement about their approach to the new Union treaty. Nazarbayev and Yeltsin told Gorbachev at this meeting that several of his close associates were opposed to the Union treaty and to the introduction of the free market, and would have to go. Between them they named Pavlov, Kryuchkov and Anatoly Lukyanov, who as chairman of the Soviet Parliament ranked second to the President himself and had been Gorbachev's friend and associate for forty years. At one stage, according to interviews which Yeltsin, Nazarbayev and Gorbachev himself gave to the BBC, Yeltsin became agitated and went out onto the balcony to see if anyone was listening there. Nazarbayev and Gorbachev laughed at his reaction at the time, but were later forced to agree that he had been right.

Pavlov, Lukyanov and Kryuchkov had plotted against Gorbachev earlier. On 17 June, two months before the coup, they attempted to strip Gorbachev of his powers by constitutional means. At this stage the Union treaty was under discussion but had not yet been negotiated. The conservatives in the Party were already becoming nervous about its likely outcome, however. Gorbachev was not present in the Parliament, and Lukyanov announced that Pavlov was going to ask the House for emergency powers. Pavlov waddled to the rostrum.

> Pavlov: Some things are nothing to do with the President. The Cabinet [which was headed by Pavlov himself] has to be responsible for them. Not everything can be done by [Gorbachev's] presidential decree. I'm sorry, but it's technically impossible.
> Speaker from the floor: Has Gorbachev agreed these powers?
> Pavlov: I'll be completely honest with you: we've never discussed the subject.
> Speaker from the floor: Do you disagree with the President's economic and social policies?
> Pavlov [slowly]: I think I've answered that.
> [Laughter from the floor].

Later, it was announced that the Parliament would go into closed session. The television cameras were ordered to be switched off, and Kryuchkov and two security ministers gave secret reports to the members. Kryuchkov's speech was however recorded clandestinely:

> The KGB has reliable information about a plot by the CIA. It has been subverting senior officials of the Soviet state. Its agents now occupy important positions in the economy and government of the USSR. . . Our country is on the brink of catastrophe. Unless urgent measures are taken, our worst fears will be realized.

This was a heavy hint that some of the men closest to Gorbachev were in the pay of the Americans; it was Kryuchkov's lumbering explanation of the proposals for changing the power-structure of the Soviet Union. The conservatives, with the vociferous backing of the Soyuz ['Union'] group, demanded an urgent vote on the question of emergency powers. But the carelessness and lack of planning which later characterized the August coup were evident at this stage also: Lukyanov was not in the

House when the vote was called for, and his deputy, who knew nothing of the plot, refused to put the matter to a vote since neither the President nor the chairman of the Parliament were present. Gorbachev soon found out about it and was furious. But he did not sack the plotters. He did not believe that men who organized things so badly could altogether be taken seriously.

On the afternoon of Sunday 18 August a researcher working for one of Gorbachev's aides at the presidential villa at Cape Foros, on the Black Sea, was the first to notice a long line of official cars heading into the driveway. The villa was an attractive place, with a steep roof of red tiles, large windows with rounded heads looking out across the delightful waters of the bay, and a covered walkway down to the shingly beach. Inland the house was overlooked by a magnificent rocky hillside. Cypresses had been planted in the grounds, which were well kept even if to an English eye the grass was allowed to grow too long.

At 4.50 p.m. the head of Gorbachev's bodyguard came and told him that a group of people wanted to see him. Gorbachev was affronted; he had not invited anyone to the villa. The security man said he had let them in because his own commanding officer, General Plekhanov, was among them. Gorbachev headed off to see them.

> I went to invite them up, but they had already gone into my study. I wasn't used to such behaviour.

As he said these words at his press conference later, he seemed far away, and he scarcely looked at the audience of journalists in front of him. He was fidgeting with a fountain-pen, twisting it around in his fingers.

> They were led by the head of my presidential staff, Boldin.

There was a silence. Gorbachev seemed to be reliving the moment when he saw Boldin standing there in his private study.

> We chose Boldin very carefully.

By 'we', Gorbachev meant his wife Raisa and himself. This was not simply a political challenge to Gorbachev, it was an act of personal betrayal. Boldin was his chief of staff and had been a friend and protégé since the days when Gorbachev was the local Party boss in Stavropol. He was a boyish, pleasant-faced man with glasses: a natural follower. Knowing the influence he had on Gorbachev, the conspirators had set out to recruit him, and at the meeting in the KGB compound the day before they had chosen him to lead the delegation to Cape Foros.

In his book, hastily written to cash in on the interest in the coup abroad, Gorbachev left out his sense of personal bitterness against Boldin, and scarcely mentions him.

> At the very beginning of this encounter I put the question: 'Before continuing our conversation I want to ask you who sent you?' The reply was 'The Committee'.
> Then the following dialogue took place:
> 'What committee?'
> 'Well, the Committee set up to deal with the emergency situation in the country.'
> 'Who set it up? I didn't create it and the Supreme Soviet didn't create it. Who created it?'
> What the visitors had to say was that people had already got together and now needed a decree from the President. They put the situation facing me like this: either you issue the decree and remain here or you hand over your powers to the Vice-President.

Gorbachev's refusal to go along with the demands of the men who had betrayed him was one of the best things he had ever done. After the crisis, as before it, his judgement was often poor and his touch seemed to have deserted him. But he would not agree to anything un-constitutional or undemocratic, even to save his own power.

He obliged the slightly sheepish deputation to give him a list of the names of those behind the plot. Lukyanov's was the last on it, and Gorbachev put a question mark beside it; he was unwilling to accept that the guardian of the constitution could have betrayed it, as well as a friendship of forty years' standing, so easily. Raisa Gorbachev told the BBC:

> When we discovered who the conspirators were we were terribly hurt. We had a bitter sense of betrayal.

All the telephones in the house were cut, including even the military hotline, which was kept under a special cover and could not even be dusted. Gorbachev was unable to make contact with anyone.

As for the plotters, they had failed to oblige Gorbachev to step aside quietly, and had to fall back on the less satisfactory plan of declaring that he was too ill to continue in office. This obliged them to make the distinctly sub-standard Vice-President, Gennadi Yenayev, their putsch's figurehead. He had been sounded out and had agreed to take part, but he had little enthusiasm for it and was extremely nervous. Nevertheless it was essential to have his name at the head of the junta:

that way a sort of legality could be maintained, sufficient to ensure the support of the Soviet system throughout the country. All the traditional steps for taking power in that system had been followed. The announcements were made on radio and television. The tanks were deployed on the streets. The conspirators sat back and assumed that they had achieved their aim.

*

Through the haze of sleep I took in what had happened as I listened to the 7 o'clock news on BBC radio in London. I was alone: Tira was in Moscow, filling in for a colleague. The previous evening she had telephoned me to say how boring it was with most of the Western correspondents away on holiday. She didn't know, she said, how she was going to get through the next three weeks.

That Monday I was scheduled to present the BBC programme 'Newsnight'. It was depressing to think that I could not go to Moscow myself to report on the coup, but the authorities seemed unlikely to be issuing visas. It was unclear at that stage whether planes would be allowed to land, or satellite transmissions permitted. I sat gloomily at the presenter's desk in the 'Newsnight' office, while the deputy editor Keith Bowers whispered something to Tim Gardam, the editor.

'Let's go for it,' Gardam said decisively, and they both turned to me. Bowers, a calm, thoughtful man, had remembered that 'Newsnight' had applied for a Soviet visa for me some weeks earlier to cover the summit meeting between the Soviet and American presidents. Quietly, he had checked the visa: today, 19 August, was its last day of validity. A Soviet visa is not a mere stamp into your passport: it comes as a separate document, folded up like a leaflet. I looked at it in wonderment. Keith had also checked the times of the flights, and the last available one left at one o'clock. It was five to twelve, and I stopped looking at the visa.

I checked in my briefcase: I had nothing I needed for the trip except one of my passports. It wasn't the one for which the visa had been issued, but I thought I could talk my way through. I didn't mention it to the 'Newsnight' people in case they changed their minds about my going. Everyone there and in the Newsroom rallied round generously: someone cancelled a lunch appointment for me, someone else took down a series of messages, a third person lent me some money and a fourth got out his car and drove me to the airport. I arrived at Heathrow with twenty minutes to spare, and still had enough time to buy myself a large notebook and enough paperbacks – Chekhov, Hardy and Robertson Davies – to see me through the journey.

I changed planes at Frankfurt, where I bought a horribly expensive set of shirts, underclothes, ties, shaving gear and a bag to keep them in at the Harrod's shop. The Lufthansa flight was full of Western correspondents who were based in Moscow but had been away when the coup took place. A friend of mine, James Blitz, passed me the wire copy from Reuters which had been faxed to him at Frankfurt. When I had finished reading that I set about my passport. Knowing the literal-mindedness of Soviet border guards, I decided that I should alter the number of my passport to the one which appeared indelibly on my visa. It seemed a rash thing to do, but I could not bear to be turned away once I had reached Moscow itself. The result was deeply unconvincing.

The man behind the immigration desk signalled to me to wait, and called his superior. They both looked at my visa, then at me. 'Do you realize,' said the superior, 'that your visa runs out in two and a half hours?' A kindly Australian journalist standing in line behind me translated my halting reply: a replacement was being arranged with the Foreign Ministry. For all I knew, it was true. The man behind the desk gave me a thumbs-up sign, and I was through.

It was raining, and everything and everybody looked exceedingly depressed. By the time I had found the BBC driver and we began the drive into Moscow it was dark. Cars loomed out at us in the gloom, with only sidelights showing. The vast blocks of flats beside the road glimmered faintly in the darkness, the lights in the windows a dull brownish colour. We rumbled along the uneven road surface. Was there, I asked the driver, a general strike as Boris Yeltsin had demanded? He shook his head, and the fact that buses seemed to be working normally and shops were open supported the idea. 'So the coup has succeeded?' The driver shrugged his shoulders, too gloomy to talk about it. Disconsolate pedestrians waited at the bus stops in the pouring rain, waving their hands despairingly at us as we drove past, hoping we would stop and give them a lift.

At the sign which marks the Moscow city boundary a dozen light tanks had parked in a side road. I asked the driver to stop so that I could walk over and talk to them. A slovenly soldier in a yellowish uniform stood puffing on a cigarette and watching me. I had read in the wire-copy on the plane that the troops had not been issued with ammunition. 'Is that true?' I asked. He laughed and showed teeth almost as yellow as his uniform. 'No bullets,' he said. The other soldiers were friendly, bored, and a little nervous. I was reminded strongly of the troops who had been sent in to deal with the demonstrators in Tiananmen Square, but had refused to take action. Eventually Deng Xiaoping had found soldiers who would obey orders; would the State Emergency Com-mittee do likewise, I wondered. Eduard Shevardnadze, the former foreign minister who had resigned the previous December in protest at Gorbachev's sudden swing to the right, said that evening, 'We can expect a repression.' It seemed extremely likely. None of the friends and contacts I spoke to by telephone that evening had any serious hope that Gorbachev could be reinstated or the coup defeated.

Yet the one critical mistake had already been made, which ensured that the conspiracy would fail. The state commission which investigated the origins of the coup reported in February 1992 that three alternative plans had been prepared for the arrest of Boris Yeltsin, and the KGB's anti-terrorist group Alpha was supposed to pick him up, together with forty other political leaders in Moscow. For some reason, which the commission was unable to explain, the KGB leadership failed to give the order that Yeltsin or any of the others should be arrested. Yeltsin returned to his flat in Moscow after an out-of-town visit that morning, and later took sanctuary in the so-called White House – the vast white block which was the old headquarters of the Russian Soviet and which Yeltsin had turned into the lively centre of opposition to Gorbachev's Kremlin.

As the crisis developed, the White House became the symbol of the resistance to reaction. Yeltsin's career had been in some ways rather like that of Gorbachev, but altogether less refined and easy. Whereas Gorbachev had tended to avoid the more embarrassing forms of grovelling to superior authority which were required of an aspiring politician, Yeltsin had felt no such restraint. As Party boss of Sverdlovsk, the city where the last Tsar and his family had been murdered in 1918, Yeltsin bulldozed down the house where it had happened, because in the late 1970s it was turning into a place of pilgrimage. He was a hustler, a man who was perfectly willing to play rough when that was required. He had none of Gorbachev's instincts for democracy.

Yet when the coup took place he knew what was required of him, just as much as Gorbachev did. That morning the speaker of the Russian Parliament, Ruslan Khasbulatov, went to his flat to see him. They agreed together that there was no alternative but to resist. Then they moved across to the White House, where they and others composed a brief statement condemning the coup. By afternoon a sizeable crowd had gathered beside the tanks which had been deployed outside the building, and Yeltsin, overcoming the protests of his security men, decided to go out and read the statement to them. The crowd roared its pleasure at seeing him: only a few minutes earlier, a rumour had gone the rounds that Yeltsin had been arrested. Now Yeltsin looked round for some vantage point to climb. There was nothing for it but to hoist himself up onto one of the tanks.

With an Orthodox cleric on one side of him and armed security men behind him and to his right, he grabbed one of the handles on the side of the vehicle and began to clamber on to it. An even bigger roar went up as those on the edges of the crowd saw the familiar bulky figure. Characteristically, seeing the cameras (Tira's being the most conspicuous of them) he arranged his abundant white hair. As his security guards took up position alongside him, hands hanging loosely by their sides, ready to go for their guns at the first sign of trouble, Yeltsin shook hands with the tank commander. The man was wearing his helmet, like a 1930s aviator, and was half in and half out of the hatch. He seemed a little embarrassed. By now someone was holding a Russian flag, which fluttered behind Yeltsin as he prepared to read from a couple of sheets of Russian Parliament notepaper:

> Citizens of Russia! On the night of 18 August 1991 the lawfully elected President was deposed. Let us be clear. We are dealing with a reactionary, unconstitutional coup. . . I call on all soldiers: do not join in this reactionary coup! We demand a general strike!

It was a moment to match Lenin's speech from an armoured car in Petrograd in 1917, and people cheered him lustily. A superbly insouciant figure in a windcheater and dark glasses, one of Yeltsin's chief bodyguards, took his hands from his hips and started applauding.

At the Soviet Foreign Ministry that afternoon some of the members of the State Emergency Committee gave a press conference. The leading figures behind the coup – Pavlov, Yazov and Kryuchkov – stayed away, and Yenayev, the Vice-President, had to do most of the talking. From the Committee's point of view it was a disaster: Yenayev was unused to answering difficult questions in public, and the journalists gathered at the Foreign Ministry were for the most part deeply hostile. With the live cameras of Soviet television on him, Yenayev gave several different versions of what was going on, sometimes praising Gorbachev for his achievements, sometimes criticizing him, sometimes hinting that it had been necessary to push him aside, sometimes insisting that the original story about his ill-health was true:

> Mikhail Sergeyevich is still resting and recuperating at his holiday place in the Crimea where he was vacationing when he became ill. He was very tired after all his years in power, and it will take him a long time to recover his health. . . I hope that when he is better it may even be possible for him to return to his presidential duties.

He tried to reassure:

> We have the support of the regions and of most of the leaders of the
> Republics for our efforts to restore order and save the country. . . We will
> do everything to ensure that no force is used against civilians. We must do
> everything to prevent excesses.

As he spoke, Yenayev fiddled continuously with a paper clip, with the
cord of his headset, with his glasses case. In the pitiless close-up shot it
was quite plain that his hands were shaking. Later, one of the members
of the Committee who was watching on television said he began to have
his doubts when he saw Yenayev's hands. Things were not going as the
conspirators had assumed: Gorbachev had not capitulated, and Yeltsin
was openly defying them. In some areas of the system there was quiet
defiance. At Ostankino, the headquarters of Soviet television, the order
had been received to end all foreign news transmissions by the Louche –
the main satellite system. The man in charge decided to wait an hour
before passing on the order, and since no one repeated it and nothing
more was said when the foreign transmissions continued he took no
action.

Elsewhere in the Party system the Committee's instructions were
obeyed to the full. The habit of accepting the requirements of authority
without questioning whether that authority was legitimate remained,
despite six years of glasnost and open discussion. They army did what it
was told, with the exception of a few units from the Tamanskaya
Guards division, which sent their tanks to the Russian Parliament to
defend it. The previous year there had been frequent rumours that the
Tamanskaya's officers were considering a coup against Gorbachev.
When I went there with a camera crew the officers insisted they would
always uphold constitutional authority. I didn't believe them; yet they
did precisely that when the moment came.

At the offices of *Pravda*, the newspaper of the Party's Central
Committee, things were much more difficult. Most of the younger
members of the staff wanted the paper to condemn the coup, but their
seniors were still imbued with the spirit of obedience. In any Soviet
enterprise the highest-ranking official was obliged to sign a form taking
personal responsibility for what was done; it engendered great reluct-
ance to take risks. The acting editor of *Pravda*, Gennadi Seleznev,
agonized for some hours with his heads of department before deciding
how to cope with the awkward situation. The edition they had
produced on Sunday, before the news of the coup broke, had been
standard post-glasnost fare, with articles openly discussing the

difficulties of the economy and a picture of a pretty girl on the front page.

Now Seleznev decided to obey orders. The paper he edited on Monday for publication the following day was a complete reversion to the old Brezhnevite days. Its front page was entirely filled with dense blocks of type – verbatim accounts of the speeches and statements of the new Committee. The foreign affairs editor, a bold and experienced correspondent named Vladimir Snegorev, protested loudly at an editorial meeting. One of his superiors came over to him afterwards. 'Why are you making all this fuss, Vladimir? You've got a good career in front of you. Take my advice – don't rock the boat. Just keep quiet for a bit and see how things turn out. You're a fool to throw everything away like this.'

All over the Soviet Union, senior Party members must have been saying and thinking identical things. They knew their reaction would probably determine their entire career for better or worse. The foreign minister, Alexander Bessmertnykh, had known nothing about the plans for the coup. He was told to go to Pavlov's office, where he found many of the conspirators. They asked him to join the Committee, and he refused. But he clearly felt the requirement to obey which had been instilled into every Party member from earliest youth; so that when, the following day, Yevgeny Primakov, who was a member of the Presidential Security Council and a Gorbachev loyalist, came to him and asked him to sign a declaration condemning the coup, Bessmertnykh refused.

Soon afterwards he went to a meeting of senior officials at the Foreign Ministry and told them he was planning to resign. He was persuaded not to. One official said, 'We cannot leave [the Committee] to alter our foreign policy.' Bessmertnykh rationalized his decision by telling himself it was his duty to explain the change-over of power abroad; yet in fact, at that stage, his decision meant he was joining what appeared to be the winning side. The Soviet system, which rewarded obedience and punished independent thinking, had become a part of him. He was unable to change.

That night, after midnight, I went down to the White House. There was no sign whatever of the supposed curfew. 'I think tomorrow will be many, many vodka in the shops, and many, many meat,' said a girl who had hitched a lift with us. She was completely cynical about what had happened, dismissing equally the reason for the coup, the coup itself, and the political future of the country. 'Everything here is just fuck,' she said. She despised Gorbachev, and the people who had taken over from him. Our car was in bad shape: every time we hit a bump in the road the interior light went on. We drove round Dzerzhinski's statue in the square named after him. There were many lights burning in the KGB headquarters. Police cars raced up and down the slick roads, but apart from the tanks which were blocking Manezh Square and Pushkin Square there was little sign of activity.

Outside the White House I shouted questions at an officer on one of the tanks. These were the ones from the Tamanskaya Guards regiment which had gone over to Yeltsin's side. Over the drum-like rumble of the engines, as the fumes from the exhaust hit me squarely in the face, the officer said it hadn't been his decision to come here but that he was in wholehearted agreement. 'I don't think many soldiers support the coup,' he said. 'But they have their orders, just as we had ours.' Inside the White House a large blonde woman weighed down by a vast bust, her hands and arms red with some unpleasant-looking rash, announced that she was Boris Yeltsin's press spokeswomen. He was resting in his office, she said. There was an internal radio station in the building, spewing out an endless discussion programme. 'If we allow this outrage to continue,' one of the speakers said, 'it will be like. . .' I couldn't hear what it would be like.

What would happen tomorrow? I asked the large blonde woman. 'I don't know, and I am afraid,' she said. She tapped her plastic watch and shook her head. Her phone kept whirring like an insect on a window-pane, and each time she would get up and walk across to her desk to answer it. She was in almost constant motion. 'Gorbachev has arrived back in Moscow as a prisoner,' she called over at one point. 'The airport workers have just told us.' Another call. 'It's not Gorbachev after all,' she said, and came to sit beside me for another ten or fifteen seconds. 'This man will fight,' someone else told me, pointing to a man with a young figure and an elderly face. He was in his thirties, but looked far older. 'I was a prisoner in the camps,' he said, shaking my hand vigorously. He made a movement towards his belt. 'I will kill anyone who comes here. No more prison.' The security guards inside the White House wore the blue and white striped vests of special forces troops. They were Afghanistan veterans who worked for one of the new private security firms. Upstairs was Yeltsin's second in command, Alexander Rutskoi, swaggering and handsome, a gun in his belt. 'I'll stand and defend the President,' he had told the television cameras earlier; 'blood will flow from this.' It was said with a certain relish.

Outside they were building barricades, hauling lumps of concrete and lengths of scaffolding. The events described in this book had made me something of a connoisseur of barricades, and these seemed reasonably effective. It was raining steadily, and the drops splashed onto my open notebook, making the ink run. A man in a see-through plastic raincoat which had the general colour and appearance of a giant condom was tugging at a heavy box. 'What's inside?' I asked. He frowned and raised his hand to indicate it was something secret. Then, 'Bullets!' he said, with a conspiratorial laugh. In the darkness and the rain huddled groups of men were working away at some task, their coats acting as a cover. When they heard I was from the BBC they moved aside to let me into the ring of coats. They were filling Coca-Cola bottles with petrol and stuffing rags in them. *'Molotovski Koktel!'* said a wild-looking character proudly, and laughed. 'Inside I feel afraid. Outside, no,' he added confidentially: and indeed I would not have been able to tell.

I went back to the BBC office and got an hour's sleep on the floor before writing and editing a report for the Breakfast News programme in London. The staff in the office were working with great enthusiasm: a young, recently married picture-editor happened to have a tourist visa and had been intending to have a holiday with her husband in Moscow. Instead she volunteered to come and work. My report was a sombre one; but it was not borne out by events:

> It is by no means certain that there will be violence. The most difficult decision the members of the so-called State Emergency Committee have to make is, what to do about Boris Yeltsin. If they leave him alone, he's a continuing threat to them. If they move in and arrest him, the probable bloodshed will change everything. But for all the determination of the crowds round the Parliament, they're in a small minority. Most people seem apathetic – and that could well be the greatest problem for Boris Yeltsin and the remaining reformers.

As Tuesday went on, Yeltsin's chances of success still seemed slight. The strikes he had called for were by no means widespread or extensive: eight out of the thirteen mines in the Kuzbas, Russia's largest coalfield, were still working, and at the Tynmen oil field in Siberia the men had decided that if they went on strike it could lead to civil war. Yeltsin was unable to match the Committee's control of the media. To compete with the state television service he had only a feeble short-wave radio station. Worst of all, it seemed to me, was the weather. The steady downpour made it difficult for people to stay out in the open around the Parliament building. By Tuesday afternoon a jacket I had bought at great expense at Frankfurt airport had been thoroughly soaked through twice. My shoes were sodden.

That afternoon it seemed as though something was about to happen. As the camera-crew and I clambered over the barricades, gripping onto the pieces of scaffolding that stuck out like pikes at a sixteenth-century battle and hoisting ourselves over the strange collections of metal and concrete that blocked the ways to the Parliament building, it was painfully obvious that the crowds were melting away. By 4 p.m. we estimated that there were only about two hundred people. A determined rush by a single platoon of soldiers would have cleared the place. I remembered Tiananmen Square yet again: how, towards the end, the support drifted away. I clambered onto a tank like Boris Yeltsin the day before, and, miserably wet, recorded a piece to camera. I had rarely, I said, been in a crowd which was quite so passive and silent. There was so little sound from the defenders of the Parliament that you could hear the heavy lorries changing gear on the other side of the river, two hundred yards away.

As afternoon turned to evening the rumours that tanks were coming grew stronger. Boris Yeltsin, always something of a self-dramatist, had broken off a telephone conversation with the British prime minister John Major, saying he thought he could hear a hundred tanks coming. More probably he had heard his own mechanical diggers driving up to deposit more concrete slabs to act as tank traps. All along the steps on the river side of the Parliament now was a line of diehards, most of them wearing antique-looking gasmasks with long rubber tubes descending from them. 'Down With The Black Junta Of Red Bandits' said a more than usually complex banner. Someone was playing the accordion as the rain lashed us, but the loudest noise was still the shuffling feet until, as it grew dark, there was shouting and cheering from a group gathered around a radio set. 'Yazov's resigned!' someone shouted, and a little impromptu dance began in the rain. A girl with some rosary beads of ivory crossed herself, her face tilted up to the sky, the rain striking it directly. 'So has Pavlov!' Then came a correction: 'No, Pavlov's ill.' There was a snort of uncharitable amusement. 'His heart, maybe, or his blood-pressure.' 'What about our blood-pressure?' I tried to do another piece to camera, saying that the news of the two resignations had brought the crowd back to life, but it was raining so hard that it was ridiculous even to try. By this time, anyway, the report of Yazov's resignation had been denied.

Back at the office, we started to hear reports of serious violence. It was infuriating to have to wait for the slow process of editing a report to come to an end before I could get out onto the streets again. Things seemed too serious for me to be able to rely on my rudimentary grasp of Russian, so I asked if anyone in the office was prepared to come with me. Sarah, a quiet, dark-haired producer in her early twenties volunteered. It was past ten o'clock, and we headed down the familiar pathway in the darkness to the Parliament building. There was an electrical charge in the air that always comes when violence is expected. I was worried that we were too late, as we splashed through the mud and puddles, working our way through the barricades. Most people seemed to be heading away from the Parliament, but that was all to the good: it seemed to indicate they thought something was going to happen soon. Beside me in the drizzle Sarah was nervous but very determined.

We were beside the Parliament when we heard gunfire a hundred yards or so away. The earlier reports of violence had been untrue, but now a squadron of armoured personnel carriers had been trapped in the underpass on the main ring road near the entrance to the Arbat. The wilder spirits in the crowd attacked them, and when the APCs were halted and the soldiers got out, two of them opened fire at random into a crowd. Altogether three men were killed. The APCs was captured and held by the crowd in the underpass, but none of the soldiers was badly hurt.

It seemed likely to me that this was merely the beginning of the night's violence. The rumour was going round at the Parliament that special KGB troops from the unit known as Alpha would attack at 3 a.m. I was determined to be inside the building when that happened. That, it seemed, would be where things would happen. Eduard Shevardnadze arrived as we were waiting, his quiff of white hair showing above the heads of the crowd. He was extremely nervous, and had to be helped along. Yet he had decided that he could not allow himself to sit at home when such important events were happening; he had to line up with those who were defending democracy. Someone put a microphone in his hand and he made a brief and moving speech:

> Our fate is being decided. The future of democracy and freedom is being settled. Long live the people! I salute you all!

There were heroics inside too. Shevardnadze said afterwards he would never forget Boris Yeltsin's words inside the White House: 'I'll do what a real leader does. I'll stay here till the end, till my last drop of blood. I'll stand firm.'

For us, waiting outside, it was proving frustratingly difficult to get in. Sarah and I met a small group of European reporters, including Alfonso Rojo of *El Mundo*, the journalistic hero of the Gulf War. I had known him in Baghdad eight months earlier when the missiles began to fall, and now here we were trying to force our way in from the rain and cold into a building which would soon be under attack. 'Why are you stopping the BBC from entering?' I asked, taking advantage of the popularity of the BBC among Yeltsin's supporters. It worked. We even got Rojo and his friends in as well.

Inside, it was mostly dark and felt like being in the Roman senate before the Gauls attacked. There were piles of gas-masks, clothes, food containers and weapons in the hallway. Tough-looking soldiers with the cut-down Kalashnikovs officers were issued with in Afghanistan clanked around the darkened corridors and stood by every door. We made our way to the debating chamber, where a few determined figures were arguing with each other. I started to write an article for the *Spectator*, then drifted off to sleep over my open notebook. I woke to find a bulky man, a deputy, announcing that the troops would be there at any moment. Three o'clock came, and we looked out of the window. The vast, stolid crowd was still there, saying little, not singing or chanting but enduring the rain and waiting. It seemed to me a critical moment had passed.

Afterwards it was reported that the KGB force Alpha had been given orders to attack the Parliament building at 3 a.m., to clear the two lower floors with automatic fire and to take Boris Yeltsin dead or alive. The men, it was said, had decided to ignore their orders, on the grounds that their own friends and relatives could be outside the building. The head of the state commission into the coup found no evidence, however, that the conspirators had ordered Alpha to attack. Instead, it was authorized to undertake reconnaissance. Nevertheless, we felt at the time we had been lucky.

A feeble light, neither quite yellow nor quite pink, appeared in the sky. It was 5 a.m., and I wanted to take a turn around before going back to the office. The camera crew and I wandered into the underpass where the APCs had been held. Now they were getting ready to drive off, their upper works covered with enthusiastic civilians: deputies, workers, men and girls carrying Russian flags, old women, an Orthodox priest. There were nine vehicles altogether, and the thunder and stench of their engines in the tunnel was extraordinary. If this had been Tiananmen or East Berlin, Prague or Bucharest, there would have been loud chanting and singing. Here, even at the supreme moment of revolt, everyone was quiet and serious. At last, very slowly, the APCs moved off down the road, heading for the Russian Parliament in the grey, drizzling dawn of Wednesday morning, taking control for the first time in their lives.

This time it was a masseuse who noticed the line of limousines arriving at the presidential villa at Cape Foros in the Crimea. Lukyanov, Kryuchkov, Yazov and several others were there. Gorbachev's aide Anatoly Chernayev knew the coup had collapsed when they started bowing to him. Gorbachev said he wouldn't see them until they had reconnected his phones. They pointed out that it would take some time. Gorbachev said he was in no hurry. Not long afterwards a party of Yeltsin's men arrived too. With them was an enterprising British correspondent, Jonathan Steele of the *Guardian*, who thus obtained the scoop of a lifetime. Gorbachev attacked Lukyanov: 'You're our top lawyer – why didn't you uphold the law. . .? You should have thrown yourself at the tanks to defend that constitution you're always waving around.' Lukyanov answered feebly that he hadn't been able to do anything. Gorbachev said, 'Why didn't you go and line yourself up with Yeltsin? Go on, get out of here.'

They flew back to Moscow. Rutskoi, Yeltsin's vice-president, lured Kryuchkov on board the plane with the promise of a meeting with Gorbachev, then kept him there for the duration of the flight as a hostage. No one knew what was going to happen when the plane landed in Moscow. The security chief, a tough wiry man with a large moustache hung out of an emergency door as the plane touched down. It there was trouble his orders were to jump out and keep on firing till the last, so the plane would have a chance of taking off again. Gorbachev, looking tired and relieved, came down the gangway. Someone clapped, and he raised his hand in acknowledgement. Behind him came Raisa in a white dressing-gown, her arm round her granddaughter. A photograph taken by TASS showed the unbearable strain and sadness on her face. It was no surprise when, a short time later, she suffered a mild stroke. Yazov, interrogated a few days later, told his questioners:

> I wanted to sink into the ground. I felt eternally guilty for what we'd done to Gorbachev and Raisa. I felt guilty in the eyes of the people and of the Party.

He sat there, looking smaller now, his hands resting on his knees, his ten absurd rows of medal ribbons on his uniform, talking in a faint voice and using the terms of self-abasement which those who had lost political battles had habitually used in the Soviet Union for more than seventy years. It is possible Yazov may even have meant them.

15

THE FALL OF GORBACHEV

It is a great personal tragedy for me. I put all my energy into reforming the Party. I wanted to make it truly democratic – a Party for the people, and not for the elite.

MIKHAIL SERGEYEVICH GORBACHEV

The events with which this book has been concerned – the collapse of the Communist Party and of Soviet domination throughout Central and Eastern Europe, as well as its near-collapse in China – were all powerfully influenced by the policies followed by Mikhail Gorbachev. The last outpost of empire proved to be, not surprisingly, the Soviet Union itself. Gorbachev's influence, like Simon Bolivar's, moved from country to country, liberating them one after another. Bolivar intended to do so; Gorbachev merely wished to restore the Communist Party in each country by stripping out the old decaying elements and replacing them with new, democratic ones. He was a convinced Marxist-Leninist who simply wanted to clear away the accretions of seventy years. Instead, he found he had weakened the structure to the point where it fell down of its own accord. Marxism-Leninism had become, in Hazlitt's words, crazy and rotten. It had no political strength left in it: it merely stayed standing because it was shored up by habit and an unpleasant police system.

A few days after Gorbachev's return from the Crimea a cameraman, a producer and I managed to get into the headquarters of the Central Committee of the Soviet Union in Moscow. We were, quite probably, the first foreign television team to be allowed to wander round at will. The cameraman was Rory Peck, who has appeared elsewhere in these pages. We had made an extraordinary series of films together during that week: films which would have been unthinkable even a month before. We had been shown around the KGB's headquarters, had investigated the deaths of Party officials thought to have been involved in the transfer of vast sums of money out of the country, and visited the dachas vacated by a number of leading figures. Now we had obtained entrance to the Central Committee building.

It was a Friday, and the office staff and Party officials who worked in the building had been given until that evening to clear out their desks. No one bothered about us as we went from floor to floor and office to office. Downstairs at the entrance people were being searched, sometimes quite roughly, to check that they were not taking out important documents. Upstairs, in the long corridors, it was silent. Copies of the internal telephone directory which related to the topmost communications network linking the various members of the Party leadership lay on the abandoned desks. No one wanted them now: there was no one to answer the phones. Some of the offices had been sealed by order of the Mayor of Moscow, whose men were investigating various forms of wrong-doing.

In one office we came across Piotr Luchinski. The office seemed like any other belonging to a high Soviet official: the yellowish furniture, the pictures of Lenin and Gorbachev, the glass-fronted bookcase filled with bound volumes of speeches, resolutions, philosophical writings. A secretary came in with a tray of good tea and a plate of expensive, probably Western, biscuits. Outside, we had heard her complain to her colleague how difficult it was to get these things now. The office was not Luchinski's, nor was she his secretary. He had taken refuge there because his own office was sealed and his own secretary had walked out.

Luchinski stopped and reflected for a little when I asked him what his rank was now. 'Since Mikhail Sergeyevich [Gorbachev] has resigned from the Party, and everyone else who was senior to me has either resigned or been arrested' (he checked them off, one by one, on his fingers) 'I think I must be the head of the Party.' He laughed, but it was an uncomfortable laugh. At the end we closed the door on him. He had only a few hours to clear out the few things he could get together and leave. The corridors of the building were entirely empty now, and our shoes squeaked on the parquet floors. It was like walking the deck of an abandoned ship.

Mikhail Gorbachev was an impressive man in many ways, but although he often talked of the need for new thinking he was unable to imagine a world beyond the intellectual confines of Marxism-Leninism. When he returned from the Crimea on the evening of 21 August he should have declared then and there that he was disgusted by the behaviour of many of the most senior members of the Communist Party, and was leaving it. Yet even when he gave his major press conference the next day he had still not understood the immense change the rest of the country had gone through. Communism, for almost everyone else, had died during the coup, and they wanted it buried as fast as possible. Gorbachev still appeared to feel it merely required another blood transfusion:

I see it as my duty, and shall to the utmost of my ability see to it that there are no restrictions on ridding the Party of reactionary elements. We must do all we can to make certain that the Party is reformed and becomes a real force behind perestroika.

Already such expressions had an antique flavour to them. The Party was dead, and only Gorbachev had failed to realize it. Alexander Yakovlev, the original influence behind perestroika, told him afterwards it was probably the worst press conference he had ever given. It also marked the beginning of the end of his political power.

Boris Yeltsin, altogether quicker-minded on tactics though lacking Gorbachev's philosophical cast of mind, had left the Party long before and had won an enormous political reward for it. He now set out to humiliate Gorbachev and remove him as a rival. On Friday 23 August Gorbachev went to the Russian Parliament to thank its members for supporting him during the coup. Soon, faced with an audience fiercely loyal to Yeltsin, he found himself in difficulties. It became clear that Yeltsin had laid a trap for him. The two men were side by side at two desks. Gorbachev held a sheaf of papers in his hand:

Gorbachev: Boris Nikolayevich [Yeltsin] has given me a summary of my ministers' reactions to the coup, but I haven't had a chance to read it yet.
Yeltsin [waving a finger in his face]: Read it out. [Laughter, applause] Read it – they're the minutes of the Soviet cabinet.
Gorbachev: I. . .
Yeltsin: A meeting held when the Russian Parliament faced an armed assault.
Gorbachev: But. . .
Yeltsin [turning to the audience]: Mikhail Sergeyevich cannot escape some responsibility for the coup.
[Gorbachev says nothing, and licks his lips nervously.]
Yeltsin: Permit me now to sign a decree. We are going to ban the activities of the Russian Communist Party. [Loud applause]
Gorbachev: Boris Nikolayevich, Boris Nikolayevich. . .
[The applause is even louder now, and the deputies are starting to rise from their seats to give Yeltsin a standing ovation.]
Gorbachev [struggling to make himself heard]: Be democratic. Show toleration in everything you do. That's the only way to keep the people on your side.
Yeltsin [putting away his pen]: The decree has been signed.

It was a deeply humiliating moment for Gorbachev, and demonstrated (as it was intended to) Yeltsin's total superiority in the wake of the coup.

That morning an old woman, ugly and badly dressed yet with a certain style came up to me in the street and started haranguing me. 'I can see from your clothes you're a foreigner. I don't know what country you come from, but I want you to know that we don't want Gorbachev any more as our president. We have a president and his name is Yeltsin. That's all. Gorbachev is a Communist, and we don't want Communists now.'

On the evening of Thursday 22 August a group of crane drivers and willing helpers came to Dzerzhinsky Square to remove the statue of the eponymous Feliks Dzerzhinsky, the founder of the KGB's forerunner. The job of lifting it off its eighteenth-century marble plinth was done with surprising speed: the statue was hollow. I had been there earlier in the day, and noticed how, even now, there were three levels of opposition to the old régime. The statue stood like a cartoonist's desert island in the middle of a sea of traffic. Around its base was a small patch of grass. No one ever came there without permission: you needed an official form even to place flowers at the statue's feet. The most eager of the demonstrators that day had swarmed across the road and settled on the plinth itself. A few climbed up Dzerzhinsky's gloomy figure and painted slogans on it. A second group gathered in an outer circle on the grass: less ardent, but determined to participate in the symbolic destruction of the KGB's power. The third group left a clear space between the grass and themselves, and stood on the pavement around it. They, it seemed to me, represented the instinctive Russian response: they wanted to watch what happened and even participate a little vicariously; but they also wanted to have an alibi in case of trouble.

Now, however, there were no distinctions as people gathered to watch the statue being taken away. For a moment or two, as the steel cables around it took the strain, there was no sign of movement. Then, very slowly, Dzerzhinsky lifted up and swung a little, like a highwayman at Tyburn. There was a wild, ragged cheer; some people started singing the old Tsarist anthem. 'I never thought this day would come,' an elderly man told a Western television reporter; 'I never expected to be this happy.' 'That's the end of them,' said another man, much younger. 'Of whom?' 'Of the Communists.' The statue was lowered onto the back of a flatbed truck. As it was driven off it seemed to shine silver in the light from the street lamps. It was only as you went closer that you could see the silver was spit from the bystanders.

As Mikhail Gorbachev's power waned throughout the autumn and early winter of 1991, his plans for the future of the territory which had once been the Soviet Union disappeared too. Efforts to revive the Union treaty which had brought about the coup against him ran into serious difficulties. What remained of the Soviet system, with a centralized structure based in Moscow, started to fall apart. On 1 December Ukraine had registered a 90 per cent vote in favour of independence; Russia and the other republics were refusing to finance the centre, and there was very little money left in the Soviet treasury. Government officials, teachers, soldiers, were all warned that they might not be paid beyond December. Yeltsin, as tactically-minded as ever, said Russia would pay the salaries of all army officers, and give them almost double their old rates of pay.

On 10 December Yeltsin, together with the Ukrainian President Leonid Kravchuk and the Byelorussian leader Stanislav Shushkevich, agreed after a lengthy meeting not far from the city of Brest, near the Polish border, to form a Commonwealth of Independent States. They left out the fourth most important republic, Kazakhstan, and its leader, Gorbachev's ally Nursultan Nazarbayev, may have been correct to regard this as the contempt of Slavs for Asiatics. Nevertheless the C.I.S. was Yeltsin's notion of a loose grouping of states, based on a slight misunderstanding of the nature of the British Commonwealth.

Those former Soviet republics which wanted to join would be invited to do so. There would be no function for what Gorbachev had called 'the centre': no function, that is, for Gorbachev himself. It seemed to be part of Boris Yeltsin's plan for getting rid of Gorbachev as a rival, once and for all. One by one, other republics declared themselves ready to join, and Gorbachev's Union treaty was finally killed off. It was an unedifying little episode, and the Brest agreement even had to be renamed the Minsk agreement; the Treaty of Brest-Litovsk in 1918, under which the new Soviet regime agreed to the loss of large tracts of land to the Germans in order to safeguard its political existence, made Brest an inauspicious place in which to plan the future of the former Soviet empire.

Gorbachev had threatened to resign if the Union treaty were not passed. It was a threat he had made frequently in the past, and it had lost its force. Now, indeed, there seemed very little to resign from. On 12 December he gave a news conference for Soviet journalists in the Kremlin. He walked slowly into the room, head down, and made as though to sit at the head of the table: his natural place for nearly seven years. One of his officials tactfully pointed to a seat halfway down the side of the table. As I watched the Soviet television pictures I remembered the old spring in his step as he would leap out of a limousine and plunge into the crowd, shaking hands and trying to convince people that things had really changed – that socialism had a human heart as well as a human face. I remembered too the intense look in his eyes as he locked his gaze on someone and for that minute or so gave himself and his fullest attention to them and to their problem. Now the eyes were dull, and did not always meet those of the journalists sitting opposite him.

> The main work of my life is finished. I have done everything I could. I think that if they'd been in my shoes most other people would have given up long ago. Still, I've managed to drag through the main ideas of perestroika, even if there have been mistakes. . .
>
> I want society to make its choice consciously. But I cannot shake off the impression that the collapse of the state is taking place. They have started carving up the country like a pie. . . I'm worried that we are priming a bomb which will sooner or later blow our society apart.

It was a depressing occasion. Even Russians who had come to hate him felt the pathos of the moment. After it, to be sure, a little of his old buoyancy returned and he started to talk about finding another role for himself and more scope for his ideas.

In China, at the time of Tiananmen Square, it became fashionable to say that Deng Xiaoping had got the order of his reforms wrong: he had given the country economic liberalization but prevented any political liberalization. This, the commentators said, was the reason for the sudden explosion of demand for greater freedom of expression. By contrast, it was said, Gorbachev had had greater success by allowing people greater political freedom and then moved on to the economic sphere. Yet after the collapse of his power it started to be said that Gorbachev had done it wrongly too: the fact that people could complain openly, noisily, about the poverty of choice and the increasing difficulties of everyday life which resulted from the failure to liberalize the economy quickly enough meant that trouble was inevitable.

The truth is that it was probably never possible to take a society as damaged as that in the Soviet Union and reform it with any real success. Marxism-Leninism seems to have weakened the necessary fibres of human existence. No single solution, no single leader, can suffice to put it right. All that was possible was to set people free from the old burdens, and that is what Gorbachev did. I watched the television pictures as he ended his news conference after two hours – even now, he was incapable of speaking briefly or concisely – got up from the table, and walked slowly to the door. For some reason it brought back the memory of the first day I saw him: an unscheduled glimpse in a side-room at the British Museum. Spotting a mirror, he whipped out a comb and arranged his thinning hair. It seemed to me then, as it seems now, the action of an eager provincial, anxious to make a good impression on everyone he met; not vain, so much as keen to please.

On 25 December, the Western Christmas, I was back in Moscow. After days of uncertainty and delay, it was Mikhail Gorbachev's last day in office, and he ended it with a sombre television address.

> Dear compatriots, fellow citizens. Because of the situation which has developed with the formation of the Commonwealth of Independent States, I am ceasing my activity in the post of USSR President. I adopt this decision as a matter of principle. I have been firmly in favour of independence and the self-determination of peoples, but at the same time in favour of preserving the union state and the country's integrity. Events took a different course.

He ran through his achievements:

> The process of renovating the country and of key changes in the world community has turned out to be far more difficult than could have been predicted. However, what has been done should be assessed on its merits. Society has acquired freedom and liberated itself politically and socially, and this is the main achievement we have not yet fully realized, since we have not yet learned how to use freedom.
>
> Nevertheless, work of historic significance has been done. A totalitarian system which has deprived the country of an opportunity to become wealthy and prosperous a long time ago has been eliminated. A breakthrough on the road to democratic transformation has been accomplished. Free elections, a free press, religious freedoms, representative bodies of power and the multi-party system have become a reality, and human rights have been recognized as the supreme principle.

He read through his speech steadily, allowing no sign of emotion to show. The end was brief.

> With all my heart, I wish to thank those who during these years stood alongside me for a right and good cause. Some mistakes could probably have been avoided, and there is much that could have been done better; but I am sure that sooner or later our shared efforts will achieve results. Our peoples will live in a flourishing and democratic society.
>
> I wish every one of you all the best.

The camera lingered on him a little, and he didn't quite know what to do. He looked to the side, then back to the camera: that steady gaze I remembered from the first time I had met him, at Hampton Court seven years before. Then he relaxed and started to put his papers away, and at last the picture changed. Mikhail Sergeyevich Gorbachev had handed over the Soviet nuclear arsenal to Boris Yeltsin, and was a private citizen in the country he had changed out of all recognition.

That night my colleagues and I walked through Red Square. It was cold, and the small crowd which had gathered in front of Lenin's Tomb was mostly silent. The red flag with its hammer and sickle, which had been the last evidence of the Union of Soviet Socialist Republics and had flown there for as long as almost anyone could remember, had been pulled down. In its place was the Russian tricolour. Boris Yeltsin had lost no time in taking over from the old régime, and the following day he would change the name on the door of the presidential office before Gorbachev had had time to go in and remove his belongings. There was a new, cruder spirit in the Kremlin, like a Chekhov story in which the farm manager takes over the property from the old landed gentry. Mikhail Gorbachev was not really like a Chekhovian landlord, but he was thoughtful and sensitive and intellectual – and the Russian people disliked him for it. Yeltsin was none of these things; but he was a traditional Russian mujhik, and they instinctively felt happier with him. They needed to believe in something, and Gorbachev had raised their hopes for a better life only to dash them. Now they had someone new to believe in. Gorbachev, the Liberator, was forgotten.

POSTSCRIPT:
A DIFFERENT WORLD

Of course, completing a book gives one a sense of crossing a frontier, of finality. As Pushkin put it, 'Why this strange sadness troubling me?' At the same time, there is an awareness of the powerful flow of life, which began before us and will continue after us.

ANDREI SAKHAROV, *Moscow and Beyond*

It was the last day of 1991. Moscow was cold and dreary, the thin snow lying grey on the ground like the hair on an old man's pate. Outwardly, nothing was different: the queues, the heavy trucks grinding past, the sense of life as an unceasing battle. Yet the entire country had changed out of all recognition. In the streets, drivers who had once been so meek and careful now ignored the traffic lights and the police; outside the ludicrously-named 'gastronomes', Stalin-speak for food shops, there was violent pushing and shoving instead of the usual patient queuing, and friends told me of three recent cases in which elderly people had suffered heart attacks as a result. Colonels and generals now came to the offices of Western television organizations to sell the most secret pictures imaginable: one brought a video filmed in the cockpit of a nuclear bomber on exercise close to the German frontier, another had a collection of official film of the numerous disasters of the Soviet space programme. Once, merely to have looked at these things would have been to risk a long prison sentence as a spy; now I had the feeling that a Westerner could experience no problem so serious that the discreet payment of a hundred-dollar bill would not solve it.

Every principle, every ideal, every last trace of the ethic of Marxism-Leninism had evaporated from Russia. All that was left was the crude unwanted residue: the inhumanity, the queues, the short-ages, the injustices, the brutalities, the corruption, the dirt and sickness and destruction which had welled up from three-quarters of a century of reckless exploitation of the natural environment. Once the Marxist state had denied that such problems existed. Then it accepted that some of them were the unfortunate but inevitable accompaniment to the creation of true socialism. Now no one bothered to deny that they were all that was left of a social experiment which had failed within four years of its introduction, yet had lingered on through sheer state violence for seven more decades.

Outside the Kurskiy Station a puddle of melting snow glinted in the street lights; a film of oil and an unravelling cigarette butt lay on its surface. Kurskiy is not one of those places where you could imagine Anna Karenina alighting; it was built in 1960 in the general style of Euston Station (suitably, since the Russian word for a railway terminus is *voksal*, from Vauxhall in London) and is ugly and depressing. It seemed to embody every one of the most urgent of the problems that Gorbachev had bequeathed to Boris Yeltsin: collapsing services, inadequate funding, poverty, crime and despair. It was midnight, and my colleagues and I were there in the hope of finding a beggar woman whom we had met and filmed earlier outside the Intourist Hotel in the city centre. She usually spent the night in the station with her seven children, she said.

We pushed through the heavy double doors and were assailed by the old smell of Soviet public places. Here, though, there were nasty additions to the usual flavour of sweat and wet clothing and cheap cigarettes: urine, vomit, sleeping bodies. If Gustav Doré had illustrated Hobbes *Leviathan* it might have looked like this. People pushed past each other in the dim light, arguing, drinking, searching for lost relatives. Someone was making constant, incomprehensible announcements over a loudhailer. All round the sides of the concourse young men were hunched over electronic games, shouting as they zapped their targets. Others slept or defecated or copulated in corners.

On the stairs I stumbled across a man being loudly, liquidly sick: he turned an empty face towards me, blood running down his chin. Hundreds of people sat in utter silence, waiting in the dark for a train that would not now be leaving because there was insufficient fuel. They dared not leave their seats for fear someone else might take them, and they would have to squat down on the dirty floor with the gypsies. We didn't find our beggar woman; maybe she had been chased away by the professional hustlers, who paid a percentage of their earnings to a mafioso who controlled them like a pimp. Instead we were surrounded by small gypsy girls, each holding up a tiny wizened baby and making the imploring gestures of saints around the Cross, each touching her mouth and whispering '*Signor, signor. . .*' In a society undergoing an inflation level of 250 per cent in 1991 and preparing for 750 per cent in 1992, only those with access to dollars prospered.

*

All around us in Moscow the streets and Metro stations were being renamed, so that Dzierzynski, Sverdlov and the rest of the Communist saints were no longer commemorated in everyone's daily life, and snow settled on their fallen statues which had been gathered together on the edge of Gorky Park. Only Lenin remained, still too big to be moved aside. Changes that would have been unthinkable a year or so before had become commonplace. For thirty dollars you could join an Intourist guided trip around the KGB's headquarters in the Lubyanka, and there was now a café in the building which anyone could visit, and even pay in roubles. The red stars still glittered on the spires of the Kremlin, but as my friend had once forecast they seemed unlikely to stay there much longer. Outside Lenin's mausoleum there were occasional demonstrations by tiny groups of unrepentant Communists, protesting at any notion that the body of the founder of the faith should be removed.

Russia was alone, as it had not been for centuries. The Baltic states of Latvia, Lithuania and Estonia had gone, Belorus and Ukraine were independent, the empire in the east and south which had taken two hundred years to build up had evaporated in a matter of weeks. Strange anomalies had arisen: Kazakhstan, by virtue of the missiles weapons left on its territory, had become the world's fifth biggest nuclear power, well ahead of China, Britain and France; the foreign minister of Armenia was an American; the defence minister of Lithuania was a former lieutenant-colonel in the U.S. Army. On 30 January President Yeltsin came to London and signed an agreement, forming the basis of the first full treaty of amity and co-operation since the one George III signed with Catherine the Great in 1766. International diplomacy had reverted to the days before the rise of the great ideologies.

Behind it, on the shore, the Marxist tide had left four régimes stranded: China, North Vietnam, North Korea and Cuba. None of them seemed likely to survive indefinitely, all showed some signs of changing their habits. Syria and Iraq, whose rival Ba'ath Parties had once based themselves heavily on the Soviet and Eastern European model, now went in for a concerted campaign of privatization. Lesser imitators in the Third World had already shifted their position. Colonel Gadaffy in Libya was emphasizing his Islamic origins. Angola and Mozambique had come to terms with their pro-Western and pro-South African rebels. President Mengisthu of Ethiopia, who had overthrown the imperial government of Haile Selassie in the interests of the workers and the peasants, drove his presidential Rolls-Royce up the ramp into the belly of a Russian transport plane and was given refuge and a country estate in Zimbabwe by President Mugabe. It was noticeable that Mugabe himself spoke less and less of the desirability of the one-party state and the socialist economic model. The PLO and the ANC found the funding and the ideological input from Moscow had been completely switched off: which in turn made the pursuit of peace agreements possible in the Middle East and South Africa. In the West, Communist Party after Communists Party voted itself out of existence and started life again as a branch of social democracy. The radical chic of the 1960s and 70s became as outmoded as nostalgia for the days of colonial empire.

Slowly, Western public interest in the countries which had freed themselves from the former Soviet empire faded. As each of them held generally acceptable free elections, they seemed to move from the category of a political problem to that of a purely economic one. Nevertheless there was a sense of dissatisfaction and unease in most of the ex-satellite countries. The Forum-led coalition government which came to power in Hungary on 23 May 1990, with three leading academic historians taking the posts of prime minister, foreign minister and minister of defence, ran quickly into serious difficulties in shifting the economy onto a market footing. More than two million people earned less than 1,500 forints a week, which was regarded as the poverty level. Inflation seemed likely to reach 50 per cent, interest rates 35 per cent. There were demonstrations, blockades, a mutiny in the army and a small amount of rioting in the streets. Despite their grasp of history the prime minister, Jozsef Antall, and the foreign minister, Geza Jeszenszky, made some elementary blunders in Hungary's relations with its neighbours, upsetting the governments in Bucharest and Prague by stirring up the feelings of ethnic Hungarians and recalling memories of the Austro-Hungarian Empire by allowing 10,000 Kalashnikov rifles to be sent to Croatia. The Forum and its coalition allies were soon deeply unpopular at home.

In Poland the Solidarity movement, having in some ways begun the process that brought independence to the whole of the European branch of the Soviet empire, had fallen apart by the end of 1990. Resentment had grown at the apparent inability of the government headed by Tadeusz Mazowiecki to root out the old Communist officials who had managed to cling on to positions of power as a result of the 1989 Round Table agreement. Lech Walesa began angling for the post of President, and intrigued against the Mazowiecki government whose members had once been his friends and allies. He seemed to suggest that Poland's problems were being exacerbated by the Jews, and spoke of the need for 'mass social action'. He also indicated that, as President, he would rule by decree if he saw fit. In the first round of the presidential election on 25 November 1990 Mazowiecki was humiliated, and the run-off was between Walesa and an unknown emigré businessman who had lived in Peru and Canada, Stanislaw Tyminski. A fiercely personal campaign by Walesa's supporters uncovered all sorts of dubious facts about Tyminski, but Walesa's views and methods had given rise to so much concern that Tyminski still obtained a quarter of the vote. As President, Walesa was less extreme than his speeches during the campaign; but the failure of the Polish economy to shake off the old patterns of command socialism kept his government relatively unpopular.

By the end of 1991 the process of integrating the old German Democratic Republic into the Federal Republic of Germany had long ceased to be a pleasurable one, and Germans were paying the price in an inflation rate of more than 4 per cent high wage demands in the steel and other industries, and an unfamiliar degree of industrial strife. Far right-wing groups paraded in the cities of eastern Germany and their recruitment increased. There were dozens of attacks on hostels where groups of non-Europeans lived. The burden of the Communist past was particularly heavy in one respect: as records from the East German secret police, the Stasi, became available to its victims more and more informers were unmasked, from football players to leading figures in the democracy movement. One woman who had played an important part in the campaign discovered in December 1991 that her husband had informed on her for years. 'We are now going to spend Christmas together, my husband and children and I,' she said. 'You can imagine for yourselves what sort of Christmas it will be.'

Czechoslovakia, a more instinctively moderate and democratic society than most of the other former Soviet satellites, nevertheless experienced the same difficulties as the rest. The intense pressures of government split Civic Forum, which like Solidarity had led the way to independence, along its fault lines. Catholics and conservatives went one way, radicals and social democrats another. StB files were used to discredit a number of people, among them Jan Kavan, who had to wait until January 1992 before it became clear that he had been unjustly accused of informing and collaboration. Vaclav Havel, though rigorously loyal to the programme of morality and justice which he and Charter 77 had worked out during the long years of repression, found it hard to keep the popularity which had swept him into the presidency in the election of 29 December 1989. He was re-elected on 5 July, but his position was weaker. There were fewer economic problems than in Poland or Hungary, yet once again the movement towards a liberal economic system was sluggish and disappointing. Industrial productivity dropped, food prices rose alarmingly. Having once been the most effective member of Comecon, Czechoslovakia suffered accordingly when Comecon collapsed.

At first, an even greater worry was the possible breakup of the country itself. The end of Soviet control brought another upsurge in Slovak nationalism, which had played its part in the 1968 reform movement. Civic Forum's counterpart in Slovakia, Public Against Violence, split into moderate and nationalist wings. Havel managed to defuse much of the demand for outright independence on the part of Slovakia, but was obliged to agree that either of the two republics could secede from the federal system. There were stirrings, too, in Moravia and Silesia. The country had been an awkward conglomerate since its creation at the end of the First World War, and its sufferings under the Nazis and the Russians after 1938 were in part the result. Even in freedom, the problem had not finally been dealt with.

The National Salvation Front in Romania endured the same pattern of difficulty and unpopularity as the other umbrella groups that had taken over from the old régimes – with the added difficulty that its enemies were able to accuse it, with some reason, of being nothing more than Communism with a more human face. Even the human face was in question when the Front bussed groups of workers into the centre of Bucharest and encouraged them to use chains and batons to attack anti-Front demonstrators. The Front was later obliged to take in members of opposition parties, and held presidential and parliamentary elections on 20 May 1990. By that time there were eighty-two registered political parties, but the elections resulted in a landslide victory for the Front's leader, Ion Iliescu. There were many irregularities and dirty tricks, and the Peasants' Party (headed by an emigré millionaire) suffered threats and violence; but most foreign observers accepted that the result was broadly accurate.

Four weeks after the election the NSF reverted to its old habits and laid on special trains to bring in seven thousand miners, armed with sticks and iron bars, and beat up the students and opposition figures who were occupying University Square in the heart of Bucharest. Foreign opinion was horrified by this reminder of the methods of Ceausescu and the Securitate, and Romania was cold-shouldered by the countries of the West at a time when its disastrous economy most needed help. Its request to attend a summit of former Soviet bloc countries in Central Europe was turned down by President Havel on the grounds that the ambitions of Czechoslovakia, Poland and Hungary to secure integration into Western Europe might be damaged. As a result Romania turned its attention eastward. Its problems with ethnic

Hungarians, which had led to the fall of Ceausescu, and with other minority groups, refused to go away, but its hopes of regaining the territory of Moldavia which it had lost to Stalin's Russia in 1945 and which, renamed Moldova, was now independent, seemed a partial reward for all the difficulties Romania had gone through. Yet Ceausescu's rule had left it with a curse it seemed unable to exorcize.

One country made a relatively easy transition from Soviet clientship to independence. By the end of the 1970s Todor Zhivkov, who had come to power in Bulgaria in 1954, was becoming increasingly monarchical and discredited. His security service had planned the murder by a poisoned projectile of the BBC commentator Georgi Markov, who had made fun of him in a series of broadcasts; it was also suspected of having hired a Turk to murder the Pope in 1981. There was discontent at home over worsening economic standards. Zhivkov's only answer was to try to rouse the Slavic, Bulgarian-speaking majority of the population against the million or so Turks. It became an offence to speak Turkish in the street, or even to have a Turkish name.

In 1989, while more striking events were starting in East Berlin and elsewhere, opposition groups in Bulgaria began a series of protests in support of the Turkish minority. Zhivkov, the longest-surviving dictator in Eastern Europe, was voted down at a plenum of the Communist Party's Central Committee on 10 November. The Party proceeded to reform itself, and managed (with the help of a good deal of deeply unfair electoral practices) to win the elections of June 1990. The difficulty the opposition parties had was in finding a suitable candidate around whom support could rally. As in so many other former Soviet bloc countries, several leading figures in political life were discredited when the secret files were opened, and the new government was unable to settle down. Economic problems grew. Bulgaria's largest hard-currency debtor was Iraq, against whom the United Nations declared mandatory sanctions in August 1990, after the invasion of Kuwait. The exodus of tens of thousands of Turkish-speakers from Bulgaria damaged agriculture badly. The prime minister, Andrei Loukanov, who had never entirely given up the Communist Party cast of mind was forced to resign in November 1991. Fresh elections in January 1992 confirmed the reformist president, Zhelyu Zhelev, in power. His main rival had the support of the former Communist Party, now renamed the Socialists. Zhelev, a one-time dissident and a Christian, had been appointed President in 1990, but now, following the adoption of a constitution along Western lines, his role was to be a purely ceremonial one.

For Albania, which had gone to extreme lengths to remain untainted by outside influences, the infection from the death of Communism nevertheless penetrated as fast there as it did everywhere else. Enver Hoxha, who had set up his Communist state in 1944, died in 1985, seven years after breaking with China, his only ally anywhere. His successor, Ramiz Alia, slowly began to open the country to the outside world, unsealing the border with Greece in 1985 and establishing diplomatic relations with Spain in 1986, West Germany in 1987 and Canada in 1988. Slowly there were economic reforms, and the Communist Party began to change its ways. The right to a defence in court was introduced. In December 1990 it was even agreed that political parties could be set up. At the start of 1991 the first religious service in nearly a quarter of a century was held, political prisoners were being released, and on 20 February Hoxha's huge statue in the centre of Tirana was uprooted and taken away. In the election of 31 March the governing Albanian Workers' Party won two-thirds of the seats, though President Alia himself was defeated in his own constituency. He continued in office, but appointed a non-Communist prime minister. Within a matter of weeks there were more political unheavals, and throughout the rest of 1991 the country was faced with an unprecedented wave of crime and political violence.

*

It is a considerable irony that the greatest loser from the collapse of the Soviet empire in Europe was the country which first escaped from it. By another irony, a version of Marxism-Leninism lasted longer there than it did in Russia itself. Yugoslavia was effectively handed over to the Communist Partisan leader Josip Broz Tito by Britain during the Second World War. By 1948 he had broken with Stalin, and become Stalin's biggest hate-figure since Trotsky. An even more cumbersome portmanteau of nationalities than Czechoslovakia, Yugoslavia could be governed as an effective entity only by tough methods and an elaborate federal system. It worked because of Tito's powerful grip on the country and his ludicrous cult of personality, but the old hatreds, which had been intensified by the massacres of Serbs by Croats and of Croats by Serbs during the War, were simply waiting to re-emerge. Tito's death in 1980 began a slow and increasingly painful disintegration.

The slightly absurd system of rotation in office which he introduced meant that each of the different republics and autonomous regions was represented in each major branch of the executive for six months at a time: a scheme which made effective government impossible yet did nothing to assuage the deep internal tensions. In particular, Serbia's feeling that although it formed the largest part of Yugoslavia's population (35 per cent) it had only a fraction of its rightful influence, was seized upon by the unashamed populist and nationalist Slobodan Milosevic, a long-term Communist apparatchik who had nevertheless made himself highly popular with the Serbs by finding enemies for them.

The other republics were making their own tracks away from Communism. Some parts of Slovenia, for example, seemed indistinguishable from Austria because of the increasingly liberal economic system it had introduced. Croatia, for its part, became more and more hostile to Serbia as it watched Slovenia's success. As the atmosphere deteriorated, the mutual hatreds were greatly inflamed by the fact that the various population groups were so intermixed: 11.6 per cent of the population of Croatia were Serbs. After Milosevic won a big victory in Serbia's first multi-party election in December 1990 he began a deliberate campaign to undermine the governments of Bosnia-Hercegovina and Croatia by stirring up the national sentiments of the Serbs who lived there. Milosevic's counterpart in Croatia (like him, a right-winger whose earlier Communism was overlaid by a large degree of nationalism) was Dr Franjo Tudjman.

As Slovenia and Croatia moved closer to outright separation from the old shell of Yugoslavia, the outside world paid more attention to them. The German government was openly in favour of recognizing their independence, and (with the support of a few individual politicians in other countries such as Margaret Thatcher in Britain) forced the hand of the European Community as a whole. Whereas Slovenia slipped its bonds with some ease, Croatia's independence exacerbated the feelings of Serbian nationalists, who believed that Germany intended to continue what they insisted was a long campaign against them, dating back to 1914 and culminating in the invasion of 1941. Serbian tactical stupidity seemed to know no bounds: their forces murdered Western television crews, shot down a helicopter containing EC observers, and did serious damage to Dubrovnik, the one beautiful and historically important city in Yugoslavia known to most Westerners; it had no serious strategic value. German diplomatic clumsiness played some part in the outbreak of civil war between Serbs and Croats, on which thirteen cease-fires brokered by the European Community and the United Nations had no effect. Nevertheless after so much bloodshed the hope was that the arrival of United Nations troops would achieve peace of a sort. As a country, however, Yugoslavia was dead.

*

So was an entire phase of history. Marxism-Leninism could not have come to power without the European convulsion of 1914-18. The Russian monarchy was foolish and ramshackle, but it would not have collapsed in the way it did without the appalling loss of life caused by the Russian high command's misconduct of the war. The simple miscalculation which Kaiser Wilhelm II made in July and August 1914 ('It ran away with me and it will run away with him,' he said glumly in his Dutch exile when he heard that Adolf Hitler had started another war in Europe) was reinforced by another: his military leaders' decision to allow Lenin to travel in the sealed train to Petrograd in 1917, in order to undermine the Russian state.

The revolutions of 1989–91 brought about the end of the order ushered in by the Kaiser's war, and greatly reinforced by Hitler's war: a revolutionary Russia, the new nation-states packaged up at Versailles, the growth of Soviet power, the terminal weakening of Britain and France, the division of Europe into two mutually hostile camps, each dominated by a super-power. As the smoke begins to clear, the landscape looks very different. Russia is exhausted, America is in retreat, Western Europe assuming something of its pre-1914 importance. A more traditional form of diplomacy is springing up, free of the great post-war ideological blocs. The shameful carve-up of central and eastern Europe, as proposed by Churchill to Stalin, has ended.

It used to be that anyone who criticized the Soviet Union or its satellites too strongly would be accused of having a Cold War mentality. Nevertheless as the evidence of human rights abuses grew, criticism became more widespread. Nikita Khrushchev's half-hearted reforms were succeeded in 1964 by Brezhnev's return to the old, heavy, unquestioning control of the Communist Party. If it had developed or eased up significantly under Brezhnev, it might well be in power in Russia and in central and eastern Europe even now. As it was, its harshness towards personal freedom brought about its eventual collapse.

It would be wrong to forget the idealistic element in Marxism. It was intended to be a liberating, life-enhancing force, not a method of control. Vladimir Mayakovsky wrote in his poem 'Khorosho!' ('OK!') in 1927:

> Life
>   is marvellous,
>   life
>   is beautiful!
> May we live
>   to a hundred years
> until our first
>   grey hair appears.

May the future
　　　　　bring
joy in everything.
Verse and hammer,
　　　　　　glory sing
to the land
　　　　of Spring!

By that stage, probably, Mayakovsky was starting to realize that life under Stalin was unlikely to be marvellous, and only three years later he shot himself. Nevertheless he had felt the same sense of vast possibilities that usually comes with genuine revolution. It is a young man's feeling, and young men and women in dozens of countries gladly devoted their lives to the new dawn. Kim Philby, Guy Burgess, Donald Maclean, Anthony Blunt, Alex Cairncross and their equivalents in other countries betrayed their countries and their closest associates for this ideal, and felt the sacrifice a hundred times worth it.

Yet the ideal was undermined at the very outset by its own errors and inconsistencies. 'The Internationale unites the human race,' says its anthem, and the founding fathers, Marx and Engels, wrote in *The Communist Manifesto*: 'The workers have no country. . . National differences and antagonisms between peoples are vanishing gradually from day to day [;] the supremacy of the proletariat will cause them to vanish still faster.' It is a noble thought, but it was not true at the time and is scarcely truer even now. By the time the Bolsheviks came to power it had already been proven comprehensively wrong by the outbreak of war in 1914. They made certain of ultimate failure by forcing the people to be good and noble in the one way their ideology prescribed. When the people failed, and tried to hold onto their land or their animals or their old ideas or their personal integrity, the labour camps and mass graves were opened up for them. Nazism killed its millions, but Bolshevism its tens of millions. 'No peace without freedom,' said a badge I saw on the lapel of a demonstrator on the streets of Prague during the revolution; and it was more accurate than all the slogans which Marxism-Leninism had placed on all the buildings of its capital cities, or all the banners carried at all the May Day parades in its seventy-four years in power. 'Marxism was better in theory than in practice,' said an elderly Moscow writer who had spend much of his life criticizing the Soviet system but was too honest and proud to relinquish Marxism simply because it had suddenly become unfashionable.

Near the TASS building in the centre of Moscow is a street that has survived the destruction and unplanned rebuilding of the Communist years. It is lined by buildings two storeys high, painted a pleasant green, from the 1860s and 70s. There was ice like black quartz on the pavements when I went there last, and a light snowfall made it dangerous. I walked a little way down the street, then turned into a courtyard which could have come from a Gogol story. Part of an old cart still lay against one of the walls, and there was nothing there to suggest that life had changed for a century. A sign said 'Bukinist': secondhand bookshop. Snow was settling even on the upper surfaces of the flaking paint.

Inside there was the comforting, university smell of old paper. The proprietor was an elderly man with thick pebble glasses; looking at his eyes was like peering down a tunnel. His wife was there, and a stoutish young woman with a pasty face who was nevertheless not unattractive and may have been his daughter. They had an indefinably bourgeois air, survivors of the decades during which to be middle-class was to be a potential enemy of the state: booklovers. I gave them a vague idea of what I was interested in, though I scarcely knew it myself. A large sepia photograph of Mayakovsky was pinned to the side of one of the shelves; two out of three volumes of an illustrated, pre-revolutionary edition of *War and Peace* (the third was missing) lay next to Lermontov and Turgenev.

The proprietor directed me to a large packing-case full of books, papers, magazines, ephemera of all sorts. It was, I slowly realized, a time capsule, striated over the decades with materials from the past. Close to the top lay a medal of Lenin with a red and gold ribbon in a red plastic case: 1870–1970, said the legend. Beside it was a medallion of Lenin from the 1950s, older, more faded, but still an icon, empty-featured, of a figure who had long ceased to be a real man and was simply an institution, the only thing that kept the state together in the absence of a monarch or a god, a waxwork lying in the darkness of his Mausoleum in Red Square. It was hard to associate the smiling face in the jaunty cap with the documents which were starting to emerge from a special nuclear-proof vault in the Kremlin: letters authorizing the execution of several dozen priests, of peasants who refused to take down the Tsar's portraits, perhaps of the Tsar and his family themselves.

There were pamphlets by and about Brezhnev: 'The Little Land', a ludicrously exaggerated account of his wartime service as a Party ideologue attached to fighting units which he claimed to inspire and no doubt bored and frightened in equal measure. There were placards and stamps and badges celebrating the greatest moments of Khrushchev's reign: the flights of Sputnik and of Yuri Gagarin. Below them lay the deeper layers of Stalinism: portraits of the great man looking quizzically at the camera much as he is said to have looked at the departing figures of his generals and ministers and secret policemen, wondering if it was time to have them arrested and shot. It was, it seems, as they walked away that he made up his mind about them. There was an edition of *Pravda* from 28 January 1937, the day of one of the most important treason trials, with the headline 'Trotskyist – Saboteur – Diversionist – Spy' and a picture of the evil dwarf Yezhov who was heading the NKVD for the time being, and who looked like a thoughtful chorister. On an inside page was an account of Vyshinsky's cross-examination of the chauffeur Arnold, who was supposed to have tried to murder Molotov by driving into a ditch. By all accounts Stalin was so amused by his evidence he ordered that he, alone among his co-defendants, should be sentenced to prison rather than the execution cellars of Lefortovo.

Below that, smelling of damp and must, was a pile of copies of the monthly magazine *Communist International*, dated 1919. A fiercely moustached worker was wielding a hammer to break the chains binding the world. 'Moscow Kremlin – Petrograd Smolny' said the cover, and the price in those inflationary times was 20 roubles. Zinoviev (later executed under Stalin) was the editor, and the editorial committee included the names of Lenin himself, Trotsky (murdered by Stalin), Bukharin (executed under Stalin), and Kamenev (executed under Stalin): all the Party luminaries of the period. Stalin himself, being of lesser importance at that date, was not listed. I looked back at a twentieth anniversary history of the Revolution which I had come across elsewhere in the box, published in 1937 – a difficult year for the historians, with so many Old Bolsheviks appearing in court and charged with sabotage and treason. Stalin's picture appeared next to Lenin's, clearly faked, trying to give the impression that as early as 1919 he was the natural heir. And then, below the revolutionary level (marked by a large lime-green banknote for 1,000 inflationary roubles issued under the Kerensky government in mid-1917) lay the Tsarist period: a dozen or so turn-of-the-century portrait photographs on thick board. Each had the photographer's name and the address of the studio stamped in gold underneath. The faces looked out from the fading sepia at a world changed beyond their comprehension: army officers, Orthodox priests, young girls in pinafores, boys in sailor suits, patriarchs and matriarchs, newly married couples, stern cadets, jovial lawyers, and self-aware, fast actresses. It was a pleasant, careless, idle, nervous world. Perhaps, like the characters in Chekhov's plays and short stories whom they so much resembled, they worried incessantly about the future but did nothing about it; and soon their lives would be overwhelmed by the plotting of a few extremists. With them were theatre programmes for light comedies and the occasional tragedy.

underneath everything lay a single long glove of indeterminate colour, maybe yellow, maybe lilac, a little stained by age and damp. Perhaps it had belonged to one of the fast actresses and someone had kept it as a memento, taking it out sometimes and holding it to his nose to recall the perfume. I held it to my own nose: nothing but damp and old documents. It had waited there, under the accretions of the twentieth century, the revolution and the treason trials, Barbarossa and Sputnik, the ossification of the system and its collapse, the renewed hope for freedom and affluence. I put it back in the box where it belonged. It had been a long wait.

INDEX